Lutherans in Kerala

Christian Heritage Rediscovered

The Series, as the name suggests, is meant to focus on Christian Faith & Living vis-à-vis topics like Literature & Poetry, Indigenous Philosophizing, Ethical response towards Agriculture, Health & Healing, Science & Technology, Eco-feminist Theology, Sociological approach towards Human Rights, Law & Politics, Arts, History of Ideas, Ancient Civilizations, Cultural Contiguity, Religious Cosmologies & Mysticism, Footsteps of famous Theologians, World Peace & Harmony, Global Capitalism, Network Marketing, Cybertheology, Population & Demographics, Epigraphic Studies, Contextualized Education, and many others. We welcome a Mss. on any topic/s mentioned, whether they are original works, scholarly monographs, collections of conference papers, revised dissertations, or translations of historical documents. Through the Series we, the Publishers, are striving to put forward published works that may help Institutions, Academic Bodies, Researchers, Scholars and the World at large in furthering their respective knowledge and understanding on the concerned subject. We welcome your comments on our efforts and further suggestions on how we can foster the upcoming thought provoking theologically grounded books.

Christian Heritage Rediscovered - 69

Lutherans in Kerala

Mission Perspective Towards Subalterns and Their Socio-Religious and Secular Context

D. Christu Das

CWI
Christian World Imprints

First Published in 2019 by

Christian World Imprints
Christian Publishing & Books from India
H-12 Bali Nagar, **New Delhi-110015**
info@christianworldimprints.com
www.ChristianWorldImprints.com
Phone: +91 11 25465925

ISBN: 978-93-5148-288-8

Cataloging in Publication Data--DK
Courtesy: D.K. Agencies (P) Ltd. <docinfo@dkagencies.com>

Christu Das, D., author.
Lutherans in Kerala : mission perspective towards subalterns and their socio-religious and secular context / D. Christu Das.
pages cm. -- (Christian heritage rediscovered ; 69)
Includes bibliographical references.
ISBN 9789351482888

1. Lutherans--India--Kerala--History. 2. Lutheran Church--Missions--India--Kerala--History. I. Title. II. Series: Christian heritage rediscovered ; 69.

LCC BX8063.I4C47 2019 | DDC 284.15483 23

Printed in India.

Contents

List of Abbreviations

ADS	Ambur District Synod
BCC	Bible Correspondence Course
BCF	Backward Christian Federation
BEF	Bethel Evangelism Fellowship
BFMS-LCMS	Board for Mission Service-Lutheran Church Missouri Synod
BL	Board for Literature
CBO	Central Business Office, IELC
CC	Church Council
CLHS	Concordia Lutheran High School, Peroorkada
CMC-I	Christian Media Centre-India
CSI	Church of South India
CTSN	Concordia Theological Seminary, Nagercoil
DPI	Director of Public Instruction
FC	Finance Committee
GC	General Conference
GCM	General Conference Minutes
GMCM	General Missionary Conference of MELIM
GWC	Gospel Work Committee
HS	High School
IELC	India Evangelical Lutheran Church
KER	Kerala Education Rules
KLBS	Kerala Lutheran Backward Synod
KLVS	Kerala Lutheran Vanitha Samajam
LCMS	Lutheran Church Missouri Synod
LEF	Lutheran Employee's Fellowship
LLL	Lutheran Laymen's League
LPF	Lutheran Prayer Fellowship
LPS	Lower Primary School
MELIM	Missouri Evangelical Lutheran India Mission
NLCWS	Nadar Lutheran Christian Welfare Society
OBC	Other Backward Community

SC	Scheduled Caste
SF	Southern Filed
SIUC	South India United Church
SNPCA	Samvaranam Nastapetta Pinnokka Christian Association
SSLC	Secondary School Leaving Certificate
ST	Scheduled Tribe
TA	Trust Association
TDC	Trivandrum District Conference
TDCM	Trivandrum District Conference Minutes
TDS-EC	Trivandrum District Synod Executive Committee
TEC	Trivandrum Executive Committee
TS	Trivandrum Synod
TSC	Trivandrum Synod Convention
TTS	Teachers Training School
TX	Trivandrum Synod Executive
UPS	Upper Primary School
UTC	United Theological College
UX	United Church Organization Executive

Introduction

Background of the Research

Lutheran Christians in Kerala is a Christian subaltern community having a century of unrecognized history. This re-reading is to trace the various factors which brought together different people groups into the Lutheran fold and to analyze historically how Lutheranism became a liberating force for the socially alienated people from their age old slumber and why the historians ignored their history for the past one century.

An Elaboration

Though a Christian Church existed in Kerala long before one was established in many sections of Europe, the rest of India had to wait for more centuries to hear the good news. It is clear that only after the coming of the Portuguese, Roman Catholic Christianity was introduced in South Travancore among the *Parava* community. The arrival of St. Francis Xavier in 1542 further progressed its growth in the South. The Protestant work in India is the result of Missionary activities of different protestant societies during the 18th and 19th centuries. German Lutherans were the first Protestant Missionaries to come to India (1706). The Danish Halle Mission that sent Bartholomew Ziegenbalg (1682-1719) and his co-worker Henry Pluetschau (1677-1746) laid the foundations of the Protestant Church at Tranquebar on the East coast of South India. The first Protestant Christian in South Travancore, Maharasan Vedamanickam was baptized by a Lutheran Missionary and was also ordained as first Protestant pastor in South Travancore in the Lutheran order. The first Protestant Missionary to South Travancore was a German Lutheran, William Tobias Ringletaube (1770-1816) who came with the help of the London Missionary Society (LMS). Until the arrival of the LMS Missionary called Charles Mead in South Travancore, the first Protestant community in Kerala remained in character Lutheran.[1]

[1] For more details on the Lutheran presence in the origin of Protestant Christianity in Kerala, see C.M. Agur, *Church History of Travancore* (New Delhi: Asian Educational Services, 1990), 467-

Missouri Evangelical Lutheran India Mission (MELIM) began its work in South India in 1895. They started their work at Krishnagiri, a town in Dharmapuri District mostly among the marginalized people called Praiahs (Sambavars). In Kerala, then South Travancore, over the years, the major mass movements came from the Shanar (*Nadar*) communities. The conversion of Shanars to Christianity and the fight for their rights and equality went together.[2] Christians from a very poor and low caste felt that mission work among them was neglected. They, therefore, approached the MELIM Missionaries at Krishnagiri with a plea to serve and to work among the 30,000 Sambavars of other faiths in that area. This request called for a revision in the Missionary policy (comity)[3] of not working where other Christians were already working. The objections came from LMS Missionaries, who argued that they could take care of all the people of the area. The investigations held by the Lutheran Missionaries convinced them that the Sambavars were neglected. However, they had no intention of disturbing the work of the LMS Missionaries. In 1907, the MELIM began to work in Nagercoil.

After some years a joint invitation came to MELIM Missionaries at Nagercoil from Christian Malayalees of Sambava and Ezhava castes under conditions similar to those of the earlier one. They were also the members of the LMS, but had left it. They felt that the Lutheran Missionaries could best serve the religious situation. By moving to Trivandrum in 1911, the Lutheran Missionaries entered into another language area and gained a foothold among the people of several castes. This move raised challenges and problems. The relationship between the missions, namely, LMS and MELIM was shaken. Yet, the Lutheran Mission was progressing in Kerala through various extensions, such as literary works, social services, education and healing missions, socio-economic development programs, geographical expansion. In 1956, Lutheran Churches in Kerala were organized separately as a Synod in order to form an autonomous Church called the India Evangelical Lutheran Church (IELC). In 1958, Mission and administration were handed over to the native Lutherans.

MELIM's entrance to Kerala opened up a new era for the most downtrodden people of these areas which touched all phases of their lives. Christian Church is an assembly of believers and a people's movement. As an Eucharistic community churches should challenge the existing evil caste structures, a structure which supported individually and nurtured institutional oppression based on caste and colour. But, unfortunately most of the Christian missions in Kerala knowingly or unknowingly became the safe guarders of the caste structure. For the practical

481, 617 and 701 and R.N. Yesudhas, *A Peoples Revolt in Travancore, A Backward Class Movement for Social Freedom* (Trivandrum: Kerala Historical Society, 1975), 56-57.

[2] J.W. Gladstone, *Protestant Christianity and Peoples Movement in Kerala, 1850-1936* (Trivandrum: The Seminary Publications, 1984), 138.

[3] J.H. Maclean "Missionary Comity." *National Christian Council Review* Vol. LXIV, No.1 (January, 1944), 12.

purpose most of the Christian denominations in Kerala focused on and dominated by one particular caste people. London Missionary Society (Nadars), Salvation Army (Pulayas), Mar Thoma (Syrians), and Latin Catholics (fishermen) are a few examples. It badly affected the consciousness of inter-ethnic solidarity among all people and caused more inter-ethnic contradictions and conflicts even among Christians. But the Lutheran Missionaries realized that the power of the Christian gospel would be the main source for the freedom of the most downtrodden people. The Lutheran Missionaries concentrated among the various people groups of that area like Sambavars, Nadars, Ezhavas, Pulayas, Kerala Muthaliyars and many tribal peoples. They loved them as brothers and sisters and taught them that they were as valuable and acceptable to God just as Brahmins. The parenthood of God and Christian love opened the said group's eyes which helped them to build up their self esteem. The socially alienated groups were attracted by MELIM Missionaries and so joined the Lutheran Church. In this view, Lutheran Christian community in Kerala is a graphic design of a united people who came from very distinctively different caste as well as socio-economic background. They are united as one body purely on the merits of the grace of God bestowed upon them in Jesus Christ. The faith in Christ liberated everyone from all bondage and through re-birth they all were united in one confession, one body and one spirit; breaking every barrier and crossing all boundaries. By the systematic and conscious efforts of the Missionaries slowly the people of the land were able to attain the social dignity along with the spiritual salvation. Lutheranism became a liberating force for the socially alienated people from their age old slumber. Lutheran Church in Kerala is having 98% of her membership with Subaltern Christians. It is a unique Subaltern solidarity which brought together about 19 Backward & other Backward Class and tribal people groups into the Lutheran Christian fold. The slaves of the land became the people of the land and a community of equals. They were able to come out of seclusion and fight for their equality in society. The liberated people from different ethnic groups formed a unique Christian subaltern solidarity under the Lutheran Christian fold.

Lutheran Church in Kerala has now about 124 congregations under Trivandrum District Synod, 18 New Evangelism Centers, 24 schools including two High Schools and one Higher Secondary School and two Hospitals. Among them about 30,000 Lutherans are high government officials, politicians, professionals, national award winners. Even though Lutheran Christians have more than one century presence in Kerala, they remain as a people with an unwritten history. There are a lot of historical works related to the Churches in Kerala, Protestant Christianity and people's movement in Kerala, Directory of Kerala Churches. But almost all historians both secular and Christian have ignored the history of these people movement towards identity and selfhood. State Government had given more attractive benefits to the low caste Hindus but treated Lutheran Christians as 'forward' people ignoring their caste/tribe identity. Among the other flourished

Christian communities, the position and prestige of Lutherans are weakening. Yet, they remain as an unacknowledged subaltern community holding on to the hope of a promising future. A thorough account of the history of Lutherans in Kerala is long overdue. The people who lived at the time of starting the work are no longer alive. Important source materials are lost or untraceable. The memories and experiences and the views of the people have never been collected or written down. Thus the present researcher is attempting to construct a history of the people who were ignored for a century by the historians. An underlying issue in this study is the question of historical identity. For this study the researcher tries to explore: what are the various factors that brought together different people groups into the Lutheran fold; how Lutheranism became a liberating force for the socially alienated people from their age-old slumber. Lutherans in Kerala had a unique one century presence, and why the mainstream Christians and secular historians ignored their history. Attempts are made to search the major problems and prospects of Christian Lutherans in Kerala as a unique subaltern solidarity in this thesis.

Significance of the Research

New perspectives in historiography are emerging to find proper relevant, sufficient sources for the reconstruction of a holistic history. After the collective subaltern studies,[4] the subaltern groups are coming forward to write peoples' history from 'below'[5] – the history of the oppressed and the exploited. This is a search to identify the politics of the people that are left out in the "unhistorical historiography".[6] "Maker of his/her own destiny" is the claim by the subaltern school. It opened the possibility of many local, regional and communitarian histories. In this context, it is highly important to bring to light the lowest sections of the Christian Lutheran people in Kerala. They also need to find space in the common history of Christianity.

The unique contribution of subaltern historiography is to challenge researchers to identify signifiers of these subjectivities in the local area that the researcher is studying. Subaltern methodology is the recognition and restoration of the people who were either silenced or ignored by elite discourses. Here the subalterns are not just the objects of history but the very subject themselves. Subaltern history is the history of a suffering people of the oppressed and the

[4] The most significant moment in the development of this school happened when the subaltern study series were published. *Subaltern Studies 1: Writings on South Asian History and Society* (1982) and Ranajit Guha's Pioneering work, *Elementary Aspects of Peasant Insurgency in Colonial India* (1982) were published first. Since then eleven volumes and several other books have appeared representing the school of history. Ranajit Guha edited the first six volumes of subaltern studies.

[5] Panikkar, K.M., "Alternative Historiographies: Changing Paradigms of Power." *Jeevadhara* Vol. XXXII (January, 2002): 11.

[6] George Oommen, "Historiography of Indian Christianity." *Journal of Dharma* 28/2 (April-June, 2003): 212-231.

marginalized. As their history is being given attention to, they are moving from the periphery to the centre.[7] Moreover, subaltern studies are the effort to hear the people and their voices which have been silenced in the dominant discourses; it is an effort to make the subaltern people speak in their own language, a language of protest, resistance and negation. In this view, the present study is an understanding of Christian subaltern history and its significance lies on the theory and the kind of a tool in the hands of the researcher.

Each Minority Christian Movement has a story which needs to be told. Often their memories and stories represent the experiences of minorities. They are vulnerable to distortion, exploitation and suppression. History must do justice to their concerns and perspectives. Roger C. Hedlund observes the importance of the inclusion of "Little traditions". "In a civilization there is great tradition of a reflective few, and there is little tradition of the largely unreflective many".[8] The two traditions intersect and are interdependent. One is the tradition of the philosopher, the other that of the little people. One is literary, the other is oral. In Indian Christianity great tradition represents the mainstream Churches and little traditions represent Christian sects, Pentecostals, small Churches and other indigenous movements. Our understanding of contemporary Christianity will be incomplete, if we ignore these little traditions. There are various studies about Christianity and Churches in Kerala by both the Christian and non-Christian historians. But most of them ignore the history of Christian Lutherans in Kerala. Therefore, all perceptions of available history and assumption were deficient and incomplete. Against this background the present research is extremely important for human right concern and for scholarly truth. A historiography with the perspective of those neglected in the past will give to history a holistic approach.

During the period in study, the social settings were determined according to caste. It was not merely a social or economic order of the society, but a 'religious institution'. After the firm establishment of caste system as a religious institution, it had rigidity made the upward mobility of persons from one caste to another impossible in Kerala. Therefore, conversion of the low caste people to other religion needs special attention. There is a clear relation between conversion and the desire for upward social mobility.[9] These groups wanted a social reform and a rise in the social rank, and not just for some material benefits. In the period of study, there were a lot of people's movements among Hindus according to caste, such as Nayar Movement (Chattampi Swamikal 1854-1924), Ezhava Movement (Narayana Guru 1854-1928), Pulaya Movement (Ayyankali 1863-1941) and Nadar Movement (Vaikunda Swamy 1809-1851). It was also an expression of

---

[7] V.V. Thomas, *Understanding Subaltern History: Theoretical Tools.* (Bangalore: BETSSC/SATHRI, 2006), 7.

[8] Roger E. Hedlund. *Quest for Identity: Indian Churches of Indigenous Origin: The "Little Tradition" in Indian Christianity* (Delhi: MIIS/ISPCK 2000), p. 107.

[9] V.V. Thomas, *op.cit.*, p. 44.

communal caste resentment against certain disabilities and struggles that they had been unjustly subjected to long or short periods of time. Therefore, the role of secular factors in the process of conversion of the backward people to Lutheranism should be noticed. Mission offered to this subaltern not only the Gospel of a new religion but also the possibility of secular salvation from the clutches of the tradition which had for centuries burdened them with social disabilities and economic dependence. This research assumes "a new religion" is not only 'imposed' by an outside agency, but also consciously 'adopted' by certain groups of people who have their reasons for accepting a new religious tradition. In the midst of awakening among separate caste movements, how and why different marginalized communities form Christian solidarity under Lutheran Mission needs to be researched.

Hypothesis

The primary aim of MELIM in Kerala was to spread Christian Gospel among the most backward peoples. Power of the Gospel created in them self-consciousness that they too were valuable in the sight of God. There is a clear relation between the conversion to Lutheran Christianity and the desire for upward social mobility. Mission not only offered the Gospel of a new religion to the subaltern people but also the possibility of secular salvation. The MELIM Missionaries tried to form a fellowship of different caste people under the Christian Lutheran fold. Comparing with other mainline Christian Churches in Kerala the Christian Lutheran Community is a unique subaltern solidarity. The history of Lutherans in Kerala was unrecognized until today because it was and is the movement among the socially backward communities in Kerala. The history of Lutherans in Kerala needs to be understood as a part of Christian Subaltern history.

Definitions

Caste

Caste is derived from the Portuguese '*Casta*' signifying race, mould or quality. Varna (<skt = colour) and jati (<skt = birth) are the two terms which explain the nature of caste as a religious institution.

Community

In modern epistemological understanding, community is a social order in which relationships are connected externally and determined by contracts rather than custom or tradition.

Dalits

The word 'Dalit' is derived from the root *dal* which implies open, split, downtrodden, scattered, crushed, destroyed. Sanskrit root word 'Dalit' means broken, oppressed, and the Hebrew root word *dal* (week, frail). In the Indian context the word 'Dalit' is used to denote the people considered as 'out-caste' on the basis of caste distinction.

Historiography

Art / method / techniques of historical research and writings. It is the history of the history, or, the history of the historical writings; the historical perspectives. The way of representing the past.

History

From Greek/Latin *istoria* = inquiry, research, explanation (or) information. The German word *Geschichte* = the explanation of the past. Generally, the story of the past.

Lutheran

A branch of the protestant Christian Church adhering to the views of Martin Luther (1482-1546).

Subaltern

Subaltern is a general attribute to subordination expressed in terms of class, caste, gender, religious orientation or in any other way, a generally inferior rank of people.

Tribe/Tribal

The English word 'Tribe' derives from the Latin (*tri* = three, *bhur* or *by* – to be). In India this term popularly used to denote those who live in a relatively isolated life and are technologically backward. They are historically victimized communities especially the out castes or untouchables.

Methodology Adopted

The perspective of research employed is socio-historical, analytical method based on the subaltern approach.[10] The introduction of Christianity through the western Missionaries posed fresh problems to society. To understand the impact of this mission upon society, it is necessary to know what have been the social conditions of its origin, and the social groups which had adopted this new faith. The role of social factors in the process of conversion needs to be critically evaluated. Therefore the research makes a socio-historical analysis of Kerala.

A content analysis of historical documents and Missionary records is studied thoroughly to analyze the Missionary strategies and their effects in the responded people. This work will seek to analyze history on the basis of subaltern experiences.

---

[10] The book by V.V. Thomas: *Understanding Subaltern History: Theoretical Tools* (Bangalore: BETSSC/SATHRI, 2006) is an excellent contribution for the study of Christian Subaltern Historiography.

In conducting historical research this study will do an empirical research using both quantitative and qualitative methods of data collection and analysis. A structured questionnaire was distributed to 300 lay and ordained people to collect data. Personal interviews with 50 peoples were conducted among the leaders of all the groups; who were both in various age groups including men and women. Their education and profession could also be taken into consideration. Apart from this, the researcher carried out 10 focus group discussions. Unpublished as well as published sources such as the Minutes, Church records, reports, letters, journals, magazines, books, newspapers, manuscripts, statistical records, non-ecclesiastical sources were also be consulted.

Content

A brief survey of the land and history during the period of research work are discussed in the first chapter. Second chapter tries to trace the historical developments towards the entrance of Lutheran Christianity in Kerala. The next two chapters discuss the expansions and developments of Lutheran Christianity in Kerala. The fifth chapter is about the significance of Subaltern Studies in Kerala and the emergence of the major Subaltern movements in their immediate context. The unacknowledged situation of Lutherans in Kerala is analyzed in the sixth chapter. Final chapter is an exploration of the challenges and hopes of this unique solidarity. The study ends with the general findings and evaluation.

Scope and Limitations

The scope of the study is to analyze the impact of Christian Lutheran Missionary Movements among the backward class communities in Kerala. The major focus of this research is a critical analysis of the Missionary attitudes and approaches towards subalterns and their socio-religious and secular context. Different Lutheran agencies have their mission among the Muslims in Kerala like 'Gospel to Muslim' at Manjeri and 'Call of Hope' at Kayamkulam. There is one another small independent Lutheran Christian denomination in Kerala namely 'India Bible Lutheran Church' with its headquarters at Trivandrum. MELIM also worked among Muslims and Tribal peoples in Malabar areas. Now, the Mission in these places is under the Board for Mission IELC and not with the Trivandrum District Synod. In order to limit this research, Lutheran works in Kerala other than by MELIM and IELC are not included in the present research.

This research is intended to create a historical identity for the Christian Lutherans in Kerala. Even though the Lutheran presence is clearly evident in the beginning of Protestant Christianity in Kerala, this research likes to focus from 1911, when MELIM started their work in Malayalam-speaking area and ends with 2011. The main focus area of this research is the Trivandrum District Synod of India Evangelical Lutheran Church.

Previous Research

Few studies are available regarding the history of Christian Lutherans in Kerala. D. Christu Das' "Impact of Lutheran Mission among the Sambavars in South Travancore from 1907-1956" (M.Th. Thesis, 2000) gives an overview of the history of the Christian Lutherans in Kerala, its origin and impacts among one people group namely, Sambavars, and it is upto 1956 only. But the proposed research, beyond the perspective shift, is an attempt to do an indepth study of the history of the Lutheran Christians in Kerala with the inclusion of all people groups and covers half more century of its history, which is the period after the formation of the Trivandrum district Synod. Sam Thompson's M.Th. thesis (March, 2008) "Evolving An Ethical Critique In Relation To The Leadership Crisis Of The India Evangelical Lutheran Church (IELC) With Particular Reference To The Trivandrum Synod" focused on the ethical and leadership issues among the Lutheran Christians in Kerala. Neither Christian historians nor non-Christian historians tried to have a detailed study about this Church so far. As for the best of knowledge, the present researcher understands this as a pioneer attempt to study the whole history and its impacts in a systematic way.

Sources of Data

The present researcher uses available resources from different archives and Libraries, IELC headquarters and local churches. Primary resources are firsthand accounts of information. Along with personal diaries, letters, eye witness accounts of events and oral histories, the primary source materials include Missionary reports, proceedings of mission boards, Trivandrum District Conference minutes, letter of Missionaries and native workers, Church records. Records of Government proceedings, Administration reports, Census reports, Gazette reports, Government notifications, Travancore information and Listeners, News Paper cuttings from the Kerala State Archives are the valuable secular sources for this study. Secondary sources of information are records or accounts prepared by someone other than the person, or persons, who participated in or observed an event. For this study secondary sources include published books, articles from various journals like *Christiani*, *Lutheran Sabdham*, *Christian Patriot*, *Lutheran Witness* and previous study papers in Seminars and Souvenirs. The study materials are available at Concordia Seminary, Nagercoil, Synod headquarters at Trivandrum and Concordia Historical Institute, St. Louis. The existing works on IELC, the Records of Statistics, and unpublished thesis are also been consulted. Other information are collected through interviews and questionnaires.

Chapter 1

Socio-Cultural and Historical Context of Kerala

1.1. Introduction

The work of Christian Missionaries, which resulted in the humanization of the subjugated classes in Kerala, can be explained only against the socio-cultural and historical background of the period of their work. Though their work came as a peripheral factor in the life of the society, its direct and indirect impact functioned as one of the forces beyond many movements within the society. Therefore, it is necessary to know what have been the social conditions of its origin, and the social groups which had adopted this new faith. The role of socio-cultural factors in this process of adaptation needs to be critically evaluated. In order to analyse the context of Kerala during the period of study, a brief survey of the land and history, the people and their socio-cultural life settings including the caste system, untouchability and the communal awakenings are discussed in this chapter.

1.2. A Brief History of Southern Kerala

1.2.1. General

The State of Kerala was formed on 1st November, 1956. Before that date the region known as Kerala was divided into two political units, the United State of Travancore and Cochin and Malabar. Malabar was a district of the neighbouring Madras Presidency. Travancore and Cochin was the result of an integration of the two independent princely States on 1st July, 1949. Kerala was never a single political unit under one government prior to 1957, but the region has to credit a long and glorious history as a cultural, linguistic and ethnic unit, distinct from other parts of the country. Kerala, the home of Malayalam speaking people is one of the smallest States in India. The capital of Kerala is Thiruvananthapuram and this State has 14 districts.[1] Now the total population is 3.34 cores[2] of people, with 90.92% literacy rate[3] living with their tradition, culture, language, hopes and aspirations constitute the Kerala society.[4] Kerala represents 1.18% of the total area of India but 3.4% of the total population.[5] The southern part of Kerala with which this study is concerned formed the old Venad and later the Travancore State, consisting of the Taluks of Quilon, Kottarakara, Chirayinkil, Nedumangad and Trivandrum.

1.2.2. The Land

Kerala is a small strip of land lying at the South-west coast of India. It extends over an area of 38,863 sq. km.[6] The land strip is sandwiched between the Western

---

[1] No. of Taluks-63; No. of Revenue Villages-1478; No. of municipal Corporation-5; No. of Muncipalities-60; No. of District Panchayats-14; No. of Block panchayats-152; No. of *Grama* Panchayat-978. 5. *Diary 2013*, Government of Kerala, General Administration Department, 2013, 212.

[2] *Malayala Manorama Daily Newspaper*, 1 April 2011, Friday, 1. Census 2011 put Kerala's population at 33,387,677 persons who included 16,021,290 males and 17,366,387 females. Sex ratio (Females per 1,000 males)-1,084. Although, Kerala accounts for only 1%of the total area of India, it contains about 3% of the country's population. Rural population 17,455, 506 and Urban population 15,932,171.The population density of the State is about 859 people per square kilometres, three times the national average. Kerala is one of the densest States in the country. Kerala with a sex ratio of 1084 females' per 1000 males is the only State in India with a positive figure. In the human development and related indices it occupies prime position among the Indian States. (Source: Census 2011.) *Diary 2013*, Government of Kerala, General Administration Department, 2013, 212.

[3] According to 2011 Census it is 93.91% (Male 96.02 and female 91.98%).

[4] Census of Kerala: The earliest authentic account of census in this part of India is available from "Geographical and Statistical Memoir of the Survey of Travancore and Cochin States" conducted by Lieutenants Ward and Conner during the period 1816-20. Thereafter, censuses were taken in Travancore State in 1836 and Cochin state in 1854. But there are grounds to believe of frequent attempts made by the earlier rulers of the State to collect statistics of the population and the resources of the country. The first modern census of Travancore-Cochin was taken in 1875. From 1881 onwards the constitutional units of Kerala State had taken the census at 10 year intervals with the rest of the country. The first census of Kerala was taken in 1961. Thereafter, census is being taken every 10 years. The last census was taken in 2011. Census 2011 put Kerala's population at 33,387,677 persons who included 16,021,290 males and 17,366,387 females. Although, Kerala accounts for only 1% of the total area of India, it contains about 3% of the country's population. The population density of the State is about 859 people per square kilometres, three times the national average. Kerala is one of the densest States in the country. Kerala with a sex ratio of 1084 females' per 1000 males is the only State in India with a positive figure. In the human development and related indices it occupies prime position among the Indian States. (Source: Census 2011.)

[5] According to 2001 census Kerala's population is as follows: 31,841,374; Males: 15,468,614; Females: 16,372,760; Urban population: 25.97%; SC, 3,124,000 (9.81%), ST, 364,000 (1.14%); Literacy (%) 90.92; Males: 94.20; Females: 87.86. Kerala has 1,364 villages and 159 towns. (*Manorama Year Book* 2011, 573).

[6] Percentage of area of the State to the area of Indian Union-1.18.

Ghats (also known as the *Sahyadri*) in the East-the hill ranges with spices and tea plantations, wild life reserves, and small settlements- and the Arabian sea in the West. Kerala State locates north Longitude between 8' 18' and 12'48 and East Longitude between 74'52' and 77' 22'.[7] Geographically Kerala is small strip of land lying at India's south. It has formed by the annual deposit of mud brought by the rivers from the Western Ghats.[8] It can be viewed as a joint gift of the sea and the mountain.[9] The geographical location of the land surrounded with the sea and hills played a major role in the shaping of Kerala's history and culture. Kerala is "… a long fish-shaped land squeezed between the ranges of the Ghats and the beaches of the Arabian Sea."[10] Kerala has a total coast line of 580 Kms. Its width varies greatly from west to east. It is about 120 Kms at its maximum and just 30 Kms at its minimum. The mountain wall of Western Ghats forms an excellent frontier in the East with about 20 miles in the Palaghat region. Kerala is boarded by land on three sides and by the Arabian Sea in the west. It shares its boundary with the State of Karnataka at the north and the rest of Kerala shares its border with Tamil Nadu. In fact, almost the whole of the western and southern frontiers of Kerala is surrounded by Tamil Nadu.[11]

This land of antiquity is mentioned in the earliest writings in all literatures.[12] Most of the rivers of Kerala originate from the Western Ghats.[13] Kerala has a unique cropping pattern. Kerala is famous for plantations like tea, coffee, rubber and various spices. They cultivate cashewnuts, coconut, and areca nut, tapioca, banana, ginger, vegetables and rice. Kuttanad region of Kerala is the area of paddy cultivation and it is one of the very few places in India where cultivation is done below the sea level, 50% of people are engaged in agriculture. Kerala accounts for 91% of India's Rubber, 70% of Coconut, 60% of Tapioca and almost 100% of Lemon grass oil.[14] Coir and cashew are two large industries. Handloom and bamboo-based industries are well developed. Kerala accounts for about 1/3 of India's marine exports. Water is the main mode of Transportation in these areas.

[7] *Administration Report of Kerala State*, 1956-57:5. *Diary 2013*, Government of Kerala, General Administration Department, 2013, 212.

[8] K.V. Krishna Ayyar, *A Short History of Kerala*; Ernakulam: Pai & Co., 1966.1.

[9] A. Sreedhara Menon, *Social and Cultural History of Kerala* (New Delhi: Sterling Publishers, 1979), 9.

[10] George Wood Cook, *Kerala, a Portrait of the Malabar Coast* (London: Faber & Faber, 1967), 25.

[11] Anamudi (8841'), the highest peak in India after the Himalayas is in the Munnar division of Western Ghats. It ends at *Aramboly*, near Cape Comorin. This Cordomens Hills in the East isolated Kerala from the rest of the Peninsula. Arabian Sea in the West opened up Kerala to traders from the Middle East and Europe.

[12] V. Nagam Aiya, *The Travancore State Manuel, Vol.1,* (Trivandrum: Government Press, 1906), 229-231.

[13] No of rivers-44.

[14] *Manorama Year Book 2011* (Kottayam: Manorama Publications, 2011), 574.

Kerala is a land affluent in water resources with rivers and back waters. The back waters form especially attractive and economically valuable features of Kerala. The biggest backwater is Venad. Apart from 44 main rivers, countless number of streams and rivulets cross the land making it green and fertile and also serves as inland water wages. The number of lakes and back water lagoons enhance the beauty of the land. The wealthiest temple in the world is at Trivandrum, the capital city of Kerala, namely Sri Padmanabha Swamy Temple.[15] The history of this ancient land, obviously famous for overseas trade and rich cultural heritage has not been recorded systematically.

1.2.3. The Legend

The ancient history of Kerala is obscure. Traditions, legends and myths exist to narrate the founding of Kerala. One of the major legends is connected with a renounced Brahmin hero and one of the ten forms of the God Parasurama. After defeating some of the 'wicked' king, Parasurama was engaged in observance of penance. He threw an axe across the sea and the sea god *Varuna* and *Bhoomidevi* (the goddess of the earth) granted the coastal land, which later came to be known as *Keralam*. Thus *Keralam*, from Gokarnum to Kannyakumari, which had been submerged under the ocean in a former age, was recovered.

There are many versions for the Parasurama myth.[16] Kerala is occasionally referred to as *Bhargavaksethram* or *Parasuramaksethram* which means the land of Parasurama.[17] The land was also called as '*Dharma Rajyam*' because it was presented to the Brahmins by Parasurama. Parasurama myth can be best taken as the conquest of *Keralam* by the Brahmins.[18] It might be the explanation of the "Ariaynization of the west-coast.[19] "According to E.M. Sankaran Namboodhiripad, "...These stories of origin are the intensions of the land lords, most of who are either Namboodhiri Brahmins or very close to them.[20] This legend "... Embodies some geographical and geological facts pertaining to ancient Kerala."[21] However, the attention needs go to other stories of origin which speak about the glorious pre-Brahmin Kerala and Dravidian supremacy.

---

[15] *Malyala Manorama* (Mal.) Daily Newspaper, 2011 July Sunday, 1.

[16] P. Shangoonny Menon, *History of Travancore from the Earliest Times*, New Delhi: Asian Educational Services, 1985 (first published, 1878), 16-17.

[17] A. Sreedhara Menon, *Cultural History of Kerala*, 9.

[18] Samuel Mateer, *The Land of Charity* (London: John Snow & Co. 1871), 14.

[19] T.V. Kuppaswamy, "Reflections on the Genesis of Kerala" *Journal of Kerala Studies, Vol.1* (March, 1975), 8.

[20] E.M.S. Namboodhiripad, *Kerala: Yesterday Today and Tomorrow* (Calcutta: National Book Agency, 1968), 14.

[21] A. Sreedhara Menon, *A Survey of Kerala History* (Kottayam: NBS, 1970), 10.

1.2.4. The Ancient Dravidian Kerala

Sanskrit scholars derive the term Keralam from *Kera*, which means coconut. Persians and Arabs refer to this region as Malabar. Malabar is a synonym of the word *Mala Nadu* (which means the land of mountains). The state was known in different names at different times like *Venad, Vanchidesam, Thiru adi desam, malayala nadu.* Malayalam in its Tamil name signifies *mala* (hills) and *azham* (depth) i.e., the hill and dale country or the land at the foot of the mountains. Being hilly in the early Tamil records it was called as "kurichy."[22] Kerala was very likely a part of the larger Tamil country having common language, culture, beliefs and aspirations till the turn of second millennium AD. Once it was ruled by the *Cheras,* hence was called as *Chera* nadu. Slowly this *Cheranadu* changed to Kerala Nadu. Dr. Gundert, the author of a monumental Malayalam dictionary, observes that the word *'Keralam'* is 'the canaries' pronunciation" of the word *'Cheram'* and he describes "*Keralam*" as *"Cheram"* - the country between Gokarnam and Cumari.[23] The age of the *Chera* empire was a significant epoch in the history of Kerala.[24] The word *"charal"* in Tamil means the declivity of a hill or a mountain slope and according to some writers the word must have got itself corrupted in course of time into *charal,* giving its name to the Kerala or Chera country.[25] The people of Kerala were, by and large of Dravidian origin, with an earlier mix of Negroid and Australian races.[26] There was a ceremony at the Ambalapuzha temple called *Bhumiyarannu pattu.* This is a song used to be sung at the time of the temple festival relating to the search for a lost land. In this song they used the word *Malanad* instead of *Keralam.* Besides stating the divine origin of the *Vetan* community (the traditional exorcist) this song, mentions Christians as well as Ezhavas. That means this song might have been composed after the dawn of Christian era and before the spread of Islam. While speaking about the origin of Kerala, this song never mentions the name Parasurama.[27] It may mean that the Parasurama myth may be a later composition.

The *malanadu* broke away from the dominance and influence of Tamil following the death of Raja Raja Chola. Though freed from the Tamil power, *malanadu* could not continue to be a centralised imperial state. During the 12th century AD, it was broken up into a number of kingdoms. But a certain cultural identity (*Kerala maryada*) began to take definite shape from this time

---

[22] T.V. Kuppaswamy, *op.cit.*, 3.

[23] A. Sreedhara Menon, *Kerala History and its Makers* (Madras, 1990), 3 see also P. Sangoonny Menon, *History of Travancore,* 53.

[24] A. Sreedhara Menon, *Social and Cultural History of Kerala,* 51.

[25] T. Madhava Menon, *Hand Book of Kerala,* vol. 1 (Thiruvananthapuram: The International School of Dravidian Linguistics, 2000), 2.

[26] K.K. Kusuman, *Issues in Kerala Historiography* (Trivandrum: University of Kerala 2003), 185.

27

on.[28] After the 13th century, Kerala culture became more and more Sanskritic and Namboodhiri Brahmins and Nairs started flourishing both economically and politically.

1.2.5. Early History of Kerala

The period before the arrival of the Portuguese in 1498 is not clear, since historical facts are mixed with myths and puranic stories.[29] From the 15th century through the 17th century, the middle region of Kerala remained a powerful State. The rulers of this region were said to be the direct descendents of the ruling dynasty.[30] During the 18th century the small southern kingdom of Travancore, which the Brahmins named as *Dharma Bhoomi*[31] became powerful under the leadership of Marthanda Varma.[32] During the second half of the 18th century Haider Ali and

---

[28] K.V. Krishna Ayer, *A Short History of Kerala*, 51.

[29] Sachriya Zachariya (ed) Herman Gundert: *Keralolpathiyum Mattum* (mal) (Kottayam: DC Books, 1992).

[30] L.A. Krishna Ayyar, *Social History of Kerala, vol. 1. The Pre-Dravidians*, (Madras: Book Centre Publications, 1968), 2.

[31] Samuel Mateer translated this term as '*The Land of Charity*. Samuel Mateer, *op.cit.*, 1.

[32] The Travancore Royal family claiming decent from the *Kulasekhara* line of the *Cheras* ruled over the Indian State of Travancore until 1949. The royal family alternately known as the Kupaka royal family, *Thripappur swaroopam, Venad swaroopam,* etc., has its seat today at Trivandrum in Kerala. Marthanda Varma (1729-1758), the maker of modern Travancore and Dharma Raja were powerful rulers who re-established the power of monarchy in the State and destroyed that of nobles the *Ettuveettil Pillamar*. By the early 19th century the kingdom became a princely State under the British. Swathy Thirunal (1829-1846) was one of the most popular rulers of the 19th century. The regency of Sethu Lakshmibai (1924-1931) was a time which heralded many new reforms which were continued by Chithra Thirunal Balavarma (1931-1949). (Travancore kings. Marthanda Varma 1729-1758; Dharma raja 1758-1798; Balavarma 1798-1810; Gowri Lakshmi Bai 1810-1815; Gowri Parvathy Bai 1815-1829; Swathi Thirunal 1829-1846; Utharam Thirunal 1846-1860; Aayilyam Thirunal 1860-1880; Vishakom Thirunal 1880-1885; Moolam Thirunal 1885-1924; Sethu Lakshmibai 1924-1931; Chithra Thirunal 1931-1949.) The Legislative Reforms Act of 1932-33 by Chithra Thirunal, provided a bicameral legislature to Travancore. *(Travancore Administration Report, 1939-40,* 8.) Abolition of Devadasi system (1930), the University Act of 1931 and the Temple Entry proclamation of 1936 were the other important reforms of his reign. (Travancore Administration Report, 1939-40, 8.) Caste system and social distinction were provided in the Hindu society from time immemorial. The low castes were not allowed to enter into the Temples. After a long series of social revolutions the maharaja issued temple entry proclamation on 12th November 1936.(*The Regulations and Proclamations of Travancore, Vol.IX*, Trivandrum, 1936, 21.) The Travancore royal family style themselves as *Padmanabha dasas* (or servants of Padmanabha). (Travancore Directory for 1938, Part 11, 47). Since 1750 when maharaja Marthanda Varma made over the State to the deity of the Sri Padmanabha Swamy temple and vowed that from that day on, the royal family would rule the State on behalf of Him. The title of *Padmanabha dasa* is pre fixed to the name of every Travancore king, while females call themselves *Padmanabha Sevinies*. The important donation of the State to the temple was known as *Thripady danam*. The British government accorded the maharaja of Travancore a high 19 gun salute, whereas for all temple festivals, the highest salute of 21 guns was given. The Indian Constitutional amendments of 1971

later his son Tipu Sultan of Mysore were able to exercise political dominance and supremacy over the Malabar region for a short period. As per Sreedhara Menon, it was a "Shock Treatment" to the traditionally conservative Kerala society in favour of the less privileged minority.[33] The high caste Hindus were persecuted and made to flee for their lives. This condition indirectly created a new sense of self confidence and self respect - it also hastened the decline of feudal policy. British established their power over Malabar region in 1792.[34] Though rulers accepted British power, the patriotic element as represented by Pazhassi Raja in the north and Velu Thampi *Dalawa*[35] in the south challenged British supremacy in vain. 19th century Kerala witnessed the declension of Brahminical dominance and the supremacy of western power and influence.

1.2.6. Kerala under British Supremacy

It was in the 18th century that the British established themselves as the dominant political power in Kerala. The alliance between British East India Company and then Travancore king were renewed and strengthened in 1805. According to the arrangement they enhanced the subsidy. The native government felt it as unwanted and an enslaving one. Serious differences of opinion arose between the King, the Resident and the *Diwan.*[36] The *Diwan* justified his rebellion against the Resident and the Company due to the following reasons: the native Government had a heavy monetary loss; the Resident involved in the administration of the local government and due to the personal influence of the Resident there was a possibility to spread Christianity in Travancore. No doubt, it was a time when native rulers were guided, controlled and directed by the British Residents.[37] The prestige and dignity of each native king and his state were also determined by the British administration.[38] The Resident's powerful influence was evident on occasions like the promotion of the deputy *Peishkar* Krishna Rao to the

---

terminated the status of the royal families of the erstwhile princely States as rulers and abolished their rights to receive privy purses. However, the other clauses of the agreements signed between the government of India and princes in 1947 legally still hold. The royal family of Travancore has no administrative authority since 1971. The rights of the royal family over the Sri Padmanabha Swamy temple were respected and the head of the family still fulfils his duty towards the temple as the Maharaja of Travancore. The allowances of all the family members born prior to 1949 are also still paid by the government of Kerala.

[33] A. Sreedhara Menon, *Social and Cultural History of Kerala,* 55.

[34] The Travancore King Ramavarma entered into an alliance with the British power and renewed later in 1805. In 1809, Cochin State also entered into an alliance with the British.

[35] *Dalawa* was a title used in the 18th century to designate the head of the administration and by the latter half of that century it was changed to *Diwan.*

[36] C.M. Agur, *Church History of Travancore* (New Delhi: Asian Educational Services, 1930), 530.

[37] Dick Kooiman (ed.), *No Elephants for the Maharaja* (New Delhi: Manohar, 1994), 2.

[38] Lala Lajpat Rai; *Young India* (Delhi: Publication Division, 1965), 89-90.

position of Diwan.[39] "Even though, the British Resident involved in the internal administration, Travancore enjoyed complete liberty" says Yesudasan.[40] British presence also influenced the native government to introduce reforms in the administration itself. With a view to obtain popular support for the introduction of reforms into the administration the 'Legislative Council of Travancore (1888) and Sree Moolam Popular Assembly' (1904) were formed.[41] A gradual transmission from individual rule towards a more democratic form of government took shape.

1.2.7. Modern Kerala

Present day Kerala consists of three former principalities; Travancore, Cochin and Malabar. The move towards democracy and social change started in Kerala towards the end of the 19th century.[42] The political confrontations continued until 1947 when Travancore became free from the British and the *Diwan* of the king. On July 1, 1949, the two separate States of Travancore and Cochin were united as one Travancore-Cochin State under the guidance of the Home Minister of the new State. The legislatives of these two States were combined. The capital of the united State reminded at Trivandrum but the High Court was moved to Cochin. The first elected government was headed by T.K. Narayana Pillai. The internal discussions within the ruling Congress party led to the formation of a new Ministry in 1951 under C. Kesavan whose Chief Ministership lasted only a few months. After the Nair and Ezhava chief ministers, came a Christian Chief Minister A.J. John. He could stay in office only for about two years because of support was withdrawn by the Tamil-speaking legislators from Kanyakumari district.[43] They demanded the merger of Kanyakumari with the Tamil-speaking Madras State. John's ministry was succeeded by the Praja-Socialist party (PSP) Ministry headed by Pattom Thanupillai in March 1954 as Chief Minister. The Tamil agitation in the South took a violent turn when police opened fire and seven people from the agitator's side were killed. As a result, the PSP ministry quit office and was replaced by a Congress ministry headed by Panampally Govinda Menon in February 1955. This cabinet also fell in 1956 due to the internal fights

---

[39] P. Sangoonny Menon, *op.cit.*, 420-42.

[40] R.N. Yesudasan, *British Policy in Travancore, 1805-1859* (Trivandrum: Kerala Historical Society, 1977), 53.

[41] Ibid.

[42] Since the State Peoples Conference of Ernakulam, in April 1928, the people of Kerala demanded the formation of an all Malayalam-speaking united Kerala (*Aikya Kerala*). By the early 20th century, leaders like E.M. Sankaran Namboodiripad, A. K. Gopalan and T.M. Varghese, used communist ideologies to organize political mass movements both against British rule and the Travancore State. The *Aikya Kerala* movement also gathered momentum during the forties, during the struggle for independence and after. This was also a period when a lot of lower castes rose against caste subjugation and gained their rights to enter temples, and the women to cover their breasts. The Travancore state began to include elected representatives in the political administration.

[43] *Report of States Re-organization Commission,* New Delhi, 1955-81-84.

within the ruling party. This led to the imposition of President's rule in the State through the Governor.[44] It was during the President's rule that the States of the Indian Union were re-organized on linguistic basis. Under the State reorganization Act, the four Tamil speaking Southern Taluks; namely Thovalai, Agastheeswaram, Kalkulam and Vilavancode were separated from Kerala and added to Madras. The districts of Malabar and Kasargod Taluk of South Canara district were added to Travancore-Cochin to constitute the new Kerala State. The united Kerala came into existence on November 1, 1956. The first general elections held in Kerala in 1957 produced a surprise. In an assembly of 127, the Communist Party secured the majority. On 16th March 1957, for the first time in the history of the world, the Communist Party had come into power through democratic means with the first legislative Assembly of Kerala.[45] Kerala is a very politically sensitive State

---

[44] No. 4351/RC/56 *Government of India Ministry of Home Affairs Notification*, New Delhi, 23rd March, 1956.

[45] E.M. Sankaran Namboodhiripad was the Chief Minister. (*Times of India*, March 20, 1957 wrote "If the communists succeed in establishing an efficient and uncorrupted administration, they surely endear themselves to the people of the State." This was the general feeling both inside and outside the country). The ministry was dismissed in July 1959 because the opposition parties launched an agitation called *vimochana samaram* (Liberation struggle) which led to clashes between the police and mass protestors (Government of India. Ministry of Home Affairs, No.G.S.R.900, New Delhi, 31st July, 1959). During their period in power, the Communist Party passed two significant bills, the Education Bill and Agrarian reform Bill. After the Presidential rule, in February 1960 the second assembly was formed with Pattom Thanu Pillai as Chief Minister. (*Manorama Year Book 2004* (Kottayam: Manorama Publications, 2004), 176). This was a coalition of the Congress, Praja Socialist and Muslim League parties. The ministry lasted until September 1964. On 6th March 1967 again EMS became the Chief Minister. In October 1969, EMS resigned and C. Achutha Menon became the Chief Minister. In October 1970 the fourth assembly was formed with C. Achutha Menon as the Chief Minister. This was the first ministry in the history of Kerala which not only lasted five years, the full term, but also extended its term thrice. A fifth Kerala assembly witnessed the rule of three Chief Ministers; K. Karunakaran (March 1977 to 78), A.K. Antony (27 April 1978 to Oct. 19780), and P.K. Vasudevan Nair (1978 to Oct. 1979). (*Manorama Year Book 2004* (Kottayam: Manorama Publications, 2004), 177). In January 1980 seven political parties formed a coalition, the Left Democratic Front (LDF) under the leadership of Communist Marxist party and succeed the election E.K. Nayanar became the Chief Minister, After 22 months the ministry lost its support and Nayanar resigned. A new ministry with K. Karunakaran of the Congress party as the chief minister came to power in December 1981 and lasted until March 1982. In May 1982 United Democratic Front (UDF) won the election and again K. Karunakaran became the Chief Minister. Eighth assembly in March 1987 was formed under the leadership of E.K. Nayanar (LDF). During this ministry in April 1991 Kerala was declared as a totally literate State. In June 1991 again UDF won the election and K. Karunakaran became the Chief Minister. In 1995 A K Antony took over the Chief Minister position. In 1996, E K. Nayanar of the LDF again came to power. During this period, Kerala Govt. introduced the people's plan and campaigned for the planning and implementation development programmes at the grass root level. The peoples plan became a model for development and attracted worldwide interest. In June of 2001, the 11th assembly was formed with UDF in power with A.K. Antony again (3rd time) as the Chief Minister. *(Manorama Year Book 2004* (Kottayam: Manorama Publications, 2004), 180). 31 August 2004 to 18th May 2006, Oommen Chandy was the Chief Minister of Kerala. V.S. Achuthanandan became

to the extent that one can find heated political discussions even in the remote villages. Kerala is one of the states in the world where the leftists are democratically elected to power. The political sensibility of Kerala is the result of decades of political movements and people's participation. People are politically committed to reforms and changes in society.

1.3. Religious Context of Kerala

Kerala has a unique record in India for the harmonious coexistence of diverse religions compared to other states. Though geographically a small country, Kerala had given room for almost all religions of the world to set foot and flourish in their own ways. Hindus, Christians and Muslims are the major religious communities of the state, although a small population of Janis, Sikhs, Buddhists, Jews and some others are also present.[46]

1.4. The Socio-Cultural Life in Kerala

1.4.1. Caste System

Though the caste system was "an all India phenomenon", it was unknown in Kerala in the early years when it was a part of *Thamizhakam* and her people shared with it common cultural heritage.[47] The origin of caste lies deep in India's past. Caste system is a social hierarchy which determines social status and it is the worst form of oppression that exists in Indian society. Caste is an elaborate system grounded in Hinduism which may almost be said to be without parallel in the world. It consists in the division of society into hereditary classes or castes by colour, races, tribes, clans. The word caste is not of Indian origin, but it is derived from the Portuguese word *Casta* signifying race mould or quality,[48] *Varna* and *Jati* are the two Indian terms which explain the nature of caste. '*Varna*' (<Skt *varna*=colour) and '*jati*' (<Skt=birth).[49] But *Varna* is not the same as *jati*. The former represents the four-fold division of society and the latter represents the smaller groups other than the four *Varnas*. Recent studies bring forth the contradictions of these two categories. Sangeetha Rao clearly summarises it as follows: "*Varna* is dynamic and flexible as it is based on worth (quality), where as "*jati*" is fixed by birth and rigid and there is no place for worth (quality). This is the contradiction. It appears that

---

the Chief Minister of Kerala on 18th May 2006. In 2011 again Oomman Chandi of UDF leads the ministry of Kerala.

[46] As per the census of 2001, Hindus who constitute 56.20%, is the most prominent religious community in the State. This is followed by the Muslims who form 24.7% of the population and Christians constitute 19% of the total population of the State.

[47] A. Sreedhara Menon, *Social and Cultural History of Kerala*, 44.

[48] R.V. Russel and Hiralal, *Tribes and Castes of the General Provinces of India* (Delhi: Cosmo Publications, 1984), 8.

[49] J.H. Hutton, *Caste in India* (Delhi: Oxford University Press, 1946), 64-65.

'*varnavyavastha*'and '*jati*' have different origins and developments."[50] Therefore, *Varna* appears to be based on religion but *jat*i determines one's social position through life.[51] Caste has religious significance and religious sanction. The four fold caste division of the Hindu Community was defined by Manu. Manu is the mythical figure believed to have given Dharma Sasthra (ethical codes and caste duties) for the people of India. Thus, beyond a social or economic order it is a 'religious institution.'[52] The Census Report (1901) states that there were nearly 500 castes among the Hindus.[53] The theoretic foundation of caste made on the firm belief that it was a divinely ordained institution. "*A Brahmin is born not made, so is a Sudra... A Brahmin by neglect to perform his religious ceremonies and caste observances may become an outcaste; but no member of a lower caste can rise to a higher one, as the Hindu religion by its peculiar constitution does not allow converts from one form to another of its own fait ....*"[54] Hence, the upward mobility of persons from one caste to another is made impossible in Kerala through the rigidity of caste system.

An alien system of society based on caste was introduced by the advent of *Aryans* by uprooting the indigenous people who lived during that period. During the eighth century AD the *Aryan* invasions in Kerala reached its peak.[55] Kunjan Pillai observes: "before the arrival of the Aryans the caste system was unknown in Dravidian society". And he continues "Brahmins who reached Kerala from the Deccan were able to subjugate the land during the period between the 8th and 11th centuries AD. Kerala was enclosed in the straitjacket of the caste system."[56] The thousands of years of friendly and peaceful co-existence had come to an end in the 12th century; the caste system was firmly established in Kerala. From then, "Caste has been the dominant factor in the economic and cultural life of Kerala."[57] In course of time, the distinctions between castes increased. This process was known as '*Aryanization*' or *'Sanskritaization.'*[58] They spread the *'chathurvarnyam'* or four

---

[50] R. Sangeetha Rao, *Caste System in India Myth and Reality* (New Delhi: India Publishers and Distributers, 1989), 66.

[51] For detailed study on of the term *jati, varna* and *caste*, see Sharti Swarup Gupta, *Varna, Caste and Scheduled Castes*, (New Delhi: Concept Publishing Company, 1991).

[52] *Travancore Census Report 1891, Vol 1.* 615. This census report gives a scholarly account of the caste system in Kerala.

[53] T.K. Velupillai, *op.cit.*, Vol. 1, 401.

[54] *Travancore Census Report, 1891,* Vol, 1. 614.

[55] A. Sreedhara Menon, *op.cit.*, 66.

[56] E. Kunjan Pillai, *Studies in Kerala History*, 311.

[57] Ibid., 312.

[58] "Sanskritization is the process by which a low Hindu caste or Tribal or other group, changes its customs, ritual, ideology and way of life in the direction of a high and frequently," twice-born' caste. Generally such changes are followed by a claim to a higher position in the caste hierarchy than that traditionally conceded to the claimant caste by the local community" for more discussion see

caste groups, i.e., Brahmins, Kshathriyas, Vaisyas and Sudras. High caste Hindus called themselves as *Savarnas*'[59] (people with *varna* or followers of *varnadharma*) and others as "*Avarna*' (outside the *varna* discipline). Implementation of the new social laws which followed the introduction of the caste system was exclusively for the comfort of the *Savarnas,* especially the Brahmins. Among the *Savarnas,* Brahmins stood at the top of the hierarchy. The Hindu Nambudiri or Malayali Brahmins, non Malayali Brahmins (*Pattar or Ayyar*), Ambalavasies, (temple servants), Potris, Elayathu, etc., were the sub castes among the *Savarnas.* The Kshathriyas are the Nairs of Malayali Sudras. The *Avarnas* the non Hindus, include the Nadars, Ezhavas, the Christians and Muslims. The outcastes include the Pulayas, Parayars, Kammalars, Baratas, Chakkilians, Kaniyars, Kavathies, Mukkuvans, Panas, Tantans and Velans.[60] Apart from these polluting castes, there were the Nayadies, Arayans and the hill tribes like Kanikkars, Mala Pandarams, Kuravans and Vedans. According to the common law of the country, they were considered untouchables. They were strictly prohibited into temples, barred from using public wells, tanks, and *chathrams.*[61] All social relationships, such as marriage, were limited within the caste and only exemption granted for Brahmin men to have concubine with any women from the *Savarna* caste.[62] The society in Kerala generally presented a picture of social disabilities and inequalities due to caste rules. The rule of pollution made it necessary that the *Avarna* people should not even approach the *Savarnas.* Popular versions regarding the origin of caste are based on the colonial theories by quoting the Manu Dharmasasthra (V111, 413-414) and Rig Veda (X90: 11-12). They identify the *varnas* as based on 'purity of blood' with what is assumed to have been the Aryan invasion. These theories of Aryan conquest and racial hierarchy originated during the colonial period. They have been abandoned by critical modern scholars.[63] Madhava Rao says: "...The people being orthodox and conservative; strictly the ancestral norms of conduct and religion."[64] A brief description about the major caste will help us to understand the people's relationships.

M.N. Srinivas. *The Dominant Caste and other Essays* (Madras: Oxford University Press, 1987) and M.N. Srinivas, *Social Change in Modern India* (Los Angeles: University of California Press, 1986), 6.

[59] *Savarnas* (the first four castes in the hierarchy) are generally called upper caste Hindus or simply caste Hindus." Christians and Muslims were regarded as castes too, and accepted such a state". M.N. Sreenivas, *Religion and Society among the Coorgs of South India* (London: Asia Publishing House, 1952), 31.

[60] C. M. Agur, *Church History of Travancore*, 569ff.

[61] E. Kunjan Pillai, *op.cit.*, 432.

[62] E. Kunjan Pillai, *Kerala Charithrathile Iruladanja Edukal* (Mal.) (Kottayam: NBS, 1970), 2.

[63] William Logan, *Malabar, vol. 1* (New Delhi: Asian Educational Services, 1995), 109; Gabriele Dietrich and Bas Wielanga, *Towards Understanding Indian Society* (Madurai: TTS, 1977), 40.

[64] T. Madhava Rao to the Resident dated Trivandrum 24, November, 1868, *Political Proceedings, 1869,* vol. 111, 442.

1.4.2. The Nambudiri Brahmins

As said above, in the hierarchical order, the Brahmins were given the highest place. The whole frame work of Hinduism was conceived for the comfort and exaltation of the Brahmins. They dominated the whole society in all spheres of life. They claimed to have come out of mouth of Brahman and considered them as the very image of Brahma on earth and were respected and worshiped. The Brahmins were, twice born, who alone could legitimately rule the country through certain special religious ceremonies. According to Thurston, the traditional view of a Nambudiri is: "His person is holy; his directions command; his movements are a procession; his meal nectar, he is the holiest of human beings, the representative of God on earth."[65] Although their numbers were not very great, the Nambudiris were the most influential section who dominated the social scene of Kerala. About their high and singular superiority Prof. Kunjan Pillai writes: "The Namboodiris were the real rulers of Kerala from the 11th century to the 16th. The kings were mere servants of the Nambudiris. The Nambudiris in Kerala were masters in the arts and science of war as well as learning and scholarship…"[66] They enacted the laws and even controlled the kings. As the royal astrologers they designed the destiny of the state and fixed the times for the auspicious functions of the land.[67] Brahmins were exempted from all social and religious disabilities. According to their sacred laws killing a Brahmin is a serious sin. A king cannot even think of it, because they believed that they were the law givers and the visible presence of Brahman. Therefore, Brahmins totally escaped from capital punishment,[68] and the crimes committed by them were viewed very lightly.[69] They became rich by virtue of their claims and rights. They were large land-holders and most often absolute tax-free owners of the soil.[70] As head priests and trustees of the temples many of them became enormously rich. The accumulation of wealth made them idle pleasure seekers and unfit for hard work. Education was their sole privilege because it was taboo for the low castes. According to the Aryan rule, the Sudras or the low castes were not allowed even to hear learning.[71] They were the priests, philosophers and scholars who interpreted the scriptures and dictated all social, political and religious law of the land. The rulers considered it their privilege and sacred duty to keep them happy. The kings spent large sum of money for

[65] E. Thurston, E, *op.cit.*, vol. 1, 160.

[66] E. Kunjan Pillai, *Studies in Kerala History*, 195.

[67] Ibid., 265.

[68] Francis Buchanan, *Journey from Madras through the Countries of Mysore, Canara and Malabar, Vol.111,* (London: Asian Educational Services, 1807), 325; T. Krishna Kurup, *Kerala Charithram Parasuramaniloode* (Mal.) (Kottayam: NBS, 1962), 87.

[69] S. Mateer, *Land of Charity,* 311.

[70] J. H. Hutton, *Castes in India*, 14.

[71] Kunjan Pillai, *op.cit.*, 116.

the support and comfort of them. Free feeding inns known as *ootupuras* were established all over Kerala to feed them at the expense of the State. The practice of polyandry among Nair women led to creation of the Nambudiris for their personal comfort. It was called as "Sambandhom."[72] It began to demoralise society. The thrusting of prostitutions on young girls and the heartless denial of 'paternity' became sociological factors that seriously affected the morale of the society and tended to degrade the status of women.[73] The Brahmins also practised child marriage but remarriage of widows was strictly prohibited. This created a large number of widows and unmarried women among this community and many of them died as virgin widows.[74] N. Subrahmanya Aiyar gives a detailed description of how Nambudiri women suspected of immorality were tried and punished by the Nambudiris.[75] Kerala society witnessed many changes in the 19th and 20th century and naturally Brahmins became the losers. This community also underwent many changes.

1.4.3. The Nairs

Next to Brahmins in the social scale in Kerala was Nairs, the largest single caste.[76] There are various theories regarding the origin of the Nairs and "no two opinions agree" on the subject.[77] According to Brahmin tradition, the Nairs are born of the union between Nambudiris and Deva, Gandharva and Rakshasa women introduced by Parasurama.[78] Henry Bruce suggests that "the Nairs may have come from Nepal."[79] Chattampi Swamikal, K.P. Padmanabha Menon and others assert that they are the decendents of the Nagas who held sway over Kerala.[80] They like to call themselves as *Kshathriyas* which comprised the *Coil Thampurans*, the Rajas or the *Tirumulpads*.[81] Even though they were considered as Sudras, the studies do not accept this. They might not be Sudras, but the people who were ready to serve the Brahmins were formed as a new caste, the Nairs. Later they became a unique community with power and influence, in almost all temporal

---

[72] *Sambandham* was legally abolished only by the Namboodiri act of 1933.For more discussions see Peter, H. R. Prince, *A Study of Polyandry* (Hauge: Mouton & Co 1963), 167-68 and K.P. Padmanabha Menon, *op.cit.* 94.

[73] Joy Gnanadason, *Forgotten History*, 36; P. Raman Nambudiri, *Nambudirimar* (Mal) Trichur, 1918.85ff; see also F. Fawcett, *Nayars of Malabar* (Madras 1901), 225ff.

[74] 'The Re-marriage of Hindu widow', *Keralopakary*, April 1905: 54.

[75] *Census Report of India, 1901,* vol. XXVI, Travancore, Part 1-report, 311ff.

[76] K. Thulaseedharan, Studies in Traditional Kerala Society, *TCDR, vol. 1.CC No.1* (February, 1910), 90.

[77] K.P. Padmanabha Menon, *History of Kerala*, vol. 3, 161.

[78] E .Thurston, *op.cit.*, vol, 284.

[79] Henry Bruce, *Letters from Malabar and on the Way* (London: W.H. Allen & Co, 1909), 284.

[80] K.P. Padmanabha Menon, *op.cit.*, 161.

[81] *Census of India 1931,* Vol. XXV11, Travancore, Part 1, report, Trivandrum, 1932:369.

and spiritual affairs of the State.[82] They acted as the body guards to the kings and to the Namboodiris.[83] They were the protectors of Brahmins in all respects.[84] Though the Nairs were subordinate to the Brahmins, they dominated the other castes. Though the entire land of Kerala was under the Brahmins, in practice, the Nairs were the real owners. In the 19th century, Kerala became feudal in nature and the Nairs owned most of the land. These feudal lords exercised their authority through assemblies or *Koottoms/pidagai.* They were wealthy merchants, farmers and skilled artisans.[85] The Nairs were great warriors and extremely skilful to use arms. The Nair children were trained in their military gymnasium called *kalaris.* They formed the military and police. They also were the principal owners of slaves in the South[86] and were highly oppressive in all respects.[87] Their alliance with Brahmins gave them enormous power and influence. The Brahmins had concubine relationships with Nair women. The Nair women practised polyandry without reservation and had several husbands.[88] Their women were the worst sufferers of the system called *sambandam.* Consequently, their inheritance was matrilineal known as *marumakkathayam.* The inheritance and succession were through the sister's children in the female line.[89] The administration of the family was entrusted to the eldest male member of the family, who was known as the *Karanavar.*[90] Naturally they were against British authorities and Christian Missionaries. Because of that, often they challenged existing customs and social norms of the high caste dominance over the lower castes.

1.4.4. The Nadars

Below the Nairs in the social pyramid of Kerala were the peoples from the working class marked as outcastes. Of these, are the *Shannars,* also known as Nadars, in the South and Ezhavas in the North occupied the highest position. Francis Buchanan equates both *shannars* of South and Thiyas (Ezhavas) of the North together.[91] The high caste called them *Shannars* while they called themselves as Nadars. In the Census Report of India 1921, on the representation of Nadars, the government of

---

[82] *Ibid.* 376. They were the protectors of Brahmins in all respects; E. Elamkulam Kunjan Pillai, Studies in Kerala History, 314.

[83] *Census of India 1931,* Vol. XXV111, Travancore, Part 1, report, Trivandrum,1932: 37-60.

[84] E. Elamkulam Kunjan Pillai, *Studies in Kerala History,* 314.

[85] B. Sobhanam, "*Fall of Nair Dominance in Kerala*" *Ithihasa,* (Hyderabad, 1980 vol. 111, no. 2), 94.

[86] Samuel Meter, *The Native Life in Travancore,* 291.

[87] C. M. Agur, *Church History of Travancore* (New Delhi: Asian Educational Service, 1980) (1903), 569.

[88] E. Sredhara Menon, *Social and Cultural History,* 94-96.

[89] Ibid., 83.

[90] R. Muthookrishna Naidoo, *The Law of Inheritance among the Sudras of Malabar* (Kottayam: NBS, 1971), 2.

[91] Francis Buchanan, *A Journey from Madras.* Vol. 2. 415.

Madras chose to recognize them as Nadars and issued an order to that effect in July 1921.[92] They were considered as a 'half polluting' caste but were free from some of the restrictions placed on the still lower classes. There are different opinions about the place of origin of the Nadar caste. According to Robert Caldwell, Ceylon is the place of their origin.[93] The Nadars claims that they had a glorious past as a warrior class. The Nadars of Kerala claimed that they had migrated into this state at the request of the Kings of Travancore to serve them. This could lend credence to the fact that they were patronised by the early kings of Travancore. Because of migration, they adopted various professions such as practising martial arts, doing agricultural operations, manual labour and extracting sweet toddy from the Palmyra tree. During the 19th century Nadars were one of the agricultural castes.[94] Some of them claimed that they belonged to the Saivaist religious tradition.[95] The hereditary occupation of the Nadars was cultivation and climbing the Palmyra palm, the juice of which they boil with a coarse sugar.[96] During the 19th century many of them turned to different occupations other than the traditional one.[97] The Nadar occupied "a social limbo somewhere between the Sudras and the outcaste untouchables."[98] Caldwell observes: "They may in general be described as belonging to the highest division of the lower classes; or the lowest of the middle classes: poor, but not paupers; rude and unlettered, but by many degrees removed from savage state."[99]

More serious were their social bondages. The government and the caste Hindus oppressed the Nadars. The government imposed oppressive taxes and the most oppressive was a capitation tax they collected even for the deceased members of the family. There were a large number of taxes such as *purushadhanam* (*talai Irai* = poll tax) levied on all the male members of a family, living and dead. A tax of 25% nominally levied by the government on all inheritable property like – *Iray panam, velai padivu*. There was a tax for the hair one grew and for the breast of the women called a breast-tax.[100] They did free services (*ooliyam*) to government. They are expected to supply the things like Palmira leaf to government for writing purposes. A Christian missionary John Cox wrote about the sufferings of Nadars as follows: "…it is not beyond the reach of the Government officers and of their oppressive doings. These men find their way into every corner seizing the people's

[92] The Government of Madras–Law (General) Department G 6 no. 785 dated July 7th, 1921.

[93] R. Caldwell, *The Tinnevely Shannars* (London: ISPCK, 1850), 5.

[94] Samuel Matteer, *op.cit.*, 66.

[95] E. Thurston, *op.cit.*, vol. V, 372.

[96] E. Thurston, *op.cit.*, vol. V, 4.

[97] Ibid., 372ff.

[98] R. L. Hardgrave, *The Nadars of Tamil Nadu*, 21.

[99] R. Caldwell, *Tinnavely Shannars*, 5.

[100] A detailed account of the various taxes collected from the Nadar and the brutal way in which they were collected are given in C M. Agur, *Church history of Travancore, op.cit.*, 585-586.

goods and forcing them in the name of their government, to labour without pay.[101] Up to the middle of the 19th century they were not permitted to build good and tiled houses. When the Nadars attempted to build decent houses, in the late 1870'such houses were destroyed by Nairs.[102] They were not allowed to carry umbrellas, to use foot-wear or carry water pots on their hips. They had to keep spatial distance from the high castes. They could not milk cows. The Nadar women were not allowed to cover the upper part of their body. Socially degraded and economically exploited, the Nadars lived in a state of fear, humiliated and despised until the middle of the 19th century. In this social bondage, Nadars got attracted to Christianity.

1.4.5. The Ezhavas

Scholars differ in their opinion of origin of Ezhavas and their earlier social status. According to Herman Gundert, a generally acknowledged authority, they had come from *Ezham* (Sri Lanka) during the pre historic period.[103] They were also known as Tiyas.[104] On account of their traditional profession as well as character, Ezhavas were suspected of having a common origin. But "all Ezhava sub-castes speak Malayalam, whereas the Nadars are Tamilians."[105] While Ezhavas are thickly populated in northward starting from Trivandrum, Nadars are mostly populated in the Tamil region downward from Trivandrum.[106]

They were known by different caste names, "....In the Central Travancore as *Ilavars*; from Quilon to Paravoor, Chogans; in Malabar, as far as Calicut they are called *Teers.*"[107] Like *Nadars, Ezhavas* were also one of the lower castes, the *Avarnas* or the out castes. Their traditional occupation was the cultivation of coconut palms and produce toddy from it. They are also agriculturists, weavers, boatman, petty traders, teachers, priests, doctors and like. Because they belonged to the polluting castes an *Ezhava* was obliged to keep a minimum distance of 36 feet from a Brahmin. They were compelled either to leave the road at the approach of a Brahmin or to announce their own approach by a special cry "*Hai, Hai.*"[108] They were also exploited and harassed by higher castes as well as by the

---

[101] John Cox, letter in Annual Report of the London missionary society 13th May 1841, 72 quoted from J. W. Gladstone, *Protestant Christianity and People's Movement in Kerala*, (Trivandrum: Seminary Publication, 1984), 30.

[102] *The Indian Evangelical Review*, July 1874, vol. 1, No. V, 10.

[103] Herman Gundert, *Keralolpathiyum Mattum*; (mal) (Kottayam: D C Books, 1992), 261-26.

[104] K.V. Krishna Ayyar, *op.cit.*, 15.

[105] Samuel Mateer, *Native Life in Travancore*, 83.

[106] Robin Jaffery, *Declain of Nair Dominance; Society and Politics in Travancore, 1847-1908*. (New Delhi: Manohar Publications, 1976), 20.

[107] S. Mateer, *Native Life in Travancore*, 83.

[108] V.T. Samuel, *One Caste, One Religion, One God: A Study of Sree Narayana Guru* (New Delhi: Steerling Publications, 1977), 27.

government. The missionary work saw some conversion among them and the Lutheran missionaries expected a mass conversion from them. Their aspirations for social development found its fulfilment through the work of their own people like Dr. Palpu, and Sree Narayana Guru and the movement initiated by them.

1.4.6. The *Pulayas*

The *Pulayas* and the Pariahs constituted the slave castes and occupied the lowest section in the Kerala society. The term *Pulaya* is derived from '*pula*' which means ceremonial pollution. During the second Chera Empire, the *pulayas* were an influential and dignified community. Once they were the rulers of the land.[109] The Pulayanarkotta (fort of the Pulayas) at Trivandrum, the capital city of present Kerala is a visible sign of their royal ancestry.[110] Caldwell opines that the Pulayas were the earliest race or inhabitants in Kerala.[111] Whatever the glory of their past, later they became one of the most degraded castes. They were slaves of the higher castes and were bought and sold like cattle and not valued as human being. They were punished very brutally.[112] Their houses were miserable huts and they were not permitted the free use of the paths. They were not permitted to the entrance to the public market for purchase or sale of things. The *Pulayas* who made umbrellas, reed baskets and other small articles placed on the public path and went back to scheduled a distance. From there, they shout the price and the customers take the articles and place the money there. If a *Pulayan* wanted to make a purchase, he had to place his money and under a stone and retired to the scheduled distance. When the merchant or the seller comes, the *Pulayan* would shout out his needs. The merchant would take the money and keep on the stone whatever he needs. This was always a disadvantage for the slaves. Ironically, though the nearness of low castes polluted the high castes, the rice they produced and other things they made did not pollute them! Freedom was beyond the imagination for them. The abolition of slavery (Trivandrum 1853; Cochin 1855) did not help them to attain the upward social mobility. A new awakening appeared in this community during the second half of the 19th century through Christianity. They converted to Christianity in large numbers hoping for social and human dignity. They are still on the way to progress.

1.4.7. The *Sambavars*

The word '*Sambava*' means the worshipper of Siva. *Samban* is Siva, Hindu God.[113] *Sambavars* are found throughout *Southern Kerala* but are more common

---

[109] K. K. Kusuman, *Slavery in Travancore* (Trivandrum: Kerala Historic Society, 1973), 25.

[110] S. Mateer, *Native Life in Travancore,* 35 and E. *Thurston, The Castes and Tribes in South India,* vol. ii, 47.

[111] J. W. Gladstone, *op.cit*., 33.

[112] J. W. Gladstone, *op.cit*., 34.

[113] K.S. Singh, *op.cit.,* 1138.

in the southern taluks. Singh observes that, "they are also known as '*paraiyan*' and '*adi dravida.*'"[114] According to Velupillai, "in South Travancore *paraiyas* call themselves as Sambavars."[115] In the 19th century the term '*Sambavars*' was used to denote the people of the *paraiyah* community. During the 20th century onwards they did not like to call themselves as *paraiyahs* thinking that it dehumiliate them. Robert Deliegue points out "In Tamil Nadu calling someone a '*parayar*' implies contempt and will be taken as an insult."[116] The Tamil Nadu Government has also accepted the term '*Sambavar*' equal to '*Paraiyah*'.[117] They will vehemently oppose if someone calls them as *paraiyahs* in these days. They prefer to address them as 'Adi Dravida.'[118] There are different local traditions about their origins. While writing on *Paraiyas* of Kerala J.W. Gladstone says thus:

> "*It is believed that they exercised much power and enjoyed a high position as masters of the land before the arrival of the Brahminic races. The Paraiahs claimed that they ruled over the land in ancient times. In the past there were many people of repute from among them such as poets, men of wisdom etc. It has also been traced that in many traditions and customs there are many points of similarity or connections between the Parayahs and Brahmins.*"[119]

Some of the recent scholarly research works point to the fact that *Dalits – Paraiyas* – could have been '*Palaiyars*', which means ancient or original people who lived in small independent kingdoms and owned large tracts of land and that they were mostly agriculturists.[120] Their traditional occupation was drum production and drum beating. But H.A. Stuart argues that "it is only one section of *Paraiyas* that act as drummers. Nor is the occupation confined to *Paraiyas.*"[121] Hutton says

---

[114] Ibid.

[115] T.K. Velupillai, *op.cit.*, vol. 1, 297.

[116] Robert Deliege, *op.cit.124*.

[117] They are notified under different names such as '*praiyan*', '*prayan*', '*paraiah*' and '*sambavar*'. At present they are called as Adi Dravida. *Parahiya* is a small hill tribe or caste in Mirzapur district of Uttar Pradesh, Hutton: *Caste in India*, 292.

[118] In 1918, the *Paraiya Mahasabha* appealed to the Govt. of Travancore to abandon their disgraceful name '*Paraiya*' and to give them the highly respectable name 'Adi Dravida', denoting the original inhabitants of the Dravidian land. In 1922, the Provincial Legislative Council of Travancore passed a resolution recommending that the name 'Adi-Dravida' should be given to the *Paraiyas* (G.O.817 Law (Gen) 25 March, 1922) Kshirasagar, *Dalit Movements in India and its Leaders*, 72.

[119] J.W. Gladstone, *op.cit.*, 57.

[120] F.J. Balasundaram. "Set us free A Cry of the Marginalised: Dalit Perspective," *NCC Review* 119/4 (April, 1999), 275-294.

[121] E. Thurston, op.cit., 78; Bishop Robert Caldwell (1814-1891) is of the opinion that the name 'parayan' is from the Tamil word 'parai' – a drum; as certain parayans act as drummers in various occasions.

that "they were field laborers and village servants."[122] While describing their life and work, Nagam Aiya observes: "*The Parayas are a most patient and industrious class of people and the occupation of a vast majority is agricultural laborers. They are mostly serfs attached to the soil and generally very faithful to their masters. Most of the domestic servants of the Europeans in South India are drawn from this class.*"[123] They manufactured wickerwork, drums, bamboo mats and baskets, and caddie umbrellas.[124] They were the gravediggers, scavengers and watchmen. They irrigated their master's field and also tended horses, cattles and elephants. They were also known as carriers, sweepers and manual laborers. *Sudras* and *Shanars* employed them.

They were the lowest among the slave castes. Slavery among them was common but not all were slaves.[125] Tamil was their mother tongue in South Travancore and they spoke a unrefined form of Malayalam.[126] Education was prohibited to them as it was a taboo. Barely one in a hundred is a literate.[127] Owing to illiteracy they were at a very low position in the social scale. Their approach was considered polluting by the high castes. They should stand 72 feet away from the higher caste to avoid pollution by touch or approach.[128] Their houses were, therefore, situated away from the residential quarters and were built outside the ordinary village limits. They were called '*paracheris.*'[129] They were highly ignorant and superstitious and were steeped in poverty. They were prohibited from drawing water from the wells of other castes; they had their own wells near their habitation, around which they place the bones of animals and waste.[130] If anyone of them happened to enter the Brahmin quarter or street, they would greet him with cow-dung water.[131] They were normally Saivaites but were really zealous demon worshippers.[132] Their chief demons being *Madan* (the cow one), *Mallan*, *Karumkali* (Black Kali), *Chevas*, *Bhutam*, etc.[133] Devil dance, sorcery, magical charms were parts of their religion. Samuel Mateer observes that "in Trivandrum this caste people are rather strongly built and bold. They live in

[122] J.M. Hutton. *op.cit.*, 292.

[123] V. Nagam Aiya, *op.cit.*, 403. K.S. Singh also supports this view. The Scheduled Castes, op.cit., 1060.

[124] T.K. Velupillai, *op.cit.*, vol. 1, 860.

[125] Samuel Mateer, Native Life in Travancore, 82; John C. Webster. *The Dalit Christians: A History* (Delhi: ISPCK, 1992), 23-39.

[126] John C. Webster, *The Dalits Christians: A History* (Delhi: ISPCK, 1992), 27.

[127] T.K. Velupillai, *op.cit.*, 438.

[128] C. Achutha Menon. *The Cochin State Manual* (Trivandrum: Govt. of Kerala, 1995), 251.

[129] T.K. Velupillai, *op.cit.*, vol. 1, 860.

[130] Edgar Thurston, *op.cit.*, 78.

[131] G.S. Churge, *Caste and Race in India* (Bombay: Popular Prakasam, 1979), 1.

[132] V. Nagam Aiya, *op.cit.*, vol. 11, 402.

[133] J.W. Gladstone, *op.cit.*, 38.

hamlet and eat the purified flesh of dead cattle, tigers and so on."[134] Among them unity is almost non-existent even though they feel themselves to be members of the same caste. Being a *Harijan* he is like being a member of a family which has the plague – the best thing is to leave it.[135] They are divided into four endogamous subgroups, namely, *Melakkaran* (drummers), *Pettipottupavar* (who makes boxes), *Samsari* (agriculturist) and *Ur Paraiyan* (village *paraiyan*). The basis for these divisions appears to be occupational. Now-a-days intermarriage between subgroups is reported.[136] It was only during the later part of the 19th and early part of the 20th centuries that a new awareness about progress became visible among them. They are still on the way to progress.

1.4.8. The Tribals

Apart from the above polluting castes, there were the ***Nayadis*** and the hill tribes. The *nayadis* were one of the most degraded and wretched of all the debased tribes of Kerala. Almost naked and shunned by all classes, they lived far away from villages in small huts erected in solitary places.[137]

1.4.8.1. The *Araians*

Among the other tribes the ***Araians*** are the prominent ones. They were usually called as Mala Araian (Mala=Hill). Their home is mainly in the mountains. Unlike many other hill tribes they had fixed villages. They were severely oppressed by government officials who exacted free labour from them particularly for carrying hill products to the plain.[138] Their headmen were supposed to offer food products to Nairs and certain quantity of forest resources to Brahmins and Maharajas. Christian and Muslim traders also exploited them to collect many articles from the jungle for export and trade.[139] They were a people open for exploitation by many other groups, having no protectors to save them. They were the people who were victims by frequent epidemic and natural calamities. They had a practice of worshipping their ancestors as heroes. Later they found Christianity as a means for their prosperity, liberation and leadership.

1.4.8.2. The *Kuravars*

The *Kuravars* are one of the early tribes who mainly inhabited the southern part of Kerala. They believe that they had their own kings and kingdom. The *Kuravans* consisted of two sections, one living in the plains and the other in the jungles. The former was known as *Kuravans* and the latter as *Malankuravans.*

---

[134] Samuel Mateer, *Native Life in Travancore*, *op.cit.*, 82.

[135] Robert Deliege, *op.cit.*, 127.

[136] K.S. Singh, *op.cit.*, 1138-1139.

[137] Sherring, *Hindu Tribes and Castes*, London, 1881, vol. 111, 191.

[138] Samuel Mateer, *op.cit.*, 78.

[139] J.W. Gladstone, *op.cit.*, 41.

They were nomadic agriculturists and moved to new areas within few years. They also have exorcist and foretelling people among them. Till the middle of the 19th century, they were also slaves who bought and sold along with land. They were also excluded from the possibility of education. Their progress towards socio-economic and educational fields has been very slow. Many of them embraced Christianity in the beginning of the 20th century.

1.4.8.3. The *Kanikar*

They are a jungle tribe inhabiting the mountains of southern Kerala. They are strong and sturdy race well fitted for the wilds they inhabited. As they were nomads, they did not put up permanent dwelling places.[140] They are said to be characterized by high standard of honour, straight forwardness, honesty and truthfulness.[141] Some of them are engaged as coolies on plantation estates or cutting bamboo for contractors. They live by collecting and selling honey and many of nature's produce. There were a number of exorcist and fortune tellers among the *Kanikars*. Many of them were converted to Christianity, but most of them remain socially, economically and educationally backward due to the lack of education.

1.4.8.4. The *Vedans*

They were formerly hunters and soldiers and this tribe furnished a considerable and valuable contingent to the early Hindu kings and later armies of Hyder and Tipu. Living in jungle clearings or working in the rice fields, they were sold and bought as slaves. E. Thurston says "they have to wander about in seasons of scarcity in search of wild yams, which they boil and eat on the spot, and are through gluttons, eating all they can get at any time, then suffering want for days. Polygamy is common, as men are not required for the support of their wives."[142] *Mala vedans* live in wretched huts amid the rice-flats at the foot of the hills and are employed by farmers to guard the crops from the ravages of wild beasts. Some of them have been converted to Christianity and have shown rapid improvement in their general status.

1.4.8.5. Other Tribes

The ***Velans*** are the caste devil dancers, sorceress and magic practitioners. The word *Velan* has been derived from *vel* (a spear) and also from *vela* (=work). The usual title of the *velans* is *Panikkan* (worker). The ***Malapandarams*** were the nomadic tribe who did not remain in a place for more than a week and lived in families of two or three locality. They considered themselves superior to *kuravans*

---

140 L.A. Krishna Iyer, *The Travancore Tribes and Castes*, 8.

141 E. Thurston, *op.cit.*, Vol. 3, 162-167.

142 E. Thurston, *op.cit.*, vol. V11, T-Z, 333.

and *Vedans*. In case of pollution by any of these two castes, they would re-enter the jungle only after a purification bath.[143]

1.5. Caste Classifications

In post-independent Kerala, castes are classified as general category, other backward classes, Scheduled classes and finally Scheduled tribes. Forward castes come under general category; include castes such as Nambudiris, Samanta Kshathriyas, Nairs, Vaishyas, Ambalavasis and Syrian Christians. Due to their relatively better economic and educational status in the pre-Independence Kerala, they are not given reservations in government jobs and educational Institution. Nadars, Ezhavas, Muslim Mappilas, Latin Christians, Arayan, Ezhuthachan, Kalasi Panikkar, Kaniyar Panikkar, Kalari Kurup, Kaniyar Panikkar, Kusavan, Viswakarmas, Veluthedans and Vilakkithalavan have been classified as backward castes by Kerala government due to the discrimination faced by them historically. Paravan, Cheruman, Mannan, Nayadi, Pallan, Thoti, Vetan, Vettuvan, Panan. are some of the castes who have been included in the scheduled castes list of Kerala. These castes were generally in the bottom of a caste hierarchy, and faced, worst kind of discrimination. According to 2001 census, Scheduled castes along with Scheduled tribes form 10.95% of the total population.

1.6. Untouchability

The caste rules operated in the most irrational manner. The concept of pollution assumed serious dimensions. Being the bottom rung of the social ladder the outcastes were considered polluted and impure by other castes. They did not have the right to leave the village to which they were attached. They were linked to waste, excrement and evil spirits.[144] Untouchability is the English translation of local expressions like '*Tittu*' in Tamil and "*pula*" in Malayalam which generally convey the meaning pollution.[145] Another word used on those days was *Theendal* (= distance pollution). B.R. Ambedkar defines untouchability as "the notion of defilement, pollution and contamination and the ways and means of getting rid of that defilement."[146] The distance to be kept between castes were fixed by rules to avoid pollution, for example, a *Mukkuvar* (fisherman) had to remain 24 feet away from *Nambuthiri* Brahmin, an *Ezhava* 36 feet, Kamakkan 48 feet, a *Pulaya*

---

[143] L.A. Krishna Iyar, *op.cit.*, 81.

[144] Robert Deligue, *The World of the Untouchables, Pariyars of Tamil Nadu* (Delhi: Oxford University Press, 1997), 146.

[145] The words Untouchables and Untouchability were in fact, first coined by the British (Refer, Census of India 1911, Part 1, 117).

[146] B.R. Ambedkar, *The Untouchables: Who are they and Why they Have become Untouchables?* (Jalandhar: Bheem Patrika Publications, 1998), 1.

64 feet, and a *Nayadi* / Ullatan 72 feet.[147] Even the mere sight of a Pulaya or Nayadi was enough to make a Nambudiri consider himself polluted. They had no admission to the markets and they had to stand apart at some distance.[148] They could not enter the village temple and could not draw water from the well. They were forbidden not only to enter into the temples but also to use the roads around it.[149] The high caste never went to the *Ceri*, where the outcastes dwell together.[150] The house of a slave was called "madam" which means a hut. A high caste neither accepted food prepared by untouchables nor water. The untouchables could not dress like others. They constantly maintained an attitude of reverence towards the high caste. They had to speak to a superior with eyes lowered and holding their hand to the mouth lest the breath should go forth and pollute the person. He could not look at the face of his master and speak freely. In their language they used specific terms, e.g. when speaking of his children, she/he had to call them as calf or as monkey, and of the high caste man and even their children as "Lord."[151] A force bath in a tank or stream was the method of washing off pollution. The orthodox and conservative Hindus strictly observed the ancestral norms of conduct and religion. Any deviation from the established system was looked upon with suspicion and superstitious dread.[152] Untouchables could sit only in an inferior position. "Kuppa Katcha" was a house tax collected from the low caste people. For low caste marriage a fees was levied.[153] *Pulappedi* and *Mannappedi* was another strange custom of untouchability.[154] There were instances when untouchables like the Paraiahs were persuaded to transgress the pollution limits deliberately so that pseudo cases could be filed against them.[155] Cases of pollution of pagodas were decided by the local authority (the Huzur) and if they were unable to pay the sum required for *sudhikalasam* (purification), some other punishments followed.[156] Freedom was beyond the imagination of

[147] M.S. Rao, *Social Movements and Social Transformation: A Study of two Backward Classes Movements in India* (Delhi: Macmillan, 1970), 21.

[148] Samuel Mateer, *The Land of Charity*, *op.cit.*, 36 ff.

[149] Travancore Legislative Council Proceedings, vol. X, 249.

[150] Robert Deliege, *op.cit.*, 147.

[151] Robert Deliege, *op.cit.*, 147.

[152] Neettu vol. 20, 63-64, Proclamation by the Rani of Travancore, 3 February 1829, Central Archives, Trivandrum.

[153] C.M. Agur, *op.cit.*, 573.

[154] The practice of pula pedi or Pulaya terror was held in the month of 15th July to 15th August. During this period if a Pulaya threw a stone at high caste women after sunset she would lose her caste and accompany the Pulaya and thus she became a slave. Pulappedi in Kerala, *Journal of Kerala Studies,* Vol. 1, part. 1. 63-64.

[155] Cover file no. 1627, letter dated 21-12-1892 (English Records, Kerala Secretariat, Trivandrum).

[156] Cover File No. 15855, Letter dated 12-10-1849 (English records, Kerala Secretariat, Trivandrum).

this people. Thus, the socio-cultural condition of this caste presented a dark and gloomy picture. On 12 November 1936, Sri Chithra Thirunal Rama Varma (1913-1992) the then Maharaja of Travancore, on his 25th birthday announced the temple entry proclamation. It was the bold step to theoretically eradicate the painful untouchability practice.[157] It was said, "no act of any reform of any ruler in India has so far stirred the hearts, roused the enthusiasm or evoked the gratitude of the people to the extent that this proclamation has done."[158] But still in this century it is not an uncommon sight to see the evils of untouchability among our people. The old prejudices which ignore and negate the basic human rights of the weaker sections in one form or the other, are still prevalent in the performance and conduct of the dominant caste –ridden bureaucracy.[159] There is an immense gap between the legal abolition of untouchability and the actual state of affairs.[160]

1.7. The Communal awakening

Before we take up the depressed castes movements in Kerala, it is appropriate to speak about the social awareness created by the Christian Missionaries among the depressed castes of Kerala such as Nadars, Pulayas, Ezhavas and Sambavars. Christian Missionaries belonging to the London Missionary Society and Church Missionary Society came increasingly into contact with the lower castes. The lower caste who had been under enemy control to various disabilities and social restrictions looked up to the Christian Missionaries for their redemption. Among the converts from the slave class developed a widespread social awareness due to the systematic Christian teachings and inspiration of liberal human values. This awareness created a feeling that they were in bondage and that they had various rights which it was their duty to fight for. There is no doubt that the Christian missionaries in South India successfully created an ideological climate which was ideal for the birth of several social justice and social emancipation movements.[161] The 19th and 20th centuries witnessed the emergence of a new social order in Kerala under the impact of diverse social, economic and cultural influences.[162] The war

---

[157] The Regulations and Proclamations of Travancore, Vol. 1x, 1937, 3; Prohibition of slavery on 1029/2/30. Vol. 61, 97.384.

[158] Report of the Temple Entry Proclamation Memorial committee, 1.

[159] The incident happened on 1st April, 2011- in Modern Kerala shows the deplorable insignificant and ineffective stage of the subaltern people. After the retirement of A.K. Ramachandren the registration I.G., an officer from backward caste; the new registrar a person from high caste before using the official car, furniture and office room purified with Cow doge water according to the Hindu tradition for his use. Malayala Manorama, Daily Newspaper (Malayalam) (dated 7 April, 2011), 2 and the editorial in the same paper (on 8th Friday, April 2011), 10.

[160] This proclamation was only a belated as well as a calculated gesture of a theoretic regime propped up by an obscurant orthodoxy to arrest the growing power and influence of Christians.

[161] S. Manickom, *Depressed Class Movements in South India*, in K.A. Manikumar (ed.) *History & Society* (Madras: FIGA, 1996), 124.

[162] For more discussion on mass based movements see 5.3.

against caste disabilities and inequalities was being waged by progressive leaders among the affected people groups. Untouchability and inapproachability were looked upon by them as great social evils. They devoted their time for propaganda against the evil systems in the then Kerala society. The caste groups were properly institutionalized and formed into a mass-based movement, because the process of socialization was possible only through organizations. Thus several organizations came into existence towards the decisive phase of people liberation. There were Hindu awakening and Hindu movements during this period and moreover lot of Hindu leaders visited Kerala.[163] The awareness of social and religious disabilities led both the higher castes and the lower castes to search for the possibilities of emancipation.[164] As we had seen earlier the role of the Christian missionaries in the spread of western education and liberal ideas deserves special mention in this context.[165] Similarly there were some social reformers from among the backward class who worked for their betterment in all spheres of life. Vaikunda Swamikal (b.1803, at Swamithopu), Sri Narayana Guru (1856-1928), Sri. Ayyankali (1863-1941), Poikayil Yohannan (1879-1939) etc. were prominent social reformers in that period.[166] They did their best for the progress of the depressed classes, but their ways were different. They sowed the seeds of emancipation but the expected results were not to be harvested by them.

The work of the Christian missionaries and the spread of western education helped to bring about radical social changes. The history of the Protestant missionary activities in South Travancore clearly shows that it was their efforts to social liberation that attracted people of the lower classes to Christianity.[167] The evils in the Hindu social organization also created an atmosphere in favor of radical religious and social reform.[168] The English education system offered all castes of people opportunities of learning. As a result, the spread of education created awareness and a vision of progress and improvement among the people of the lower strata of society.

---

[163] C. Rajagopalachari, E V. Ramaswamy Naicker, Pandit Madan Malavya, Swamy Vivekananda, Gandhiji, etc., were few among them.

[164] J.W. Gladstone *op.cit.*, 81ff. For Vaikkom Sathyagraham and the crusade against untouchability got leadership from the High caste Hindus, the Nairs.

[165] A. Sreedhara Menon, *A Survey of Kerala History*, 369.

[166] For more discussion see, 5.4.

[167] Abolition of slavery (1843), Castes-disabilities removal (1850), Proclamation of permission for upper cloth for women (1865), Prohibition of untouchability (1950) and Proclamation of Temple Entry (1936) were the other milestones in the people's movements in Kerala.

[168] A. Sreedeshara Menon, *A Survey of Kerala History*, *op.cit.*, 380.

1.8. Conclusion

The 19th century was an epoch-making period in the history of Kerala. Up to that, there were centuries old traditional stances on matters pertaining to socio-religious concerns of life. The political set up that prevailed in Kerala in the past days was highly unfavorable to the general welfare of the vast majority of her people. It is because society was divided in terms of caste and caste decided the nature of the social relationship of individuals. Its principles made major section of the people mere slaves of the dominant privileged classes. They were systematically excluded from all positions of power and were subjected to exploitation and humiliation. Slowly severe changes took place in the life of individuals as well as communities. People were organized under the leaders with definite ideologies to fight for their self hood and identity. Knowledge about their own backwardness and an awareness of their right led the castes to organize themselves under leaders from their own castes. So, these movements naturally influenced each other. People were aware that something strange was going to happen in their life. A new sense of social awakening, self respect and vision of a new life took shape in the hearts and minds of many people. This openness and awareness led the people towards new realities and changes in society. The process of change among the depressed classes in Kerala has been gradual and was towards a purposeful reformation to form solidarity. It was the meaningful incorporation of changes for the individuals and groups that exercised freedom and purpose. In this formation of a unique solidarity there is a process of selection, interpretation and integration which will be seen in the following chapters.

Chapter 2

The Lutheran Mission to Kerala

2.1. Introduction

Christianity is an Asian religion with a worldwide family, not influenced by racial, cultural or political boundaries. Jesus Christ was sent to an Asian nation, called as among the Palestinian Jews and from them to the whole world. The resurrection of Jesus Christ is the starting point of Christianity. It is a fellowship of the followers of Jesus of Nazareth. Christian Mission[1] cut cross all the geographical borders as a

---

[1] The word mission as such is never in the Bible. The term *missio* is derived from the Latin word *mittere*, which corresponds to 'going' or 'sending' in the English translation. Biblical scholarship has related the terms to sending and mission for the equivalent terms in the Old Testament *shalach* and *apostello (pempo)* in both the Septuagint and the Greek New Testament. [David Udayakumar, "Church-in-Mission: facing Contemporary challenges" in Abraham P. Athyal & Dorathy Yoder Nyce, eds., *Mission Today: Challenges and Concerns*, (Chennai: Gurukul, 1998), 10.] Even though it is not a Biblical word, the concept of mission inherits a cardinal space in biblical theology. Traditionally, mission meant 'propagation of faith', 'expansion of reign of God', 'conversion of heathen', 'founding new churches', etc. These continue to be the dominant features of many mission agencies today. Many Christians in Asia are not quite happy with the word *mission* [For more discussions see, *Mission Today*, 45-46.], because the word originally belongs to the military vocabulary and the history of missions runs parallel to the history of colonial western domination. The missionary activities were to a large extent promoted and supported by colonial powers. The word *mission* has the connotation of the imperial expansion of the western Christianity. [Gnana Robinson, "Solidarity As missionary Principle", in Milton Jaganathan, ed., *Mission Paradigm in the New Millennium*, (Delhi: ISPCK, 2000), 62.] New shifts of thinking are emerging about the concept of mission. Mission is *Missio Dei*; i.e. God's mission. Mission is the heartbeat of Triune God. God is a God in mission or a 'Missional God'. After the Willingen conference of the International Missionary Conference in 1952, ecumenical missiology became strongly influenced by the *Missio Dei* theology, which is rooted in a holistic witness. The renowned Indian theologian Dr. M.M. Thomas saw the Church in mission in its four aspects; *kerygmatic, didache, diakonia* and *koinonia* tasks. No definition should be regarded as final.

movement. Jesus Christ sends His disciples into the world as the extension of His incarnation. Therefore mission work is the life-blood of the Church. It is believed that in obedience to Christ's Mission, St. Thomas, one of the Apostles, came from Palestine to Kerala, South India, in AD 52 to preach the Good News. There are no documentary evidences to show that Apostle Thomas started Christianity in Kerala. However, the people of Kerala undoubtedly possessed a rich oral tradition about the early history of the Christian community in Kerala. The present St. Thomas Christians in India also known as the Syrian Christians claim as the direct descendants of the Apostle's early converts.[2] So, one has to rely primarily on the tradition of the community. Certainly there was a well established Church in Malabar by the third century.[3] Solid historical written datas are available regarding the existence of Christianity in Kerala from the end of the third century.[4] We have no evidence that any Christian of early Church in Kerala ever attempted to record the history of this Church during the first thousand years of its existence. The Church was limited to 'Syrian Christians' and did not reach outside. Though a Church existed in South India long before one was established in many sections of Europe, the rest of India had to wait more centuries to hear the Good News. It is clear that only after the coming of the Portuguese and particularly after the arrival of St. Francis Xavier in 1542, Christianity progressed in the South. The first Protestant Mission in India was begun in Tranquebar by the German Lutherans. Since this study is an attempt to research the history about Lutherans in Kerala, a short description about Lutheranism and its beginning in India will be helpful. Moreover, the following chapters discuss the formation of a unique subaltern solidarity. Along with the other factors the Lutheran theology will play a major role for this formation. In this context, an overview of Lutheranism will be helpful to proceed. This Chapter is an attempt to trace the historical developments towards the entrance of Lutheran Christianity in Kerala. The first chapter is a brief history of the reformation and the origin of the Lutheranism in Europe. The next part is about the history of the arrival and spread of Lutheran Mission at Tranquebar, South India. The formation of Missouri Evangelical India Mission, and its entrance in Krishnagiri is discussed in the following part. In the final parts the direct influence and presence of Lutheranism in the first Protestant Mission in South Travancore is relooked along with the arrival of MELIM in Kerala.

2.2. Reformation and the Lutheran Church

Sixteenth century in Europe was an age of unrest and which was unhappy with a lot of problems and longings. People were discussing and planning on a number of different ways to renew the Church. Many thought about the changes and

[2] A. Mingana, *The Early Spread of Christianity in India* (Manchester: University Press, 1925), 18.

[3] G.T. Mackenzie, *Christianity in Travancore* (Trivandrum: Travancore Government Press, 1902), 4.

[4] George Evers, *The Churches in Asia* (Delhi: ISPCK, 2005), 445.

worked for it but they did not agree on that which needed to be done. The major influence behind this change was the doors opened by the renaissance. In order to accelerate the thrust for transformation they needed a leader and a dramatic incident which would unite the various groups into one party. God raised a person with a purer spiritual life and free from the political control of the Pope. That was a profound, biblical and scholarly theologian, a courageous servant of the Lord formed in the words, actions and writing of a German monk and Professor of Biblical Studies Martin Luther[5] (1482-1546) of Wittenberg. Sixteenth century reformation in Europe,[6] the Protestant Revolt, changed the course of World History. The Christian Church was reformed in many ways which were not in accordance with Luther's ideas.

2.2.1. The word 'Lutheran'[7]

Martin Luther was opposed to attach his name to any organization in Christianity. The expression "Lutheran" and 'Lutheran Church' at first was a nickname applied to the followers of Martin Luther in the days of the Protestant reformation. In 1522, Luther himself protested against this use of his name. "I ask that man to make no reference to my name and call themselves, not Lutherans but Christians. What is Luther? After all the doctrine is not mine nor I have been crucified for anyone. St. Paul in 1 Corinthians 3 would not allow Christians to call them Pauline or Peterine, but Christian. How, then should I, a poor evil-smelling maggot sack (Maden sack) have men give to children of Christ my worthless name? Not so dear friends, let us cast out party names and be called Christians after Him whose doctrine we have."[8] Luther's conception was like that of Paul, that the Church was an invisible body consisting of the communion of saints which Christ had drawn into himself as members. Luther was an ecumenist, not a sectarian. To become a follower of Luther meant merely to go over the faith of Jesus in his pure, original form and to drop certain outward abuses which had crept in. Such views did not assume an outward organization separate from the established Church; the hope

---

[5] Family name Luther variously spelled. Eg. *Luder, Ludher, Luther, Lutter*, etc. Here we prefer to use the word Luther. Baby Luther was baptized on St. Martin's (of Tours) day. Therefore, he was given the name Martin which means "*Warrior*". Later events proved this to be an appropriate choice, for Martin Luther became a warrior for the Lord in a very real sense. For the details about the life and work of Luther see, Bernhard Louse, *Martin Luther* (Philadelphia: Fortress Press, 1986).

[6] For the Reformation history, see: Ronald H. Bainton, *Studies on the Reformation* (London: Hodder & Stoughton, 1963); Owen Chaldwick, *Reformation* (Baltimore: Penguin Books, 1964); Thomas M. Lindsay, *Luther and the German Reformation, Vol. III* (Edinburgh: T & T Clark, 1935) and Lewis W. Spitz, *The Protestant Reformation* (New York: Harper & Row, 1985).

[7] For more discussion see, D. Christu Das, *Tranquebar to Travancore* (Delhi: ISPCK, 2008), 9-12; D. Christu Das, The Indian Christian Lutheran Communion: Challenges and Hopes, *Gurukul Journal of Theological Studies* XXX11 No.2 (June 2011): 66-75.

[8] Julius Bodensieck, *The Encyclopedia of the Lutheran Church* (Minnesota: APH, 1965), 856-57.

was that the concept would result in better Catholics. In later days, Luther silently agreed to call his adherents as Lutherans.

2.2.2. Distinctive features of Lutheranism[9]

One of the earliest English names for "Lutheran" was 'confessionals.'[10] The non-Lutherans often criticize the divisions among the Lutherans. But actually they are not divided as they may see. Among various Lutheran groups all the churches represent a single type of Protestant Christianity, built on Luther's principle of justification by faith alone – Faith in Jesus Christ' it centers in the Gospel for fallen humanity. This Bible is the inspired Word of God and the infallible rule and standard faith and practice. Lutherans confess their faith through the three general creeds of Christendom – Apostles', Nicene and Athanasius – which they believe to be in accordance with the scriptures. They also believe that the unaltered Augsburg Confession is a correct exposition of the faith and doctrine of Evangelical Lutheranism. The Apology of the Augsburg Confession, the two Catechisms of Luther, the Smalcald articles, and the Formula of Concord are held to be faithful interpretations of Lutheranism[11] and of the Bible. The two sacraments – Baptism and Lord's Supper – are not merely signs of memorials, but channels through which God bestows forgiving and empowering grace upon humankind. The theories of consubstantiation, transubstantiation, and impanation are rejected. Infants are baptized, and baptized persons are believed to receive the gift of regeneration from the Holy Spirit. Universal priesthood of all believers, Justification by faith are the keys to interpret the Bible, Law and Gospel distinction, Two Kingdom theory, the Four alones, Theology of Cross, Hidden and revealed God, importance of Gospel Preaching, Means of grace invisible and visible church, local congregation, Christian ministry, Saint and sinner are the distinctive doctrines of Lutheranism. The Lutherans highly recognized their heritage. These features are common among all Lutheran communities. These show that the real unity among Lutherans is based on faith than organization. Pastors are called by the congregations. Congregations are united in Synods (conferences or districts) that composed of pastors and lay representatives. Worship is liturgical, centring on the Altar. To this day Lutherans retain much from the tradition of the ancient

[9] For more discussion see, D. Christu Das, *Vachanathinte Vineetha Dasan: Martin Luther (Mal.) (The Humble Servant of the Word: Martin Luther)* (Thiruvalla: CSS, 2010) (2008); D. Christu Das, *Tranquebar to Travancore*, (Delhi: ISPCK, 2008), 9-12; D. Christu Das, The Indian Christian Lutheran Communion: Challenges and Hopes, *Gurukul Journal of Theological Studies* XXX11 No. 2 (June, 2011): 66-75.

[10] *The Oxford English Dictionary 11* (Oxford: Oxford University Press, 1993), 802. Werner says as such because the Lutheran Church defined itself in a series of Confessions but never adopted an official Liturgy or union of polity. The old German name for denomination was *Konfessionen*.

[11] More discussions on Lutheranism see Eric W. Gritsch and Robert W. Jenson, *Lutheranism* (Philadelphia: Fortress Press, 1976) and Werner Elert, *Structure of Lutheranism* (St. Louis: CPH, 1962).

and Medieval Church, including a sense of participation in the historic people of God and the traditional liturgy revised in accord with Protestant Theology.

2.3. Lutheran Mission to India

2.3.1. Formation of Missionary Movements

Eighteenth century European political and religious context had a direct link on the Christian Mission in India. A revival movement began in the late 17th century called pietisms,[12] in Germany, largely as a reaction to the prevailing unproductive confessionalism (denominationalism).[13] The movement later on spread to England where the movement came to be known as the Evangelical Revival and then to America where it was referred to as the Great Awakening.[14] The movement which began in North America then spread to all over European countries stressed personal Christian commitment and awareness for social reform. Three features appeared wherever the Evangelical awakening spread; such as International Christian inter-course, action of Missionary Societies and efforts directed to social reform.[15] The Evangelical awakenings, German Pietistic movement and the geographical discoveries gave the evangelical zeal to spread the saving grace both in their own countries and in other parts of the world. Consequently, German Lutherans were sent to South India as the first Protestant Missionaries and Denmark play a great role in the establishment of the Protestant Church in India.[16]

---

[12] Pietism began as a movement to recover the 'first love', the primary religious experience of the early Christians. The strong emphasis was upon personal conversion, purity of life, lay initiative, non-resistance and the claims of the "great Commission".

[13] Philip Jacob Spener (1635-1705) a Lutheran pastor influenced by both mysticism and John Conrad Dannhauer (1603-1666) became the founder of pietism. Spener writing *Holy desires (Pia Desideria 1675)* is the manifesto of pietists. Pietism was a protest against the Lutheran orthodoxy. Spener stressed the importance of Bible study, personal life and new life style. True Christianity is not just doctrine to be believed, it is an experience of the Holy Spirit in conversion and new life. For more discussions on Pietism and Confessionalism see Richard L. Gawthrop, *Pietism and the Making of Eighteenth Century Prussia* (Cambridge: University Press, 1993).

[14] Williston Walker, *A History of the Christian Church* (New York: Charles Scribner's sons, 1958), 464-465 and Herbert Hoefer, *Debate on Mission* (Madras: Gurukul, 1979), 83.

[15] Louise Pirouet, *Christianity Worldwide, Church History 4: A.D. 1800 onwards* (New Delhi: SPCK, 1993), 2.

[16] For more discussion on the circumstances surrounding the founding of the Danish Halle Mission in Tranquebar see Peter Vethanayagamony, *It Began in Madras* (Delhi: ISPCK, 2010), 15-57.

2.3.2. The Royal Danish Halle Mission[17]

Most of the historians believe that the founder of the Tranquebar Mission, King Frederick IV (1699-1730), of Denmark was a very pious Lutheran ruler and was deeply interested in the spiritual welfare of his subjects in Denmark's various overseas outposts. Martin Luther emphasized the duty of the Government to provide for the preaching of the Word of God to all their subjects. Philip Jacob Spencer (1635-1705), the Father of Pietism, also urged the Lutheran Princes to give proper evangelistic concern to their own people.[18] This idea provided fruitful insights to the mission among non-Christians where Lutheran countries began to acquire colonies in foreign parts of the world.[19] In 1699 Frederick IV ascended the Danish throne. This king felt that it was his duty (*Rajadharma*) to care for the spiritual welfare of his non-Christian subjects of the colonies.[20] The domestic crisis in the royal family in 1704 also made an impact on the decisive beginning of the "mother of all Protestant (Lutheran) Missions.[21] As we noted earlier this was the policy known as *cuius region, eius religio* (the ruling prince of the country decides what religion his subject shall have). For instance, he sent the first Protestant Missionary to one Danish colonial outpost of Tranquebar.[22]

Tranquebar was a Danish tenant colony (1619-1845) on the Coromandal coast in Tamil Nadu,[23] having been ceded to the Danish East India Company by the Raja of Tanjore.[24] In 1705, King Frederich IV ordered Franz Julius Luetkens

---

[17] D. Christu Das, *Impact of Lutheran Mission among Sambavars in South Travancore*, Unpublished MTh. Thesis, Senate of Serampore, 2001, 29.

[18] J. Sandegren, *The Song of Tranquebar* (Madras: CLS, 1955), 7; Daniel Jayaraj (ed), *Ordination of the First Protestant Indian Pastor Aaron* (Madras: Gurukul, 1998), 2.

[19] C.H. Swavely, (ed), *The Lutheran Enterprises in India* (Madras: FELCI, 1952), 1.

[20] Perhaps over a period of time several things seem to have shaped his determination. For more discussion on this subject see Daniel Jeyaraj, *A German, Exploration of India Society: Ziegenbalg's Malabarian Heathenism* (Delhi: MIIS & ISPCK, 2006), 18-20.

[21] Daniel Jeyaraj (ed), *Ordination of the First Protestant Pastor Aaron*, 3; Daniel Jeyaraj, "Early Tamil Bible Translation in Tranquebar", Dharma Deepika, 1.1 (July-December 1997): 68, (67-77).

[22] The Tranquebar mission has many different names like "*Missionarri danci*", Royal Danish missionary in East India, The German Halle Lutheran Mission, Danish-Halle mission, The Tranquebar mission, etc.

[23] Tamil Nadu as a name of the present geographical area began to be denoted as a result of States Reorganization Act of 1956. By that time, the earlier British Presidency of Madras had lost its northern districts to Andhra Pradesh and its western districts to Mysore now Karnataka. Under the 1956 Act, it also lost the district of Malabar but gained four Taluks (sub divisions) from Trivandrum and another Shencottah taluk of Quilon District, when the new state of Kerala was formed. H. Tony Samuel & D. Rajendren, *Tamil Nadu Before the Throne of God* (Chennai: People of India, 1999), 18. But, during the time of Ziegenbalg, it was only known as the land of Malabarians or Damilians.

[24] The name 'Tranquebar' was an European form. Danish spelt it as *Trankebar* and *Trangeber*. Missionaries `used "*Tranquebar*" for their correspondence. The Tamil word is 'Tharangampadi' which means 'village of waves', 'wave dancer', and the songs of the waves or even as 'wave singer'. Tharanganpadi is situated on the seacoast nearly 250 kms south of Chennai and about 30 Kms

(1650-1712), his new court preacher to find Danish Missionary candidates, but no Dane was willing to become a Missionary. As suitable Missionaries could not be found in his own country, Lutkens wrote to his colleague friend, Rev. Joachim Lange (1670-1744) in Berlin, Germany and asked him to find appropriate missionary candidates for Danish colonies in East India, Africa and the West Indies.[25] Thereupon a call was sent to Halle. Two young German Lutheran students of Halle, namely Bartholomaeus Ziegenbalg (1682-1719)) and Henry Plutschau (1677-1746), were found as suitable for the purpose. Ziegenbalg was an orthodox Lutheran and a practicing pietism.[26] At first Ziegenbalg declined to accept this offer because he thought that he was too young and inexperienced, he also hesitated to do a long voyage due to his sickness.[27] Later, he accepted this call at the age of 23. He then went with Plutschau to Copenhagen, Denmark and there they were ordained as Missionaries. On November 11, 1705, the Missionaries were charged to transplant a Danish Church among the non-Europeans living on Danish colonies. Ziegenbalg and Plustchau signed an official job description which was attested to by King Frederich IV with his signature.[28] They were then sent out to Tranquebar as 'Royal Missionaries' at the personal expense of the king.[29] Ziegenbalg arrived at Tranquebar on the East Coast on the 9th of July 1706. Thus, Tranquebar became the cradle of Protestant Christianity in India and origins of Lutheran World Mission, later it opened the doors of Serampore. The first Protestant Missionaries who started work in the Danish trade settlement of Tranquebar took pride in having been sent and being maintained by the king of Denmark.

---

north of Nagapattanam. It covered about 45 square kilometers. It had direct trade relationship with many European and Asian countries like Ceylon, Burma, China, Rome, Portugal, Denmark, France, England, Holland and Russia from 11th century A.D.

[25] Daniel Jeyaraj, *A German Exploration of Indian Society, op.cit.*, 20.

[26] German pietism got its big break in 1688, when the German elector Frederick 1 became the first King of Prussia. He invited them to start Halle University. The pope objected that he had not consented to the creation of Prussia, but his consent and objection were becoming increasingly irrelevant. From Halle, pietism thawed the churches of Germany. Stephen Tomkins, *A Short History of Christianity* (Grand Rapids: W.B. Eerdmans Publishing Company, 2005), 186.

[27] Daniel Jeyaraj, *Bartholomaus Ziegenbalg: The Father of Modern Protestant Movement*, (Delhi: ISPCK, 2006), 58.

[28] For more details about the Letter of Royal appointment and the instructions to the first missionaries by R. Frederick, Capenhagen, 17 November 1705 see, Andrew Gross, Y. Vincent Kumaradoss, Heike Liebau (eds.) *Halle and the Beginning of Protestant Christianity in India,* vol. iii; *Communications between India and Europe* (Halle: GmbH, 2006), 1337-1339; M.K. Kuriakose, *History of Christianity in India: Source Materials* (Delhi: ISPCK, 1999), 57-59.

[29] E. Arno Lehmann, *It began at Tranquebar* (Madras: CLS, 1956), 7-12.

2.3.3. Lutheran Mission at Tranquebar[30]

There was some lack of systematic coordination on the part of the Danish crown, clergy, and the company, leading to mutual distrust and suspicions. Capton of the ship *Princess Sophie Headwig* was very unfriendly to the Missionaries.[31] The voyage took seven months. The Royal Missionaries never received a warm welcome at the Danish port. The Governor of Tranquebar, Johann Sigismund Hassius (1704-171) and other Europeans in the colony, made all possible hindrances to these Missionaries. The officials had nothing personal against the Missionaries, but they were opposed to Missionary enterprises because they thought that Missionary activities would put at risk their commercial interest.[32] Although, the first Lutheran Missionaries in India entered in the wake of Western colonial expansion, Lutheran work in India very fortunately has been remarkably free from association with colonial powers from the West.[33]

The strong commitment to the holistic mission concept of the early Tranquebar Missionaries amazes any mission student of today. They considered schools to be a preparation for evangelism and agents of evangelism. They also believed that education would help improve the society. They did not deny the education for girls. The Missionaries were able to start gradually schools, churches, printing press in the locality.[34] They learned Tamil and Portuguese and produced Christian literature in Tamil for the new converts. Communication in the language of the people was given prime importance. Besides, they were able to translate and print the New Testament in Tamil, in 1712 which was the first translation of the New Testament in any of the Indian language. Ziegenbalg prepared Tamil Dictionaries and translated Luther's Small Catechism and Luther's Hymns. In a report sent to Halle in 1712 Ziegenbalg mentions 38 printed books in Tamil, written or translated by him.[35] "…this *Malabarien heathens* are very clever and intelligent people who can only won over with great wisdom. They have just as accurate an analogy in their religious beliefs as we Christians have… ."[36] Ziegenbalg's letter to Mission Board shows his positive observations about the Indian people.

Zeigenbalg's first converts were from the slaves of the local European population. Together with Indians he introduced the message of Jesus Christ to

---

[30] *Impact of Lutheran Mission among Sambavars in South Travancore, op.cit.*, 30.

[31] Erich Beyreuther, *Bartholomew Zeigenbalg. A Biography of the First Protestant Missionary in India, 1682-1719.* Trans. S.G. Lang and H.W. Gensichen (Madras: CLS, 1955), 64.

[32] E.R. Hambye, *History of Christianity in India,* Vol. 111 (Banglore: CHAI, 1997), 119.

[33] Arno Lehmann, ed. *Handbook Lutheran World Missions* (Germany: LWF, 1952), 13.

[34] E. Arno Lehmann, *It began at Tranquebar*, 16.

[35] Swavely, *op.cit.*, 4.

[36] For the full version of the letter dated 1 October 1706 from Tranquebar to Hermann Franke see, Andreas Gross, et.al., *op.cit.*, 1341-1346.

others. He was not a colonial person, but was dedicated to improve the lifestyle of downtrodden Indians in his time. He recognized the dignity of the local people and genuinely respected them. He interacted with them as trustworthy friends and equal partners.[37] As a Christian Missionary he tried to help the indigenous community to orient their world views and life style toward Jesus Christ. Daniel Jeyaraj observes: "Ziegenbalg being a German Lutheran Pietist is convinced that the Church in South India should be contextual so that it does not blindly imitate any form of western Christianity or uncritically takes over every aspects of South Indian society and religions, but carefully chooses a middle path between continuity and discontinuity."[38] With regard to caste,[39] Ziegenbalg was of the opinion that it was chiefly a social institution, which could be tolerated to a certain extent, at least as long as it did not come in direct conflict with Christian principles. He took no radical step either to eradicate it or to tolerate it.[40] This attitude towards caste he left as a heritage to subsequent Lutheran Missions in India.[41] For the effective mission he selected and trained the catechists in regional level and gave them ordination. Within three and a half years of ministry there were about 160 converts. After his 10 years of service in India Ziegenbalg died on 23 February 1719. The first Tamil pastor S. Aaron, was ordained in 1733. Ten Missionaries were working in the mission. The number of Christians rose from 280 of the time of Ziegenbalg's death to 3766.[42] By the time Ziegenbalg died 140 converts were from Sudras, the dominant high caste people of that area on those days.[43] Danish Missionaries, as with the other Protestant Mission in India, received large converted populations from subaltern backgrounds.[44] While assessing the contributions of Ziegenbalg, Varun Rodriguez says: "He was a bridge as he interacted with the socially and religiously marginalized and played a catalytic role in promoting Tamil culture in and outside India. It has been a curious fact that the works of G.V. Pope, Caldwell, and Beschi were printed at Tranquebar in

[37] Daniel Jeyaraj, *A., German Exploration in to Indian Society*, 362.

[38] Ibid., 365.

[39] As Dr. Manickom observed, the Tranquebar missionaries did not have any idea about the caste system and the missionaries thought it was part of Hinduism so ,it did not want to touch it. K. Manickom, *Dalit Liberative Ideology* (Madras: DRC, 1992), 21.

[40] Peter Vethanayagamony, *It began in Madras* (Delhi: ISPCK, 2010), 99.

[41] Swavely, *op.cit.*, 6-7. But the recent works on this subject shows that Ziegenbalg condemned caste Differences as an expression of superstition. He did not tolerate them in his church at Tranquebar. See also D. Dennis Hudson, *Protestant Origins in India, 1706-1735* (Cambridge: W.B. Eerdmans Publishing Company, 2000), 82-95 and Brijraj Singh, *The First Protestant Missionary to India, Bartholomaeus Ziegenbalg, 1683-1713*. (Oxford: University Press, 1999), 57-59.

[42] J. Sandegren, *The Songs of Tranquebar*, 10.

[43] Arno Lehmann, *op.cit.*, 111.

[44] George Oommen and Hans Raven Iversen (eds,) *It Began in Copenhagen* (Delhi: ISPCK, 2005), 26.

a nice touch of ecumenism."[45] This mission became the model for future missions in India.[46] In schools, he never allowed caste discrimination to be practiced, and children from different castes studied, ate, and lived together, partly because space was so tight.[47] When they constructed "New Jerusalem Church" in Tranquebar in 1717, it was constructed in the model of a cross so that the Sudra adherents would be accommodated in the side wing and non-Brahmins in the main portion. In a way Tranquebar Missionaries helped the Sudra adherents to worship with their upper caste masters and to feel comfortable and proud to be worshipping with their masters. Accommodating Sudras inside the Church with the Dalits was a revolutionary and liberative act at that time.[48] In the Holy Communion no separate chalice was used and every one drank from the same cup. But people from the low caste origin were communed only after the high caste people. At Ziegenbalg's funeral; people of all castes, high and low, crowded into the New Jerusalem Church, standing together and rubbing shoulders without any regard for caste.[49] One aspect of the social character of the Lutheran communities seems to have been fairly constant, that they were the people from the socially alienated. The Missionary paradigm developed by the pioneer Tranquebar Missionaries, was holistic in approach. They were convinced that "service to the body" should receive equal emphasis with "service to the soul.'[50] They were totally convinced that they should cater the physical needs of the people with whom they came to contact.

From Tranquebar the work then spread to other stations of the central and Southern portions of the Madras Presidency including Tanjore, Madras, Cuddalore, Nagapattanam, Trichinapally and Tinnevely.[51] Tranquebar had been sold by the Thanjavoor Kingdom to the Danes. But close to it at Tillaiyadi, and in the kingdom proper, there were 1,722 Lutheran Christians, all of them were subalterns.[52] The successful pioneering of Ziegenbalg and Henry Plutschau was followed by the painstaking labors of Benjamin Schultze (1689-1769) a great Linguist, Johann Philipp Fabricius (in India 1742-1791) a linguist and a great

[45] Varun Rodrigues, "Bartholomaeus Ziegenbalg" in Anand Amaldass (ed.) *Christian Thinkers in India, vol.3* (Chennai: Satya Nilayam Publications, 2007), 289.

[46] Arno Lehmann, *op.cit.*, 97-98.

[47] Daniel Jeyaraj, Inculturation in Tranquebar, quoted in *It began at Madras, op.cit.*, 99.

[48] R. Christopher Rajkumar, "Liberative Missiology: Serampore and Tranquebar Missionary Models" in Solomon Rongpi, ed. *Mission and the local Congregations* (Delhi: ISPCK/NCCI, 2011), 34.

[49] Peter Vethanayagamony, *op.cit.*, 101.

[50] Erich Beyreuther, *Bartholomew Zeigenbalg. A Biography of the First Protestant Missionary in India, 1682-1719.* Trans. S.G. Lang and H.W. Gensichen (Madras: CLS, 1955), 77.

[51] J. Fred Fenger, *History of the Tranquebar Mission* (Madras: M.E. Press, 1906), 186.

[52] Arno Lehman, *op.cit.*, 204.

Lutheran Leader in North Tamil Nadu and Christian Frederic Schwartz[53] (in India 1750-1798) the *Raja guru* being the greatest of all.[54] The work of these Missionaries was strengthened by the financial support from the Society for Promoting Christian Knowledge (SPCK),[55] which was started in London in 1698. From 1709, the SPCK, contributed towards the funds of this Lutheran Mission, and after 1734 the main responsibility for the mission outside Tranquebar rested on them. From Tranquebar Mission activities spread far and wide.[56] The cooperative nature of the first Protestant Mission in India must be noticed.

2.3.4. Turn down of Danish Mission

The differences in mission ideology and the probable financial constrains turned into an open conflict resulting in immense discomfort and mental agony for the Missionaries working in India. At the end of the century the influence of pietism weakened at Halle. The king of Denmark started the Tranquebar Mission without any formal support from the Church of Denmark. The king's failure to consider some basic organizational structures caused difficulties for the early Missionaries. The absence of Missionary manuals detailing mission policy, mission administrative structures, relationships between mission and colonial powers, and decision-making process in the mission filed, resulted in confusion among the Missionaries on several critical occasions.[57] Within a century, growing rationalism in Europe caused lack of Missionary zeal and the discontinuation of the Danish Mission.[58] This led to the gradual decline of Danish Mission. Europe was involved in the Napoleonic wars. And the mission fell into decline. In 1826, the S.P.C.K. handed

---

[53] All the missionaries who came under the auspices of the Royal Danish–Halle Tranquebar Mission were from Germany, Denmark and Sweden. They included pastors, laymen, printers, doctors, nurses, wives of missionaries and others. The first evangelical women missionary was Dorathea. According to Wolf, the Danish-Halle mission had send to Indian the 18th century no less than 56 men. The most conspicuous of these after Zeigenbalg was Schwarts. L.B. Wolf, *Missionary Heroes of the Lutheran Church* (Philadelphia: The Lutheran Publication Society, 1911), 64.

[54] M.E. Gibbs, *From Jerusalem to New Delhi* (Madras: CLS, 1964), 215.

[55] SPCK was formed by a group of Anglicans in England in 1698. Its aim was 'to promote Christian Knowledge at home'. Thus, its focus was mainly in the field of education and publishing. Beth Walpole, *Venture of Faith: A Brief Historical Background of the Church of South India* (Madras: CLS, 1993), 34.

[56] From Tranquebar people went out and started new stations in Cudallore, Madras, Tanjore, Trichnopally, Palayamcotta, Tinnevely, and Travancore and even in Calcutta. Even the Serampore trio were inspired, when they came to Calcutta almost a century later. Joseph G. Muthuraj, *We Began at Tranquebar,* Vol. 1 (Delhi: ISPCK, 2010), 104-121.

[57] Peter Vethanayagamony, *op. cit.*, 247.

[58] The recent studies show that the economic crisis resulted from the war between the Danes and the Swedish and the changed view of the Christian Mission activities among non-European people were the main reasons for the decline of Tranquebar Mission.

over its responsibilities to S.P.G.[59] In 1813, the first CMS Missionaries arrived in south India, and in Tinnevelly the CMS Mission soon became more numerous than the earlier missions. The first CMS Missionaries were also German Lutherans.[60] But by this time there were Anglican bishops in India, and though the Anglican societies accepted the Lutheran orders of existing Missionaries and Indian clergy, they required that in future all ordinations should be in accordance with Anglican practice. The question of caste within the Church was another issue in Danish Mission. While describing the spiritual paralysis of this mission, Arno Lehmann observes the following five issues. 1) During this period of decline there were still violent quarrels between the Mission and the Government, 2) the Tranquebar Mission was paralyzed due to the mother church's negative attitude towards the deep scriptural foundation and healthy spiritual life, 3) rationalism was the method of thinking and social Gospel was the message for preaching, 4) the mission was ridiculed from its task of saving the souls to making 'good people' and 5) the decline in the moral life of the clergy and quarrels among them worsened the situation. The dying mission, the mother of all other missions, had sunk down to a small institution in the locality.[61] In the light of this Arno Lehman concludes as follows: "But the Tranquebar Mission, who between 1706 and 1806 had gathered in 36,970 souls, had come to an end, it was not a glorious end. It was a sad sign of the selfishness and poverty of Christians and Church in Europe, as especially in Germany, that the exits of the once famous Lutheran Tranquebar Mission touched them so little."[62] Hence, the growth and mission of first Protestant Mission of India were paralyzed. As the Danish Halle Mission was losing its dynamism, the Leipzig Missionary Society[63] arose in Germany to counter the effects of rationalism.

---

[59] The Society for Propagation of the Gospel (SPG) was the second Anglican Mission Society to be formed. The first meeting of the society was held in 1701. Rev. Dr. Thomas Bray was responsible for starting both ISPCK & SPG. The main purpose of starting SPG was to support the Anglican Church in the American colonies and the West Indies. This SPG decided to begin its work in India and Ceylon also from 1818 onwards. Consequently, SPCK handed over its mission work in India in 1826. Beth Walpole, *op.cit.*, 47-51.

[60] M.E. Gibbs, *op.cit.,* 215.

[61] E. Arno Lehman, *op. cit.*, 171-176.

[62] *Ibid.,* 17.

[63] Leipzig Missionary Society was founded in 1836 in Dresden, Saxony, as the Missionary arm of the newly awakened European Lutherans. Under the leadership of Dr. Karl Graul it found its field of work in South India where it revived the heritage of the Danish Halle Mission, centered in Tranquebar, with special emphasis on high professional and linguistic qualifications of mission workers.

2.4. The Leipzig Evangelical Lutheran Mission

2.4.1. Leipzig Lutheran India Mission[64]

Seeing Lutheranism in India slip on a downward trend, away, the Leipzig Evangelical Lutheran Mission society sent out its Missionaries to take care of the Lutheran legacy in India. The Leipzig Evangelical Lutheran Mission (LELM) was founded on 17th August, 1836. While Danish Halle Mission becoming defunct, the Leipzig Missionary Society arose in Germany to encounter the effects of nationalism. This developed from a Mission Society, which mainly supported the Basle Mission. The desire of Lutheran circles to establish a decidedly Lutheran Mission was understood on the part of the Basle Mission, and the society sent out its Missionaries to re-establish the Lutheran cause.[65] Meanwhile, in 1845 Denmark sold her Indian possessions to English East India Company in India. Hence all fruits of the blessed labours of the Old Lutheran Missionaries in the 18th century fell into the helping hands of Anglican Missionaries and to the SPCK.[66] Though there was a move to include the Tranquebar Mission in the transaction, the king of Denmark decided that the Tranquebar Mission would remain Lutheran and be handed over to the German Home Board. The Christians, church, schools and lands within the limits of the former Danish colony, Tranquebar, by an order of King Christian VIII, were entrusted to the Leipzig Evangelical Lutheran Mission on 7th March 1847. Thereafter the Lutheran Mission in South India had a field of her own. They utilized this opportunity to revive the Old Danish Lutheran centres in India. The Missionaries of Leipzig Mission worked hard and sacrificed everything to re-establish the Lutheran understanding of the Gospel in South India.

2.4.2. Resignation of Missionaries

The Leipzig Missionaries who were working in South India had to face dogmatic and personal differences. The dogmatic differences landed them in deep trouble that led to misunderstanding, bickering and internal disunity among the Missionaries. In 1875, five young Missionaries raised the issue of the Confessional stance of the Leipzig Mission. The Confessional controversy was mostly based on the doctrine of verbal inspiration.[67] The greatest reverse to the work of the LELM was caused by the great war of 1914-1918 due to internal disunity and controversies that arose within the community and from outside.

---

64 *Impact of Lutheran Mission among Sambavars in South Travancore, op.cit.*, 33.

65 C.H. Swavely, *op. cit.*, 15-16.

66 H.M. Zorn, *The Background and First Twenty-five Years of the Missouri Evangelical Lutheran India Mission, op.cit.*, 23.

67 F. Dean Luekening, *Mission in the Making* (St. Louis: CPH, 1964), 203.

Between 1840 and 1894 four major splits happened within the Mission.[68] The Mission Board sent 44 Missionaries to India to intensify its Missionary activities. But by the said four controversies 14 Missionaries left the Mission.[69] The latter two of these controversies were closely connected with the establishment of MELIM. Director Karl Graul (1814-1864) came to India to mediate and the dispute ended with the dismissal of two Missionaries and resignation of another two. On January 1, 1893 Karl Gustav Theodore Naether (1866-1904) and Theodore Franz Mohn (1867-1925) were dismissed from the service of the Leipzig Mission in India.[70] J.F. Zucker (1842-1927) and C.M. Zorn, (1846-1928) the former Leipzig Missionaries, already resigned and went to America. The controversy and other related developments brought four men into MELIM from the Leipzig Mission by 1897. These four were born in Germany and trained in America and were conservative Lutherans. J.M. Kempff (1860-1945) another Missionary in India also had left Leipzig Mission due to misunderstandings. But he remained in India and became a coffee planter in the Shevaroi Hill. Consequent upon the splits, the Missouri Evangelical Lutheran India Mission could gain a foot hold in South India.

2.4.3. Lutheran Mission in USA

The Lutheran Church in America is as old as the American nation and much older than American republic. According to Abdel R. Wentz "The Lutheran Church in America is an integral part and potent part of American Christianity. The people in the Lutheran Churches of the land are constituent and typical element of the American nation."[71] It was mainly from Germany and Scandinavia that Lutheranism came to the United States. A Lutheran Christian service was held at Hudson Bay in 1619. The people from Holland arrived in 1623 at Manhattan; they were the first European Lutherans to remain in country permanently. The first Independent colony of Lutherans was established at Fort Christina, New Sweden, along the Delaware in 1638. The Lutherans started to worship as a congregation in 1649 at Amsterdam. From 1664 onwards, when English assumed control of New York, Lutherans enjoyed full freedom in their worship. The New York Lutherans were largely Germans. The Napoleon war caused much devastation in Germany. There followed economic insecurity, political persecution and religious oppression. These motivated a huge emigration to America a land of economic stability, political freedom, and religious liberty. During the 19th century a total of

---

[68] B. Sobhanam, *op.cit.*, 161.

[69] *Ibid.*

[70] H.M. Zorn, *op.cit.*, 7.

[71] Abdel Ross Wentz, *A Basic History of Lutheranism in America* (Philadelphia: Muhlenberg Press, 1955), v.

5,009,280 Germans arrived in American ports.[72] The early American Lutherans were through the migrants from various Lutheran communities.[73] Later American Lutherans increased and numerous synods were formed. The Saxon immigrants from the land of Luther came to America and settled at Mississippi valley. Later, they formed as Missouri Synod of Lutheran Church. This orthodox/conservative Lutheran group sent its Missionaries to South India and then to Travancore.

2.4.4. Missouri Evangelical Lutheran Synod and LELM

Rev. Carl Ferdinand Wilhelm Walther (born.1811), one of the Saxon migrants in 1839, became the pastor of Trinity Church in St. Louis in 1841.[74] In 1844 he and his congregation began a publication in German language, called *Der Lutheraner*.[75] They used much place in this news letter to explain true Biblical and Lutheran doctrine Lutherans in the different parts of the country read *Der Lutheraner* and found that they agreed with Walther and his group. In September 13-18, 1845 the likeminded people assembled together at Cleveland, Ohio, to discuss the possibility of forming a Lutheran synod.[76] In the year 1846 two meetings were held at St. Louis (June 25) and Fort Wayne (July) for the same cause. *Der Lutheraner* of March 23 enclosed the announcement: "Those concerned are herewith again reminded that the first session of the German Evangelical Lutheran Synod of Missouri, Ohio and Other States will take place on Monday after Jubilate Sunday, April 26, 1848, at Chicago, Illinois."[77] The Missouri Synod was finally organized in Chicago, Illinois, at the meeting which began on April 26, 1847, and lasted for eleven days. The governing boards and officers were elected. Pastor Walther, of the German Evangelical Lutheran Church of the Unaltered Augsburg Confession, St Louis, Mo, was made the President.[78] From the very beginning itself, it was mission minded.[79] First, attempts were made to bring the Gospel to the American Indians.[80] In the first four decades, members of Missouri

---

[72] Walter A. Baepler, *A Century of Grace: A History of the Missouri Synod, 1847-1947* (St. Louis: CPH, 1947), 7.

[73] For the detailed history of the Lutheran church in America 1619-1857, see Carl S Meyer (ed.), *Moving Frontiers* (St. Louis; CPH, 1964), 1-46.

[74] W.G. Polack, *Fathers and Founders* (St. Louis: CPH, 1938), 87.

[75] On September 7, 1884, Walther issued the first number of *Der Lutheraner*. The very first article announced the reason, purpose, and contents of this paper.

[76] For more details about the formation of LCMS see W.G. Polack, *Fathers and Founders* (St. Louis: CPH, 1938) and Walter A. Baepler, *A Century of Grace*, *op.cit.*, 7.

[77] The "other states" besides Missouri and Ohio were Illinois, Indiana, Michigan and New York. Walter A. Baepler, *A Century of Grace, 97.*

[78] August R. Suelflow, "*The Beginnings of "Missouri, Ohio, and Other States "in America*" in Carl S Meyer, *op.cit.*, 90-141.

[79] At the very first Convention of LCMS in April 1847 a committee on mission was established. Carl S. Mayer, *Moving Frontiers* (St. Louis: CPH, 1964), 184.

[80] C.H. Swavely, *op.cit.*, 184.

Synod supported European Lutheran Mission societies, principally of Leipzig and the Hermannsburg Missions.[81] Later on the Missouri Synod had come closer to an opportunity to open a mission to non-Christians and foreign lands. In 1876, four German Missionaries of the Leipzig Society arrived in India. Lutheran Church Missouri Synod (LCMS) financially supported the Leipzig Mission.[82] On viewing the issues, Missouri Synod felt that too much liberal doctrinal position was infiltrating the Leipzig circles. In 1876 four German Lutheran Leipzig Missionaries joined the Missouri Synod and later served as members of its foreign board. Two of those were F. Zucker and C.M. Zorn. At this moment Missouri Synod stopped its financial support to Leipzig Mission.[83] In the convention of 1887 the Synod resolved to take introductory steps toward the opening of a *heathen* mission.[84] In 1893, the general Mission Board resolved a plan for mission work in Japan.[85] Preparation was made to start the work by Japanese national who graduate at Springfield Concordia Seminary, Henry Shigetaro Midzuno with another Missionary. Due to some cultural and personality conflict the Japanese Mission project was dropped, and a formal resolution to begin mission work in Japan was diverted.[86] The Mission Board convention included C.M. Zorn and J.F. Zucker, the former Leipzig Missionaries who had left India in 1876 as its members.[87] They always urged the Missouri Synod to begin its Mission field in India, since India's circumstances was brighter. Zucker was appointed as Director of Missions in 1896. Meantime Theodore Naether and Mohn were dismissed from LELM due to clashing differences on the doctrine of the verbal inspiration of the scriptures.[88] The conflict among the Leipzig Missionaries and the consequent dismissal of Naether and Mohn paved the way for the establishment of the MELIM.[89] Through mutual friends in Germany and America, they had heard about the Missouri Synod and through its periodicals they became familiar with its doctrinal position.[90] The immediate reaction of the LCMS was to get in close touch with these men to decide whether their doctrinal stand coincided with

---

[81] *Ibid.*

[82] H.M. Zorn, *Much Cause for Joy*, 8.

[83] F. Dean Lleukening, *op.cit.*, 806.

[84] Proceedings of the 5th Delegate Synod, (Fort Wayne, IN: 1887), 63.

[85] Hermann O.A. Keinath (ed), *Documents Illustrating the History of the Lutheran Churches in America: with Special Emphasis on the Missouri Synod* (Illinois: Concordia Teachers College, 1947), 72 and *Proceedings of the 22nd Regular Convention,* 1893, 83.

[86] William J. Danker, In to all the world, in Carl S. Meyer, (ed) *Moving Frontiers* (St Louis: CPH, 1964), 294.

[87] *Missouri Synod Proceedings,* 1893, 141.

[88] Hermann O A Keinath, *op.cit.*, 141. The conflict was mainly with the understanding of the verbal scriptures.

[89] H.M. Zorn, *op.cit.*, 36.

[90] C.H. Swavely, *op.cit.,* 185.

conservative Lutheran teachings. These former Missionaries had experience in India and could speak a native language the Tamil, fluently. Thereafter be able to begin effective work at once without further teachings. In the meantime, request for starting a mission in India reached the Missouri Synod.[91] Immediately a special meeting was convened at Fort Wayne on May 1, 1894. In that meeting the question of starting a mission in India was considered. Then things moved fast and the Mission Board decided that the field should be changed from Japan to India.[92] The President of the Synod H.C. Schwan (1878-1899) contacted the Districts for their approval to transfer the new area of work from Japan to India. Upon favourable response from the District Synods, the Missouri Evangelical Lutheran India Mission (MELIM) was formed in 1894.

2.5. The beginnings of LCMS Work in India[93]

After fixing India as the first LCMS mission field, the things were moved fast. The Foreign Mission Board of Missouri Synod extended an invitation to Missionaries Naether and Mohn to come to America for a discussion with the board. They arrived there in late summer and were examined regarding their doctrinal position. The Board met with them on 12–13 October 1894, and extended them a call to India. They accepted the call and in turn they were accepted into membership in the Missouri Synod. The commissioning service was held at Immanuel Church in St. Charles, Missouri, on 14 October 1894, and they were accepted as the first foreign Missionaries of MELIM.[94] Zorn preached the commissioning sermon based on the text Matt.28.18-20. He explained the circumstances of this event, defending the defecation from Leipzig and also the Board's decision to go to India instead of Japan. Zorn said: "*very well, we take them and send them back again to the Tamilians. We are certain and say clearly: This is God's will and God's guiding .... We are not sending them to the territory where they can interfere with the congregations of the Leipzig mission, much less of any other heterodox mission. On the contrary, we have instructed them to begin in a place that is as far away from Leipzig mission stations as possible*". Regarding the dealings, Zorn added; "*We wish to go to the heathen with nothing but the Word. The teaching of Christ, the gospel, knowing that nothing else can help and that this is the means which the Almighty saviour has entrusted to us. At the same time, it must not be said under any circumstances that we bring the Word to the heathen in only one way; only one must make sure that what we bring is always the Word. To speak more specifically, we do not want our missionaries to restrict themselves to public and private Preaching of the Word to the heathen. We have instructed them specifically to erect schools, where possible, in which the word of Christ may be taught along with worldly wisdom. Tamilians are eager*

91 *Proceedings of the Missouri Synod*, 1984; 82-86.

92 F. Dean Leukening, *op.cit.*, 203.

93 *Impact of Lutheran Mission among Sambavars in South Travancore, op.cit.*, 38.

94 Missouri Synod *Proceedings*, 1896, 77-79.

for education. We want them, so to speak, to flood the town and environs, where they make their residence, with good, clear, and brief tracts. Tamilians are eager to read. If they perceive another means or way to bring the Word to the heathen, they should use it or follow it. But it must always be the Word and nothing else. In and with it is the almighty Lord; that is His means by which to make heathen into Christians."[95] This message clearly shows their understanding about the then Indian people, and the Missionary strategies. The next step was the establishment of working principles under which the new Missionaries would conduct their programs abroad. The following eight points of instruction were then formed.

1. The purpose of our mission is to make Disciples of Christ out of the heathen (*sic*) and to gather them into congregations built on the pure teachings of the Word of God as the same is witnessed in the Confessional writings of the Lutheran Church. 2. The means to be used by the Missionaries for the achievement of this purpose is the proclamation of the Gospel through the Christian Education of the youth, and particularly through instructions in schools, private discussions and the distribution of Christian Literature, especially doctrinal tracts. 3. The Missionaries are the emissaries of the Synod to the heathen and also, by their call, have entered into a formal churchly relationship with the synod. In these performances of their office they are put under fraternal regulations of the Synod, particularly under the Board established for this purpose. 4. The direction of the mission is in the hands of the Board established by the Synod and takes place through the Director, who shall establish and maintain contact between Missionaries and the Board. 5. The Missionaries shall report on their work monthly and account for the Mission money which pass through their hands. 6. The Missionaries shall seek fellowship one with another and to that end is to found a conference, with a Chairman chosen by them. He is to be the legal representative of the Mission in India as far as the Board is concerned. 7. At these conferences doctrinal matters were discussed and Mission business was taken care of. Detailed minutes of these transactions are to be sent to the Director. The Board names one of the Missionaries in India as the official correspondent between the Missionaries and the Board. 8. Synod provides an established annual salary for the support of the Missionaries. Synod also provides the Missionaries with a free home and takes care of the necessary mission travel expenses by rail and other vehicles.[96] It shows that they set forth these working principles for their mission in obedience to the "Great Commission" (Matthew 28: 18-20). It was marked by courage, evangelical insight and foresight. MELIM was founded on strict confessional principles.[97] In 1894, the Missouri Synod accepted the action of its Mission Board to establish

[95] Report of C.M. Zorn, *The Lutheran,* vol. L (4 December, 1894): 211-212. Italics are in the original.

[96] F. Dean Leukening, *op. cit.*, 207-208.

[97] H.M. Zorn, *The background and the First Twenty Five Years of the Missouri Evangelical Lutheran Mission (1894-1919),* Unpublished STM thesis (St .Louis: Concordia Seminary, 1969), 115.

a new Mission in India. The founding principle of MELIM also includes a strict avoidance of interfering with the work of other Mission Societies. Hence the Missouri Evangelical Lutheran India Mission, known as MELIM came into existence and the work had thus begun.[98] The Mission Board's policy and strategy are described as follows: "The first Missionaries sent out by the Missouri Synod were charged not to built on ground previously occupied by other missions, but to select a territory where the Gospel had not been preached before."[99]

2.6. It began at Krishnagiri

LCMS owes a debt of gratitude to the manpower resources of the Evangelical Free Church in Saxony. The roster of the earliest LCMS Missionaries to India (1894-1913) shows the Saxon influence in a big way.[100] Karl Gustav Theodore Naether and Theodore Franz Mohn left for Germany immediately after the commissioning. Naether, after becoming engaged to Miss. Johanna Naumann, left for India at the end of December 1895. Mohn was in poor health and, with his wife, remained in Germany until he was well enough to begin his new work.[101] Naether arrived in Tuticorin on January 20, 1895. He met his former colleague J.M. Kempff[102] (1860-1945). As soon as they stepped into the Indian soil, they understood that the Missionaries of other denominations such as the London Missionary Society and the Salvation Army also had established stations. They were instructed that one group should not interfere in the mission fields of the other group. Hence, they were forced to seek new fields for their work. With Kempff's help, they selected Krishnagiri in the present day Dharmapuri district as the starting point. It was rather a virgin field but still within the area of Tamil language with which the first mission workers were familiar.[103] A Leipzig Missionary Georg Otto Kellerbauer (1868-1914), who arrived in India in 1893, resigned from Leipzig Mission on 16th March 1895 and met Naether at Krishnagiri on 3 April 1895. Following his wide correspondence, which included a detailed statement of Kellerbauer's doctrinal stand, the board issued a call to him to serve in the India Mission. This call was dated 25 November 1895.[104] In the beginning he worked with Naether at Krishnagiri for ten years and later in

[98] Missouri Synod *Proceedings*, 1896, 77-79.

[99] W.H.T. Dau, ed. *Reviews of the Missouri Synod during Three Quarters of a Century* (St. Louis: CPH., 1922), 395.

[100] Hans Kirsten," Pioneer Missionaries of MELIM ", *Concordia Historical Quarterly*, 56/3 (Fall 1983): 116-132.

[101] "Life of Missionary K.G. Theodore Naether" recorded by his daughters, translated by Martin Naumann, *Concordia Historical Institute Quarterly*, XXXIX (January, 1967): 184.

[102] There is some doubt on the spelling of Kempff. Some places it was Kempf. MELIM records mostly used as Kempff,

[103] O.H. Schmidt, *Globe-Trotting for the Gospel* (New York: Vantage Press, 1962), 14.

[104] Missouri Synod Proceedings, 1896, 80.

Bargur, ten miles away from Krishnagiri. Mohn arrived in India in the beginning of 1896. He started his work at Ambur, North Arcot District, 43 miles east of Krishnagiri. The fourth and final man to MELIM from Leipzig Mission was Reinhold Freche (1862-1924).[105] After the correspondence with the board a call was issued to Freche on 24 February 1898 to serve MELIM. He joined the mission in the interim between the Missouri Synod meeting of 1896 and 1899. He was assigned to work at Vaniyambadi about 16 miles west of Ambur. Having thus established a series of four stations with one Missionary at each station gained success, and expansion was expected. All missionaries considered schools as a basis to their calling. They started schools manned by Indian teachers but under the supervision of the Missionary.[106] In 1900, and the following years new Missionaries came to join the original four. A. Huebner came in 1900 and John Foster and George Naumann in 1902. They were Germans by birth but trained at Concordia Seminary, St. Louis. These Missionaries preached the Gospel to the natives and slowly converted them to Christianity. The first convert was an 18 year old Chinnaian (later he took the Christian name *Devasahayam* means "God is my help") in Ambur on March 11, 1900, Easter Sunday.[107] He was the teacher in one of MELIM schools at the time of his baptism. Other early converts were often the family servants of the Missionaries. The first statistics were announced at the Missouri Synod convention of 1902. Total Lutheran Christians at that time was 45. Among them 15 were with Mohn, 8 with Naether and 22 with Freche. Kellerbauer had not yet gained any converts in his short time in Bargur.[108] Early results were extremely poor and disappointing to members of the Missouri Synod in America.[109] Though it was pioneering work, the Missionaries were in need of great faith and much patience.

After years of patient and preserving labours the Missionaries were able to see small results. At the close of the year 1900, the total number of baptized Christians was only 45. Most of the converts were from outcaste groups. Few high

---

[105] *Ibid.*, 1899, 75-76.

[106] O.H. Schmidt, *op.cit.,* 15.

[107] B. Sobhanam, *op.cit.,* 162. Some record says the baptism date as on march 10.

[108] Missouri Synod Proceedings, 1902, 83.

[109] At the close of the first decade of mission activity, the Missouri Mission published the following statistics: Stations Missionaries' Native Wives & children Christian School Children.

Stations				
Krishnagiri	9	9	2	116
Ambur	3	18	3	170
Bargur	2	--	4	136
Vaniyambadi	6	29	11	55
Total	20	56	22	477

The cost of maintaining the Mission was a little more than $ 7000.00 annually. IELC Statistics file No. 3, Concordia Seminary Archives, Nagercoil.

caste individuals had been obtained as teachers but they did not remain long with the Mission. As we had seen earlier, problems of caste were familiar to the former Leipzig Missionaries. Most converts in the northern district of MELIM were from the outcaste community, therefore caste did not represent a significant problem in the early years. In 1900, Naether's two children died due to dysentery. One of Mohn's children also died and was buried in Ambur. But it was followed by another shock, namely a terrible epidemic of plague in and around Krishnagiri in 1904. A number of Christians were afflicted by it. When Naether heard that the plague had struck the family of a school teacher, he hurried to help. While nursing them Naether contacted the disease and died within a week on February 13, 1904.[110] Naether's death at the early age of 37, after concluding a nine-year term of faithful service and leadership with MELIM, was deeply mourned. Certainly, he did his share in laying the foundation for the Missionaries who were to follow. Mrs. Naether waited for her youngest daughter, Ida, who was born in India on 26 July 1904. In April 1905, Mrs. Naether returned to Germany and settled there with her three daughters. She died in Germany on 15 March 1935.[111] The work had progressed slowly and the blow to Mission work was serious. In addition to Naether's death, the plague brought many losses to the Christian community. The number of baptized dropped from 45 to 38 between 1901 and 1904, largely as a result of these plague deaths. Such misfortunes befalling a new Christian community were interpreted as a sign of divine anger upon these invaders of the Hindu and Muslim faiths. But the next decade witnessed the expansion of the Mission. The Missionaries decided to shift their activities to the south adjoining Travancore State to get relief from their frustration. With new men, MELIM expanded its Mission unexpectedly towards South Travancore in 1907.[112] There the Missionaries found an open door in many villages.

2.7. Lutheran Presence in Early South Travancore Protestant Mission

The first Protestant Christians in South Travancore were directly related to the Tranquebar Lutheran Mission. They were converted and baptized by the Lutheran Missionaries. South Travancore was considered as part of Thirunelveli Mission. Certain officers of the East India Company like Colonel Trotter and certain Danish merchants like Samuel Sawyer took much interest in spreading the Gospel in South Travancore.[113] According to John A. Jacob, Bishop Robert Caldwell (1814-1891) also made references to the Dutch factories established in Cape Comorin and other places in South India, and the possible Protestant evangelistic work

---

[110] Life of Missionary K.G. Naether, *op.cit.*, 185-187; H.M. Zorn, *Much Cause for Joy*, 15-16.

[111] *Concordia Historical Institute Quarterly*, XXXIX, 187.

[112] In the Mission records the area were the first work was began is referred to as Northern field and the Travancore area as southern field.

[113] *The Travancore Times* 81/5 (25th June 1952): 2.

in South Travancore.[114] The early Evangelists in South Travancore had Lutheran roots. Sathyanathan (1745-1815) a native Christian was baptized in 1772 by the Lutheran pastor J.C. Kohlhoff and then ordained in Lutheran Orders on 26 December 1790 by C.F. Schwartz and sent him as a pastor to Palayamkottai.[115] During the years 1795-1805 Rev. Sathyanathan served Rajakrishnapuram and Karumkulam villages. At Pichaikudiyiruppu the new converts were Lazer Nadar and his family and Swaminathan catechist and his family.[116] In a letter to J.C. Kohlhoff the successor to Schwartz, dated 15 December 1804, Sathyanathan, states that, "he sent an evangelist by the name Yesuadian, to Travancore."[117] J. W. Gladstone says: "Sathyanathan one of the early Indian ministers who served under SPCK sent an evangelist by the name of Yesudian to Travancore, but owing to the opposition from the higher castes, he could not establish any Church in Tranquebar."[118] That means Yesuadian also worked in South Travancore. Certain people who used to go much to the Tinneveli district for tapping Palmyra juice and as merchants became Christian converts and were baptized and returned to South Travancore. The congregation at Kudangulam was established on 25.11.1802.[119] James Hough, the first Government Chaplain in Tinneveli, in his report of 1815 states that "out of the 3100 Christians in the churches, 270 live in a village in Travancore."[120] Moreover, citing a leaf from Ringaltaube's church register[121] of the congregation at Pichaikudiyiruppu,[122] Robinson says, "most of the people were baptized at Karungulam by Sathyanathan, a native priest, the date of baptism is unknown. The marks 'X' denotes the persons all who died in 1803 during the famine."[123] That means before 1803 there were baptized Christians in South Travancore.[124] While describing Ringaltaube's Mission in Travancore,

114 John A. Jacob, *A History of the London Missionary Society in South Travancore, 1806-1959* (Nagercoil: 1956), 17.

115 Sathyanathan was a son of a Hindu agriculturist from Uthamapalayam; his earlier name was Karpakam.

116 James Town CSI Church, Bi-centenary Souvenir, 16/5/2010, 33.

117 J.W. Gladstone, *Protestant Christianity and Peoples Movements in Kerala, 1850-1936* (Trivandrum: KUTS Publications, 1984), 58.

118 J.W. Gladstone, *op.cit.*, 58.

119 *The Travancore Times*, *op.cit.*

120 *Ibid.*

121 For the copy of hand written page by Ringaltaube's Church Register see appendix no.

122 The former name of this congregation was Kananpottal up to year 1810. From 1840 this church moved to James Town.

123 William Robinson, *Ringaltaube the Rishi* (Sheffield: Independent Press, 1902), 99.

124 V. Thiraviyamony told that there were graves of Christians at Kannanpottal, the old Pichaikudiyiruppu with the marking the year on 1802, but at present the land is under the Hindus and they have demolished them. Interview with Mr. Thiraviyamony, the secretary of James Town CSI Church, on 22 October, 2011.

J. Duthie writes, "he expected to find a good number of Christians there."[125] J.W. Gladstone also indicates the conversion of a few people to Christianity before Maharasan's baptism.[126] These evidences clearly support the argument that there were Christian Protestant converts in South Travancore even before the London Mission started its work. And they were not from the *Sambavar* community, but most probably *Shanars*.[127] The work by the LMS clearly witnessed the Lutheran presence.

The first LMS Missionary Ringaltaube was also an ex-Danish Halle Lutheran. Before the arrival of Ringaltaube in South Travancore the form of worship adopted by these early Protestant Christians was Lutheran. The form of Church worship and Church government was Lutheran, same as Tharangampadi and Tanjavur. Several rituals and festivals of the Lutherans were observed. Women were taught to cover their head when they assembled for worship and were seated separately. For sermons and discourses, he was aided by the tracts and books published by the Tranquebar Missionaries.[128] Further, C.M. Augur, while describing the agreement made between Ringaltaube, the new Travancore Missionary and J.C. Kohlhoff, the then head of the SPCK Mission said as follows: "*The reason why Mr. Kohlhoff entered into such an agreement with Mr. Ringaltaube was that Mr. Ringaltaube was equally with himself in Lutheran orders, and so he had the assurance that though put in temporary charge he would maintain the churches in conformity with his own Lutheran principles ....*"[129] While describing the works of the first Protestant Missionary of South Travancore R.N. Yesudasan says: "*Ringaltaube, who was a German Lutheran, had taught Lutheran Catechisms for forms of worship. The Tamil prayer books and Catechism (Gnana Upadesa Kurippadam) of the Lutheran Church of Tanjore were in consequently used by the majority Christians and their brethren in the mission.*"[130]

Even though, Ringaltaube was the pioneer Protestant Missionary with the ground breaking ministry of twelve years at Travancore, the credit of "Father of South Travancore Protestant Mission" goes to Rev. Charles Mead, the later LMS Missionary. Mead's mission was the transformation to Methodism from Lutheranism. Augur writes: "one of the most important events of the earlier years of Mr. Charles Mead's period of administration of the mission was the gradual transformation of the Lutheran Church practices of the early Church

---

[125] J. Duthie, "A Century of Protestant Missionary Work in South Travancore," *Harvest Field* 17 (1906): 412-414. This was a paper read at the Kodaikanal Missionary Conference in May 1906.

[126] J.W. Gladstone, *op.cit.*, 58.

[127] Since this subject does not come under the present study, this may be dealt with in a future research.

[128] Joy Gnanadasan, *A Forgotten History* (Madras: Gurukul Publication, 1994), 59-60.

[129] C.M. Agur, *op.cit.*, 487.

[130] R.N. Yesudhasan, *A People's Revolt in Travancore, A Backward Class Movement for Social Freedom* (Trivandrum: Kerala Historical Society, 1975), 56-57.

into Methodist forms of worship". We have seen that the early converts of Vedamanickom and the members of the church formed by Mr. Ringaltaube were brought up in Lutheran ways and latter adapted to the Church of England form of worship. The church at Mylaudy was constituted after the model of Tanjore and Tranquebar Churches which mostly followed German Lutheranism. The Tamil prayer books and Catechisms of the Lutheran Church of Tanjore were used by early Mylaudy Christians and their brethren in mission. When Ringaltaube ordained Vedamanickam, he put on him his own surplice and called him a "native priest."[131]

It is clear that before the conversion of Vedamanickam of Mylaudy into Christianity, there were Protestant Christians in South Travancore in Tinavely and Tranqueabar mission and most probably they were the Shannars/Nadars. The historians of South Travancore Protestant Christianity have so far only acknowledged Vedamanikam of Mylaudy and Ringaltaube, the harbingers of Protestant Christianity in Kerala. Even then, the first Protestant Christian, the first Protestant Missionary, the first Protestant Church and the first Protestant native pastor in Kerala was a Lutheran. The above facts prove the connection of Lutheranism in the first Protestant efforts in South Travancore. But for the direct Lutheran Missionary work in South Travancore had to wait for another century.

2.8. Conversion of Vedamanickam Maharasan

Maharasan from an obscure village called Mylaudy near Nagercoil heard the Gospel while he was on a pilgrimage to Chidambaram from the Lutheran Missionary Kohlhoff of Tanjore. He was converted to Christianity and baptized by the Lutheran Missionaries there and he took his new name Vedamanickam.[132] He returned to his village and preached the Word of God which he had learned during his stay in Tanjore. This happened in 1804. Certain Catechists from Tanjore and Tinnevely came and worked for some time in South Travancore. Vedamanickam felt the great need of the presence of a European Missionary for effective mission. So he went again to Tanjore with one of his friends to beg for a Missionary. He, however, commended his eager friends to the brethren at Tranquebar, where Ringaltaube of the LMS was residing and waited for providential guidance to labour in the Mission field. He accepted the earnest entreaty of Travancore as a divine call to labour in that country. So he promised to visit South Travancore. In Mylaudy, Vedamanickam gathered those who would listen to the Gospel and read to them the Scriptures and taught them the Catechism called *Gnana Upathesa Kurippadam*. There were about thirty persons.[133] He also gave Christian names to his wife and relatives who accepted Christianity. A Catechist from Palayamkottai

[131] Augur, C.M., *op.cit.* 701.

[132] C.B. Firth, *An Introduction to Indian Church History* (Madras: CLS, 1992), 156.

[133] C.M. Agur, *Church History of Travancore* (Madras: SPS Press, 1903), 447.

visited him occasionally to help him. But Ringaltaube's entrance to South Travancore opened a new era to South Travancore touching all facets of life.

2.9. Ringaltaube's Mission at South Travancore

The London Missionary Society (LMS) at first was non denominational, later on mainly Congregationalists was founded in 1796. This was an international enterprise aiming to spread the knowledge of Christ among the "heathen" and other unenlightened nations.[134] William Tobias Ringaltaube (1770-1816) was destined to be the first Protestant Missionary to Travancore. He came to Travancore by travelling in a Danish vessel 'Kind Packet'. He was a German Lutheran and a graduate of the University of Halle. As Ringaltaube moved towards the South by the LMS, he began to learn Tamil.[135]

Ringaltaube reached South Travancore on 25th April 1806. Then he returned to Palayamkottai, after two days, which became his headquarters for the next three years. He came back again in March 1809 and settled at Mylaudy in South Travancore upto 1816. He founded seven congregations including Mylaudy. He earned many converts to Protestantism.[136] One of the local helpers and protectors of Ringaltaube from Pichaikudiyiruppu was Lazar Nadar.[137] He received financial help from some of his friends in Travancore and from outside, in particular, from British Army Officers and Civilian Officers of the East India Company. After 12 years of labor in South India, he handed over his charge to Vedamanickam and returned to his country due to ill-health. The meritorious services of the LMS Missionaries attracted the people of the depressed classes and this in turn resulted in group conversion movement towards Christianity in South Travancore.

2.10. MELIM moves to South: Helpful Factors

2.10.1. Sambavar Christians and L.M.S.

The LMS had been working in the Southern tip of India since 1816, when an ex-Danish Halle Missionary, W.T. Ringeltaube, began to work there. Over the years, most of the converts came from the *Nadar* caste, a group of people with strong community bonds and eagerness to improve their rather miserable lot.[138] Only a few converts came from the other castes. The Christian Missionary centers were confined to strongholds of *Nadars*, who were numerous in South Travancore. Major William Johnson founded the Salvation Army in South Travancore in 1890.[139] As Christians of very poor and low origin, the *Sambavars* felt that LMS

---

[134] G.P. Fisher, *The History of Christian Church* (London: Hodder & Sloughter, nd.), 985.

[135] Samuel Mateer, *The Land of Charity* (London: John Snow and Co; 1871), 158-159.

[136] John A. Jacob, *A History of the LMS in South Travancore, 1806-1857* (Nagercoil: Diocesan Press, 1990), 45.

[137] *James Town CSI Church, Bi-centenary Souvenir*, 16/5/2010, 57.

[138] H.M. Zorn, *Much Cause for Joy, op.cit.*, 17.

[139] Harry Williams, *Miracle of Medicine Hill* (London: 1970), 11.

work was concentrating only among the *Nadars*. J.W. Gladstone says, "*In 1891, the Paraya Christians in southern part of LMS expressed their feelings that they were neglected and not properly cared by the missionaries, and that more opportunities were given to the Nadar Christians. They had the reason enough to feel neglected. In 1891, according to them, all the higher posts in the mission were given only to the Nadar Christians and out of the 18 ordained ministers and 24 Evangelists of the mission there was not even a single member from the Paraya caste.*"[140] The same situation continued in the Nagercoil local LMS congregations also. P.N. Peter writes as follows:

"*The Nagercoil LMS Church is the largest one in Southern India and the congregation is also the largest one. There are seven deacons (elders) to manage this church. The Christian love is so great that there is not a single non-Nadar deacon. A Nadar Catechist is gladly accepted by the non-Nadar Christians but if a non-Nadar Catechist is posted to a Nadar village he will not be accepted.*"[141]

His agitation against *Nadar* domination was clearly expressed in his letter. He adds: "The first Protestant Christian was of the Valluvar Caste, ie., Adi-Dravidas, who are called Sambavars in Travancore. In the earlier this community pushed up the LMS. But today there is not a single ordained agent from the Sambavar, Ezhava, Cheramar (Pulaya) etc., communities while the majority of them belonged to the Nadar community. The LMS is working for the last 125 years and yet the Missionaries are unable to uplift these people to the position of a pastor. Their present teaching is might is right.[142] In a Hindu conference held on December 27, 1925 one of the *Sambava* leaders Subramonya Sambavar, observed that the conversion of the men belonging to his community to Christianity was due to the lack of education on their part and sympathy on the part of their high caste brethren. The Christian *Sambavars* felt that they were neglected. Christian converts were oppressed even by high caste Christians. They gained no equality of status even under the Christian fold. Subramonya Sambavar entreated the high caste Hindus to extent him a helping hand in his mission of re-converting his men to their original faith and creed.[143] This kind of anti-*Nadar* consciousness and protest against Missionary approach forced them to unite and even to demand for a separate district for them. The agitation was noticed by the Missionaries also. L.M.S. Missionary, T.W. Back, made a reference to it as follows: "In some churches the *Shanars* have been refusing the low caste *Pulayas* and *Parayas* admittance to the public service, whilst in other they have only allowed them to enter under protest, and then huddled them together in a remote corner of the building."[144] But nothing concrete was done immediately to alleviate their grievances. They felt

[140] J.W. Gladstone, *op.cit.*, 137.

[141] P.N. Peter, *Depressed Community, Christian Patriot* 37/7 (August, 1928): 11.

[142] *Ibid.*

[143] *Travancore Daily News*, 2 January 1925.

[144] LMS, *One Hundred and Second Report* (1897), 144.

that the Missionaries were not recognizing the claims of *Paraya* Christians. They had suffered all the humiliations of non-Christians as slaves. But the discovery of the existence of caste inside the mission shattered their hopes and was too much for them to bear. The lack of integration and the feelings of neglect within the Church led many *Parayas* and *Pulayas* to join new Christian missions.[145] One congregation, whose members were from *Sambavars*, separated from LMS and became independent at Vadassery[146] near Nagercoil.[147]

2.10.2. Role of Gnanamuthu Jesudasan

Gnanamuthu Jesudasan was the leading figure towards the MELIM's move to Nagercoil. Nagercoil, literally means "the city of a snake" is a city at the very southern tip of South India. At the end of the 19th century this place contains more than 30,000 *Sambavars* in the 1900's. Only a few of them were Christians. One of the prominent members of this congregation was Gnanamuthu Jesudasan (1872-1952). He was born in a Christian family for four generations. He was educated up to the University level. At the end of the year 1896, he went to Trivandrum and joined work in the office of the British resident as a clerk. Later he rose to the position of a Secretary to the British Resident at Trivandrum. He was mindful of the improvements of foreign Missionary enterprises.[148] He wrote many articles under a pseudonym in the *Christian Patriot*, in which he stated that the local *Adi Dravidas* were being neglected by the mission agencies then in Travancore and he pleaded for another mission to come and bring them the Gospel. He appealed to the Baptist Mission.[149] In reply, he was told that this mission was working only in Telugu area and they would not venture to undertake in a new linguiostic area. Then he approached a Salvation Army Captain, Pothenchary, an English man stationed at Trivandrum. Initially he reciprocated positively. But they never stepped into his area with an organized plan for Missionary work as it goes against the established protocol on those days. According to A. Huebner, Jesudasan was not satisfied with the Salvation Army and their teachings. He did not like the *Panchamas* belonging to the Salvation Army. So he approached the Lutherans who were considered to be true teachers of the Scriptures.[150] A request to the Madura Lutheran Missionary in and through *Christian Patriot* by Hazan

---

145 J.W. Gladstone, *op.cit.*, 138.

146 Vadassery village is situated four kilometers North-West of Nagercoil.

147 H.M. Zorn, *Much Cause for Joy*, *op.cit.*, 17.

148 For more details refer 'Nagercoil' an article in *Homiletic* Magazine, 48/7 (July, 1924).

149 G. Jesudasan, *Early History of the Evangelical Lutheran Mission in Nagercoil District* (Unpublished Manuscript). Hereafter referred to as EHELM.

150 A. Huebner, "Nagercoilil Sthapikkappettittulla Namathu Missionin Arambha Charithram." (History of the origin of our Mission at Nagercoil) (Tamil) *Sathia Satchi* 24/8: 162-173.

was also not answered.[151] One day Jesudasan saw an advertisement in Concordia Publishing House (St. Louis) about a book written by Henry Nau. Later on, he sent a letter to Nau along with the petitions signed and sent by the people of Aralvaimoi and others requesting the MELIM to send a Missionary and asking whether they could take up this work.[152] After 28 days he got a reply from H. Nau asking him to write all details clearly and that it would be good if this would reach him before the conference of the Missionaries to be held in Krishnagiri shortly.

Henry Nau raised the following questions: 1. Are those people of the five villages Hindus from the beginning or whether they were Christians of other missions who later turned back. 2. Why do they desire to join our mission? What is their aim? 3. Why should they not join the missions which are already working there? 4. To which mission do you belong? What connection do you have with them?[153] Jesudasan sent appropriate answers to Nau. He was able to state the cause effectively. Moreover, he wrote to his friend Heinrick of the Baptist Mission asking him to write a letter of recommendation stating the needs to Nau. Since, Heinrick was a man of concern for the *Panchamas* of Nanjil Nadu, he wrote letters both in German and English immediately to Ambur, the then headquarters of MELIM, and encouraged them to do Gospel work in Nanjil Nadu straight away.[154] In this way, Jesudasan played an essential role in bringing the MELIM to Kerala, the then South Travancore.

2.11. MELIM to South Travancore

2.11.1. Ambur Missionary Conference

The request from Travancore made a mixed feeling among then MELIM Missionaries in the field. For a number of years the thought of establishing a new station in Madras section had been under consideration. To the Missionaries the opening of the station was only a matter of location. The man to undertake this work was Albert Huebner (1877-1947), who had just been relieved from the charge of Keller Bauer's station at Bargur. When the appeal from Travancore came to his hand, it was examined with a great deal of caution, because this request called for a revision in the policy of not working where other Christian Missions were already working.[155] The Travancore issue was discussed at great length in the Missionary Conference held from 2-6 February 1907 at Ambur, but it did not meet with very much approval at first. The Missionary Conference expressed

[151] *EHELM*, 11. Fact might be, for purely material reasons many of them were looking to the Christian missions for aid. Yet some of their requests were sincere. Among them a certain Jesudasan was appealing to various church bodies for aid which was refused by all until he finally approached the Missouri Mission. Huebner's words justified this move on the basis of their doctrinal stand.

[152] Letter by Jesudasan to R.M. Zorn on 5th October 1941, 2.

[153] *EHELM*, *op.cit.*, 12.

[154] 'Nagercoil', *Homiletic* 48/47 (July 1924).

[155] H.M. Zorn, *Much Cause for Joy*, *op.cit.*, 17.

its opinion on the appeal thus: "If all these things are represented, it is evident that this is to be regarded as a call of God to another mission field which it is our duty to follow even though it means restricting our wok here."[156] After long deliberation, the Conference of the Missionaries decided to examine the matter. Two Missionaries, George A. Naumann (1877-1949) and A. Heubner, were sent to Travancore in the latter half of February 1907[157] to investigate and report the matter.

2.11.2. Reports of the Enquiry Commission

The recommendations of the enquiry committee were positive. Nauman, as a member of the Committee, and Heubner were deputed by the Northern District Conference to discover the conditions in Travancore. They were expected to visit the Vadassery congregation that was independent for more than ten years. The people were to be interviewed to find out whether they were merely dissatisfied from another mission or as represented, a congregation which was independent for reliable reasons and which was minded to submit to instruction from God's work.[158] The Committee visited the congregation, surveyed the field and gathered information wherever they could. Furthermore, they interviewed the LMS Missionaries to find out if they had any objection to the Lutheran Mission opening work among the heathen *Panchamas* in Nanjilnad.[159] They summarized their report in such a manner that the reasons for undertaking the work and reasons against undertaking the work were stated.

The first stated argument for undertaking the work was that it was a call of an independent congregation, which in reality had been an independent congregation for years.[160] Besides, it wished to join a mission and its pastor appeared to be a true and upright man.[161] Secondly, as far as the heathens were concerned, there were many thoroughly heathen villages with people who were not opposed to their preaching. Again, many hindrances, which kept people from joining MELIM, were lacking here and the London Mission was not in a position to take care of the people. Further, the LMS agents were *Shanars* and therefore not willing to work among *Paraiahs*. In addition to these there was the great danger of the Roman Catholics taking over the work of the Salvation Army, which was also working there and could not carry on proper mission work. The reason against starting work in Travancore could be mainly the strengthening of caste spirit. The *Paraiahs* evidently wanted a mission of their own. So they wanted to pledge

---

[156] Swavely, *op.cit.*, 186.

[157] *EHELM, op.cit.*, 13.

[158] Jesudasan. Letter to Heubner on 12 June 1907.

[159] *EHELM, op.cit.*, 14.

[160] Palany Andy's Reports and letters support these facts. But the present writer could not find out these sources.

[161] Nathaniel was the local pastor and Lazarus was another helpful companion.

the Missionaries to work only among *Paraiahs* for three or five years.[162] Besides, the situation would be different with the proximity of the LMS and many LMS Christians from ulterior motives seek acceptance with MELIM. Over and above all these there was a feeling that this Vadassery congregation was reformed and might turn away when things became very much Lutheran in coming years.[163]

2.11.3. MELIM Decides to Move

Members of the Enquiry Commission felt that the work among the masses of heathen *Sambavars* could be justified since they were not evangelized yet properly. Nagercoil lies 400 miles South to Krishnagiri – Ambur field. The Northern District Conference debated regarding this more at length and agreed only half heartedly. The records do not show the exact nature of the decision. Anyhow the Conference decided that A. Heubner be sent to Travancore experimentally for one year and definite decisions might be made after a year. He reached Nagercoil on 21 February 1907. Within a short time he left Travancore and went back to Ambur. They found that there were many outcaste people groups to whom the gospel was not being reached. Records are not available to find out the exact nature of the report. According to H. Nau this move was not unanimously approved by the Missionaries of MELIM.[164] The LMS Missionaries in South Travancore too raised objections against this Lutheran move but they were not considered valid.[165] Rev. Heubner once again at the end of July visited Nagercoil for further enquiry. On his return to Ambur, a conference was again held in which it was finally decided to begin mission work in South Travancore.[166] The Missouri Synod later gave permission to move to South Travancore and start the work having Vadasery as the base.[167] C.M. Zorn was the strong defender for this move. He affirms: "We shall remain here and build God's Church … We are urgently called here."[168] A. Huebner moved to Nagercoil. LMS people tried to give all possible troubles to him including in getting a rented home for his residence. The news about the discontent of LMS went around and so none of the local Christians rented him quarters. Finally, he managed to rent a house from Ambrose, a pastor of the local

[162] This pledge was, of course, not given. See the letter by the Nagercoil District Conference, dated 5 December 1941 and April 1942 to Jesudasan, 1-3.

[163] C.H. Swavely, *op. cit.*, 187.

[164] H.M. Zorn STM Thesis, *op.cit.*, 71.

[165] G. Jesudason, "Extension of work of the Missouri Evangelical Lutheran Mission in India." *The Lutheran Witness* 26 (17 October, 1907): 157.

[166] *Ibid.*

[167] There was another version also about this move. The MELIM conference voted negatively by a narrow margin, but was overruled by the Board H.M. Zorn STM thesis, *op.cit.*, 71.

[168] *The Lutheran Witness* Vol.LX1V, 14 July, 1908, 219.

mission.[169] Ambrose was harshly criticized for this act, but no other action was taken against him. Another man who offered assistance during the early days was a Muslim named Musthapha.[170] He acted as banker, builder, expediter and a person employed to do all types of work for the new men. This gentle man a Muslim had a habit of speaking of "our mission" whenever he came into contact with the people and strangers. Since LMS Pastor Rev. Ambrose and Muslim Mustapha were bold enough to extend a helping hand to the MELIM, the mission was able to expand its work in South Travancore.

2.12. Early Developments

Theodore Gutknecht (1883-1960) was the first colleague of Huebner. He arrived in India in 1907. Jesudasan and his associates cordially received the two Missionaries. The newly arrived Missionary Gutknecht was required to devote his time to the learning of Tamil, the language used in South Travancore.[171] The members of the Vadassery congregation met under the shade of a tree.[172] Gradually it grew and planned for a building. The congregation was very enthusiastic. In 1907, Jesudasan presented a piece of land to build a church at Vadassery. Thus, the first church of Lutheran Mission was established at Vadassery.[173] The church was extended in 1910 by purchasing 7 more cents of land. At the outset, the Missionaries selected twenty youth and recruited them to mission service. G. Jesudasan also assisted the Missionaries in all their activities. An analytical outlook clearly indicates that, the Southern field had grown far quicker and sudden than the Northern districts.[174] The work expanded to places like Oottuvalmadam (1909), Thathiyarkulam (1909), Palkulam (1909), Kulathucheri (1911), Puliyadi (1908), Villavanputhoor (1908), Thazhakudy (1910), Maruhalthalai (1911) and Mangulam (1912). The places like Oottuvalmadam and Thathiyarkulam had strange experiences from the landlords and their supporters.[175] Jesudasan, the prime mover in the MELIM's South Travancore work, was forced to resign the Government job and became a worker for the Mission as teacher and Evangelist. He was given training and instructions by the Missionaries and was ordained as the first national pastor in 1921.[176] New Missionaries were sent out so that by 1911, there were 11 of them, including the two pioneers. Others were Henry

[169] Ambrose's son, A. Gunamony, was a retired Government official, who served as lawyer for IELC.

[170] Musthapha was a prominent politician in Travancore.

[171] Missouri Synod *Proceedings*, 1908, 105.

[172] Minutes of the 14th Nagercoil District Conference, 10 October 1928, 118.

[173] Seminary Board letter, 3 September 1937, 4.

[174] Proceedings of the Missouri Synod, 1908, 104.

[175] Minutes of the 13th NDC, April 8, 1928, 1.

[176] Goerss, R.W., "Rev. Jesudasan's Ordination." *Lutheran Witness* 60/10 (September, 1921): 312-313.

Nau (1909), F.R. Zucker (1913), Richard W. Goers (1913) and Otto A. Ehlers (1914). There were 25 catechists at that time.[177] Besides, there were 223 baptized Christians in nine different places.[178] The Missionaries had to travel 10 to 15 miles in various directions to reach the village. In addition to the Gospel centres, schools were also established at Vadassery and Checkadi in the first year itself. Nagercoil was the main station. Only two congregations were located in the city proper.

2.13. MELIM in the Malayalam Speaking Area

2.13.1. Joint Request from Trivandrum

Similar to Jesudasan's appeal, many other requests followed in quick succession. But many of these were declined.[179] One such request was accepted in 1911. This was a call of Trivandrum,[180] a Malayalam-speaking area, about 50 miles North-West to Nagercoil. While the work of the LMS was progressing, there were some conflicts among the various sub castes and LMS christians at Kuttichal area. This was the context of inviting MELIM into the Malayalam-speaking area.[181] The local persons who were involved in this new venture were Masillamony Paulose,[182] Joseph Kanchanam[183] and Arulanandam. Joseph Kanchanm was an educated and active member of Kuttichal[184] LMS Church and Arulanandam was a catechist in LMS. Kanchanam's farther-in-law Lalus was the catechist in Kuttichal LMS Church. The personal conflict between these two caused a division in Kuttichal church and Kanchanam started a new evangelism centre at Kuttichal with the help of his intimate friend Arulanandam.[185] They started an independent worship service in a *Kalari* of Madan Markose.[186] It was a successful mission. With this inspiration, they started the work at Puliyoorkonam, Puthukulangara, Kurungalloor and Kattakada. This was an independent mission work. Paulose son of Markose was a teacher in LMS School Kuttichal. He married Emma the

---

[177] Missouri Synod Proceedings, 1912, 127.

[178] Swavely, *op.cit.*, 188.

[179] B. Sobhanam, *op.cit.*, 163.

[180] In the early mission records it was as Trevantrum. Presently it is as Thiruvananthapuram.

[181] P. Cubert, Sabha Charitram, (Church History), Souvenir, 170 Annual, published by CSI Paruthipally (Kuttichal), 2010, 19-23.

[182] Some of the missionary records spelt this name as Paulus.

[183] In the early missionary records this name is spelt as Canjanam.

[184] Kuttichal Village is situated 25 Kms east of Trivandrum.

[185] N.C. George, "*Adhiyathe Anchu Varshangal*" (Malayalam); "The First Five Years." In *Christiany* 52/11 (November, 1976): 70.

[186] Madan was a devil dancer. He was a leading man of *Parayan Thullal* (Exorcism of Devil) in that area. Later he became a Christian and his shed had been converted into the Christian worshiping place.

daughter of Arulanandam catechist in1908.[187] After this, he also actively joined with this evangelistic group. Josepeh Kanchanam and Arulanandam heard about the Missouri Evangelical Mission working in Nagercoil among the low caste people. Kanchanam was a member of mixed caste and Arulanandam belonged to Sambavar community. Arulanadam went to Nagercoil again and again and contacted MELIM Missionaries for further help. He was not happy while returns. The MELIM Missionaries were not willing, to invite more rift from LMS Missionaries. Moreover, it was not easy for them to study a new language for the further extension of their work.[188] Jacob deacon from LMS Church Kattakada now joined this Kuttichal independent evangelistic team. Once again they met Gnanamuthu Jesudasan at Nagercoil for the service of MELIM Missionaries. MELIM Missionary Hubner along with Gnanamuthu Jesudasan went to Kuttichal for further enquiry.[189] They got a warm welcome from the native people. They were convinced that the poor *panchamas* of these areas were not receiving the Gospel. They discussed with them about the possibility of relating the independent evangelism centres with MELIM. After hearing the details, the MELIM Missionaries felt this invitation to be God's call which was similar to those of earlier moves. Mr. Lalus spread a lot of lies against the Lutheran Mission among the people, but Yesudasan was a classmate of Lalus.[190] After a visit, Jesudasan was able to convince Lalus the need of a new mission among the panchamas at Kuttichal. Jesudasan in his second visit to Kuttichal in 1910 brought 12 *Sambava* youth from Kuttichal who were admitted in the MELIM School at Nagercoil.[191] Henry Nau (1881-1956) who, by this time had joined the Southern field received a request to begin work in Trivandrum. Now, Masillamony Paulose (1879-1960) became the chief among them to contact the Missionaries.[192] This man, a member of the *Sambavar* caste, had worked as a Catechist, teacher and evangelist with the London Mission.[193] Since they were from the low caste, like the majority of the LMS Christians, they felt that their fellow caste people's chances were inadequate for advancement of education and other benefits. After discussing the matter with a Missionary of LMS, Paulose made his request to Nau.[194] The move to

[187] N.C. George, *Phalangal Mundirivalliyil* (Malayalam) (Fruits in the wine) (Trivandrum: IELC, 1975), 75.

[188] N.C. George, *First Five Years*, 71.

[189] B. Sobhanam. *op.cit.*, 61.

[190] *Early History of MELIM, 28.*

[191] *Ibid.*, 29.

[192] M. Paulose, in 1930, became the first ordained *Malayalee* pastor of MELIM. A. Rash, "Ordination of M. Paulus at Trivandrum", *The Lutheran Witness*, 51/8 (August 1930): 307.

[193] Herbert M. Zorn, *First 25 years of MELIM*, 79.

[194] *Life History of M. Paulus,* autobiography, 5th June 1928, 1.He resigned from LMS and went to Nagercoil in 1911 and there he served as the boarding master and Malayalam teacher along with the confirmation classes with Rev. F.R. Zukker for the two years.

Trivandrum earnestly in 1911,[195] was taken chiefly on the initiative of Henry Nau. The initial interest in the Lutheran Mission was not doctrinal but the desire for better opportunities and advancement.

2.13.2. The First Five Years

Henrich Nau arrived in India in 1905 and served a few years at Ambur and then moved to Nagercoil.[196] Nau was a capable man with strong will and conviction that the Lord would approve of aggressive action. Later on he informed the Board of his action.[197] He simply ignored the objections of LMS since it had failed in 1907. The correspondence at this time does not show any dissatisfaction on the part of the Board. Nau later on wrote a book – *Vanji Bhumi* – describing the life in Travancore.[198] With this move into Trivandrum in April 1911, the Lutheran Missionaries would not only be going into another language area but would also be gaining foothold among people of several castes.[199] Nau, a keen linguist, rapidly learned Malayalam language and initiated the new work with extraordinary energy. The worship place was now moved from Madan Markose *panthal* to David *Moopan's* house at Konam for more participation of the people.[200] They converted the former independent preaching centers as the base for the MELIM"s works in Malayalam speaking area. During the first few years he established a number of congregations, preaching centers and schools. The native workers team helped him were Joseph Kanchanam, Jacob Deacon, Arulanandam and Paulose.[201] As we have seen earlier, they were directly related to the LMS as church workers, catechists and teachers and now they joined the Lutheran fold. With the help of a dedicated local evangelist Nau was able to organize six Lutheran congregations within a few months. They are, Kuttichal, Puliyoorkonam (Kattackode), Kattackal (Luthergiri) Kurungalloor, Puthukulangara (Chalikonam) and Chullimannoor. During the year 1914, the church at Kuttichal was considered as one of the important churches of Lutherans. Puliyoorkonam is situated 18 Kms east of Trivandrum.[202] The congregation was organized by Overhaul. Gradually the congregation grew up and planed for a building. Ponnambi is another village situated 10 Kms South east of Trivandrum, and the mission work was started there in 1912.[203] In 1912, Fritz started gospel work at Pudukulangara village which is

---

[195] *Sathya Satchi* 1932, 179.

[196] H.M. Zorn, *Much Cause for Joy*, 20.

[197] H.M. Zorn, *First 25 Years of MELIM*", 80.

[198] Henrich Nau, *Vanji Bhumi* (German) (St. Louis: CPH, 1913).

[199] Swavely, *op.cit.*, 188.

[200] *Panthal* means temporary shed and *moopan* means elder of the people group.

[201] N.C. George, "First Five Years", *Christhiani* 52/11 (November, 1976): 70-75.

[202] *Minutes of the Local Conference,* Trivandrum, May 1, 1924, 1.

[203] *Minutes of the Local Conference*, Trivandrum, September 21-22, 1923, 3.

situated 22 kms south-east of Trivandrum.[204] Thachancode and Aryanad were the other places where the Missionaries started their work in 1912. Anthiyoorkonam and Tholicodu works were started in 1913. On 31 October 1911 all Lutherans from this six congregations assembled together at Kuttichal for a reformation festival. At that time all MELIM Missionaries in India were present there. This was the first general gathering of Lutherans in Kerala. On 13 May 1913, Paulose was posted as the catechist at Chullimannoor and Chalikkonam. He says "By God"s grace after some three years nearly one hundred people were examined and baptized by J.R. Zukker, in both places."[205] He served there until 18 May 1924. The Missionary work in this area was intensified with the arrival of Frederick R. Zucker (1910-1930), John C.W. Harms (1912-1928), Otto A. Ehlers (1913-1923) and A.J. Lutz (1912-1948). The First World War broke out in 1914 which created problems and difficulties to the Lutheran Missionaries. During the war period the Missionary work met problems because the Missionaries were of German origin. The Missionaries who were working in Travancore area did not face much problem in their Missionary work because Travancore was a partner of the British by the agreement of 1805. But the Missionaries who went on furlough faced problems. Nau left for furlough in early 1914 and he could not return to the mission field.[206] This move to Trivandrum received very little notice in the minutes and correspondence, which is surprising in the light of its importance.[207] Working near Christians of different denominations thus had its problems.

2.13.3. Problems with LMS

MELIM's entrance into a field of another linguistic area raised challenges and problems. This was against the policy of not working where other Christian Missions were working. As it was a strong LMS Missionary centre the LMS objected to the service of the new mission. The Lutheran Missionaries came in with the purpose of bringing the Gospel to the people who were excluded to hear the Gospel due to the social pressures of caste.[208] They had no intention to interfere with the work of other Missions. Later experiences showed that it was extremely difficult for the two Missions to work side by side without co-operating with each other. The marriages between the members of LMS and MELIM were not possible on those days. Playing one Mission against another became a common practice.[209]

Missionaries of the LMS complained to their headquarters that the Lutheran Missionaries were pocketing their members and entering into their congregations

204 *Sathya Satchi,* 1932, 179.

205 *Life history of M.Paulus,* Autobiography, 5th June 1928, 2.A hand written manuscript.

206 H.M. Zorn, *Much Cause for Joy*, 23.

207 H.M. Zorn, "Relation between MELIM and LMS", *ICHR* 1/2 (December, 1967): 133 -143.

208 Ibid.

209 H.M. Zorn, *Much Cause for Joy*, 20.

whenever disputes arose. The Board in London complained to the Board in St. Louis about the unspoken sheep pocketing. Director Brande of St. Louis gave an assurance that Lutheran Missionaries would not take the members from other missions. A delegation was appointed to investigate the facts in the case. But on the mission fields, the members of the LMS approached the Lutheran Missionaries with reports of false doctrines and wrong practices in their congregations. Some of them quit the LMS and returned, asking for spiritual care. The Lutheran Missionaries tried to provide such care. Conferences spent long hours and wrote detailed minutes on the stands to be taken towards other Christians who might come for spiritual care. Since MELIM ran boarding schools, it needed and hired teachers and catechists. They also gave certain amount of charity to poor people. It was difficult to tell how many of these requests were sincere for spiritual care and how many were prompted by other motives. The Lutheran Missionaries ignored all objections and gave new thrust to religious activities. H.M. Zorn argued, "The relation between MELIM and LMS was cool and strained."[210]

2.13.4. Courageous Vision

Moving into the Malayalam area meant that Missionaries would have to study a different language, literature would have to be duplicated, and theological training would face special problems. Moreover, it was a move that began to involve the MELIM in the problems of caste. This was not immediately evident, though the implications were present. At the time of the move, Paulose and his father-in-law, one Arulanandan and several others demanded that the Missionaries should agree to work exclusively among the Sambavars for the first fifteen years.[211] The request must have puzzled the Missionaries, because there was J. Canchanam, a mixed caste in the group. The Missionaries refused to agree to this demand. They did begin their work among the people who had invited them. They accepted the offer with a hope that they will gain foothold among several other castes too.[212] In 1912, the first MELIM Missionary to Trivandrum Hendrich Nau himself declared it as follows: "We decided to work among the most downtrodden people at Travancore, who were oppressed and separated from the common people from a long period back. We will first start our work among the Paraiahs those who suffer most. God willing then we will move to the Pulayas and Shanars. We are not trying to do something on the surface level. We need to do something which is urgent and basic to their needs. As explained earlier, I personally witnessed in several occasions about their deplorable and sad situations. I want to show them hope and comfort."[213] That means MELIM Missionaries were consciously aware about the need of forming solidarity of subalterns. During the period of the

[210] H.M. Zorn, "Relation between MELIM and LMS", *ICHR* 1/2 (December, 1967): 133-143.

[211] H.M. Zorn, *First 25 years of MELIM*, 81.

[212] H.M. Zorn, *Much Cause for Joy*, 19-21.

[213] H. Nau, *Vanchi Bhoomi* (German) (St. Louis: CPH, 1913), 45.

Missionaries they controlled the Church organization completely, and the caste difficulties were not obvious. But there were a clear willpower that mission work should be expanded to all those who are in need without any caste distinction. The Home Church, LCMS through the board, was engaged in the largest fund raising effort, with the aim of taking advantage of the favourable opportunities for the spread of the Gospel throughout the world. In these circumstances MELIM made various expansion plans for the fruitful mission.

2.14. Conclusion

Christianity found its continuous history in India from at least fourth century A.D. onwards. The Church was confined with 'Syrian Christians' and did not spread outside. Introduction of Christianity into other parts of India came through the colonization of western Countries. Portuguese paved the way to plant Roman Catholic Church in South Travancore among the fisherflock. The first Protestant Mission to India was made possible by German Lutherans at the beginning of the 18th century at Tranquebar. After a glorious beginning, the Tranquebar Mission almost went astray and Leipzig Mission came to be forefront to continue the mission. Lutheran Church Missouri Synod financially supported the LELM. Quarrels among Missionaries over doctrinal differences collapsed the relationship and Missouri Synod started its own Mission Board, the MELIM. MELIM sent its Missionaries to Krishnagiri in South India. The main beneficiaries of this mission were members of the *Subaltern* community. In South Travancore, Protestantism found its growth through Vedamanickam and the LMS Missionary Ringaltaube. However, before that, there were Protestant Churches and Christians in Travancore who had clear connection with Lutheranism. Though the LMS Mission was started among the *Sambava*r community, the major converts were from the *Nadar* caste. Since the *Sambavar* felt that they were neglected by LMS, they decided to have another mission among them. For that purpose they approached the MELIM Missionaries and invited them to South Travancore. They accepted their request and decided to expand their mission in Nagercoil, then a part of Kerala. This was the beginning of Lutheran Christian Mission in Kerala. The significant things in this Missionary move were firstly, it was an invited mission not an imposed mission like many of the other mission works in the colonial period. Secondly, it was not the Missionaries or the mission board that founded the place and people group for their work, but the people selected the place and the partners of mission. Thirdly, it was consciously a mission to the most downtrodden people. Fourthly, the first people groups who were involved in this mission were not passive recipients of Lutheranism but active participants of mission. Finally, this was a Christian mission started by the joint invitation of the two subaltern groups which eventually led to the formation of a wider subaltern solidarity in Kerala. In the next chapter we will discuss the further expansions and developments of Lutheran Mission in Kerala.

Chapter 3

Lutherans in Kerala till 1956

3.1. Introduction

The history of Lutherans in Kerala from 1911 to 1956 can be understood as the Missionary era. Trivandrum is the youngest of the Indian Districts of MELIM. The increase in the membership of MELIM indicates the growth of individual congregations. New preaching places sprang up and the mission was invited to move into new places. Frequently the invitations came through relatives of the members of MELIM. These relatives lived in a neighbouring area and would invite Missionaries to serve their village as well. Such moves were usually within the caste being served in the original congregations. From the beginning onwards, Missionaries tried to reach the different people groups with the liberating Gospel. The magazine *Sathia Satchi* and *Christiani*, Minutes of NDC and TDC, Congregation Reports by Missionaries, Survey Reports, Autobiographies of the old pastors, Seminary and Board letters give detailed history of the origin of major Lutheran congregations and the mission strategy of MELIM Missionaries in Kerala. This chapter tries to analyze the historical development of MELIM in Kerala till 1956, when the district synod was formed in connection with formation of an autonomous and indigenous Church called IELC.

3.2. Mission Before the First World War

3.2.1. A New Start with Peace

The Mission was divided into Northern and Southern districts. These two districts worked independently under MELIM. The Southern district brought greater results. The move to Travancore brought some internal problems to MELIM. Increase in Missionary staff increased the business of MELIM. Distance made it impossible for the Missionaries to meet together frequently. Moreover, the move to

Travancore that is to a new linguistic area. There were clashes among Missionaries and the need of districts conflicted with one another.[1] The correspondence from the Board to the fields indicates that there was a serious rift between Northern and Southern districts in 1910 and 1911 mostly due to the allocation of Missionaries. Misunderstanding arose and the future of the MELIM was threatened. The cable sent from the field to the Board with one word "peace" was received with joy in the United States in early 1912.[2] O. Ehlers arrived in 1913 as a Missionary to the Northern field. But he disobeyed the Board and Missionary Council and later moved to Trivandrum.[3] The early Missionaries suffered untold miseries due to poverty, bitter epidemics, monsoon rains and lack of transportation.[4] Julius Friedrich, the Director of the Board for Missions of LCMS visited the Indian field. He remained in India from September 1912 to March 1913. He visited all the stations and met all Missionaries in two General Conferences.[5] Friedrich also worked toward establishing harmony among the Missionaries. In fact, this visit did much to increase understanding between the fields and the Board.[6] Thus, MELIM was ready for a new surge of growth.

3.2.2. The First Missionaries

Henry Nau the first MELIM Missionary to Malayalam-speaking area[7] arrived here at the age of 35 and started his mission based on the independent congregations

[1] H M Zorn, first twenty five years of MELIM, *op.cit.*, 82.

[2] File of Board letters, 10 February 1912. Concordia Seminary Archives. Here after refer only as Concordia archives.

[3] MELIM Proceedings, February 1914, 110-123.

[4] Sobhanam, *op. cit.*, 164.

[5] MELIM *Proceedings*, October 1912 and October 1913, 127-137.

[6] MELIM *Proceedings*, January 1913, 92-93.

[7] Dr. Henry Nau was born near Marburg, Germany, on 21 Sep. 1881. After graduation from the high school in Marburg, he went to USA for ministerial training. After the completion of his studies at Concordia Seminary St. Louis Mo, in 1905, he was commissioned as a missionary to India. On his way to India he passed through Germany and met Helan Hempfing of Cheminitz, who later became his wife. From 1905-1914 Henry Nau served as a missionary in the Salem and in the North Arcot districts of Tamil Nadu as well as in the Nagercoil and Trivandrum areas. He worked both in Tamil and Malayalam fields. During the years of First World War he served as a hospital chaplain in Germany. After the war he worked for his doctorate in the department of Oriental languages at the University of Halle –Wittenberg, Germany and was awarded the degree of Doctor of Philosophy in 1920. In 1921 he accepted a call to the faculty of the Luther college of New Orleans, USA. From 1925 he served as president of this institution which during his years of service was merged with Immanuel Lutheran College at Greeshro, North Carolinas. He retired from the presidency of this school in 1950. During the years 1921-1956 Dr. Nau answered the call to work on assignments in the interest of extending mission frontiers of the Kingdom four times. In 1932 he was asked to survey mission possibilities in Peurto Rico. In 1935 the mission Board requested him to take a similar survey in Nigeria, West Africa. Once more, in 1950 he went to Iraq, Iran, and India with the purpose of helping his church's mission. In 1951 he himself together with his wife at

in and around the Kuttichal area. He selected some educated members including Paul Joseph Kanjanam and Arulanandam (Kuttichal) Markose (Konni), Raman Vadhyar (Kurungallooor), Jacob, Arulanadan Vadhyar, (Vengannoor), Appavoo Vadhyar, K.P. Masillamony (Kattakada), M. Paulose, David, James Vadhyar (Irinjayil) and V.M. Markose to train them in Bible lessons to became the early workers to help him in his work. In 1911, Nau brought 16 acres of land for Rs, 10,000 in Vattiyoorkavu at Peroorkada and started to build a bungalow there. But, when it was completed, he was not able to live in it for a single day, because at this time the First World War broke out and as a German Missionary, he had to leave India. Nau was a hardworking visionary, courageous man with good health, and respected and feared by the high castes. He faced much opposition from the Nairs, when he wanted to protect the poor Christians. He used his influence to get the help of the police to subdue the Nairs. When Julius Frederich, the director of BFMS-LCMS visited the Malayalam-speaking area, in 1913, Henry Nau with nearly 6000 members received him. Thus, Henry Nau worked for a short period of two years from 1911 to 1913 and established many congregations. Frederick R Zukker[8] arrived in India 1910 and served here till 1930. He was one of the Missionaries who worked for a long period in Kerala. In 1913, he built a boarding school in Vattiyoorkavu at Peroorkada and admitted students from different Lutheran Churches. Later, he also opened a boarding for girls. Zukker was a man involved in doing Social service. When cholera and small pox spread in his congregation at Chullimannoor, he visited each house with the doctor and supplied them with medicines and other helps. As a result he even fell ill.[9] Very soon Missionaries, O. Ehlers and J.C. Harms joined with Zukker. When Nau left India, these three Missionaries continued with their work. As a result they were able to start more churches and schools. The following are the major churches they organized before the First World War.

---

the age of 69, came to reside in India, taking up mission among the Muslims at Vaniyambadi, N. Arcot. After an active term of three years they retired from the field in 1954. Dr. Nau died at his home in Greensboro, North Carolina, in 1956, after serving his master on four different continents. In addition to normal activities as pastor, missionary, educator, and father, Dr, Nau also wrote numerous articles in church periodicals and books namely, *The move into Africa, Vanchibhoomi,.* He was instrumental in founding "Society for the Promotion of Muslim Missions" and served as first editor of the society's publication, "*The Market*". Upon the request of IELC the Society founded by Dr. Nau had granted a sum of money to hold annual lectures on Evangelism at Concordia Seminary, Nagercoil. Source: *Biography of Dr. Nau,* Concordia Seminary, Nagercoil, Archives.

[8] There is one church called Zuker memorial Lutheran church at Kavadithalakkal.

[9] D. V. Bernard, "*A Historical study of the origin and Growth of the Lutheran Churches in Kerala up to the present time*", Unpublished BD thesis, UTC, Bangalore, 1974, 24.

3.2.3. Early Churches

Chullimannoor is situated thirty kilometers south-east of Trivandrum. MELIM Missionaries started their work here in 1911.[10] They organized a small congregation on September 21, 1911. The members met under the shade of a tree. As the congregation began to grow they started building a small church on 1 January 1924. They also started a school in the church premises. The members of the church extended generous help. By 1930, this church became an important Lutheran Church in that area.[11] On 1 Dec. 1935 there were 38 communicant members in the service conducted by Oberhume.[12] Another church formed during this period was at Puliyoorkonam situated eighteen kilometers east of Trivandrum.[13] The congregation was organized by Rev. Overhaul. Gradually the congregation grew and plan for building a church was proposed.[14] The villagers though very poor generously helped the church. The Mission purchased ten more cents of land and added it to the church.[15] In 1912, they started the work at Kuttichal.[16] Kuttichal village is situated twenty five kilometers south-east of Trivandrum. On 1 October 1934, a small congregation was organized by Bro. Charles and U. Daniel. 16 members were in this congregation. The members met in a verandah.[17] Later this congregation grew into 17 families. During the year 1914 this church at Kuttichal was considered as one of the important churches of the Lutherans. Fifteen cents of land was added with the existing land in 1932.[18] Ponnambi is another village situated ten kilometers south-east of Trivandrum. In 1912, the Missionaries started the work at Ponnambi.[19] This congregation had a small building. The Mission purchased seven cents of land.[20] The members met in the small building. Nine members attended the Sunday service. In 1912, gospel work at Podukkara village was started by Rev. Fritz which is situated 22 kilometers south-east of Trivandrum.[21] A small church was build there[22] and 14

---

[10] *Sathiya Satchi,* 1932, 179.

[11] *Minutes of the Local Conference,* Trivandrum, 1 May 1924, 1.

[12] *Ibid.*

[13] *Ibid.,* 1-2.

[14] *Minutes of the 50th Local Conference,* Trivandrum, 5 January 1923, 2.

[15] *Sathiya Satchi,* 1932, 179.

[16] *Minutes of the 50th Local Conference,* Trivandrum, 21-22 September 1923, 3.

[17] *Seminary Board Letter,* 4 December 1927.

[18] *Sathya Satchi,* 1932, 179.

[19] *Minutes of the 50th Local Conference,* Trivandrum, 21-22 September 1923, 3. But some record the year of starting was 1911. See H.M.Zorn, Congregation Report 1953; Sathya Satchi 1932, 179-180.

[20] *Letter to the Board of Missionaries,* 1913, 9.

[21] *Sathya Satchi,* 1932, 179.

[22] *Minutes of the 50th Local Conference,* Trivandrum, 21-22 September, 1923, 3.

families were there. Four cents of additional land was purchased for this church.[23] Thachancodu village is situated 27 kilometers south-east of Trivandrum. In 1912, the Missionaries started to work at Thachancodu.[24] On 11 February 1928, a small congregation was organized by P.M. Kauffeld. The Vedars caste resided in this place.[25] Canchanam, who was a Hindu, who showed interest towards Christianity worked among the Vedars at Thachancodu for two years. When the work was in progress, the Mission purchased 12 cents of land for the construction of a church building.[26] Aryanad village is 28 kilometers south-east of Trivandrum and in 1912, work was started there by Lutz.[27] In the same year, they started a school there. This congregation has an old building and the Mission purchased 10 more cents of land.[28] In 1913, the Missionaries started the work at Anthiyoorkonam situated 15 kilometers south-east of Trivandrum.[29] Kauffeld served this congregation in a small shed. Later a new church building with mud walls was constructed.[30] In 1914, eleven more cents of land was purchased.[31] Tholikodu village is 15 kilometers South-East of Trivandrum and started the work there in 1913. Catechist Markose organized a small congregation there. There were seventeen members in the congregation then.[32] The members met for worship in an old building which was built in 6 cents. Three more cents of land was added in 1914. The church grew shortly.[33] The new venture of MELIM Missionaries among the neglected section of the people got attention from the surrounding areas. Different groups of people from nearby villages invited MELIM to start their work among them.

3.3. Progress of the MELIM Between the World Wars 1914-1939

3.3.1. New Missionaries

Between 1920 and 1921 more Missionaries like, P. Kaufeld, G. Oberheu, R.M. Jank, and A.C. Fritz arrived.[34] Chairman of LCMS BFMS wrote an open

[23] *Seminary Board Letter*, December 4, 1927, 10.

[24] *Sathya Satchi*, 1932, 179.

[25] *Minutes of the 50th Local Conference*, Trivandrum, 11 February 1928, 1.

[26] *Minutes of the 50th Local Conference*, Trivandrum, 26 March 1925, 11.

[27] *Sathya Satchi*, 1932, 179.

[28] *Minutes of the 50th Local Conference*, Trivandrum, January 5, 1923, 2.

[29] *Sathya Satchi*, 1932, 180.

[30] *Minutes of the 50th Local Conference*, Trivandrum, December 27, 1928, 5.

[31] *Seminary Board Letters*, December 1, 1924, 1.

[32] *Minutes of the Local Conference*, Trivandrum, May 1923, 1.

[33] *Sathya Satchi*, 1932, 180.

[34] A C Fritz (1921-1944) started his ministry at Balaramapuram. Later he became the initiator of many developments in both Balaramapuram and Ponvila Districts. He was the founder of Concordia High school at Trivandrum. He stressed the need of education in English medium and also he insisted that all the teachers in Lutheran School should be Lutheran. Most of the missionaries

appeal to the whole LCMS for serious and immediate consideration. Through that communication he asked for a few more workers and funds to the India Mission since India was truly ready to harvest."[35] Kurt M. Zorn arrived in 1927,[36] G.R. Stelter[37] arrived in India in 1926 at the Trivandrum station. A.J. Buehner[38] who arrived in 1928 worked a long period in Ponvila station. He also served as the supervisor of MELIM schools. He left India in 1951. Daniel S. Chuvala[39] arrived in December 1929 and worked in Trivandrum station. He worked as TDC chairman, Ex. committee member of MELIM General Council, Editor of *Christiani*, Executive member of Kerala Christian Council, President of Indian District *Sangam* and Chairman of Wynad committee.[40] Arther R. Rash[41] and his wife Marie reached Trivandrum station on 1 Nov. 1926. They worked in Ponvila and Balaramapuram stations. In 1942 he went for furlough and he came back to the district without his family. Then he took over the charge of Nilamel station.

---

argued for the vernacular education for the natives. But he wrote to the board and got permission to start a High School. He devoted his latter life for the development of Concordia School and the boarding school. Due to ill health he accepted another call from a church at Oxhoma. He left India mission with grief. He died on 18 Aug 1948.*Christiany*, Oct. 24/10, 1948, 111-112.

[35] Letter by Rich Krelzschmar, Chairman, BFM-LCMS, An appeal to Pastors, Teachers, Congregations, Schools, and Sunday-Schools, 14 Dec. 1920.

[36] Wife Hazel, Children Susan and Jonathan.

[37] Wife Gertrude Oberheu Stelter and children Richard Paul, Ruth Irma, Ralph Robert, and Carol Anne.

[38] He went on furlough with his family in 1942. Christani, July 21/7, 1945, 62.

[39] D.S. Chuvala was a short man and always with a smiling face.TDC appointed him as a missionary to Alleppey area to work with K M Zorn. He worked in Vadakkal, Thiruvampady and South Aryad churches. He loved the people very much. While K. M. Zorn was on furlough, he tried to revive the evangelistic work throughout the district. Night Public meetings in street, public dinners and tea parties along with sharing of the gospel were his new method. He worked hard for the literature ministry including the promotion of Christiani Monthly. Latter he was transferred to the Trivandrum field to develop the Concordia hostel Trivandrum. He was a good sportsman. His wife also worked hard to support her husband mission even though they had no children. He died in a hospital at USA, due to cancer on 20 Feb. 1953. *Christiani*, March 1953, 55-63.

[40] A special memorial service was held at 4.30 PM Thursday in connection with the sad demise of Chuvala who died on Feb.20th ,1953.Conferance decided to take a special collection and received Rs.500 from the missionary congregations for the Chuvala memorial fund which is to be used for an alter and other furnishing for the Trivandrum Central Church. *127th TDCM* (1953 February 24-27): 4.

[41] Arthur R. Rash served nearly 26 years in TDC. He was born at Bathallou, New York on 23 April 1904. He Studied at Concordia College, Branks Villa and Concordia Seminary, St. Louis. In 1926 he graduated and accepted the call to serve MELIM. They left India in 1953 due to the sickness of their son. They had eight children. In 1952 one son Paul died due to diabetes at Kodaikkanal. One of his daughters Odhri Rash worked at Ambur Bethesda hospital. *Christiani*, (Dec. 1953): 290-291.

He was in charge of Nilamel girls and boys boarding homes. Elmer E Griesse[42] arrived in India for the work in Trivandrum district on 21 June 1945. He was the one who came to this District after a long gap after the arrival of R.P. Sieving in 1937. This MELIM Missionary learned Malayalam and they started their mission as a team among the most backward communities in different parts of Kerala.

3.3.2. First Twenty Five Years and World Wars

The breaking out of MELIM's boundaries and geographical expansion within first 25 years and its growth in different fields are summarized below:

While MELIM completed its first 25 years, the Missionaries had laboured through disappointment, faced new situations and dangers of world war. The church had grown from nothing to a baptized membership of 1681. Sixty-eight schools functioned with 2657 children.[43] The policy developed more from the needs of the times than from planning. Medical Mission was tried. New areas and new kinds of works were entered. Theological training was discussed and the following period had seen its establishment. Literature efforts had begun during this period. The groundwork had been laid and had survived the storm of war. The First World War that broke out in 1914 had created problems and difficulties to the Lutheran Missionaries.[44] Great Britain and Germany were arch contenders. Most of the Lutheran Missionaries were German citizens and subject to captivity or repatriation. While in 1914, it was a force of fifteen men on the field, by 1920, this number had dried-up to four. Despite many and various efforts it was impossible to send out new workers. When the ban was lifted 18 new workers were sent out in a three years period.[45] The Missionaries who worked in Travancore area did not face much problem in their Missionary endeavours because Travancore was a supporter of the British by the treaty of 1805.[46] But the Missionaries who went on furlough faced problems. Rev. Kellerbaur who went on furlough died in 1914. Nau was in Germany and could not return to the mission field.[47] Fresh workforce could not be sent to the mission field. The existing staffs were burdened

---

[42] He was born on 7 Feb. 1919 at Miart, USA as a son of LCMS Pastor. After the Concordia Seminary graduation in 1943 he became a pastor for one year at Cassias Norton. While he continued his studies at Washington University, he met MELIM Missionary Rasch who was on furlough at that time. From him he heard about the Malayalam language and decided to work among the Malayalies. *Christiani*, 21/7, 1945, 61-62.

[43] Missouri Synod, *Proceedings*, 1930, 143-144.

[44] Missionary manpower had grown to 17 by 1914, but dropped sharply during the war to eight in 1919.

[45] Their *Blessings, A resume of 60 years of Missouri Synod Mission work in Asia*, Foreign mission department, LCMS, 29.

[46] For the full version the Treaty signed by the Maharaja on 12 January 1805 and ratified by the Governor general in council on 2 May, 1805 see 425, V, Nagam Aiya, *The Travancore State Manual, Vol.1* (Madras: Asian Educational Services, 1989 (1906), 425-427.

[47] H.M. Zorn., *op.cit.,* 23.

with heavy work. The new Missionaries who came just before the outbreak of the War suffered for want of linguistic competence. The Missionaries worked day and night.[48] The burden of the War was too heavy on Travancore. Being a partner, the Maharaja was forced to pay a huge amount as War fund. This affected the economy of the State. People who were working in Malaysia and Singapore came back to Travancore. There was large scale unemployment in the State. The country was suffering under the throes of famine and poverty. It was during this time the Missionaries, though limited in number, met their fold, extended alms to the needy and consoled those who suffered due to the War.[49] During this time, MELIM Missionaries stood with the people and won their appreciation. Even though, the difficulties of the War were severe, it did not hinder the growth of the mission. During this War period, the mission was growing surprisingly.[50] In 1914, 675 baptized members were registered and in 1920 there were 1681.[51] Statistics shows that in 1922 there were only 14 catechists in all over the Malayalam field. In 1927, there were 25 and in 1932, it was 49. Likewise in 1922, there were only 16 communicant members in the whole Malayalam area. But in 1927 it was 66 and in 1932, 503.[52] MELIM was beginning to realize that the future of its work lay in the Indian Church. The emphasis on education and theological training witnessed to that realization. However, the steps in this direction were still very tentative. Few Indian pastors and those who had acted only as "assistants" to the Missionaries in the local centre has been ordained. Decisions regarding the allocation, salary, and other needs of teachers, catechists and other workers were made by the Missionary conference. Once again, World War II tested MELIM and its work. All the Missionaries were either Americans or British and so they could continue their work. Those who remained had heavier tasks to carry on with less equipment. Wartime rationing was so severe that bicycles became the standard means of transportation, even to distant places. Wartime jobs lured many of the Indian workers away from their posts, high inflation squeezed the budget.

Even the end of the War did not bring immediate relief. Almost all the Missionaries were due and overdue for furlough. In July 1946, only a skelton staff remained. Fatigue and ill health forced a number of Missionaries to resign from service.[53] The lessons of War were learned well. They gave top priority to the training of local pastors to carry out the future ministry. The War and its difficulties emphasised the need for fellowships among Christians as imperative. When War

[48] *Ibid.*

[49] *Minutes of the General Conference*, 1919, 78-80.

[50] F Foster, *Report of the General Secretary of Missions and foreign Missions* 5 pages and document, Concordia Archives.

[51] *Their Blessings*, op.cit., 29.

[52] Delegates and Workers Meeting in TDC, 1. Concordia Archives.

[53] H.M. Zorn, *Much Cause for Joy*, 44.

threatened to remove Missionaries from the field, the Missionaries convened district delegates meetings with representatives from all the congregations.

3.4. The Mission Expansions

The earlier Missionaries started their work in the Luthergiri field and most of the churches which are described above came into this field. Another field was Peroorkada[54] where the Missionaries opened a boarding school for boys and girls. Soon, they also extended their work in the near villages of Peroorkada which included Chenamcode, Kathukal, and Karuvoollam where the people were out castes, the Panchamas.[55] Another field was Ponvila which lies nearly 20 miles South of Trivandrum at the border of Tamil Nadu. Here, the work was started in 1924 by missionary G R Stelter. Balaramapuram lies in between Ponvila and Trivandrum, nearly 15 miles south-east of Trivandrum. Missionaries A.C. Fritze, A.R. Rasch, L.M. Wetzel were the pioneers in this field.[56] Another new field was Nilamel which lies nearly 35 miles north of Trivandrum. This is a hill station and the people are mainly Vedars, Mala Arayas, Paniyars, Kuravas and other hill tribes. The work was started in 1923 in Arivarikuzhy by Missionary Robert M. Jank. He was the one who opened the medical and the evangelistic work there. As the people were illiterate a school was opened for them. Many churches were established in between 1924 and 1930. In 1927, the mission spread to another field, Alleppey, a sea cost, nearly 100 miles north of Trivandrum. The people were mainly Ezhavas.[57] Due to caste problem, some of the leaders of this caste, invited the Lutheran Missionaries, and so in 1927, Missionary P.M. Kaufeld, opened a Lutheran centre in Schertalley.[58] Even though, they had to face severe oppositions and persecutions from the Roman Catholics and the Hindus, churches were established in Alleppey by the efforts of the Missionaries, D.S. Chuvala, G. Oberheu, P.M. Kaufeld, G.R. Stelter, K.M. Zorn, and H.E. Heinlein and the active workers like the catechists A. Israel, D. Duthie, W. Alexander and J.C. Gamaliel.[59]

Another important new field was Wynad, which lies nearly 70 miles east of Calicut on the Malabar Coast, North east of Kerala. The Missionary conference in 1945 appointed a committee consisting of two Missionaries and three native

---

[54] Perurkada became the headquarters of Lutheran Church at Kerala.

[55] E.E. Griesse, *Lutheran India Missions*, 1845-1944, 31.

[56] E.E. Griesse, *op.cit.*

[57] F. Kauffeld, *Eazhava report No.2.* Letter to the Honorable Board, St. Louis, 27 June, 1927, an 8 page documents with supporting evidences. See also F.R. Zukker, *Notes on the Eazhava Movement*, 4 page typed document. Concordia Archives.

[58] K.C. Kutten, General Secretary of the North Travancore, *Sahodhara Samajam*, Schertalla, 13/10/1102, and 9/11/1102. Concordia Archives.

[59] W. Alexander, *North Travancore Lutheran Mission and Reformation, Christiani,* 10/12, Dec. 1934, 185-186.

workers to look into the field. They conducted a survey with the help of J C Albert, a superintendent of a Tea estate in Wynad. On the report of the committee, the mission sent M N Paul, to this field in 1946. Wynad is a thickly forested area full of wild animals and a very cold climate. The people were the Kurumas and Paniyars. In May 1946, M. Nallathampy was sent there and in Oct. 1949, Missionary M.J. Lutz settled at Meenngady and established churches. Muslim Missions among the Malayalies were opened in 1950. In Wandoor, 40 miles from Calicut, Henry Otten settled within the community. To contact Muslims he set up reading rooms in adjoining centers and a dispensary in Wandoor.[60] The mission through Harry D Smith opened a new centre in the large sea port town of Ernakulum-Cochin in 1951.[61] Many of the aboriginal hill tribes were meeting civilization for the first time. The Gospel could be a precious gift to them as well. Congregations had grown up among these various groups and new methods of evangelization were being tried to make a great impact on them.

The above are the summary of the work before the formation of the Trivandrum District Synod. The expansions of the mission through the Organization of local churches in the Missionary era are described below.

3.5. Expansion through Church Planting

The Missionaries' stations were the centre of their mission. Luthergiri, Trivandrum South, Trivandrum North, Balaramapuram, Nilamel, Alleppey were the main stations of MELIM. In these places Missionaries brought huge mission compounds and built Missionary bungalows and controlled their work from there. The Missionary records reported the name of the church, starting year and caste identification. The caste identification does not mean that in a particular church there were only the noted people as the members. It shows the majority of the people which may belong on those days in a particular congregation. After 1956, this identification seems to have changed because of the mixed community membership in various churches.[62]

---

[60] H M Zorn, *Much Cause for Joy*, 46.

[61] The first service was conducted in the Smith's bungalow near Ernakulum Thevara road on 11 Feb. 1951. Nearly 15 members were present at this service.

[62] The growth of church planting can be reported in the following stations. The station's status is reported in the subsequent order; First name of the church; year of starting and then the major people group. Luthergiri Station: Chullimannoor (1911- Paraiahs), Kuttichal (1911 - Paraiahs), Chalikonam (1912 - Paraiahs), Ariyanad (1912, Nadars and Ezhavas), Kattaikal (1914 - Paraiahs), Konni (1914 - Pulayas), Luthergiri (1914) is a mixed congregation with four caste people mostly from Paraiah caste. Kurungalloor (1914 - Paraiahs), Parantodu (1914 Pulayas and Paraiahs). Mylakkara (1918 - Nadars and Sambavars), Madathikomnam (1918 Sambavars and Nadars), Tholoor (1923 - Sambavars), Chettachal (1924 - Nadars, Pulayas and Vedars), Mannoorkonam (1925 Mixed community), Kannankonam (1929 - Vedars), Thachancode (1931 - Nadars), Karuvallam near Nedumangadu was started in 1931. Poovachal (1940 - Pulayas). Vallimangalam (1940 - Cheramars), Parantode (1946- Pulayas), Mandikalam (1946 - Pulayas), Churamkuzhi

The above list gives a gist of information regarding the planting of churches by MELIM Missionaries with the help of the native workers. In the late twenties, Malayalam-speaking Missionaries had established two outposts among the people who were principally non-Christians. First one among the animistic hill tribes was at Nilamel area, 30 miles North of Trivandrum.[63] Another one was on the

---

(1948 - Nadars), Devancode (1949 - Nadars and Cheramars), Kottoor (29 April 1951 - Pulayas), Pannikonam (1951 - Pulayas), Mayam (6 July 1952 - Sambavars, Cheramars and Nadars). K.M. Zorn, *Congregation Report* 1953; Concordia Archives*; Sathya Satchi*, 1932, 179-180. Trivandrum Station:Thumarichal (1914 - Paraiahs), Karode (1916 - Paraiahs and Nadars), Vattitoorkavu (1918 - Pulayas, Paraiahs and Nadars), Anthiyoorkonam (1913 - Paraiahs), Kalathukal (1921 - Paraiahs and Pulayas), Panayamcode, (1939 - Nadars), Varthoorkonam (1939 - Nadars), Trivandrum Town chapel (1947 with complexity of mixed caste people, govt. servants, printers, merchants, clerk, etc.) Trivandrum city, in between statue Junction and Post office and opposite to Puthen Kachery in 1950, in a house hall with different caste people Martin L. Wynekan, *Congregation Repots of Trivandrum Station*, 1951; *Sathya Satchi,* 1932, 179-180.; *Christiany*, 25/June 1950, 116. North Trivandrum Station: Chenamcode (1925 - Pulayas, Paraiahas and Vedars), Kusavarkal (1929 - Pulayas), Mannanthala (1929 - Nadars), Kodappanakunnu or Concordia (1931 - mixed caste but predominantly Nadars and Ezhavas), Karakulam (1931-Nadars), Kazhakuttom (1932 - Nadars), Kavadithalakkal (1932 - Nadars), Chenkottukonam (1933 - Nadars), Sreekariyam (1948 - Nadars), Puliyamcode (1945 - Nadars). D.S. Chuvala, Congregation Report of North Trivandrum station. Concordia Archives. *Sathya Satchi* 1932, 179-180. Ponvila Station: Kaliyakkavila (1921 - Nadar), Ponvila (1923, Nadar), Chenkavila (1927- Iravas),. Vanniyoor (1928, Nadar), Marayamuttom (1929, Nadar), Kolla, now known as Dhanuvachapuram (1929 - Paraya), Kalparapotta (1930, Nadar), Malakulangara (1933, Nadar Barber), Ambilikonam (Nov. 6, 1934, Nadar) by N. Samuel catechist and missionary Beenar with more than 200 peoples. Karimaram (1937, Iravan), Karakkonam (1938 - Iravan), Pacode (1939 Nadar), Melpuram (1946, Nadar) Thittakudy (1947, Nadar), Pranivila (1947, Nadar), Karumannoor (1948 - Nadar), Karavakuzhi (1948, Nadar), Mattamcode (1948), Perumpahuthoor (1951), Parassala (1951 - Nadar), Kanyapuram (1951, Nadar), Kuzhevila (1952), Moododu (1953), Panachamoodu (1954), Devicode (1955 - Nadar). R.T. Koepke, *Congregation Reports of Ponvila Station*, B P, Hahn, *Parassala District report*, 12 Sep. 1943, *Sathya Satchi*, 1932, 179- 180; *Souvenir,* Ponvila Circle, IELC Centenary Celebrations 1895-1995; *59th TDCM*, Sep. 5-9, 1932, 27, 60th *TDCM,* Jan. 2-7,1933, 8.; *Christiani* 10/Nov. 1934, 180. *Ponvila circle souvenir, op.cit.* Balaramapuram Station: Puliyoorkonam (1911 - Paraya), Kanakode (1911 - Paraya), Anthiyoor (1922, Paraya), Thumbodukonam (1922 - Paraya & Pulaya), Muzhakolkunnu (1926 - Nadar), Valiyavila (1926 - Veder), Venganoor (1928 - Pulaya & Paraya), Kaivankala (1928 - Paraya). Kottukal (1929 - Paraiah), Perumana (1928 - Pulaya & Paraya), Ponnumangalam (1928 - Pulaya & Paraya), Mulloor (1929 - Pulaya), Kaynikkara (1933 - Paraya), Venpakal (1933 - Paraya), Kuttara (1939 - Paraya), Kidarakui (1941 - Pulaya), Parachel (1947 - Nadar), Idagramam (1947 - Pulaya), Karumam (1951 - Pulaya). H.M. Zorn, *Congregation Report of Balaramapuram station; Sathya Satchi*, 1932, 179-180. A.C. Fritze, *Congregation report of Nilamel Station*; *Sathya Satchi*, 1932, 179-180. H.E. Heinlein, *Congregation report of Alleppey- Schertalay Station; Sathya Satchi*, 1932, 179-180.

[63] Nilamel Station:Arivarikuzhi (1923 - Veder), Venkattakuzhi (1924 - Veder), Melporinthamon (1924 - Veder), Idathara (1924 - Veder and Kuravar), Karaykadu (1925 - Pulayas), Kurumbayam (1925 - Veder), Nilamel (1926 - Kuravas and Sambavas), Meenkulam (1926 - Kuravas), Kulathupuzha (1926 - Vedars and Cheramas), Modayil (1926 - Sambavars), Anapara (1928 - Veder and Kurava), Kanoor (1929 - Kuravas), Karyam (1930 - Ezhavas), Vayanam (1941 - Pulayas), Madathara (1950 - Veder and Kurava), Chipponchira (1951 - Paraya), Vazhode (1952 - Veder),

sea coast of Alleppey.[64] The people in this area were the *Ezhavas* and there the Missionaries expected a great mass movement. But the work in both the places was discouraging. The list in *Christiani*[65] shows that 78 active churches celebrated harvest festival in 1943. In 1937 it was 61.[66] In 1949 there were 76 churches in the list.[67] This list clearly shows that Lutheran Missionaries expanded their work among various people groups of Kerala who were most backward in those days. The churches, Catechists, teachers and seminary students were identified by their caste.[68] This is not to show the caste distinction but to reveal that they were aware of the evils of caste and they did not restrict their work with one particular caste only. In a caste-ridden society, they challenged the various subaltern groups to stay, worship, and study and grow together as one community, as the children of the living God.

3.6. Statistics

Statistics show us that in 1922 MELIM had only 14 catechists in all Malayalam field. In 1927, there were only 66 Catechists, and as late as 1932 only 53. The statistics shows the rate of growth of MELIM over the years.[69]

Venjaramoodu and Chathannoor work was begun in July 1954. Varkala reading room among the Ezhavas was opened in Feb. 1955. A C Fritze, *Congregation Report of Nilamel Station*; *Sathya Satchi*, 1932, 179-180.

[64] Alleppey-Shertalay Station: Aattinpuram (1925 - Ezhavas). Sreekandamangalam (1926 - Velan) Thykal (1926- Ezhavas and Velan), Shertaly (1928 - Ezhavas), Thiruvampady (1928 - Cheramar), South Ayrad (1928 - Ezhavas), Padayakulam (1929-Ezhavas), Kalavangodam & Kunninpuram (1930 - Iravas), Muhamma (1931 - Ezhava), Puthanangady (1932 - Velan), Chettigad (1933 - Ezhavas and Thiyas). The successful ministry report at Shertallai, Alleppey, Sreekandamangalam, Puthanangadi and Vadakkal was reported in Christiani 1934. Aaryadu church at Alleppey was of mixed community with Cheramas and Ezhavas. Charamangalam (1940 - Ezhavas), Tottapally (1950 - Syrian and Pulaya). Rev Harry D. Smith who arrived at Trivandrum in 1950 started two works in Ernakulam - Cochin on Jan. 1951 and Feb 1951. H E Heinlein, *Congregation report of Alleppy- Schertalay Station; Sathya Satchi*, 1932, 179-180. *Christiani*, 1/ Sep. 1925, 159. *Christiani*, 10/ 6,1934, 84; *Christiani* , 10/11, 1934, 180.

[65] *Christiani*, 19/7, 1943, 282.

[66] *Christiani*, 13/2, 1937, 32.

[67] *Christiani*, 24/1, 1949, 12-14.

[68] For details see the Report on the District tours, Aug.16, 1929; The list of religious workers in TDC, Feb.1945; Assignment of Catechists and Teachers in 67th TDC Minutes, 10-11.

[69] Growth of IELC, LCMS-BFMS Statistical file, Concordia Archives.

	1913	1916	1919	1930	1940	1948
Missionaries	15	9	5	42	41	34
Indian Pastors	--	--	--	3	9	35
Evangelists	--	--	2	4	15	12
Catechists	--	--	32	31	165	141
Baptized Members	675	1378	1681	7170	14330	18351

The statistical data and related files show MELIM Missionaries were very systematic in their work. They analyzed the progress of work from time to time by the authentic survey records. They were particular to inform the survey result to their members through their publications almost every year.

Communicant Members	162	230	318	1692	4477	6786
Average Attendance	--	--	--	--	10477	11518
Contributions	698	--	4150	3832	6720	28667
Schools	--	--	68	112	136	99
Teachers	58	81	127	171	195	242
Other Christians	--	--	--	35	30	28
Other Faiths	38	47	52	37	12	13
Students	1717	2315	2657	5435	9208	9596
Baptized School Children	193	429	310	--	--	--

Following is a comparison of statistics for the years of 1932, 1933 and 1934 of Trivandrum Field.

(*Christiani,* 10/5, 1934, 69; 11/2, 1935, 32. Record says in 1934 baptized members from the Hindus were 648, confirmed 648 and the average worship attendance were 9980. In 1935, it became 478, 291, 8985 respectively. The statistical records of 1944 and 1945; *Christiani*, 12/3, 1936, 4).

The statistical records of	1944	1945
Churches	81	80
Missionaries	12	11
Pastors	5	7
Evangelists	10	7
Catechists	82	81
Lutheran Teachers	51	49
Souls	9636	4089
Communicants	2167	2326
Baptized Members	7328	7433
Baptized in 1944	384	484
Confirmed in 1944	91	128
Marriages	121	118
Burials	133	201
Average Attendance	4742	4527
Offerings	3000	3446

(Christiani, 22/4, 1946, 50.)

3.7. The Early Strategy of Missions

After establishing Missionary centres in various places in Kerala, the Missionaries planned to advance various strategies or instruments to persuade the Hindus as well as the Muslims into their fold. Starting a vernacular school along with all centres need to be noticed. The method of preaching to water-bearers, peasants at tea shops, courts and other public places did not bring the desired result. Hence, they contemplated upon various new methods to attract the people. They adopted new methods like distribution of tracts and books, visiting the sick, helping the needy, and so on. Missionaries spent most of their time on purely evangelistic work, unhampered by institutional and administrative duties. The Missionaries liked to go out in pairs, on bike, stopping overnight on longer trips at traveller's bungalow, or at any available shelter. They were always assisted by an Indian helper. They used to carry with them a violin and a collection of lyrics.[70] They adopted various methods such as personal discussions, teachings, slide shows and literatures as means for propagation of the Gospel. The Missionary methods can be described under the following heads.

3.7.1. Educational Service

Statistics shows how poor was the literacy rate of the backward class people in the early days.[71] The Lutheran Missionaries felt that the Education Mission as one of the effective means of attracting people to Christianity. To their disappointment, they found that the children of the low caste people from the remote village had no established schools. So, the Lutherans thought that without mission schools nothing was possible.[72] Hence they planned to open schools attached to all their mission stations. Travancore was one of the important centers of education. Without affecting or delinking the educational system that was in existence in Travancore, they introduced Western education. Before the Lutheran workers began the educational endeavors, the LMS and CMS had already started their educational work. While opening schools, the Missionaries adopted policies such as giving permanent literacy, minimum preparation for citizenship and discovering their aptitudes as the basis. The poor and illiterate people of the depressed classes also believed that education would be the most effective way of raising them up to a higher standard of life. But the Missionaries had maintained the principle that any proposed venture in education would be distinctly Christian, Christian in both motive and method. This principle was not popular among the parents who wanted the Mission to aid their children to obtain a good job, or to make a better

---

[70] Swavely, *op.cit*, 192.

[71] Literacy rate of men in % - Vedan, 0.1, Kuravan, 1.5, Pallan 2.4, Pulayan 4.1, Parayan 4.9, Maravan 8.8, Nadan 10.5, Thandan 10.1. Literacy rate of woman in % -Vaniyan 6.9, Paravan 4.6, Thandan 2,8, Nadan 2.7, Kudumy 1.5, Marakkan 1.3, Pulayan 1.3, Maravan 0.9, Parayan 0.8, Kuravan 0.5, Vedan 0.3, Pallan 0.1 %. *Christiani,* 11/8, 1935, 129.

[72] Herbert M Zorn, *Much Cause for Joy*, *op. cit.*, 19.

marriage. MELIM was involved in various types of educational work not merely for the sake of education, but in support of its one aim, namely, proclamation of the Gospel. With this end the Lutheran Missionaries opened schools wherever possible.[73] In 1916, it was possible to open up a vernacular school at Peroorkada Vattiyoorkavu compound with three classes, mainly to provide opportunities for the village children to continue their studies beyond the second class.[74] Most of the students were the inmates of boarding schools.

The Government was pressured by the Caste Hindus to add a "conscience clause"[75] which would exempt children, attending private schools from taking otherwise compulsory religious education. The VIII Annual General Conference of MELIM in 1917 debated the matter and the general feeling was reported as follows:

"*If, however, the number of the applicants for exemption increases, and the school is in danger of losing its character of Christian Mission School, then the pupils who refuse to take part in the religious instructions must be told that they cannot continue as pupils of the Mission school. If there is no other school in the neighborhood, the agitators should be told to agitate for another school, even if; the building of another school entailed the loss of the Government grant and recognition to the Mission school.*"[76] The conference debated the issue: *The Conscience clause or our aim in secular instruction*: "*whereas very many children in our village schools do not attend religious instruction, and we are in conscious and in duty bound to conserve the Christian character in our schools, even though the attendance may suffer, and possibly the government grant withdrawn, be it resolved, that affirm our conviction, that we are not in India to impart mere secular instruction to anybody, and that are there children who attended secular, but will not attend religious instructions, we make every reasonable effort, to induce them to do so, but if they persist for some months, they be tripped from the register.*"[77] This matter also became a more serious problem in the later years.[78] Therefore, MELIM ceased to accept Government grant in 1924.[79]

[73] A.C. Fritz, *Statement on non- Lutheran Teachers in Lutheran Schools* (n.d.)(4page report) Concordia Archives.

[74] At the beginning there were only 23 students in the entire school. The number increased within six months to 65. In the following year the fourth class was added, thus making a complete vernacular middle school. The fifth and sixth classes were added in the successive years 1918-1919. The seventh class was added only in 1921.

[75] See more detail in *TDCM* 1949, 32.

[76] O.A. Ehlers, "VIII Annual General Conference of MELIM", *The Lutheran Witness* (11/6, 1918), 183.

[77] *Minuts of the XI General Conference of MELIM*, Nagercoil, 1-9/Feb. 1922.

[78] O.A. Ealers, *The Lutheran Witness*, 11/6, 1918, 183.

[79] R.P. Sieving, "Secretary O.H. Schmidit Attends India General Conference", The Lutheran Witness, *67/12 (September, 1994). E H meinzen Secretary MELIM to The Public instruction Director, Trivandrum, 15/12, 1924, stating the withdrawal of government grant in order to continue the religious instructions in MELIM schools.*

Letter from E.H. Meinzen, MELIM Secretary wrote to the Director of Public Instruction, Trivandrum regarding the relinquishment of Government grant in aid to the MELIM schools in order to continue the religious instruction.[80] The schools had operated without Government grant for a period. Only after the formation of the IELC in 1958 this practice was resumed.[81]

Regarding the secondary schools in Trivandrum we read as follows in the Travancore Conference Minutes: "*The Salvation Army started a lower Secondary School and is planning to shift in the very neighboring area of our compound. The Director of Public Instruction, who already knows long hand our plans, says that the Education Department will not give permission for 2 schools of this kind, but promised to keep an opportunity open for us, if we open a Lower Secondary School with the beginning of the next academic year (May 1918).*" According to the urgency given by the DPI the Travancore Conference discussed at length and resolved to go ahead with this plan.[82] By the end of 1919, fifty percent of the pupils of MELIM schools were baptized members of the congregations. These schools were under the control of MELIM, with financial aid from Government.[83]

Travancore district special school conference on 8th & 9th December, 1924 met and discussed at length about the mission schools.[84] There was a feeling among the field workers that due to want of enlightenment, the people were carried away by superstitions. They were suffering from bad sanitary conditions. The missionaries firmly believed that education was a powerful instrument to win more people to the religion.[85]

The LCMS-BFMS Secretary Frederick Brand wrote to MELIM on 4 Jan. 1926 "*Hindu caste marks in school. The board is of the opinion that it would not be right to make the removal of caste marks a condition of admission to the schools, as that would be asking "the heathen"*[86]*children to do something against their convictions.*

---

80 E.H. Meinnzen, Secretary, MELIM Letter to The Director of Public Instruction, Trivandrum 15/12, 1924,

81 *Minutes of the Board of Education*, 1958, 12.

82 Minutes of the XXXVIII Travancore Conferance 18-20, Sept. 1917, 2.

83 Missouri Synod, *Proceedings*, 1920, 143-144. In 1919, the amount was Rs. 5,733.

84 E.H. Meinzen *and* B Strasen, Report on Schools, 1924, 8. Cocordia Archives.

85 They adopted the following principles while using education as an instrument. 1) Education must meet the needs of the people, but must not be a part of evangelism. 2) Strive to root Christian teachings in the total life of the community. 3) Strive to create enlightened persons who would be Christian salts who in turn would preach the gospel and the love of God to the community to which they belonged. 4) To strive to produce materials for the students who have returned from the Seminary so that they could come back home with a spirit to evangelize. 5) To inculcate and infuse in their minds the need for welfare measures, social service and agricultural training that were lacking in them. To strive hard to ward off their superstitious faith regarding contagious diseases and to teach them that these afflictions were due to want of cleanliness. Robert Day, *op.cit.*, 117.

86 This term is frequently seen in Indian History books written by foreigners. They mean it as "a person who does not belong to a widely held religion as seen by those who do". (Catherine Soanes,

However, after the children in our schools have been sufficiently instructed in the Word of God were asked to remove their caste marks under pain of being excluded from the schools that would seem to work against the very character of our mission in India, in other words it would preclude real mission work on them."[87]

The Lutheran system of school education was from Nursery to High School. The nursery schools that they started served as a base to reach the Muslim and Hindu houses. The primary schools were started with the permission of the government. In the early days, the result of the school leaving examination of the students of Lutheran vernacular schools in Travancore was very commendable.[88] Fritzy was a bold man with courageous vision. Without much support of the other missionaries he started Concordia English medium High school. He was the founder of CLHS, Trivandrum. Fritzy was very particular against appointing Hindu teachers in MELIM school.[89] In 1930 they started South Aryad School.[90] Concordia Lutheran High School Peroorkada was founded in 1931.[91]

Between 1928 and 1930, the number of children attending classes decreased considerably due to the World War. The attendance in schools dropped for want of food.[92] Missionaries with available funds made arrangements to provide at least one meal those children who attended schools. During the war period Maharani Sethu Lakshmi Bai was the Regent of Travancore. Maharani out of sympathy and upon the request of Lutheran Missionaries provided a grant to help the poor children in the school. This helped the Missionaries to provide one time meal to school children and thus attracted more students and the number of pupils in attendance got increased.[93] Most of the schools were in thatched sheds (*ola panthal*). The government did not give any grant to run the schools. Even land was not provided by the government to run the schools. So, the Missionaries collected funds from local churches. In order to reduce the expenses, the catechists

---

Compact Oxford Dictionary, (Oxford: OUP, 2004 (2001), 415. But now this term is legitimizing and brings negative impacts among the Indian society. In this research, when unavoidable, the present researcher would give the word within quotation marks.

87 Frederick Brand, *Letter to GC of MELIM*, 4 Jan 1926; *Minutes of MELIM 14th GC*, 1926, 3.

88 *Christiani*, 4/7, 1928, 198. see also, *Christiani* 25/6, 1950, 115.

89 A.C. Fritz, *Statement on Non Lutheran teachers in Lutheran Schools*, 1924, three page typed document; *TDCM*, 1924, 2-4.

90 *Christiani Special* 52/11, 1976, 11. The number of students who attended school increased to eight hundred to twenty eight hundred in 1931-1932. *Primary School Report*, 1937-38, 3. MELIM school at South Aryad dedicated its new building on June 22 1930 By K. M. Zorn. *Christiani, 6/7*, 1930, 164.

91 In 1953, there were 8 teachers one non Lutheran and only one female. Aruma Nayagom was the then Head Master. In 1953, there were 8 teachers one non Lutheran and only one female. Arumanayagom was the then Head Master

92 *Primary School Report*, 1930-1932, 1-4. Concordia seminary Archives.

93 C.H. Swavely, *The Lutheran Enterprises in India*, 185; *Primary School Report*, 1930-1932, 1-4. Concordia seminary Archives.

were appointed as teachers in these schools.[94] To provide more teachers, a Teacher Training School was started at Concordia Theological Seminary. The mission paid salaries to the teachers, fees, medical aids, equipments and teaching aids.[95] In conformity with the government policy, the Lutherans also opened fifth standard in all the schools.[96] This was for students from all castes.[97] For the purpose of higher education to the village students they started 3 boys boarding homes and 2 girls boarding homes.[98]

1935 was a notable year for the school development. Alleppey (South Aryad), Nilamel schools were upgraded with 5th Standard, IV Form in Concordia English medium school, Vattiyoorkavu Vernacular Medium School and teachers training school were also started on 1935.[99] This year MELIM Started 7 new schools in Kerala with the increase of 390 students.[100] There were a lot of discussions to start a joint teachers training institute at Nagercoil for both Nagercoil and Travancore people.[101] But it could not materialize. The curriculum in the school consisted of Malayalam or Tamil as first language based on the mother-tongue, and the crafts like handloom weaving, wood work, gardening and agriculture for boys. The girls were taught home crafts, simple Mathematics, Social Studies and Ethics.[102] Night literacy schools were opened that taught Bible lessons along with secular subjects. Bible lessons formed the major portion in the MELIM schools, and the persons who were capable of handling it alone were appointed as teachers in these schools. They were given Diploma and In-service Training to teach the children better. These facts show that the school education of the Lutheran Mission was well planned and that it was beneficial to the needy children.

In the high schools vocational courses were started in conformity with the policy of the Government. Along with regular subjects like the mother-tongue, English, Hindi, craft, citizenship training were included. Teaching was well focused to develop their personality and character.[103] The Education Committee in its meeting held in 1946, decided to start electrical engineering for the boys and sewing for the girls. Along with handloom weaving, drawing was also introduced.

---

[94] Report of Education Reforms Committee of MELIM, Trivandrum, 1933, 59. Concordia Archives.

[95] *Primary School Report*, 1930-32, 2.Concordia Archives.

[96] *Nagercoil District Conference Minutes*,1932, 14. (Hereafter only as NDC)

[97] In 1933, Lutheran mission had 2 V M schools 1 English medium school, 42 primary schools. There were in total 2391 students.

[98] Lutheran mission Schools, *Christiani* 10/5, 1934, 71-72.

[99] *Christiani*, 11/2, 1935, 18.

[100] Ibid., 32.

[101] The Travancore Joint Secondary Training School, Committee meeting 12/8, 1942, Nagercoil report, 1-5.

[102] *Education Committee Report*, 1953, 1-5. Concordia Archives.

[103] *Educational Committee Report*, 1945, 14. Concordia Archives.

To conduct the courses successfully trained persons were approached and their permission was obtained.[104]

Soon after completing the primary school education, the students who desired to study further could go to middle school which was generally attached to the high schools.[105] During those days middle schools had classes up to Six to Eight standards or Form I to III. The high schools had Form 1V to V1 or classes nine to eleven. Hostel and boarding homes for boys and girls were attached to these schools to accommodate students who came from distant places.[106] The Missionaries also started High Schools.[107] They discussed even to give free education to Lutheran children.[108]

The Travancore Government, a predominantly Hindu body, had passed laws directly affecting Lutheran schools. In order to have the desirable government recognition, a school was required to have a certain number of students and at least one teacher per class. It should not be organized within a certain distance from another school. The wall should be of a certain thickness. Classes should not be conducted in buildings used for congregational worship. Yearly inspections from government would be held to enforce the laws affecting the schools. At that time a number of schools were conducted in the buildings used for worship. The school was open for all caste and religion. A sixty minutes devotion and Bible class under the direction of a Seminary trained teacher started every working day in all mission schools.[109] As schools were attached to the local churches, the management of the schools was with the local churches. But later on the management of the schools was shifted to the hands of the Missionaries.[110] In 1952,[111] the management of the school was shifted to the local pastor. After 1953, the managements of schools came under the supervision of the executive board,

---

[104] *Report of the Educational Council,* 1946, 6. Concordia Archives.

[105] Possibility of starting 3rd class at Kalparapotta the requirements of 2nd class at Chegavila, and the completion of Nilamel High school were discussed at the 111th Trivandrum District conference in 1949. *TDCM,* 1949, 6-7.

[106] *Educational Work of the LCMS in South India* (nd) 2-5. Concordia Archives.

[107] The objectives of HS are: Cultivation of habits of effective communications in the Word; Development of intellectual curiosity, competence and maturity; Formation of a code of ethics and a philosophy for the regulation of individual life and achievement of the highest spiritual values; Acquisition of knowledge and habits necessary for maintaining sound physical and mental health; Intelligent and cooperative entrance into the responsibilities of family life. *(Current Problems in Higher Education,* 1947, 177. Concordia Archives).

[108] *Free education for Lutheran children,* committee report. TDCM, 1949, 64.

[109] H. Wenger, South India missions, *Lutheran Witness* 65/5, 1946, 161.

[110] *A General Report of the Lutheran Primary School,* 1937-1938, 2. Concordia Archives.

[111] In 1952, MELIM had 99 schools with 273 Indian teachers. Most of the 141 Catechists were also teaching in the schools.

and separate officials were appointed to supervise, and manage the affairs of the Lutheran schools.[112]

W.C. Duke Wits proposed a plan for a private college in South India to train Indian Lutherans for both teacher training and theological training. A joint meeting of General Conference, Educational Committee and Seminary Board discussed the matter in the presence of Duke Wits.[113] TDC urged the GC to establish at least a second grade college inside the Malayalam speaking area for Lutheran students. The proposal was for an "open" college staffed by Lutheran instructors and managed by the Lutheran Mission.[114] The matter of a Lutheran college in Trivandrum was discussed in MELIM General Conference at Ambur on 1950 January, 5.[115] In 1956 TDS had 2 High Schools, 4 Upper Primary Schools and 25 Lower Primary schools.

An evaluation of the educational ministry of MELIM[116] will helped to move further. Missionaries found that illiteracy was the major cause for blind beliefs and inhuman customs. So they felt the need of education for effective communication of the Gospel. Thus they started elementary schools in almost all the evangelistic centres.[117] In some places they established schools first and then started evangelistic work.[118] In early days, schools were conducted in church buildings. In order to keep students in school during the working days, Missionaries introduced noon meal system for them. The State Government put this system in practice only in the later years. A Report of the Malayalam schools dated 8th September 1943 reads as follows:

"The great majority of our congregation members are day labourers belonging to the so-called "depressed" class. When the parents go out to work in the field, they wanted the grown up children to look after the younger ones. In some cases, the children accompanied their parents to the farms to share in the meals given to their parents by employers. In this connection it is worthy of special mention that our Missionaries of Alleppey and Shertallai give noon meal to the unhappy children of those poverty-stricken areas ...."[119]

[112] *A General Report of the Lutheran Primary School*, 1957-1958, 2. Concordia Archives.

[113] For the proposal and detail of discussion see Joint meeting of GC, Educ. Com. and Seminary Board, Nov. 28-29, 1949 at Zorn's Bungalow, Nagercoil.

[114] 131st TDCM, June, 1954, 43.

[115] *Christiani,* 25/1, 1950, 19.

[116] For an analysis and evaluation of MELIMS educational ministry in Kerala see D. Christudas, *Azhangalile Anugrahathinte Uraval* (Malayalam) (the source of Blessings from the Depths) (Thiruvalla: CSS, 2007), 93-98.

[117] *See Primary School Report* (1930-1932): 104 to find the objectives of Educational Mission of MELIM. See *Education Committee Reports* (1953): 1-5. Concordia Archives.

[118] *EHELM, op.cit.* 25.

[119] *Report of the Lutheran Malayalam Schools* (8 September 1943). Concordia Archives.

The MELIM Missionaries used to hire efficient teachers with better salaries.[120] The Catechists served as teachers also. Needs of the day forced the Missionaries to start Nursery schools, Middle schools, High schools, English education, separate boarding schools both for boys and girls, teacher training schools, seminary for theological education. Students enjoyed free boarding and lodging, dress, study materials and all other educational helps.[121] With the help of systematic education, a lot of native Lutheran leaders emerged in due course.

Besides, a good number of educated men and women became teachers, pastors, evangelists and Cctechists. Some of them joined the Government services. Some of them got employment in railways, police, armed forces, mills and factories. Several illiterate converts entered into the domestic service of Europeans as attendants, butlers, cooks, gardeners and horse-keepers. Later on, the educated and employed Lutherans saved money and they cleared their debts, purchased land and built houses or invested in the education of their children. They began to realize that self-help was the basis of freedom and they slowly learned this lesson. It seems that P.D. Martin's words of gratitude are a good conclusion for the above said facts:

"From Second Form to Sixth Form (SSLC) I had the opportunity to be a boarding student in Concordia High School from where I had continued my graduate course till 1950 and passed B.A. with gold medal for Economics from the University College. It is worth mentioning that I was the first graduate from Sambava community as a result of the work of MELIM . . . I cannot but remember MELIM with gratitude for the educational facilities made available to the children of the poor community."[122] The educational services of Lutheran mission in the remote villages among the most backward people would be remembered forever. Along with other Protestant denominations, their educational service paved the way for social renaissance in Kerala.

3.7.2. Literary Service

Literature was a great need for the meaningful propagation of the Gospel in those days. From its very beginning in 1895, MELIM Missionaries prepared tracts and printed them for wide distribution in connection with evangelistic work. In 1914 and 1925 two sermon books, written by F. Mohn and N. Samuel, were published. A long list of MELIM published literature shows their concern in this regard. Besides, Luther's Small Catechism and one hundred Bible lessons were published

---

[120] *Primary School Report* (1937-38): 2. Concordia Archives.

[121] The purpose of upgrading schools and need for adding more vocational course was clearly stated in Current Problem in Higher Education (1947): 77 and Educational Work of the MELIM in South India, 25.

[122] P.D. Martin after graduation he entered into the teaching ministry of MELIM and retired as the Headmaster of Higher Secondary School. He lives at Peroorkada, Trivandrum. P.D. Martin letter to the researcher, 12 January, 2000.

in 1917.[123] In October 1921, a Tamil monthly *Sathia Satchi* (True Witness) was started. In the meeting of the TDC Delegates, held on 21 Aug. 1924, the question of a church magazine was first discussed and it was there they decided about the efforts to be made towards this end. The publication of the Malayalam monthly *Christiani* was started in March 1925.[124] This monthly was well received by the Malayalies of different people group and continued its publications till March, 1982.[125]

In 1929 a printing press was purchased and installed in Vaniyambadi. Since that time Concordia press had rendered an important service to the evangelistic outreach mission, as well as helping to further the knowledge and understanding of Indian Christians.[126] Separate order of worships and questions and answers for the celebrations like, Christmas and Reformations were widely used.[127] A long term plan with a bold vision was prepared by the Inter-conference publication committee.[128] The literature program was severely hit during the War period. Shortage of time was compounded by shortage of paper. After the War, new types of literature came through the publication committee of MELIM. The liturgical and catechetical books were revised and reprinted. Tracts and other evangelistic materials were produced. Manuscripts were submitted to larger publishers for wider distribution.[129] Another notable publication in Malayalam was the *Christava Siddhantha Deepika* (The Light of Christian Thought), a theological quarterly, published by the Concordia Seminary Faculty from 1948 onwards.[130]

---

[123] *History of ELIM Publications* (nd) 3 pages of typed document. Concordia Archives.

[124] *The Lutheran Witness*, 63/9, 1944, 303. The name Christiani was suggested by Goda Rama varman Unyathiri, a baptized Christian who worked in MELIM School at Kattaikal as a teacher and a man with some experience in news paper work. *The Lutheran Witness*, 63/9, 1944, 303. The first issue was printed at the Kamalalaya Press, Fort Trivandrum with 16 small pages. Zukker became the first editor of the Paper.

[125] More details about the history of Christiani see, D. Christudas, *Akshara sushrushyil Kerala Christhavarude Sambhavanakal* (*The contributions of Kerala Christians in the literature ministry*), Seminar Paper, 5-6.

[126] *Kastanubhava Charithram* (*Passion History*-1921), Agenda (Order of service-1924), *Sara Sangraham* (*The Essence of the Content*-1925), An order of service and Hymnal (1927, 1930, and 1931), Small Agenda (1930), Hymnal, Catechism (1931), *Veda Charithram* (Bible History -1932), Augsburg Confession, Matthew Commentary, Bible stories, were the oldest Malayalam publications Swavely, *op.cit.*, 200-201.

[127] "A Hymn book cost of 2 Anas is fully out of stock. A singing church cannot wait for its reprinting. Therefore, resolved to reprint 2,500 copies from the running expense." TDCM, 2/6) January 1933): 11.

[128] For more detail on the project of MELIM for vernacular literature see the minutes of Inter conference publication committee 2/ Dec. 1937. and 31/ Jan. 1938.

[129] H.M. Zorn, *Much Cause for Joy*, 50.

[130] *27th GCM*, 15; *TDCM*, 1950, 24.

From 1951 January onwards it was published in Malayalam.[131] Simple sermon helps accompanied with articles on theological subjects, quotation from Church fathers, excerpts from Luther's writings, and other leaders of the Church, doctrinal and practical articles, and religious news from the world brought their thoughts into vernacular for pastors and interested church people.[132] MELIM appointed full-time literature secretaries in each district to coordinate and supervise the work and the production and promotion of Literature ministry.[133]

Since India Government Press sought for more literacy classes for adults MELIM Missionaries were active in this program. Separate book depots were also opened in each district to distribute these publications. Decision was made for the production of original Malayalam literature than translations.[134] Instructional materials available from government for adult literacy program were distributed widely among the educationally and economically backward Lutherans at free of cost.[135] Ferdinand was authorized to translate a Tamil novel into Malayalam for publication.[136] Production of worthwhile Christian literature was one of the most and durable means for the propagation of Christian Gospel.[137] The contribution of Lutherans in the literature ministry was very high compared to other Christian Churches in Kerala.[138]

3.7.3. Boarding Homes

From a survey of the Trivandrum Boarding School history, it is evident that it was the purpose of the first Missionaries in Trivandrum to train Lutheran boys as teachers and catechists. The history of Lutheran boarding home in Trivandrum begins a year before the history of the work in Trivandrum district and four year before the opening of the boarding school in Trivandrum itself. As we had seen earlier, in May 1910 itself MELIM Missionaries gave admission to 16 youths from Trivandrum area at the Nagercoil boarding school.[139] The compound comprising 16 acres at Perurkada was purchased in the early part of 1912 at a cost of roughly Rs. 1000 per acre. Since no building was available in this compound for a boarding school, a house was rented in which M. Paulose and family lived with the school children until May 1916. Only 12 boys attended at the first time. At that time the day school had not yet begun and so no regular school was conducted. The

---

[131] *Christiani,* 27/Feb. 1951, 44.

[132] *Their Blessings, op.cit,* 33.

[133] *134 TDCM,* 1955, 38.

[134] *TDCM,* Aug, 1950, 54.

[135] *131th TDCM,* June, 1954, 40.

[136] *TDCM, 1950,* 62.

[137] *127th TDCM* Feb. 1953, 22. Literature report, *136 TDCM,* 1956, 17-18.

[138] For the full list of Lutheran publication in Malayalam language see, D. Christudas, *Contributions of Kerala Christians in Literature Ministry, op.cit.,* 8-9.

[139] *Early History of MELIM,* 29.

purpose of dealing with these boys was to train them as workers in the course of years. A Malayalam teacher was appointed to instruct them in their mother tongue, because on those days they spoke a colloquial language with Tamil mixing. Every morning the boys received one hour Bible study from F.R. Zukker and another hour in the evening by Paulose. In 1916, a building for boarding school could be erected. At that time a change of boarding master did also happen. Latter J. David, S. Markose, K. Francis and I. Theophilose were the boarding Masters. Because of a great increase in pupils the old quarters soon became crowded and a new boarding house was erected in 1925 at a cost of Rs.4000. The consecutive Missionary managers of the boarding house were Zukker, Ehlers, Harms, Oberheu and WetzelIn. In 1922, the Girls' Boarding School was started in a building used part time for catechist training. The inmates then were attending day school. Only 8 girls attended the first year. In 1930 some 30 girls were admitted. The special grant through the Missionary's wives enabled a new building with separate kitchen facilities built in 1931. Mrs. Canjenam, Mrs Sarah Joseph, and Achamma were the successive matrons. Nilamel boarding school was of much help for the mission among the hill tribes.[140] But later, the TDC found the main purpose of establishing the boarding home was not being fulfilled through the Nilamel home, as only a very few inmates of the home were coming up as catechists and pastors. Moreover, conducting the home for very young children was against to the policy of MELIM.[141] The later TDC resolved to close Nilamel boarding home from the 1954-55 school year[142] and ultimately closed from 1 April 1954.[143] Most of the boarding inmates later joined in Concordia high school and TTC School for higher studies. A good number among them became teachers, pastors and catechist in Lutheran institutions. Even though this boarding school was a great burden to the mission, as many village boys/girls of that institution offered to serve the Lord, the Missionaries did not count it as a waste.

3.7.4. Theological Educations

The training of Indian pastors and teachers had always taken a large place in the thinking of the Missionaries. The whole educational system had this as one of its objectives. The missionaries very often conducted special courses for the natives in the different districts and utilized them for evangelical work. But they lacked in depth knowledge in Christianity and Lutheran Doctrine. Therefore, to give them a proper education in theology, a Catechist Training School was started at Nagercoil in an old bungalow situated in the old girls boarding school compound.[144] A tentative plan for the establishment of a Seminary was submitted

[140] Trivandrum boarding Home reports, 2 page typed document. Concordia Archives.

[141] *TDCM,* 1953, 67.

[142] 130th *TDCM,* 1954, 15.

[143] 132nd *TDCM,* Nov. 1954, 55.

[144] *Minutes of the Education Committee,* Vol. I, 1943.

to MELIM in 1919.[145] In 1921, Hammann read a paper at G.C. of MELIM about starting a seminary at Nagercoil with the following emphasis: Pastors are to be adequately trained for Christian mission; workers in the church related institutions to be direct witness to the Gospel; laymen and women to be equipped to witness and to give effective leadership in their congregations; and to enable the men and women to be strong witnesses to Christ and the gospel.[146] The 12th conference constituted a committee with Heckel, Harms, Fritz, Noffke and Lutz.[147] The committee realized the immediate need for the training of native pastors after discussions, the committee resolved that

a) Practical pastoral seminary should be started in 1923
b) It should be situated in Nagercoil
c) It should be linked with teacher catechist seminary
d) The syllabus should be drawn by an ad hoc committee
e) It should be a three year course
f) The local conference should nominate the candidates
g) One of the Missionaries should be appointed as the director for the seminary
h) Two more missionaries should be delegated to assist the Director.[148]

The 23rd GC of MELIM resolved to start the first three year course at the seminary in July 1924.[149] The founding of the Seminary had to wait until September 1924. It was opened in Nagercoil to serve all the three districts and it had been in constant operation since then. As proposed in 1922 it started a three year program. Since the MELIM missionaries observed many 'defects' in other Theological Institutions, they insisted to run a theological college of their own with strict Lutheran principles. Theodore Gutnecht was the first Principal. He served up to 1928 when the first set of seven students was graduated.[150] In 1934, the Seminary instruction was divided into two separate units of two-year duration each, called the Catechist's Seminary and the Pastoral Seminary. To the former course were sent workers who already had some catechist training and experience. Upon graduation, there were prepared to do their work more efficiently as "advanced catechists". After several years of experience, some of these were chosen for the second course of two years. Thereafter, the graduates of this Pastors' seminary were declared ready for immediate ordination. Until

[145] Letter by H. Hamman to BFMS-LCMS, on 18th January, 1919.

[146] Brief Historical and statistical Survey of Concordia Seminary up to 1944, 1-2. Concordia Archives.

[147] *Report of the 12th MELIM General Conference*, 1922, 3.

[148] Ibid.

[149] *Minutes of the XIII General Conference of MELIM* 28 Nov. - 8 Dec. 1923, 19.

[150] *Concordia Seminary Nagercoil,* Handbook, 1962, 1.

1938, there were only four ordained Indian pastors in the Mission.[151] In 1959, under the leadership of M.L. Kretzman, Concordia Seminary was affiliated to the Senate of Serampore College. Since then, it has been training pastors for recognized theological degrees. Concordia Theological Seminary, Nagercoil is the only institution that trains pastors, deaconesses, and lay ministers for IELC by employing different languages like, Malayalam, Tamil, Telugu and Kannada in the same class room.

3.7.5. Deaconess Ministry

The Christian home depends largely on mothers who would themselves be well grounded in Bible Knowledge and trained in ways of worship and the relevance of the Christian Gospel in all spaces of life. The external growth of the congregation also depends largely upon the effective presentation of the Gospel to non Christian women. These women are the guardians of Hinduism and it lives largely because they weave it in to the twist and woof of the pattern of the home. This shows the importance of women ministry in the total mission. The Lutheran Church felt that this major part of the ministry was neglected. Seminary board in its 30th session listed as a point for further study and planned the introduction of a department at the seminary for the training of the women workers, and this training to be equivalent to the deaconess training offered in the Church in America.

It was resolved to start a Bible woman school at Trivandrum in 1949 by TDCM and the courses for study also listed. This course was mainly designed for the widows and wives of the workers.[152] "After the completion of her deaconess course of study, if both her class and field work reveal her aptitude for deaconess service, the student is consecrated as a Lutheran deaconess in an inspiring divine service, at that time she receives … her deaconess cross, which symbolizes Christ's love to her and her service to the church."[153] Rose Zimke arrived in 1947 and took over the leadership for the women work.[154] In order to increase and improve the work among the women of the congregations and their non Christian sisters a deaconess school was dedicated at Trivandrum on 18th June 1950 under the direction of Miss Rose M. Ziemke.[155] They selected 7 candidates out of 19 applicants.[156]

---

151 C.H. Swavely, *op.cit*, 199.

152 *TDCM* March, 1949, 22; 114th, *TDCM*, Aug 1949, 52.

153 *TDCM*, 1949, 72.

154 *Christiani Special* 52/11 Nov. 1976, 35.

155 *Some historical notes to the India mission LCMS*, 1950 nd. Three pages typed document, 3. Concordia Seminary Archives, Nagercoil.

156 Anlt (ponvila), Mary (Sreekandamangalam), Elsy (Thiruvampady, C. Chellamma (Kaivankala), Gnanamma (Mulloor), Saudamini (Vattiyoorkavu) and Snehappu (Thumarichal). *Christiani*, 25 May, 1950, 90.

The first woman organization at Balaramapuram, was organized on 5 February 1950, Sunday by Chairman Dorethy Zorn with the aim to help the pastors in their ministry.[157] Vattiyoorkavu Lutheran women's Sangh was started in 1949. Mrs Beener was its President and Ms. Sosamma David was the secretary.[158] TDCM recorded the growth of women's work.[159] For the improved program for women's work, TDC's five year planning committee reported in 1952: "With the increasing emancipation of Indian womanhood in modern times, the problem of a pastor or catechist getting access to the women of the home has practically disappeared. The need now is definitely more for the training of voluntary workers among the women, who will be influential and active in the local sphere of home and congregation. Emphasis should thus be on inculcating the spirit of Christian service to women in a large number of women as possible, rather than on the formal training course for a small number of professional women workers. Our high school and girls hostel in Trivandrum offers increasing opportunities in this respect. These girls can be of greater value and tremendous influence in the home congregation as voluntary workers among the women of the congregation neighborhood."[160] Here, we can see a clear shift in women ministry. In 1954, Miss. Ziemke took particular charge of the deaconess program, that is, training program and refresher courses.[161] Miss. Ziemke was assigned Trivandrum, Alleppey and Parasala districts. That Miss. Rink took particular charge of work with the Girls in girls boarding. This also included TTC School and college girls both in and out boarding. Miss Rink was in charge of women work in Balaramapuram, Luthergiri, Nilamel, Wynad and Wandoor.[162] A special fund of Rs 1000 was received from the home church for women's work.[163] Special ministry among the Women by MELIM proved its results. After the formation of TDS, many Lutheran women came forward to organize the ministry among women. Women candidates were even ready for the theological and ministerial training in the future years. Thus, MELIM paved the way for the future effective ministry among the Lutheran women.

3.7.6. Catechist School at Trivandrum

From the beginning itself, mission felt the need of local resource persons for the active participation in mission. They found educated people and gave them special trainings for using them as the local agents of mission. The catechist was one of the most effective helpers and church planters for MELIM. For the

[157] *Christiani,* 25/5, 1950, 96. First secretary was Ms. P. Attosa.

[158] Secretaries report, *Christiani,* 25/6, 1950, 109-111.

[159] Rose Ziemke, Women's Work Report, *127th TDCM*, 1953, 20.

[160] M.L. Wyneken, *Report of TDC Five Year Plan Committee*, 17 Oct. 1952, 3, *TDCM*, 1952, 33.

[161] *133rd TDCM*, Feb. 1955, 13-14.

[162] *130th TDCM,* Feb, 1954, 2-3. *136th TDCM*, 1956, 3.

[163] *131st TDCM,* June, 1954, 39.

training of catechists Missionaries started a lower catechist class at Trivandrum for the beginners. If the candidate proved his ability, then he would selected to do higher catechist course at Concordia Seminary, Nagercoil for two years. If they successfully completed that course they might be appointed in various fields under the strict supervision of the resident Missionary. After careful evaluation they might be admitted to the Pastor's class. This was the normal procedure which the mission followed.

The new catechist class at Trivandrum was started in 1925.[164] Trivandrum Catechist School was opened on 9 January 1928.[165] In 1949, it was resolved to send 18 men for pastor's class, 7 for joint training school and 3 men for Catechist seminary.[166] Those catechists worked as teachers, evangelists and catechists. Some of them later became pastors in MELIM. Through this local leadership MELIM was able to plant a number of new churches. They became the effective local agents and leaders of this mission. Through the local people, MELIM was able to do their mission which was a local people's movement.

3.7.7. The Medical Mission

After establishing churches in the rural areas of Kerala, the Lutheran missionaries and the church workers introduced a new method of approach. While the Missionaries were at work they saw the wounded, the sick, the disabled, the weak and those who were suffering from incurable diseases. Sometimes epidemics like Cholera and Smallpox attacked the people. The Missionaries taught the people cleanliness at the outset. Then they applied medicines to the wounds and gave medicines to those who were suffering from sickness.[167] Medical missions invariably got started at the Missionaries home, as their wives begun to do some free first aid and health care work. The Missionary wife soon found herself with a "back veranda dispensary". From there on the project grew. But they could not do much to those who were suffering from incurable diseases. Hence, they wanted to open medical centres and treat the people. This idea gave an impulse to start the Medical Mission. In Travancore area, the Missionaries of MELIM took into consideration the success of the LMS and the Salvation Army, and decided to start medical mission as a method of propagation of faith. As per the direction of the Home board a medical Mission was started.[168] They conducted small dispensaries under the supervision of the medical mission.[169] They opened medical centres at Pandikad, Malappuram, Nilamel, Trivandrum, Parassala and other places.[170]

[164] *Christiani*, 1/8, 1925, 114.

[165] *Christiani*, Dec. 1952, 268.

[166] *TDCM,* 1949, 9.

[167] *Missionaries report from the field,* 1913, 1-2. Concordia Archives.

[168] *Missionary Report,* 1921, 5. Concordia Archives.

[169] Minutes of the medical board, 1923, 9-10.

[170] Minutes of the Board for mission, 1958, 8.

Much of the present medical work in the Wandoor area[171] was started and fostered by Missionary Henry J Otten, begin MELIM Mission to Muslims in 1950. The first dispensary, *Karunalaya* (Abode of mercy)[172] was built in 1954. Karunalaya at Wandoor and Christian Welfare Centre Malappuram are the two major hospitals of Kerala Lutherans. Medical mission assumed a parallel and not a subordinate role to the preaching and teaching ministry. It was not a ministry just to open doors and homes, but rather the visible demonstration of the Gospel proclaimed by the Healer of all people's ills.

3.7.8. Youth Work

From 1942 onwards, different persons were appointed to organize the Lutheran Youth. The first youth secretary to be appointed was A. Enose. The aim was to develop the talents of youth, to build their life and character in strong Christian faith and equip them for evangelism. Within a few years they were able to start many Lutheran Youth league units. From 1947 onwards they celebrated Youth Sundays. Later J.C. Gamaliel and Sukumaran Devadas became the appointed leaders for the youth ministry.[173] Lutheran College Student's Association was founded in 1952[174] and its service also needs to be acknowledged. The Hostel Board resolved to start a new Hostel for college students at Vattiyoorkavu compound as a part of the youth ministry.[175] The service of L E Meinzen as the Youth Work Missionary advisor to budding youth endeavor in the Malayalam area was a notable event. He sent a questionnaire to all the congregations requesting information regarding youth activities. Each District *sanghom* appointed a layman as a representative to youth planning committee.[176] Through planned youth work, a new awakening among the youth in TDC was aroused. It helped the emergence of new leadership for the next generation ministry. More organized youth work among the Lutherans in Kerala flourished after the formation of the Trivandrum District Synod. The youth ministry by Rev. Paul Pollex in Trivandrum as a full time youth worker and his team shall be discussed in the next chapter.

---

[171] Wandoor is a small town near the west coast of India, almost entirely Muslim area in those days. Most of the people there were extremely poor, and majorities were not able to read and write. Almost the only industry in the area was cigarette (beedi) making. There were very few medical facilities.

[172] Another hospital by MELIM at Ambur is Bethesda (A house of Mercy) started by Louise Ellermann in 1913.

[173] *Christiani Special*, 52/11, 1976, 9.

[174] *Christiani Special* 52/11, 1976, 52.

[175] *131st TDCM*, June, 1954, 43.

[176] 132nd *TDCM*, 1954, 70.

3.7.9. Children's Ministry

Sunday schools were begun in almost all congregations from the beginning. Regular Sunday classes were conducted in the church campus. Flannel programs became a regular feature in their work. Women, children and college students were attracted by it. The life and teachings of Jesus Christ were shown at the flannel graph programs. Prayer league was another method. Sunday school in open air and houses other than the churches was another mechanism that was adopted by the Missionaries. Songs and life history of Jesus were regularly taught in the jail school too. The teachers of the MELIM schools conducted morning worships along with Bible Classes. Work for teenagers was started in the 1940's and spread vigorously in the 1950's. Sunday school and youth work in Trivandrum District level were mostly dependent on one responsible person appointed by TDC. A. Enose, Sukumaran Devadas, J.C. Gamaliel, G. Chithrabhanu and O. Lukose were the early leaders. The refresher courses which they organized from 1944 were very effective.[177] The educational Missionary L.E. Meinzen arrived in 1950 and he gave new life to the ministry among the children. He was an instrument to start the Vacation Bible Schools in the 1960's. Rose Zimke's contribution towards the children ministry must also be noted.[178] The gospel ministry among the children through the schools and boarding homes also need to be mentioned. It helped to produce future workers and leaders for the follow up mission.

3.7.10. Good News Centers/Reading Rooms

The Lutheran Christian workers opened reading rooms in the name of Good News Centers in all the places of their religious activities. They considered that the reading rooms were the effective instruments or agencies for the outreach of the Gospel. The Missionaries believed that, if a reading room was opened in a place where people assembled after the day's work or during the leisure time, or those who need rest from hard work, free and pleasant atmosphere from all worries, it would be a great service of Christian service and love.[179] Different people who came there every day to read the available literature.[180] Hence, they opened reading rooms in various centers.

An attendant – usually a student/ catechist/ evangelist or a pastor- would be present at all times to help those who come to these rooms. They also went out regularly to present filmstrip and flannel graph programs in the town and villages. The poor, the sick, the oppressed and the suppressed were visited by the MELIM workers through reading rooms for consolation and to satisfy their mental and

---

[177] *Christiani Special* 52/11, 1976, 53.

[178] *Christiani Special* 52/11, 1976, 20.

[179] *Minutes of the Muslim Mission Second Conference*, 1952, 1.

[180] *Minutes of the Muslim Mission,* First Conference, 1952, 3.

moral needs.[181] These people were welcomed to the reading rooms with friendly terms. Hence, they called these centers as Friendship centers. Such centers were well-lighted, airy, inviting reading rooms, equipped with tables, chairs, religious pictures and a variety of books, pamphlets, periodicals, magazines, and news papers. This had been a great aid to the MELIM mission. Christian tracts and other literatures were also placed there. Those who came there read all these including Christian literature. If anybody asked for more tracts they issued them happily with a welcome note. The doubts of the visitors were clarified. If they were happy and asked any doubts, they were invited for filmstrip program. The workers patiently answered all questions that came from the readers. Mostly they avoided argument and spoke to the non Christians very cordially and in friendly terms. The Bible Correspondence Course (BCC) was another work done through these reading rooms. Some of the Reading rooms grew to be organized congregations.

3.7.11. Attempts for Social Uplift

The Christian converts in the MELIM were from the socially and economically backward communities. Education helped them a lot in acquiring social awareness. Occasional helps both in kind and money by Missionaries to those people did not enable them to develop their economic stability. During the War period the Northern Travancore Missionaries distributed relief to the children and family and their door to door visit was very much helpful on those days.[182] Hence, serious efforts were taken to eradicate their poverty. Due to economic oppression suffered by early converts and catechumen an attempt to colonize them was made in 1921.[183] Mat weaving and basket making were also tried in 1915 and 1922. Brush making industry was closed in 1921 due to huge loss after two years of functioning. Similarly, Sericulture attempt and Reed industry did not end in success. The early efforts for industrial mission and rural uplift failed miserably. Both the Education Mission (1915) and Medical Mission (1921) also did not show the progress as expected. In the modern period development programs and economic development projects also met with the same fate. But the early attempts for the social upward mobility of the new converts through various means by MELIM should be appreciated.

3.7.12. Other Strategies

The Missionaries gave relief and gifts to the affected families and children who suffered either due to failure of monsoon or were afflicted with epidemics or met with the loss of earning members of the family. Hahn was the first Missionary to introduce this method. This program drew the attention of the people including

[181] Report of M. Jeyapaul, Concordia Archives.

[182] *Conference of Missionaries Report*, 22 May 1945, 3.

[183] Swavely, *op.cit.* 170.

those who opposed them. The Missionaries also distributed the tracts wherever they went. Some people tore them into pieces and threw them in the face of the Missionaries and only a few carefully read them.[184]

Unmindful of all these humiliations and criticisms, the Missionaries distributed the tracts and believed that even if they did not read them, they would carry the message.[185] The regular Pastoral Conferences helped the pastors to grow spiritually through systematic study of the scripture and doctrines. And it also provided ample opportunity to have fellowship and discus matters relating to their ministry.[186] *Pradhinidhi Sanghom* also helped the growth and smooth functioning of Trivandrum field.[187]

Paying salaries to all workers, teachers and catechists was in the hands of the Missionary in charge, who entered them all directly in his monthly statement of accounts. The upkeep of property and buildings and necessary improvements was also run in the same way. Half of the contributions of the congregations were used for the payment of salary and another half was into the church building fund account, from which money was drawn to purchase new property, erection of parsonage, digging of wells at church compound. Efforts were made constantly towards contribution either with money, labor, land or what other they may had. Baptism and Holy Communion in the congregations were conducted by Missionaries and pastors. Marriages could be solemnized by the catechists, because no marriage license was necessary in those days. Instruction for confirmation and examination of candidates for adult baptism and confirmation was usually done by the Missionary.[188]

A congregational record was kept in each congregation. It covered a full year, and maintained the following records: Attendance at all services, all lessons taught, all classes conducted, all contributions received, Baptisms, Confirmations, Lord's Supper, Marriages, burials. Attendance records were also kept of adherents, namely non-baptized people who attend off and on, and those who were under instruction for Baptism. Practically, all congregations had deacons or elders or both. The congregations themselves appointed their delegates to the various delegate Meetings. They made their own arrangements for celebrations at Christmas, Harvest festivals, Reformation festival. Normally catechists were appointed in each place by TDC and pastors were called by the local church and installation was made by the TDC. Trivandrum District had congregations made up of members from several different castes. This made MELIM work in the Trivandrum District differ greatly from the congregations and work of other sections of their work.

---

[184] *Minutes of the Board for Muslim Mission*, 1952, 3.

[185] *Report by the Missionary H.J. Otten*, 1966, 2.

[186] *128th TDCM, July*, 1953, 29.

[187] *128th TDCM, July,* 1953, 36.

[188] Wyneken, *Congregational Report*, three pages typed note, (nd.) 2. Concordia Archives.

3.8. An Analysis of Missionary Methods

The MELIM Missionaries were the by-products of German pietism. Their evangelical zeal motivated them to suffer for Christ and bear witness with all urgency to redeem the souls. When MELIM Missionaries reached South Travancore, their main aim was to preach the 'pure Gospel' and thereby convert the 'heathens' to Christian faith. They taught and preached the Gospel of Christ as the redemptive force. Even though it was against the then comity arrangements, MELIM took bold steps to uplift this poor people.[189] Most of the then Sambava leaders wanted it as exclusively a Sambava Mission.[190] It is true that some of the MELIM Missionaries had a strong affection towards this particular people group. Some of the MELIM Missionaries were called as '*Paraiah Saippu*' means the *Sambava* Missionary. They loved them as people. This acceptance gave the Sambavars hope to trust these Missionaries for all the developments. J Isaiah's words show that how they valued this affection:

"*MELIM Missionaries came and took us as we were in caste-ridden India; we were nothing then. It is only after the missionaries were prepared to accept and treat us as human beings that society in general also realized how thoroughly it had rejected us. The Sambavar Lutherans of today must deeply appreciate this unique character of the past MELIM missionaries.*"[191] But during the later years we understand that some Missionaries favoured to Nadars, some Ezhavas and some Vedars. It clearly shows how they loved the people whom they were called to serve. But it is very clear that they were against the seclusion from the beginning itself. Another IELC pastor, looking back, commented,

"*Institutions were the bedrock on which many of the churches in India were built. The Indian church is not an exception. Educational institutions, boarding schools, not only helped the people to get released from social, economic and psychological bondage, but also from the bondage of paganism. They were taught and trained to "live" a human life, and to witness for Christ. Educational Institutions were the means by which the gospel reached the people in the past. Many villagers were attracted by the witness of the Christian Missionaries who went from village to village and preached the gospel. The children of the villagers were sent to boarding homes. They were taken care of by the missionaries - free boarding, free books, and free schooling. Nearly 80% of the present day members and workers are by one way or the other connected with the mission schools. Bible teaching was considered as an important part of schooling. It was compulsory for every pupil to attend the Bible classes, but no one was compelled*

---

[189] *EHELM*, *op.cit.*, 20-22.

[190] Pattom G. Ramachandran Nair, *Thiruvananthapurathinte Ithihasam* (Mal) (Epic of Trivandrum) (Trivandrum: Sahithya Vedi, 1996), 457.

[191] J. Isaiah, letter to D. Christu Das, 12th January, 2000. Mr. J. Isaiah is the one of the oldest leaders and benefactor of MELIM Mission presently living at Peroorkada.

to believe in Christ. But many believed in Christ when they heard about Jesus as their saviour."[192]

The negative impacts also need to be noted. The evangelistic zeal motivated the MELIM Missionaries to witness Christ with all urgency to save the souls. The agenda of the early Missionaries were nothing but converting the 'heathens' to Christ by preaching the Gospel and helping to attain salvation for the souls. Thus they were not able to concentrate on the total growth of the converts. Most of the Missionaries settled down in a big Missionary compound outside the village and cities. Workers and equipments were being sent out from the Missionary compound, causing the foreign Missionary enterprise to develop into a kind of ecclesiastical imperialism. Foreign methods of church work were used almost to the exclusion of native methods. There was a lack of faith in the ability of nationals to carry out the work of the church without the aid of Missionaries. There were severe criticisms among the Missionaries against the ordination of the first native Pastor G. Jesudasan. It happened only in 1921 after 15 years of starting MELIM in South Travancore.[193] Disobedience to Missionaries and dishonesty in money matters of the native converts were recorded in Missionary records with much emphasis but their strength and ability were not appreciated. Janaka says, *"A Lutheran Missionary invented a new arithmetical table in terms of caste to the effect that a certain number of Sambavars are equal to one Nadar, a certain number of Nadar is equal to one non-Brahmin caste Hindu, and he is said to assess the value of the converts to the Lutheran Mission accordingly... The Lutheran Missionaries after all come to the same stock as the British rulers, whose policy has always been 'Divide and rule' whether in the state or in the church, the European wants to be the ruler and would not allow himself to be associated in terms of equality with the Indian without a desperate fight . . . Those modern apostles of Lutheran congregationalism are said to be highly automatic, and to be unwilling to tolerate any independence of thought or action in their converts, in whom slave mentality is sought to be developed more than anywhere else . . . It is really due to a desire to perpetuate the domineering position of the European in the India Lutheran Church."*[194] It may be an exaggeration by the non-Lutherans; mostly about the non-MELIM Missionaries, even it should be looked into for getting some lessons.

MELIM started schools along with churches. The purpose of the elementary vernacular schools was propagation of the Gospel and not elevation of people from social blindness. Most of them were not interested in upgrading the schools or starting English education. When Government rules tried to restrict religious

---

[192] Martin Jesudas, *India Evangelical Lutheran Church Growth, Expansion and Mission: An Evaluation*," Master of Theology Thesis, Fuller Theological Seminary, 1976, 86.

[193] Letter from Hentry Hamman to A.J. Lutz from Ambur, 15th July 1919.

[194] Janaka, "The Introduction of Untouchability into Christianity," *Christian Patriot* 37/13 (September, 1928): 6-9.

education through schools, MELIM conducted schools without Government grants so that they could teach Bible lessons.

Most of the development programs were Missionary-centered. When the Missionary went back, the project also came to a close.[195] MELIM Missionaries from other districts also had criticized the Mission policy in the Trivandrum District as unjust.[196] E.E. Griesse says: The Missionary took his stand as a doctrinal point and could not be moved. Doctrine was taught with typical "German bluntness", and was neither understood nor liked by the complacent Hindus.[197] Colonialism, pietism and German pride were the major influences of MELIM Missionaries. It was true that colonialism paved the way to the Europeans to come over to India with the Gospel. Their big bungalows on a large compound, unapproachability of natives to them, lack of participation of natives in decision-making, Board's policy concerning the 'locals' without any consultation with them, provided evidences to these facts. As T. Joy observes, *Most of the MELIM missionaries were German in origin; the typical 'Hitlarian' attitude was very expressive in most of the MELIM missionaries. But the other missionary groups who worked in South India were British and socially oriented than the German Lutheran missionaries.*[198] Such a Missionary mind influenced a lot in MELIM's work.

There were 124 MELIM Missionaries during 1894 to 1956 and out of that 3 died in India and 12 retired from service. But 96 Missionaries resigned from service and returned without completing their term.[199] A detailed study may reveal the real issue behind this. It may be said that there was a direct connection between the Missionary doctrine, policy and practice with the decline of Lutheran Community in MELIM.[200]

---

[195] For example former Trivandrum missionary, Rev. A.J. Lutz started different development programmes for *Sambavars* out of his personal interest. There was no direct involvement of the Board. But all the projects had to be discontinued when he returned home.

[196] E.E. Griesse, *op. cit.*, 31.

[197] Ibid., 8.

[198] Rev. T. Joy is the first Church Historian from IELC. He is a retired Professor in History of Christianity at Concordia Theological Seminary, Nagercoil, and presently lives at Chengavila, Near Parassala.

[199] L.W. Meinzen, *op.cit.*, 247-251.

[200] The historical sketch of the first period in the history of missionary work that led to the formation of the IELC had demonstrated areas of strength and weakness. The developments, struggles, tensions and progress of the IELC in its formative years were directly related to its heritage and with early missionaries. Their ecclesiastical and structural ethos was imported from the West. The impact of the Gospel on the lives of people was in diverse type in relation to the complex nature of our society. As we look into the historical background of the context an analysis of missionary polity and method may help to understand present situation and provide thought for constructive planning for the future.

3.9. MELIM's Relation with LMS

The move towards South itself was a controversial issue. Even the Missionaries had differences of opinion to this move because LMS was working there for the past one century.[201] The first helpers of MELIM at Kuttichel also had direct connections with the LMS. Many groups and congregations attached to MELIM had a Christian background either with LMS, Salvation Army or Roman Catholic.[202] Few examples are, Poovachal, Mulayara, Kazhakutam, Valiyamangalam, Kusavarkal, Mannanthala, Chalaikonam, Kattachakonam, Panayamcode, Malakulangara, etc. As Griesse pointed out that; "Missionaries thought that it was a distinct advantage to serve such congregations because they had already acquired a Christian background."[203] But it became a source of friction between other missions.[204] Other missions criticized the Lutherans that they were stealing their members.[205] Lot of 'backsliders' of other missions got favor and position among the Kerala Lutheran community. MELIM's move to Southern field raised challenges and problems. This was against the policy of not working where other Christians were working. As it was a strong LMS Missionary centre, the LMS objected to the service of the new mission. The Lutheran Missionaries came in with the purpose of bringing the Gospel to the people who were excluded to hearing Gospel due to the social pressures of caste.[206] They had no intention to interfere with the work of other Missions. Later on, experience showed that it was extremely difficult for two Missions to work side by side without either co-operating or interfering with each other.[207] The marriages between the members of LMS and MELIM were not possible on those days. Playing one Mission against another became a common practice.[208] In the later years, relation between other

---

[201] *Lutheran Witness* 28/9 (April, 1909): 277; O.A. Ehlers, The Annual General conference of the MELIM, *Lutheran Witness,* 11 June, 1918, 183.

[202] Survey of Luthergiri District Report, 1-2 and Herbert M. Zorn, "Relation between the Missouri Lutherans and the LMS," *ICHR* 1/2 (December, 1967): 133-143.

[203] Elmer E. Griesse, *op. cit.*, 11.

[204] The opinion of the Nagercoil missionaries of Evangelical Lutheran mission in India on the statement on Comity among missions in India 6 page typed document; Reply of the General Conference of missionaries of MELIM to the statement on comity among missions in India.5 page typed note .Concordia Archives.

[205] Letter from Arthur Foster LMS South Travancore Pareychaley (Sic) district, to J Harms, Lutheran Mission Trivandrum, 19 July 1917; Letter from Salvation Army Major J. Richardson dated 4.1.22 and letter from Bishop of Tinnevely, Rt. Rev. Frederic, 12th October, 1932.

[206] Ibid.

[207] O.A. Ealers, 8th General conference of MELIM, *Lutheran Witness*, 11 June 1918, 183.

[208] H.M. Zorn, *Much Cause for Joy*, 20.

missions became a serious issue and then LCMS tried to enter into an agreement with the LMS.[209]

Missionaries of the LMS complained to their headquarters that the Lutheran Missionaries were pocketing their members and entering into their congregations whenever disputes arose.[210] The Board in London complained to the Board in St. Louis about the alleged sheep-stealing. Director Brande of St. Louis gave assurance that Lutheran Missionaries would not take the members from other missions.[211] A delegation was appointed to investigate the facts in the case.[212] But on the mission fields, the members of the LMS approached the Lutheran Missionaries with reports of false doctrines and wrong practices in their congregations. Some of them quit the LMS and returned, asking for spiritual care. The Lutheran Missionaries tried to provide such care. Conferences spent long hours and wrote detailed minutes on the stands to be taken towards other Christians who might come for spiritual care. Since MELIM ran boarding schools, it needed and hired teachers and catechists. They gave certain amount of charity also to poor people. It was difficult to tell how many of these requests were sincere for spiritual care and how many were prompted by other motives. The Lutheran Missionaries ignored all objections and gave new impetus to religious activities.

An interesting outcome arose in 1935. H M Zorn observes: "Through the good offices of A Gunamony, a member of the LMS, and a lawyer with whom A. Lutz of MELIM was consulting, MELIM broached the subject of adopting some more detailed agreement on relationship between MELIM and LMS. This resulted in a meeting of Lutheran Missionaries as a Comity Committee, in 1936."[213] Later, after four years, the LMS Missionaries responded with a statement that the committees report did cover some of the important matters, but not completely adequate.[214] Comity matter was discussed at the India Mission Committee, 1944. That shows the matter was continued as unsettled.[215] Immediately after the formation of the CSI in 1947, the body issued an invitation to Lutherans in South India to consider the possibility of a wider union. Discussions began in 1949 between CSI and a number of Lutheran Churches in South India.

---

209 Letter from the Tinnevely Bishop, 12th October 1932 was not answered. So he sent a letter to the Board on 5th November 1932. Then the MELIM was forced to explain the situation to Board, viz. letter dated 16 November 1932. On 26th November 1936 MELIM submitted a statement of comity for consideration.

210 Report of the special committee appointed to consider the statement submitted by the committee of the MELIM 26th November 1936.

211 Board letter to MELIM 18 Nov. 1929; Letter from F. Brand to Philips of LMS 1 Dec. 1929.

212 See the letter from G E Philips to F Brand, 25 January, 1930.

213 H.M. Zorn, "Relation between MELIM and LMS", *ICHR* 1/2 (December, 1967), 142.

214 Correspondence of A J Lutz, 1935 and from the LMS to MELIM 22 Aug., 1940.

215 Minutes of the Board for Foreign Missions of LCMS, 29 April, 1944, 3.

Members of MELIM committee joined these discussions in 1951.[216] But H.M. Zorn concludes this matter as follows: "Succeeding years have shown a growth in cordiality between MELIM and the LMS and its successor in this area, the CSI. Efforts towards the closer relationship with CSI continued in the following years. But the presence of two denominations of this nature is always a seedbed in which dissension can grow far too easy; the balance between freedom and respect of another church is not easily maintained."[217]

3.10. Travancore Mission Conference and Representative Councils

The first delegates' or workers' meeting was instituted to provide a chance to attend communion service for the workers and their wives and for a get together with those of their own faith. The mission paid travel expenses for this quarterly meeting to a worker and his wife and a Missionary would conduct the service and administer the communion. After that, study papers based on doctrinal issues were read by workers. These meetings also provide opportunities for discussions on their work and other practical difficulties. As the church grew, and the number of workers increased, the central delegation meetings drew an ever larger crowd. The workers themselves monopolized all the meetings. As a result the congregational delegates never said anything, feeling that it was not their business. After some years each congregation had its own communion members, communion was celebrated by the Missionary in each congregation, with the catechist and his wife communing with the congregation, so that they no longer needed the quarterly Delegate meeting in Trivandrum for this purpose. It was a Representative Assembly, otherwise known as the *Prathinithi Sangam*. The central meeting for four times a year with the mission paying the travel expenses of those coming from 20 miles or more distance, were expensive for what they achieved. So as a result it was reduced to two times a year in the 1930's and the central delegate meeting was cut down to once a year in 1938.

The reason was the bulkiness of the group. In 1938, the membership was reduced and only a single meeting planned with religious workers who were in charge of a congregation together with one delegate from each congregation.[218] From 1936 onwards, two representatives from each congregation along with the workers attended such in these conferences.[219] The District delegates meetings

[216] Herbert M Zorn, "History of IELC Inter Church Efforts", A paper presented in the Joint meeting of the BTT, ICRC, MEC, and district presidents with T.F.Nickel, the second vice president of the LCMS (nd), 3.

[217] H.M. Zorn, "Relation between MELIM and LMS", *ICHR* 1/2 (December 1967), 142-143.

[218] M.L. Wynekan, *Delegates and Workers Meeting in TDC* , one page typed note. (nd.)

[219] With the reduction of the number of meetings of the whole mission in Trivandrum, District Delegates meetings were introduced in different centers, namely Alleppey, Nilamel, Ponvila-Balaramapuram, Luthergiri and Trivandrum. This District Delegates meeting met four times a year, and it was there the congregation members now spoke up and took an active part in the work of the mission. The groups were smaller, the distance to travel was less and so more delegates from each

helped more lay participation in the work of the mission. They are proved to be valuable and congregations were interested in attending them.[220]

A workers institute was organized from 1938 onwards to meet once a year normally in December in which all mission workers attended, with no congregational delegates. The delegates' meeting was held normally in July of each year, at which one delegate from each congregation and all workers in the Malayalam district were present. Every month Missionaries, catechists, pastors and teachers met at Vattiyoorkavu School. This *Prathinithi Sangams* were the very effective means to build fellowship and healthy relationships with all the congregations, workers, and Malayali Lutherans representing different ethnic group. It was an attempt to train the growing church to assume responsibility and leadership for its future, without depending on MELIM.

3.11. Formation of Trivandrum District Synod Report

There was frequent "free conference" of Indian Lutherans, which the Missionaries also attended as guests. Regarding this the Board states that "to encourage the brethren to take part in free conferences for doctrinal discussions and to speak and testify frankly in love but to commit themselves to any actual establishment of union until our church bodies in the States have united."[221] But later due to the rise of Indian nationalism, the official conferences with a view to the formation of an Indian Lutheran Church were begun. As India got its Independence in 1947 and war experience gave new lessons for the foreign Missionaries. Getting visas for long term was not easy. Indian government adopted a policy that called for progressive Indianization of all foreign ventures.[222] National and united Church of South India was formed in 1947. The "three self "movement caught peoples appeal.[223] In addition, LCMS had entered into several other countries and resources for extensive expansion in India were no longer available. Above all, the "mission" was inevitably becoming the "Church". In such a context formation of an indigenous church became an urgent need.

Regarding the development of an indigenous church the home church's resolution read as follows: "*Whereas, it is the policy of all mission boards operating in foreign lands to encourage the development of an indigenous church in our several mission fields, and to train a national ministry; and Whereas, it is likewise the policy of these boards to initiate mission work in the more popular areas, from which the*

congregation could attend. More topics which were strictly local could be tackled and discussed. The program was almost the same as the central meetings. Two or more doctrinal and practical papers, written for the lay delegates; were presented for chiefly discussions like, congregational conditions, self-help, family devotion and subjects like this.

[220] M.L. Wyneken, *Delegate and Workers Meeting in TDC,* Ibid.

[221] Minutes of Board of Foreign missions, LCMS, 17 January 1944, 3.

[222] H.M. Zorn, *Much Cause for Joy*, 50.

[223] Self Government, Self Support and Self Propagation.

missionaries can then extend their activities also into the surrounding territories, therefore be it resolved, that we heartily commend our mission boards for their vision in carrying out such practical policies."[224] LCMS's Resolution no.2 about creating an indigenous church in foreign fields read as follows: "*Whereas, experience has demonstrated that a national church with national pastors can do more effective work; and Whereas, nationalistic attitudes in many countries of the world today place obstacles in the way of foreign missionaries; therefore be it resolved, that we commend the mission boards and the missionaries in the field for their emphasis on the creation of indigenous churches in the various mission fields; and be it further, Resolved, that we send only such pastors into foreign fields who have necessary gifts, to lead and to train others for leadership; and be it also resolved, that especially in the development of new fields one or more experienced pastors be found to initiate such new work.*"[225]

Ambur Sangam or Ambur District Synod formation report by H.M. Zorn (Oct. 22, 1949), inspired the TDC to start discussions about the formation of TDS.[226] TDC approved the procedures of trying to line up the local *sanghams* into parallel working units, without losing sight of a final formal synod organization. Conference felt that when that line up is achieved, name will be the only thing lacking of the organization.[227] It was a long process.[228] The proposed synod formation was discussed in TDC and at local district levels.[229]

In 1956 October, 25 circles in Trivandrum sent 75 delegates to the organizational meeting of the District Synod held in Concordia High School, Perurkada, and Trivandrum.[230] The conference delegates accepted the new

---

[224] *Proceedings of the 42 Regular Convention of LCMS* at Houston, Texas, June 17-26, 1953 (St. Louis: CPH, 1953), 375.

[225] *Ibid., 43 Regular Convention of LCMS* at Minnesota, June 20-29, 1956.

[226] *TDCM,* 1949, 23-24; *TDCM*, 1950, 38-42.

[227] *Synod Formation Report*, 127th *TDCM*, Feb, 1953, 22.

[228] *Synod Formation Report*, 132 *TDCM*, 1954, 66-67.

[229] The representatives and leaders of the low caste of the congregations in Luthergiri District gave a petition to TDC against the Synod formation. They raised two issues: one was that the churches were not aware of how to operate properly the subsidy system. Another was a fear that if the Synod was formed the lowest caste among them would again be alienated by the upper caste groups among the Lutherans. But the TDC and its missionaries gave assurance that the proposed constitution would take corrective measures to overcome their fear. *130th TDCM* 1954, 22.

[230] The legal powers listed below were agreed upon the synod: "Synod shall have legal powers in the following matters: A.The power and right to purchase, hold, administer and sell the property of every description in the interest of its work ;B. This power and right to accept, hold and administer and if deemed advisable, to dispose of legacies, donations and documents of every interests of its work; C. Synod does not have authority over the properties of individual congregations. A congregation has the full rights over its own property" General Synod Constitution subcommittee minutes; January 1957, 1. But when the IELC Trust Association was formed this power was taken over by the IELC –TA.

Constitution on 9 October.[231] The vote was the culmination of four years of hard effort on the part of the Missionaries to establish a Synodical organization in the District. A small group of Indian leaders had worked with the Missionaries in drafting the Constitution. For four days, the delegates carefully considered each point of the proposed document and finally adopted it with a few modifications. "Discussions revealed that most of the delegates including the laymen had studied the Constitution and made valuable suggestions for improvements" wrote Wilber T. May.[232] At the meeting A. Enose presented a doctrinal essay on "The letters to the seven Churches."[233] W.T. May opines; "*The missionaries have no vote in the synodical meetings but do have vote in committees. Still the responsibility for the work of the church has been turned over to the nationals with missionaries assuming the role of advisors. This, under the blessings of the Lord of the Church, We feel confident, will contribute to the general welfare of the Church and will prepare the way for a truly indigenous Church here in India.*"[234] On 9-12 October 1956 at Perurkada the Tirvandrum Synod officially came into force with 137 churches and 14,000 members. The churches in TDS were urged to accept and sign the Constitution before 31 March 1957 so that they may get powers to send the delegates in the 1957 synod convention.[235]

3.12. Conclusion

The history of the 50 years of MELIM in South Travancore is a history of the grace of God to this people who were socially alienated for ages. The Sambavars and Ezhavas who felt negation from LMS joined to invite MELIM Missionaries to Malayalam speaking area. The Sambavars in front of this move insisted that this Mission should be exclusively for Sambavars. But the Missionaries consciously kept away from making an official commitment. Evangelistic work was carried on in many ways. First contacts were established through street preaching, which

---

[231] A lot of draft constitutions were made and distributed to all churches for study and reflections. *Constitution for Missouri Evangelical Lutheran Malayalam Synod* (Mal. 1953), *Constitution for local Sangom* (1955), Constitution for village churches (Mal. 1955) *Proposed Constitution for India Evangelical Lutheran Synod*, Trivandrum District (1956*), Constitution for India Evangelical Kerala Synod, Constitution for Indian Evangelical Lutheran Church,* Trivandrum Synod, (Mal. & Eng., 1957), *India Evangelical Lutheran Synod, Trivandrum District* (Mal. & Eng. 1957). To see the full version of the Constitution of TDS-IELC see the appendix no.

[232] W T May, People and Events, *Lutheran witness*, January, 1957, 51.

[233] The officers elected were: President, D. Vedamanikom, Vice President E. Manasse, Secretary C. M. Jacob, and Treasurer S. Markose. In addition to these officers, the Synod elected four standing committees. Four nationals and two missionaries served on each of the committees of Gospel work, Education, Finance and Building. The executive committee had nine Indian and seven male missionary members.

[234] *Lutheran Witness*, January, 1957, 51.

[235] Letter from C.M. Jacob, Secretary TDS, 1956 TDS meeting accepted Conference directions to all congregations. Discussion of constitution, 136, TDCM, 1956, 21-25.TDCM, *1956, 34-35.*

started very early in the morning and late in the evening. Schools were used to reach the children and through them the parents and communities. Literature was used to propagate the Gospel and to nurture Christian faith. Medical mission also focused to reach all people in the community. Later special recognition was given to the need of reaching youth, women and the children. Many Indian Bible women were raised to build a healthy church. Later Sunday School and Vacation Bible School ministry had proved great force in reaching the children. A good number of lay people became instrument to plant the churches and carry the gospel to their neighbors and friends. Reading rooms and Bible correspondence courses also proved as effective means to propagate the Gospel among the non Christians.

As in the beginning, most of the applicants to MELIM were the people having previous Christian background with LMS. Due to this intervention, the relation between LMS and MELIM was shaken, not only in the Mission fields but also in the Home Board, and that led to the formation of comity arrangements. Even then it remained for years an unsolved issue. World Wars, caste controversy, rift among Missionaries also affected the growth and progress of MELIM.

The war experiences and the national awakening forced them to learn new lessons like the need of properly trained native workers, formation of an Indian Lutheran Church, and need to cooperation between Missions and other churches in India. Mission records say that the interest of MELIM Missionaries were not only just to evangelize the unreached but to help the Lutheran Christians to be better citizens and help them to develop socially and economically. For this purpose they started so many development programs. But such efforts did not bring encouraging results. However, educational mission was one of the major contributions of MELIM to South India. Gradually, new congregations were established among the different people groups. This paved the way for various caste groups to enter into the MELIM's fold. But conversions from caste Hindus did not happen as expected. Yet emergence of new situations demanded new models of ministry. Thus the need of training Indian personnel to take over charge from the Missionaries was highly recognized, both in theory and in practice. It led to the formation of District Synods. However, the history of fifty years of MELIM in South Travancore was not a history of brilliant achievements by itself. But it was a history of the grace of God to His people. This means that in every sense within a half of the century, members of the MELIM had come to recognize themselves as a Church. A move from Mission to Church had its own challenges. Next chapter is about the life of Lutheran Churches in Kerala as an independent church for the next half century.

Chapter 4

Christian Lutherans of Kerala from 1956 to 2011

4.1. Introduction

Missouri Evangelical India Mission's Travancore District Conference (TDC) became the Trivandrum District Synod of IELC on 12 October 1956. IELC was formed in 8-9 January 1958 with B.H. Jackayya as the first General Secretary and was registered under Societies Act XXI of 1860; S.No. 11 of 1959 on 10 January 1959. For administrative convenience, IELC has several units such as congregations, pastorates, circles and synods. IELC has got 3 synods namely Ambur, Nagercoil and Trivandrum. Each synod has got its own Constitution submissive to the Constitution of IELC which is the apex body. Trivandrum District Synod is one among them. Before moving to the significance of Lutheran Subaltern solidarity, it is worthwhile to understand briefly the life and history of Lutherans in Kerala. The formative years of a young Church is crucial and challenging. The administrative leadership suddenly changed from missionaries to the local people without developing a next generation leadership. The formative period of the synod was led by the national leadership with limited assistance from the missionaries. From 1977 onwards may be called as the crisis years. Thirst for power, lack of administrative experience and litigations hindered the growth and life of the young church. This chapter is a brief discussion and an analysis of the history of the Lutherans in Kerala from the year of the formation of Trivandrum District Synod[1] (1956) to 2011.

[1] The title Trivandrum District Synod (TDS) and Trivandrum Synod (TS) were used to refer the Lutheran churches in Kerala in the IELC records. Therefore, this study also recognizes these names with same meaning.

4.2. The Formative Period (1956-1977)

4.2.1. Brief Sketch of TDS

The Trivandrum District Synod (TDS) of the IELC consists of 25,000 members under 62 pastorates and 117 organised congregations and 28 new fields/mission centres in five circles. The five circles of Trivandrum Synod are Balaramapuram, Luthergiri, Nilamel, Ponvila and Trivandrum.[2] The geographical surroundings of the Trivandrum Synod is spread over Thiruvananthapuram, Pathanamthitta, Kollam, Allapuzha and Ernakulam Districts of Kerala. The Trivandrum Synod is currently served by 74 Pastors, 13 Catechists/probationers and 4 theologically trained women workers. The Trivandrum Synod also has 25 Educational Institutions. The percentage of various castes are as follows: Dalit Christians, 50% (Sambavas and Pulayas), 12,500 numbers, Backward Castes 46% - Nadars about, 41% (10,250), and Ezhavas 5% (about 1250), and Tribal Christians and others, 4% - (1000 Kanikans, Kuravans, Vedans, and Forward caste-Nair). As on 2012, the caste composition of pastors,[3] women workers and gospel workers goes like this: Dalit, 45% (40), backward caste 48.3% (43-Nadars 38, Ezhava 6) and Tribal and others 69.7%-Tribals 5, Nair-1).[4] Majority of the members of the Trivandrum Synod is 2300 (72.5%) who are involved in agriculture, small cause business, and manual labour. Another 800 (25.23%) work as Teachers, Nurses, Transport Employees, Bank Employees or middle income government employees. Another 70 (2.2%) work as Doctors, Engineers, Bank Managers, Advocates, Professors and the like. This data clearly shows that the majority of members come from low income earning groups. However, there are a significant number of middle income groups also. The IELC also has a small percentage of high income earning groups.[5] TDS had 162 Acres and 61.25 cents of land in 139 plots.[6]

4.2.2. Administrative Organization

Synods are the chief administrative organizations to ensure pastoral care of congregations, supervision of workers, selection of trainees, and mission

[2] Constitution and By- laws of IELC, TS, Article VI (1), Synod by-laws. Formerly it was seven including Alleppy and Malabar. Later Alleppey circle merged with Nilamel and Malabar became a part of Board for Mission of IELC.

[3] Caste composition of TDS workers on February 1945 were as follows: Out of 129, Nadars 65, Paraians 29, Iravans 18, Pulayas 12, Velans 2, Tatchan1, Achari 1, Barber 1, Nair 2, Syrian1. List of religious workers in TDS, February, 1945.

[4] *IELC statistical survey June 2001*, and updated statistic from Central Business office and Concordia Theological Seminary on 17 July, 2012.

[5] Sam Thompson, *Evolving an Ethical Critique in Relation to the Leadership Crisis of the IELC with Particular Reference to the Trivandrum Synod, op.cit.*, 98.

[6] Information gathered from Secretary-Treasurer IELC-TA, 17 July, 2012. For the list see Appendix no.

expansion into new areas within its geographical area in consultation with circles.[7] Trivandrum District Synod has the legal powers to purchase, hold, administer, and alienate property of every description in the interest of TDS and to accept, hold, administer, and, if deemed advisable dispose of, legacies, donations, commercial papers, and legal documents of every description in the interest of TDS.[8] Trivandrum Synod was made up of representatives of congregations and so the responsibility and authority remain with the Synod rather than with the local congregations. "A Synod is a group of congregations in a larger geographical area organised into pastorates and circles and congregations for purposes of edification, co-operation and administration. It has a constitution for the administration of its work adhering to the IELC Constitution."[9] The main objectives of the Synod are the conservation and promotion of the unity of the true faith and a united defence against schism and sectarianism, the joint and enthusiastic extension of the Kingdom of God, the training of sufficient ministers and teachers for the service and their supervision the publication and distribution of Christian literature, to bring uniformity in practise, Church systems and so on, the protection of pastors, teachers, and congregations in the performance of their duties and maintenance of their rights.[10] A congregation is a fellowship of believers in one or several localities who worship together accepting the ministry of the IELC and served by ministers of the IELC.[11] An organized congregation automatically becomes a member of the IELC by virtue of its membership in one of the Synods. Such a congregation shall have at least 25 communicant members. Each congregation should have an IELC approved Constitution. Member churches should accept and confess the doctrines and confessions of the Church. Each congregation shall give a percentage of its actual income towards the IELC Support system and the administration of the Church as fixed by the Church Council (CC) in consultation with the Synods from time to time.[12] A congregation which does not contribute to the financial needs of the IELC according to the rules established from time to time by the CC shall not be eligible to make nominations or eligible for nominations as delegates, CC, Boards or committee members.[13]

A pastorate is a unit of one or more congregations in one area served by at least one pastor. The boundaries of each pastorate shall be determined by the respective synod on the recommendations of the Circle Convention.[14] The main

---

[7] IELC constitution, Article VI.A .4.

[8] Constitution and By-laws of IELC_TS, Article IV, 1-2 Powers.

[9] Constitution and By-laws of the IELC (as amended by the IELC Convention1970) Article VI, "A" 4,3.

[10] Constitution and By-Laws of the IELC, TDS, Article 111, 2;11.

[11] Constitution and By-Laws of the IELC, TDS, Article VI.A. 3.

[12] By-Laws of the IELC Constitution, section 1 Article VI A.1, 9.

[13] By-Laws of the IELC Constitution, section IX General, 8, 34.

[14] Constitution of IELC Article, VI A.3, 3.

purpose of the pastorate formation is self support. Pastorate within a geographical area shall be grouped into circles approved by the respective Synod. The circles serve as joint action units for ministry and regional concerns. "Each circle shall have a circle convention and a Circle Executive Committee elected according to the by-laws, and is to develop such other forms of organization as it considerer's (sic) necessary to implement the purpose, policies and programs of the Circle."[15]

All eligible organised congregations that have joined in TDS hold voting power.[16] TDS has an advisory council which includes all permanent workers of the church-pastors /catechists. TDS is not an ecclesiastical government exercising legislative or coercive powers in its relation to its members but it is an advisory body with respect to the individual congregations right of self government. TDS has its own separate Constitution approved by the IELC and it acts accordingly. The Synod is to be administered by an executive committee.[17] The tenure of the Synod officers is two years. This Executive Committee comprises of office bearers and also 7 members including two women elected from the circles.[18] The officers of TDS include the President and Vice Presidents, (pastors of TDS); the secretary, the appointed treasurer and a co-treasurer and Seven Executive members elected from each circle including two women representatives.[19]

The election process is to be carried out by IELC Election Commissioner with the assistance of a regional election officer.[20] The regular TDS Convention will be held once in a year. But the elections are to be held in the Synod once in two years. These elections take place at conventions held under the auspicious of the Executive committee. The presence of 1/3 of the constitutionally elected representatives is necessary for legal convention. Emergency and special convention will be held according to the Constitution. All matters shall be decided by a majority vote. The term of office is two years.[21]

4.2.3. Ups and Downs

Trivandrum District Synod was formed on Oct. 1956 with 14,000 members and since that time there is a slow but steady growth in the Church. The TDS

---

[15] Ibid.

[16] Constitution and By- laws of IELC, TS, Article IV A,3.

[17] Along with the executive committee, following standing committees are working- the Gospel work, Christian education, finance committee, Managing body and Appeal board and so on.

[18] Constitution and By-laws of IELC-TS, Article 9 C, 10 G.

[19] Ibid, Article 9A.

[20] Constitution and By-laws of IELC-TS, Section 3.

[21] First TDS president was D. Vedamonikom. He served as the president of TDS for 14 years in different terms. The pastors from Luthergiri, Paul Titus and K. Manuel also served as the presidents. Following them J. Yovas, P.G. Kunju Kunju, B. Wilson, M. Soosappan, D.S. Simpson, Y. Sukumaran, K. Stephanose, V. Jeevaraj and M. Robinson served as the presidents of TDS in different terms.

convention minutes of 1960 said: "it was evident from the reports that by the grace of God, gospel work is progressing among us."[22] In 1960, TDS had a growth of about 1000 new members.[23] But in the following years, i.e., from 1960-1967, one can see a decrease in number from 15677 to 14631 in 1967.[24] In 1966, after 10 years of the formation of TDS, its President reported that the TDS did not show much progress both in growth and self support.[25] But with the local resources, Synod was able to begin a new mission field at Gundlupet.[26] According to statistical record the TDS lost 4147 members during 1958-1966. "Although, 5,525 members were got into membership through baptism in seven years, 4,147 were lost during the same period, for every five person added, 4 persons were lost. The Gospel Work Committee (GWC) urged to take steps to discover the cause for these loses and take measures to better conserve membership. It will help know how many persons were excommunicated, how many reverted to Hinduism, how many joined other churches for marriage purposes, and how many transferred to other churches, etc."[27] The 12th TDS convention in 1967 urged to increase at least 4% of the membership every year through the conversions[28] in order to achieve the full support[29] within the next 10 years. But the 1970 data did not show any statistical growth in TDS.[30] According to the annual convention report of 1972, after the completion of 16 years of formation, the TDS included 7 *Pradesikoms*[31] (Circles) which were divided into 48 Pastorates. It had 188 congregations with 35 pastors and 30 catechists and helpers. The total baptized membership of TDS was 17,248 and the communicant members were 5812.[32] Up to 1974, the same number continued.[33] But in 1968, again there was a steady growth in the

[22] TX 60:07, 1960, 5th TDS Convention Minutes, 1960, 5.

[23] *Christiani* 52/11, (November, 1976), 38.

[24] For an analysis of 10 year growth of TDS, see, *Christiani*, 48/9, (August, 1967), 187-191, Editorial, *Christiani*, 49/11, (November, 1968), 287-290.

[25] Letter from General Secretary B.H. Jackayya regarding 5% subsidy cut from every year by Home Board, *Christiani*, 34/5 (May, 1958): 104.

[26] D. Vedamanikom, President's Report in 11th TDS Convention Minutes, 1966, 1-15.

[27] GWC 66:18, 50th TX Minutes, 1966, 23.

[28] 12th TDS Convention Minutes, 1967, 11. TX, 67:106 56th TDS-EC minutes, 1967, 5.

[29] Letter from General Secretary B.H. Jackayya, regarding 5% subsidy cut from every year by Home Board, *Christiani* 34/5, May 1958, 104; *Christiani* 34/ 9 Sept. 1958, 196-7.

[30] *Christiani*, 52/11, (November, 1976): 39.

[31] The seven *pradesikoms* were Alleppey, (1928), Trivandrum (1918), Ponvila (1924) Luthergiri (1911), Balaramapuram (1911), Nilamel (1926), Wynad (1946). The year in the brackets indicates the year of work started.

[32] T.D.S. 17th Convention Minutes, 1972, 3.

[33] In 1957, TDS had 137 congregations where as in 1974 it had come down to 126. That means within the 17 years TDS had lost 11 churches. The main reasons for this decrease were the following; Firstly, some had joined other Christian Denominations for economic help. Secondly, some Lutherans had left Kerala with their families in search of jobs in other States. Thirdly, during

churches of TDS up to 1976. Many new fields were opened up and many new churches were established during this period.[34] The Gospel Work Committee Convenor D. Vedamanikom reported in the 16th TDS convention that there were 9 new gospel work centres at Trivandrum.[35] And the same year Ponvila Circle President S. Ebenezer reported another six more centres in Ponvila.[36] As a result the number of membership increased very much. Many court cases, which were filed against the Church authorities by individuals ended. Many new Concordia Seminary Graduates were ordained. Lay ministers worked as church planters and many new congregations were organized. There was also a great movement among women under the leadership of Missionaries like Rose M. Ziemkie and her co-workers. Youth work and work among the Lutheran College Students was also started in TDS under the eminent leadership of Paul Pollex and A.R. Victor Raj. From the first convention onwards, there were lot of planning and discussions in connection with the expansions of evangelical work. But there were be proper committed ministers and lay people to implement these resolutions. The convention spent a lot of time and energy for the business sections and to take resolutions over the petitions received. There were not much record about the planned action plans for the proper evangelistic work. In 1962, IELC started its own mission field in Gundlupet, a Kannada-speaking (Hindu) area in Mysore with an IELC Malayali pastor P.K. Parameswaran as the missionary personal supported fully by indigenous funds.[37] TDS introduced in 1963, the pastorate system as a shortcut to lead the synod towards the self support system.[38] Before that there was a separate worker for each congregation. But later on, a pastorate, which is a group of congregations, came under one pastor which gradually led to inadequate pastoral care. Nurture and evangelism went beyond the limits of the local pastor. This can be viewed as the failure of Synod authorities which then failed to acknowledge. Because the mission and the factors which lead to the very life of the church is important than the administration.

After 50 years of TDS formation, the Synod lost its geographical boundary beyond the Nilamel Circle. Malabar and Muslim Mission, Gundlupet Mission,

---

this period a few got converted to Hinduism in order to get employment in the Government institutions. Fin Lutherans in Kerala come under the Forward Class people's list and there by denied the Government reservations even though they originally belonged to the Backward, SC and ST class people's list.Finally, there was also a rise in the death rate compared to other years due to contagious diseases like Cholera and Small –Pox and so on. For more discussion on these see D.V. Bernard. *op.cit.*, 31.

[34] President's report, 14th TDS Convention, 1969, 1.

[35] Kurikilmugal, Poojappura, Medical college, Karamana, Chanappara, Choyiakkodu, Maruthoorvattom, Kulathoor and Kollakonam were the 9 centers. 16th TDS Convention Report, 1971, 39-40.

[36] S. Ebenezer, Circle President's Report, Ponvila, 1971.

[37] Minutes of the 4th Central Convention of IELC, Nagercoil, 24-25 February, 1964, 18.

[38] *Christiani* 52/11 (November, 1976), 43.

Alleppey circle were lost from the map of Trivandrum Synod. The future of the Nilamel circle also was not promising. Administrative structure of the Synod demanded considerable amount of time of pastors taking them away from their parish assignments. The administrative leadership of the Synod and circles were not full time responsibilities, but they had the responsibility of local pastorate too. Hence, administration became a burden and a hindrance.

4.2.4. Malabar and Muslim Mission

The mission sent M.N. Paul[39] to Malabar field in 1946.[40] A small shed was built at Mangavayal and he worked among the Kurumars and the Paniyars which led to the formation of a small congregation and a school. In May 1946 M. Nallathampy was sent there to help him. In October 1949, Missionary M.J. Lutz got settled in Meenangadi. Very soon churches were established in Kalpatta, Meenangadi, Kurumbala, Sultan Bathery, Andoor, Moolankavu, and Kaniyampara. Reading rooms were opened in many places.[41] When M.J. Lutz left on furlough, A.J. Beahner, H.E. Heinlein and W. May went to the Malabar mission field. In 1957, new stations were opened in Chulliyodu, Kuttikulam, Manandavadi and Chittalayam. In 1952, missionary Griesse opened new station in Cheruplassery and Sreekrishnapuram.[42] In 1966, P.T. Schirmer took charge of the Wynad churches.

The work had started at Calicut, Malappuram, Wandoor and Wynad in the 1950s.[43] Rev. H.J. Otten[44] started his mission at Wandoor 48 miles away

---

[39] M.N. Paul worked at Venkattakuzhi, Nilamel, Madavoor, and Puliyoorkonam in his early days. On March 1951 he was sent to Kalpatta. He served as the Secretary- Convenor and President of Malabar circle. His wife Jessy was a member of Kanacodu Lutheran Church. She died in her 35th years of age due to a special kind of fever on 24 December 1951. She was buried at Mangavayal mission compound by M.M. Yohannan. They had 6 children and the elder son Stephenson Paul became the Secretary of TDS in 1966. M.N. Paul died on 14th January 1987.

[40] D.V. Bernard, *A Historical Study of the Origin and Growth of the Lutheran Church in Kerala up to Present Time* (Unpublished B D thesis, UTC; Bangalore, 1974), 27.

[41] The reading room in TDS was Chithalayam, Andoor, Cherplassery, Sreekrishnapuram, Peral, Kattakada, and Trivandrum.

[42] D.V. Bernard, A Historical study of the origin and growth of the Lutheran Church in Kerala up to present time, Unpublished B.D. thesis, UTC; Bangalore, 1074), 27.

[43] Wandoor, Wynad & Malappuram Gospel Work Report in 2nd TDS Convention Minutes, 14-18 October 1957, 12-15.

[44] Rev. Henry J. Otten was born on 23 June 1924 at Davenport of Iowa District, USA. By the influence of his father Henry J. Otten decided to submit his life for the full time ministry in 1938. He joined Concordia Seminary, St Louis for the ministerial training in 1943. He was very much influenced by the Islam religion and so he studied Arabic with the aim to become a missionary among the Muslims. He mastered in Islamic studies. He married Mary Esther on 26 June 1949. On 3 May 1950 he arrived at Trivandrum with his family as a MELIM missionary. On October 1951 he reached Wandoor and started his mission with a reading room. On 3 April 1952 He started the hospital- Karunalaya (house of mercy) at Wandoor. From there he expanded his service to nearby

from Calicut. He reached at Wandoor in October 1951 and started a reading room in November. He started a hospital at Wandoor – Karunalaya – in April 1952. Following that in the same year, he began a dispensary at Pandikkadu and Christian Welfare Centre at Malappuram. The main focus of the mission there was the mission among the Muslims.[45] The nursery schools in these places helped very much in proclaiming the Gospel to the children and women. The reading room in these places also played an important role in spreading the gospel to the Muslims. A Bible Correspondence Course (BCC) was also started for the Muslims and many attended this course.[46] Ronald E. Miller (1953-1977) who reached here in 1953 expanded the mission towards Wynad about 70 miles far from Malappuram. The earlier native workers include M N Paul, D. Joseph, K. Alexander, M. Abisai, L. Lazer, Nallathampi, M.M. Yohannan, Tennyson, P. Chellayyan, G. Viswanathan, B. Francis,[47] P.G. Henry and P. Madusoodananan, worked there as the pastors including a lot of catechists and evangelists. R.E. Miller and H.J. Otten were the remarkable missionaries. There were constant requests from the Malabar circle to separate them from TDS and to be included in IELC"s Mission Board.[48]As per the recommendation of Trivandrum Synod Executive (TX) the Church Council of IELC decided to put Malabar circle under the IELC-BM from 1974 October.[49] Hence, the works in Malabar area does not form part of TDS.

4.2.5. Tensions of the Young Church

The members of the young Church came from the most backward communities of the then Kerala Society, which is a mixture of many caste groups. On those days the high caste Hindus or Muslims held positions of economic, social and cultural

villages. On August 1971 Otten family moved to Calicut. There he started the House of Hope on 17 July, 1976 as a refuge to the Christian converts from Islam. The future pastors K.K. Alavi and P. P Alavi the Christian converts from Islam are the visible witness of his mission. In 1979 he was stationed at Meenangadi. While attending a meeting at Madras on 22 February, 1985 he died and was buried at Wandoor Karunalaya hospital compound. M.P. Prem Kumar, *Kadampakalkkappuram* (Malayalam) (Beyond Boundaries). Calicut: UESI, 2005.

[45] The Malabar mission was also known as Malabar Muslim Mission. The Muslim mission was centred on four fields - Calicut, Malappuram, Wandoor and Nilamel, under the supervision of four pastors who were helped by two missionaries, R. E. Miller and H. J. Otten. Henry J. Otten, Muslim work Associate, *Keralathile Musleemngalude idaile pravarthana report (The work report among the Muslims in Kerala), 1971.*

[46] TDS 16th Convention Minutes, 1971, 13-16.

[47] The work of B. Francis was appreciated by J.C. Dev, *Christhava Sabha Erupathu noottandukaliloode* (The Christian Church through Twenty Centuries) (Pathanamthitta: GLS, 2003), 560.

[48] Malabar Circle Resolution, 13 July 1971, Letter from TDS President to Secretary, Malabar Circle, 19 August 1971; Letter from P.K. George, Secretary Malabar Circle to TDS President, 30 Aug 1971; Open letter from M N Paul, Secretary Convener, Malabar Circle 7/12/ 1961.

[49] TC 71:9; TX 72:140, TX 73: 136, 19th TDS Convention Work Report, 1974, 45.

domination. Thus the leaders and the pastors of the congregations faced challenges of remarkable proportions.[50] They were not secure in their own identity nor they were very clear on the nature and extent of the mission entrusted before them. Yet they were supposed to lead God's people forward. Under these circumstances the tension between anxiety and self-protection, on the one hand, and use of all resources to equip every member of mission, on the other, was literally crucial. The 5th G.M.C met at Kodaikkanal had rightly identified three areas of priority in developing the national church to full responsibility. They were: equip the IELC for its mission; equip IELC for economic resources and equip the IELC for national leadership.[51] Pastors had worked under a variety of difficult situations. Earlier their salaries had come regularly from the mission. Now to provide the basic conveniences of life they were forced to look to the congregations. People were not able to support their pastors when they themselves were on the edge of starvation. The challenge of the lack of able national leadership required the task of building organizationally and institutionally of the young church which consisted of multiple castes which need to be noted. Luther W. Meinzen notes that in 1958, not one national pastor had received theological education to the level of Bachelor of Divinity degree.[52] This does not mean that the national pastors at that time lacked intelligence, commitment and zeal for gospel. Nor does it imply that the national leadership feared to take up the work. But it only suggests that the number of national leaders who had the kind of leadership and administrative experience and exposure which was required for the task ahead was few. Therefore the IELC general secretary B.H. Jackkayya declared: "the most urgent need for the future is the need of intellectually and spiritually qualified leaders to build the church."[53] Court cases against the Synod were begun and the proposed 1963 convention did not held due to court injunction.[54]

5% of annual cut from foreign subsidy towards the self sufficiency was another challenge for a younger Church consisting of economically poor membership.[55] Statistics shows the attitude towards giving were very negative in those days in

---

[50] Letter from General Secretary B. H. Jackayya, "IELC and LCMS are no more in mother and daughter relationship but entering in to sister relationship. We must think that, how will we survive if LCMS will stop subsidy after 20 years?" This was a serious discussion throughout IELC. *Christiani,* 34/ 9 (Sept. 1958), 196-7.

[51] Minutes of the 5th General Missionary Conference, IELC, Kodaikkanal, 18-20 April 1968, 18.

[52] L.W. Meinzen, *A Church in Mission* (Vaniyambadi: Concordia Press, 1981), 113.

[53] 3rd IELC General Convention Minutes, Ambur, 10-12 January, 1963, 8.

[54] 1963 Synod convention was declared to convene on 26 & 27 November. But One Podykutty got a stay order against the convention. *Christiani*, 30/12 (December, 1963): 226.

[55] Minutes of 1st TDS convention, 8; 2nd IELC-GC Minutes, 3; report of the 5th MELIM Conference, 20. Letter from B.H. Jackayya regarding 5% subsidy cut from every year by Home Board, *Christiani,* 34/5 (May, 1958), 104.

Trivandrum Synod compared to other Synods.[56] Administrative positions in the Synod were not a full time job. Along with one or more congregational work the Circle/ Synod authorities were supposed to carry out their administrative responsibilities and other leadership positions. This becomes visibly a difficult career, where one is unable to give full attention to either of the jobs which then causes tensions, frictions and incompetence.

4.2.6. Steps to Face the Challenges

In 1963, IELC appointed a Planning Commission to take up a scientific study of issues.[57] The purpose of this study was to guide and encourage IELC, all its congregations and committees to carefully examine the purpose for which God had called them and to plan carefully the various efforts which were necessary to fulfil their mission. The commission submitted its report in 1966.[58] Planning Commission's 320 page report covered almost all aspects of church life. This was a systematic study and assessment of the IELC with a series of practical recommendations addressing each of the respective challenges. Some of the concerns addressed were worship, stewardship, *diakonia* ministries like schools and hospitals, issues of socio-economic development of the poor and the marginalized in the Church, Church organization and administration, financial and social security to the workers, etc.[59] But unfortunately this valuable study report was ignored by the succeeding administrators including the later IELC President G. Thomas Edward who was one among in the Planning Commission.

The IELC constitution revision committee[60] proposed two major revisions. One was to reduce the power of the Synod and to develop Church life more in circle areas by providing more attention to the congregations and pastorates. Another one was to reverse the clergy-laity proportion in administration by reducing the clergy participation in administration. Both of this decentralization of power proposals were not carried out, may be because of the fear of loss of prestige and tedious nature of the authority of the clergy.

---

[56] J. Victor, "*Kodukkunnathil nam Valaruka*" (Let us grow in giving), *Christiani*, 52/11 (November, 1976): 2.

[57] V. Joseph (Harvipatti), G. Thomas Edward (Madras), Missionary Ronald E. Miller (Malappuram) were the members of the Planning Commission.

[58] Ronald E. Miller, G. Thomas Edward, and V. Joseph, *The Report of the Planning Commission of the India Evangelical Lutheran Church* (Nagercoil; IELC, 1966).

[59] For more discussion on this, *The Report of the Planning Commission of the India Evangelical Lutheran Church.*

[60] Minutes of 6th IELC- GC, Bangalore, 25-27 April. 1968, 10. The amendment process continued through the 1970 convention, the appointment of a special Constitution Continuation Committee in 1971 and the IELC Constitution Convention in 1974. Report of the Special IELC Constitution Convention (Nagercoil: IELC, 1974).

4.3. Schools and Lutheran Co-Operate Management

From the beginning itself, education received a prominent place in the MELIM program. In some instances schools were established for bringing the Gospel to certain communities. In other areas schools were an outgrowth of the already established congregations. In 1930, there were 42 schools including one Training School and two Boarding Schools. In 1954, the total number rose to 52. But in 1957, it was got to 29 with 4469 pupils.[61] Many schools were closed down due to lack of students. The memorials submitted in the 6th TDS convention, 1961, by two Missionaries Robert M. Zorn and Elmer E. Gresse gave the clear picture of the foul plays of the then General Manager of Lutheran Schools and his associates.[62] Instead of taking the corrective measures, the authorities tried to pass the resolutions against these missionaries and even send them out from the country using unchristian means.[63]

The poor management and maladministration was a continuous process in TS.[64] The only teacher training school and two boarding were closed down.[65] Another reason was the coming up of government schools. Many students and teachers left the mission schools and joined in the government schools.[66] Lutheran College Project at Peroorkada, Craft Training Centre at Luthergiri Nursing Training Course at Wandoor continued as a dream.[67] The 14th TDS convention discussed at length to upgrade Lutheran schools, to re-start the Teacher Training School, and institute a college in TDS area.[68] In the early days, LELC through Synod gave educational helps and loans for the college and technical studies.[69] When the loan repayment was not properly maintained IELC stopped this system. Then they introduced the Scholarship system according to the merit for the deserving candidates.

School administration in TDS was carried out by the Lutheran Corporate Manager through the Managing Body under TX. The IELC, as the proprietary

---

[61] 2nd TDS Convention Minutes, 14-18 October 1957, 4. But in 1971 it decreased down to 24.

[62] See the 1-9 Memorials presented to the 6th TDS General Conventions by R.M. Zorn and E.E. Gresse, 6 September 1961.

[63] See the memorial submitted to the 6th TDS General Convention by Themotheos of Kazhakutom, 1961.

[64] 8th TDS Convention Minutes, TSC, 63:13, 1963, 5-6.

[65] TTC School was started in 1952 and closed in 1958.

[66] According to present statistics, there are 24 schools in TDS which include 2 High School, one higher secondary School, 5 upper primary schools and 16 Lower primary schools, with nearly 8000 students and 200 teachers.

[67] TEC 66:9, 51 Trivandrum District Executive Minutes, 1966, 46; TX 69:36, 64th TDS –EC Minutes, 1969, 7.

[68] TDS 14th Convention Working Report, 1969, 4.

[69] For a sample list of the recipients see, 102nd Trivandrum Synod Executive Minutes, 18-19, July 1976, 12-24.

body is the educational agency and in Kerala this agency is represented by its member Synod, the TDS.[70] The Constitution of Lutheran schools was approved by the DPI by virtue of rule 2 of chapter III K.E.R.[71] The objects of the Corporate Management of Schools of the IELC-TDS are 1) to promote the Lutheran spiritual and secular education of the Lutheran Students, 2) to promote a high moral and secular education for all other students and 3) to train all students for responsible citizenship and service. During the early days, the Synod Presidents served also as the General Manager.[72] As per the Constitution the Manager is responsible to act according to the decisions of the Managing Body.[73]

Maladministration of TDS leadership, favouritism and unawareness of the Managers,[74] punishment transfers, court cases, bribery for the appointment in schools were very common in those days[75] which eventually caused the destruction of Educational Institutions. The failures of the school administration were confessed in several reports.[76] The appointment of P.D. Martin as the Headmaster of Concordia High School Peroorkada by overlooking Sukumaran Devadas[77] became a serious problem for the church for some years. The sub-committee appointed by the TDC with Missionary M.H. Grum as the convenor proposed to appoint Sukumaran Devadas as the Headmaster. Even after repeated orders

---

[70] Constitution and Bye-Laws of the Corporate management of Schools of IELC-TDS, 111 Educational Agency, 1.

[71] Proceedings of the Regional DPI, Trivandrum, Order no. K.Dis. 9082/63/G4; Letter from the Manager of Lutheran Schools to DPI, Thiruvananthapuram, 7/4/75; order no. G4-6656 /72/ R. Dis., 16/5/1975.

[72] TX 59/09, 2nd TDS Convention Minutes, 1957, 4.

[73] The duties of the Manager and the rights of the Managing body, see Constitution and Bye-laws of the Corporate Management Schools, *op.cit.*, 4-7.

[74] See the letter from Larry Meinzen to B.H. Jackayya, R.M. Zorn and H.J. Otten, 17/10/1961; Letter from P.V. David Kolath to B.H. Jackkayya, 5/10/61; E.A. Griesse, Special Financial Review meeting, TDS, 19/August, 1961, 6 page typed report; Letter from A. Sainudheen to J.Ezekiel, General Secretary of IELC with copies to Missionaries Keopke and H.M. Zorn, 20/7/1964; Open letter from K. Rajayyan, Convener, Lutheran Action Group, 18/11/1993.

[75] Letter from D. Manasseh to B.H. Jackayya, 29/9/61; Letter from R.M. Zorn to D. Vedamanickom11/10/1961; Open letter from J. Markose on 20/10/1961; The memorials against the Corporate Manager in 1969 TDS convention; Letter from AEO Chadayamangalam to the General Manager Lutheran Schools, The TDS school Management problem- for immediate action, 2 page report, Confidential file, Concordia Seminary Archives, Nagercoil.; Letter from B.H. Jackkayya, the IELC General Secretary to D. Vedamanokom, President, TDS 6 & 11 Nov. 1961; Letter from M. Yohannan to B.H. Jackkayya, 13/11/1961; Letter from N. Johnthampi to B.H. Jackkayya on 13/11/1961; Letter from IELC General Secretary, B.H. Jackkayya, to All workers of TDS, 27/11/1961.

[76] 13th TDS Convention Reports, 1968,33;The convention memorials against Corporate manager in 14th TDS convention, 1969; 14th TDS Convention Reports, 1971, 43; 18th TDS Convention Reports 1973, 51.

[77] TX 60/27; IX 60/36.

from the Government[78] and rejection of appeal from the General Manager and issued the directions to uphold the DPI's order[79] the then Manager was very much adamant for his communal preference. Finally, the DPI had warned the General Manager that steps will be taken against him if the rules are not implemented.[80] IELC, the apex body of TS repeatedly pointed out the need of implementation of the departmental orders otherwise it would be harmful to the interest of the church and for the good relationship with the Department.[81] It is also noteworthy that the General Manager who was also holding the position of the President of the Synod, which was the highest post in Synod level, had the responsibility of seeing that all things are done decently and order and should be a model for others. At last, by the court direction he was forced to revert P.D. Martin and appoint Sukumaran Devadas as the Headmaster of CLHS, Perurkada.[82] However, the Deeper Life Conferences for Lutheran teachers conducted by TDS became a turning point in the history of school administration. In one letter by J. Victor, the ex- GT and ex-Headmaster of Concordia High School states, "God has turned our schools over to the hands of unprincipled people who do not know what Christian education means. After making appointments and transfers they do not know whether there is anything else to do. Within another five years almost all the Headmasters of the TS schools will be non Lutherans. The Church authorities will have nothing to do there."[83] D. Appukuttan writes: "In the field of education, great success was achieved because the real purpose was served and fulfilled. It goes without saying that schools are great avenues of evangelism. For example, the Concordia Lutheran High School at Perurkada was a mini seminary in the past. Bible lessons were taught for two hours, from 8-10 in the morning every day. The advantage and benefits of the mission schools were beyond description in words and we should be ever grateful to the missionaries who did a lot to uplift the most downtrodden people."[84]

The following pastors and laymen served chronologically as the managers of the Lutheran Corporate Management over the years: D. Vedamanikom (Pastor), Paul Titus (Pastor), R.T. Keopke (missionary), A. Enose (Pastor), K.K. Joseph (Pastor), D. John Hus (Pastor)[85] K. Bhaskaran (Laymen), J. Rajayyan (Layman),

---

[78] DPI'S orders of 7/10/1958; 29/9/59; 5/10/59;25/4/59; 23/6/1960; Government order 25/4/1960; DEO's order 17/8/1960; 27/8/1960.

[79] DPI's order no. 56985/ A3/60/Edn. 27/1/1961.

[80] DPI"s order no. D2-137962/60 dated & /4/1961.

[81] IX 60/187; 60/248; 61/79; 61/160.

[82] Sukumaran Devadas (15 July 1916 - 6 September 2001) took over the charge 22 December 1962 and served until 1976. Sukumaran Devadas wrote his own life history – "On Myself".

[83] Letter from J. Victor to P. Joshua Siromony, 4 page typed document, 15/9/1992.

[84] Letter from D. Appukuttan to the researcher, 22 May 2012, 2.

[85] In his term as school manager D. John Hus appointed V. Jeevaraj as the correspondent to the Tamil schools under TDS. TX 80:65, 14.1.1980 and TX 80:73 12/8/1080 shows that there were

I. Titus (Pastor), J. Johnson[86] (Laymen), Y. Sukumaran (Pastor), C.H. Alfred (Pastor), M. Robinson (Pastor)[87] and R. Vijayakumar (Pastor).[88] Out of the 14 managers, 11 were ordained ministers of IELC. Even though, the schools administrations were mostly done by the synod's pastors, one cannot find a qualitative change and promising progress in this ministry. Court cases for and against the Managers approval, dispute over appointment and seniority of the teachers, litigation against the punishment transfers and bribery for appointment were very common in the past. Ernakulum High Court observes, "The dispute regarding management of Lutheran School is apparently a never ending one. The unfortunate victims are the teachers."[89]

Since the Members of the Church could not solve their problems within themselves, as per the Ernakulum High court directions, the government took over the administration of all Lutheran schools in Kerala.[90] This Order was challenged before the High Court by the Church and the High Court set aside the Govt. Order (G.O) and sent back the case to government for further consideration. This time by producing false documents and by wrong influence Simon Alexander a non Lutheran and even a non Christian was able to get a G.O in favour of him as the Manager of Lutheran Schools in Kerala from 28/11/2000.[91] The unending dispute among the Lutherans caused to skip the institutions from their hands.[92] This order was challenged before the High Court of Ernakulum and the court set aside the G.O and directed to pass further orders.[93] Later, as a conciliation candidate R. Vijayakumar was appointed and got approval as manager in 2004.[94]

---

no Specific TDS decision for this appointment. D. John Hus's term was from 15 January, 1981 to 1984.

[86] For the approval of the reappointment of S. Johnson see, General Education (F) department G.O. (Rt) No. 241/94 /G.Edn. Trivandrum, 19/1/1994; Proceedings No. ET3-3958 /89/ l. Dis. / DPI, 5/6/1989; proceedings No. ET3-35930/91, 16/10.1991; proceedings No. ET-119399/91/ DPI, 23/6/1992; Revision petition from S. Johnson, 5/7/1992.

[87] M. Robinson was appointed as Manager, with effect from 3/7/1975. His appointment was approved by DPI as per order no. ET/ 44008/95/ K.Dis., 6/2/96 for 3 years. Kerala high Court ordered that the continuance of Robinson as manager beyond 27/11/2000 as illegal.

[88] TX 7/04, 11/5/2004, Letter from J. Yovel, Secretary, TS to DPI, 12/5/2004.

[89] Kerala High Court judgement, Asha Gregarious Vs State of Kerala & others, WP (C) 5878/05 Y 29 March 2006, 1.

[90] B4-33320/2002 Education/DPI/Trivandrum, 1/1/2003; Kerala High Court judgement on 4/2/02, O.P. No. 3590/02; GO (RT)no. 3959/2/DPI, 12/11/2002; Order from District judge S9/67792/2002, 7/12/2002.

[91] G.O. (Rt) No. 4794/03/G. Edn. 21/11/2003; GO. (Rt) No. 3959/02/G. Edn. 12/11/2003; Common judgement dated 22/1/2003 in OP. Nos. 37000/02 and 37712/02.

[92] See for more discussion, D. Christudas, *Aazhangalile Anugrahathinte Uravakal (Source of blessings from the Depths),* (Thiruvalla: CSS, 2007), 93-98.

[93] Judgment by High Court of Ernakulum in W.P.(C)37459 of 2003, in 21/5/2004.

[94] TX 7/04, 11/5/2004, Letter from J. Yovel, Secretary, TS to DPI, 12/5/2004.

After his three year term, the dispute was raised again and, now three people namely, Robinson David, C.H. Alfred and Mathew Soosappan are claiming the Managership of Lutheran School Management and the dispute is pending with courts.

4.4. Ministerial Developments

During this formative period, the Lutheran Church in Kerala had some advancement in the areas of its inner life and growth. Following are the discussions about the major ministerial advancement of TDS through various units.

4.4.1. Spiritual Growth

The inner life and the inside growth of the Church determines its strength and future. The 50th Trivandrum Synod Executive (TX) in 1966 made some programs for raising the spiritual state of congregations. "The spiritual state is declining at present because neither the congregations nor the gospel workers have the impulsion on the congregational works .... If a gospel worker does not care about these and works as he likes he can be given compulsory pension and his service can be terminated. It is also necessary to put an end to the habit of gospel workers seeking their own convenience and live in other places than residing in the mission houses near the churches. If congregation does not obey instructions it may lose its membership in the synod."[95] But the records keep silent of the details of a further move. But the ministries among children, youth, college students, teachers, laymen, and women were the efforts of TDS for the spiritual growth of its members. A lot of Christian literature also were prepared and published among the Lutherans in Kerala for their spiritual growth. Pastors are the backbones of the Synod for its spiritual growth and mission. Almost all the pastors of TS were trained at Concordia Seminary Nagercoil. At the first phase, they got seminary diploma and after the affiliation of Seminary with Serampore they were awarded the L.Th. From 1970 onwards, the graduates received B.Th. Degree. Now the Seminary is upgraded to the BD level. In the near future the basic academic qualification of a pastor will be BD. A lot of pastors have already upgraded their theological education to BD or higher levels on their own. They are competent and capable of producing theological literature and engaging in dialogue with other Christians and people of other faiths which are fundamental for making a Lutheran contribution in the Indian context and opportunity to do so must be encouraged.[96]

4.4.2. Children's Ministry

Sunday school and Vacation Bible School (VBS) are the main spiritual movements for children. The TDS was very much aware of the beginning about the need

[95] GWC 66:15, 50th TX Minutes, 1966, 19.

[96] Report on Victor Raj's India Visit, 21 May to 4 June, 2012, 2.

of proper nurture among children for Christian growth.[97] They had a common syllabus and teaching materials / aids including the flannel graph ministry for children ministry. In 1960, Larry E. Meinzen arrived in TDS as a full time educational missionary. He started the VBS ministry. K.K. Joseph tried his level best to revive the Sunday school ministry in TDS. In the 1970's Rose M. Zeimke took over the charge of VBS. VBS during summer holidays with Lutheran syllabus and text books continued till the last five decades. One of the main features of the VBS is that many non-Christian students participated in large numbers. This can be seen in the VBS reports.[98] *Yuvanilayam* and the youth work team proposed a project to TDS to revive the Sunday school ministry in TS. It was approved by TX on 18th July 1976. TX appointed a committee to prepare common Sunday school text book for the use of all congregations' .The youth workers' project of home Sunday school got much attention in almost all active Lutheran congregations in Kerala. This was an effort to reach the non Christian families through children.[99] Systematic Sunday School Teachers' Refresher Courses, student's rallies, common Sunday school examinations, festivals and celebration of world Sunday School Day are the notable things related to it. *Christiani* magazine published the Sunday school lessons regularly as a special supplement.[100] In the later years, the importance and vitality of the ministry among children were lost.

4.4.3. Literature Service

The Gospel witness through Literature was a very outstanding ministry of Lutherans in Kerala from the very beginning. Before opening a new station for gospel work, they started reading rooms wherever possible. The Bible Correspondence Course (BCC) was another remarkable program. They produced the books and literatures for worship, nurture, stewardship and evangelism. Even after the formation of the Synod, the literature ministry continued in a systematic way during the formative years. A lot of new publications of Christian books had come out from the Lutherans in Kerala. There was a resolution to start a library in each congregation and some of the local churches have an open library in their compounds. Lutheran Church in Kerala was very much aware of the importance of literature for Christian nurture and they tried to produce, translate and publish it for the use of their members.[101] They also produced a lot of

[97] 2nd TDS Convention Minutes, 1957, 14.

[98] Rose M. Ziemke, VBS Report, 1972, 17th TDS Convention Work Report, 1972, 55-59. The total student participants were 2783. Out of them, 875 were Hindus, 180 Muslims and 1055 from various Christian denominations.

[99] *Christiani* 52/11, (November, 1976), 47.

[100] The main contributors were Rev. A. Enose and Rev. Gifton E. Joshua.

[101] *Vazhiyum Velichavum* (The way and Light, K. Lukose & L.E. Meinzen), *Cheviyullavan kelkatte (Hear those who have the ears,* A. Enose, *1957) Vedacharitram, (Bible History) Prarthananchali, The Prayer offerings)* Small Catechism, Bible Atlas, Medicine for Snake bite

literature for worship. The Lutheran hymnal were revised seven times during the years. For school purpose they published *Vidyalaya Keerthanangal*, (School songs) *Dhyana Manjusha (Meditations), Nompukala Dhyanangal (Lenten Devotions), Kastanubhava Charithram (Passion History),* Christmas-Reformation day-Easter worship orders, *Christhiya Ajenda* (Order of Services), *Prarthananjali (Prayers), Prasanga Kramangal (Sermon Notes),* Christmas- reformation question and answer were the major works related to the worship.

As we had seen earlier the IELC official Malayalam monthly *Christiani* (The Christian) started its publication in 1925 under the direct editorial leadership of MELIM and through national assistance. The monthly magazine *Christiani* had a new editorial board in 1957 with C.M. Jacob and Sukumaran Devadas. From May 1958 two missionaries namely, E.H. Heinlein and E.E. Greesi, were added to the editorial board.[102] Till December 1961, Sukumaran Devadas functioned as the chief editor. From 1963 January onwards, W. Frederic became the chief editor. In January1963, *Christiani* came under the direct leadership of IELC Secretary as IELC's official magazine, just like *Sathya Satchi*. The IELC Secretaries N.J. Ezekiel from Ambur and A. Enose of Trivandrum were the chief editors. Then for a short period J.C. Gamaliel was appointed as the Chief editor and K. Suseelan as the co-editor. From November 1972, K.M. Victor was the chief editor. The IELC literature board in its meeting in August 1974 at Gurukul campus handed over the charge of *Christiani* to a new team of youth. Gifton E. Joshua was the

---

(Pambu kadikku oushadam) Namukku Veendum Kanaam, (We will see again) Ella Mathavum Onnanoo? (Is all religions are same?), Sree Yesu (Mr. Jesus) W. Frederick) etc. are the few examples of publication in 1958. *Christiani*, 34/9 (September 1958), 215. The list of the works in 1959 continues as follows: *Lutheran Viswasa sweekarangal* (Lutheran Confessions - Theodore John Muller), *Karagraha Lehkanangal* (Prison Letters, E.E.Greesi) *Book of Concord* (K. Lukose), *Christheeya Valarchakku Oru Balapatam (A preliminary Text for Christian Growth* - L.E. Meinzen & K. Lukose*) Vedabhyasana Pravesika (Introduction to Bible Study- W. Frederick) Yakkob Lekhana Vyakyanam* (Epistle of James, commentary- A. Stelter), *Sisuvine Ariyan Padikkuka*, (Know how to understand the child-W Fredrick), *Bibilile vanithakal (Womens of the Bible), Walther Pandithanude Churungiya Jeevacharithram,(A small life history of Dr. Walther) Kudumbarathana – (Family worship*-F. Wheisburger) –*Vithuvithakkunnathu* - (Mark Gospel explanation). *Christiani*, 34/10 (October 1958): 239-40.

The other major books were: *Sabha Bhrasht* (Excommunication - H. Walther, 1960) *Prasanga Bhaga Kramam* (Sermon Text - H.M. Zorn, 1963), *Veda Charithra Pravesika* Introduction to Bible History - G.R. Stelter, 1964), *Karya Vicharakathwam* (Stewardship - 1965) *Oru Kristhiya Upadesa patanam* (A catechisam - H.M. Zorn 1971) *Kristhiya Aaradhana* (Christian Worship - W.L. Kretzmann, 1972), Swayam Paryapthatha (Self Support - R.E. Miller, 1972) *Daiva Rajyam* (Kingdom of God - K. M. Victor, 1973) *Veda Charithram* (Bible History - K.M. Suseelan, 1974) *Shtala Sabha Udyogastharkai (To the officers of the Local Church* - K. Suseelan, 1975), *Ningalude Chodyam Idanengi*l (If this is your Question - M.H. Findlay, 1976), *Nee pokumo* (Will you go? - R. E. Miller, 1976). This list shows that they were aware of the integral growth of their members with updated information.

[102] G.R. Stelter was a member of the editorial board from July 1954 to May 1958. Next editor was H.E. Heinlein. *Christiani*, 34/5 (May, 1958): 99.

chief editor and N.C. George and J. Paramananda Das, were the editors. T. Joy, Stanley Lawrence, and K. Suseelan served as the advisors. During this period, tremendous changes happened including the format, membership growth, and discussion of contemporary issues. A lot of new writers emerged. In 24-26 January 1976 *Christiani* celebrated its Golden Jubilee.[103] As a part of its celebrations, on 24th they conducted a Writers' Workshop, on 25th Lutherans in Kerala celebrated as the Literature Sunday[104] and 26th the Golden jubilee celebrations with a public meeting. There were criticisms also about the new format, its content and approaches.[105] There were clear differences of opinions and open quarrels between the editors and TDS administrators from 1977 onwards. The articles against the ruling groups widened the gap. The IELC Church Council, Board for Literature and TX took decisions against *Christiani*[106] including non-payment of bills, change of editor, and other issues, which finally stopped its publication.[107] In 1985, IELC Board for Literature (BL) again tried to revive *Christiani's* publication with a new editorial board. But it did not materialise.[108]

There were new efforts at the Synod level to publish news bulletins but that was short lived. IELC Bulletin,[109] *Lutheran Dharsanam*,[110] Bell,[111] Banner,[112] *Aradhana*[113] and the Lutheran[114] were some other experiments started by individuals and by like-minded people but only a few issues came out. Ponvila circle of TS are still preparing and publishing worship and nurture materials for their use. For the last fifteen years, an unofficial Malayalam monthly, *Lutheran Sabdhom* [115] a Malayalam monthly is published by a voluntary movement which is well received by not only the Lutherans but also by other Christian communities in Kerala. T. Joy was sent to Nasik for a special training to produce Christian literature. Lutherans in Kerala were able to produce a lot of writers like, *Dhosth,*[116]

---

[103] *Christiani*, 57/1 January 1976, the February issue of *Christiani* was published as Golden Jubilee Special, *Christiani*, 57/2 February, 1976.

[104] This was as per the TX decision dated 30 November 1975 in connection with the golden jubilee of *Christiani.*

[105] TX 39: 75, Aug, 1975, See *Christiani*, 54/3 (March, 1978).

[106] TX 77:95 August, 1977, TX 77:116, TX 77 :123; CC minutes 78;6; 78:81 Nov. 1978., 79:6 Feb. 1979, BL–IELC 81:13.

[107] The last issue of C*hristiani* was published on March, 1982.

[108] IELC BL, Minutes, 29, 30 November, 1985.

[109] It was published in 1985 B. Francis and Herbert Marshal was the editors.

[110] This was a publication by B. Gilbert.

[111] Bell is a news letter of Bethel Evangelism Fellowship, 2000.

[112] Sugathan Paul was the editor of Banner.

[113] This was published by the LCSA Trivandrum, 1988.

[114] By the Lutheran Pastors Fellowship of Trivandrum, 1993.

[115] First published in September 1998 and it continues.

[116] This was the pen name of Alleppey Gnanadas.

J.C. George,[117] N.C. George,[118] B. Gilbert,[119] Jaeson Abraham,[120] M.G. Louis Clement,[121] Sanandaraj brothers,[122] J. Christudas,[123] and so on.[124] It also needs to be pointed out here that all of them were very active in the Youth Work during the 70's. The literary contribution of Lutheran Christians of Kerala is much appreciable compared to other Christian mission agencies.[125]

4.4.4. Empowering Lay Leadership

Lay people are the important gift and partners of mission. The non-ordained evangelists, teachers and catechists were the main church planters of TDS. The Lutheran Laymen's League (LLL) was organised in TDS through the initiatives of J.C. Gamaliel, E. Nesan, K. Rajayyan and Silvanus on 1962. Lutheran Laymen's League functioned as an independent unit without any direct involvement from Synod authorities. They conducted very effective programs. The Lutheran Laymen's League unit at Ponvila was organised by D. James Raj, T. Joyson, and Jayson E Abraham.[126] A special Lay training course for both lay men and lay women were started in 1966 at Trivandrum. This was a two week residential course to equip lay people to help their pastor in his congregational work. Missionary E. H. Heinlein was in charge of this course. In 1967, a lay training course was conducted from 3 to 10 August at Perurkada. 24 candidates from 18 pastorates participated.[127] In 1969, another course was arranged at TDS hall from 7/4/69 to 18/4/69. The total trainees were 30; 24 men and 6 women. The study topics were Old Testament, Gospels, Epistles, Catechism, Worship, Homiletics, Liturgy and songs. Since it was proved that this course was very useful to the churches the convention decided to start new courses at the Alleppey and Malabar centres

---

[117] He was a son of a Lutheran pastor and a well known cinema script writer.

[118] N.C. George is a well recognized writer in Malayalam and published books and many articles. He served as the editor for *Christiani* and *Lutheran Sabdhom* for many Years.

[119] B. Gilbert is a son of Rev. Benjamin and a well received novelist.

[120] Son of Rev. A. Enose, and an Engineer by profession and widely known writer both in religious and secular fields.

[121] Son of Rev. Manasseh, and a short story writer and columnist.

[122] They were Sons of Rev D. Harris. John Sanandaraj became a famous novelist and columnist and Paul Sanandaraj become an Art Director in the cine field.

[123] J. Christudas is a recognized poet.

[124] TX 73: 123, 84th TDS-GC Minutes, April 1973, 14.

[125] For more discussion see, D. Christudas, *Akshara Sushrushayil Lutheran Christhavarude Sambhavanakal- Oru Avalokanam (Literary contributions of Kerala Lutheran Christians in Kerala- An Appraisal),* Paper presented on The Annual Seminar of Lutheran Voice at Perurkada Trivandrum on 24 November, 2011.

[126] *Yuva Sabdhom*, 1/2 December 1969, 22-24.

[127] 12th TDS convention Reports, 1967, 10-11., see also TX 67, 12, 54th TX committee minutes, 1967, 3.

too.[128] This training continued in the following years and it produced a lot of voluntary workers. Records indicate that there were efforts to equip the lay people for ministries. The lay training at Perurkada in 1972 introduced a new method for Bible study called "Eight Question Method."[129] Later it was stopped. As per the increasing demand of the Church, TDS failed to train and use the man/women power for building God's Kingdom. Walter Alexander observes: "*There are a good number of well educated and well placed members in the Lutheran church who could have been elected/ nominated for important positions in the Church. If those God fearing, conscientious, educated and well placed Lutherans with very strong moral and cultural backgrounds have been elected/ nominated at least in important positions such as in the Church Council/Mission Boards, etc., the fate of IELC would have been entirely different. On the contrary, party politics based on communal preference has been the regular practice. The present crisis and destruction of the IELC is basically due to this communal preference.*"[130] A church with a future vision should have a systematic effort to use and equip the lay people for effective mission.

4.4.5. Youth Work

Youth work in TDS was one of the most important and significant movements. 1946 onwards selected persons were appointed for the leadership in youth work. A. Enose was the first appointed youth secretary of TDS. The work was started in an organized way in 1952. A lot of youth league units were started at the congregational level. Records say that, from 1947 onwards youth Sundays came to be celebrated.[131] In later years, J.C. Gamaliel and Sukumaran Devadas were appointed as youth secretaries. The Lutheran College Students Association (LCSA) was started on 19 October 1952 in Trivandrum.[132] During the period 1958-59 LCSA became an effective organization.[133] Gresse formed a Lutheran College Students Choir. [134] LCSA provided future leaders to the Church.[135] TDS had taken various positive measures to co ordinate the youth work at local levels with the help of the circles.[136] Under the guidance of Lutheran Laymen's League, Ponvila, LCSA Ponvila unit was formed on 3 September 1968.[137] In 1969, Paul

---

[128] 14th TDS Convention Working Report, 1969, 8., TX 77/70 June, 1977, 3.

[129] J.P. Das, *Almenikalude Arangettam* (The Emergence of Laymen's), *Christiani*, Golden Jubilee Special 57/2 (February, 1976), 35.

[130] Letter from Walter Alexander Ph.D., to Issac Moon, President IELC, 29 August 1998, 3.

[131] *Christiani*, 52/11, (November, 1976): 9.

[132] *Yuva Sabdhom*, 1/5 (November, 1970), LCAS Suppliment, 3.

[133] *Christiani*, 52/11, (November, 1976): 52.

[134] *Christiani*, 39/12, (December, 1963): 229.

[135] Jaeson Abraham, Justus Enose, Susi Harris, Swamidas Abisai, D. James Raj, T. Joy are some of them. Interview with N.C. George, 15/7/2012.

[136] 2nd TDS Convention Minutes, 1957, 8, 10; 4th TDS Convention Minutes, 1959, 18.

[137] *Yuvasabdhom* 1/5 (November, 1970) Supplement, 10.

Pollex arrived and he renewed and expanded the youth work with new phases.[138] From that time onwards youth work was done under the Synod and it appointed youth worker. In 1971, A.R. Victor Raj was appointed as a full time Youth Worker in TDS who organized Lutheran Youth Leagues in most of the churches with the help of Paul Pollex. The main activities were Bible study, Evangelism, Group discussion on selected topics, Prayer Action groups, Youth Ashrams,[139] youth rallies,[140] *Nadaka Kalari* (Drama Group), book fare, publication and so on. They published magazines like *Yuva Sabdhom*, and youth Digest in order to edify the members, develop their talents and to spread the gospel.[141] It helped towards the emergence of a lot of notable writers and artists. They conducted regional Youth rallies which helped to raise up many future leaders and Pastors in TDS.[142] They also formed a Lutheran music Group called *Lutheran Arts Club* which staged throughout Kerala and which was well received.[143] The four watch words of TDS youth work were; Worship, Wisdom, Witness and Work.[144] The Youth worker reported in the 18th TDS conventions that the youth work team newly introduced a program, "A Bible Study group in every Church" and it was well received by the congregations.[145] Youth workers also conducted all Kerala Lutheran Youth Conventions[146] and retreats for strengthening the spiritual life of the Lutheran Youths.[147] The youth work team was able to organise the Lutheran youths from Wynad to Parassala under one umbrella. Paul Pollex started a youth centre at Perurkada namely *Yuva nilayam*[148] along with a library.[149] One of the remarkable things was that most of the expenses were collected from the Lutheran Youths and the youth participated in these functions paid registration fees which

---

[138] For the work assignment of Paul Pollex by TDS see, TX 68:110, 63rd TDS-EC Minutes, 1968, 4.

[139] For more details about the Youth Ashrams see, Youth Digest 2/5 (June, 1972): 54-55.

[140] *Christiani*, 55/9 (July, 1974): 126.

[141] For more details see, A.R Victor Raj, Youth Work Report- TDS, 5/10/1972.

[142] It is worth to mention that the youth work promoters of TDS like A Enose, J.C. Gamaliel, Sukumaran Devadas, A.R. Victor Raj, T. Joy, Giften E. Joshua, G.E. Abraham, J. Paramananda Das and so many others became leaders of the future church, Seminary, IELC and the people leaders in the Society.

[143] *Christiani* 56/9 (September, 1975), 8.

[144] Report by Paul Pollex, 6 Oct. 1973.

[145] Youth Work Report, 18th TDS Convention Minutes, 1973, 26-30.

[146] The first All Kerala Youth Convention was organized on 1971 and continued it up to 1977 regularly.

[147] Paul Pollex, Youth Work Report, 19th TDS Convention Minutes, 1974, 31-35.

[148] Later TDS gave this centre to KLVS as *Vanitha Nilayam at CLUPS compound Vattiyoorkavu Perurkada.*

[149] *Christiani*, 54/6 (July, 1973): 130; *Christiani*, 56/8 (August, 1975): 1.

was not common in those days among the Lutheran Christians.[150] A terrible and pre-planned attempt of a former TS Treasurer and his team to manhandle the youth leaders in 1977 distorted the youth ministry in TS.[151] After this incident, most of youth isolated themselves from the mainstream of the Church activities. The then TX resolved that youth work was dangerous to the Church and so dismissed the youth worker. Those who were against the youth work robbed *yuvanilayam* and closed it. The executive also punished the pastors and teachers who co operated with youth activities and the subsidy of some pastors were cut down severely. The youth department which was very strong and active at that time saw a decline and never saw its restoration to its former dynamism till date.

4.4.6. Lutheran Vanitha Samajam

In the early years work among the Lutheran women was co-ordinated by men. Later, trained women mainly, wives of Missionaries and pastors took over the leadership. Then the TDS felt the need of trained women to organize the work among the women in a systematic way. From 1957 onwards women's ministry in TDS was very active. Mrs. Stelter had organised women's organizations in most of the congregations in Trivandrum *Pradesikom*.[152] The vigour of organized mission can easily be found in their reports.[153] The 16th Synod convention recorded its gratitude to Mrs. Keopke for her eminent service among the Lutheran women.[154] The women work committee arranged '*Vanitha Sanghom* President's Institute' for the purpose of training and encouraging the leaders of ladies societies.[155] "A Bible in every home" project of women's league got much attention throughout the synod.[156] Miss. Rinke and Miss. Rose Zeimke were the full time women missionaries who served in TDS area.[157] The full time lady workers in those days were M. Snehappu, C.J. Soudamini, G. Elsi, K.M. Anlet, L. Joice. The work among Lutheran women was renamed as *Kerala Lutheran Vanitha Samajam* (KLVS) from October 1972. The central committee conducted the first All Kerala Lutheran Women convention at Perurkada in January 1973. The synod level women organization – *Kerala Lutheran Vanitha Samajam* – had an institute

---

150 *Christiani,* 55/79 (July, 1974): 124.

151 A detail of this issue is discussed under the title, 'the administrative stagnation'.

152 2nd TDS Convention Minutes, 14-18 October 1957, 9.

153 See 2nd TDS Convention Working Report, 1957, 30-33; 5th TDS Convention Minutes, 1970, 25.

154 16th TDS Convention Working Report, 1971, 41.

155 Rose M. Zeimke, argued about the need of local women leadership and the local *vanitha sanjam* should be re-organised as such the Walther league organization in LCMS. For the full version of the article see, *Sabhayile Vanitha pravarthana prasnam*, Christiani, 34/6 (June, 1958): 138-141.

156 Mrs. R.T. Keopke, Women's Work Committee Report, 17th TDS Convention, 1972, 35.

157 For more details of their work see, Rose Zeimke, " In India where Roses Bloom", Janice Kerper Brauer, (Ed.), A *Rainbow of Saris* (St. Louis: LWML, 1996), 83-112.

in Perurkada to teach women handicrafts such as knitting, sewing, basket making and so on. Record says KLVS had remarkable reports about their activities during the early periods.[158] The central *Vanitha Samajam* had a tailoring school at the *Vanitha Nilayam*, Perurkada.[159] Synod level women committee was formed by TDS in 1987.[160] At present, TDS has four theologically trained women as full time deaconesses.[161] They are commissioned as Deaconess in full time ministry. They visit the churches in the assigned area, organized the local women's fellowships called *Vanitha Sanghoms* and arrange the circle and synod level programs along with the KLVS.

4.5. Economic Development Programs

The members of the Lutheran congregations were from the lowest strata of the society. Therefore, projects were planned for the financial development of those people. 8 major pastorates and 15 congregations of Luthergiri circle were engaged in reed industry. Reed Industry was the one and only source of their livelihood. Through the formation of co operative societies this industry could develop. Therefore, IELC approved and started a Reed Industry Development Project in TDS through the IELC social Co coordinator.[162] Trivandrum district Bamboo cooperative society headed by P.D. Martin tried several projects through the financial help of IELC Economic development Committee. Synod distributed economic help from Relief fund to various peoples at different times.[163] This fund was utilized for various means like personal and medical help, help for loan repayment, money for sewing machines, for the construction of houses, to start shops, house repairing and so on.[164] There was a scheme to give loan for self help projects through the Economic Development Fund. A capital amount was deposited in the self help project at Central Bank of India, Perurkada branch in 1976 March. Loans were given for improvement of property/ of business/ of agriculture, to buy auto rickshaw/ vehicles, to purchase cow for Quarry works and so on.[165] But unfortunately people misused this fund and those who availed loan did not repay properly.[166] There was also another fund for helping the destitute

---

[158] Work Report of KLVS, 19th TDS Convention Minutes, 1974, 6-10.

[159] 18th TDS Convention Work Report, 1973, 31.

[160] TX 87: 93,163rd TDS-EC Minutes, November, 1987, 2.

[161] Pichimony Gabriel, Girija Sasidharan, Suma Chrispin , and Sheela Mohandas.

[162] For full details of this project see, Martin Jesudas, Social Coordinator, IELC, *Report of Reed Industry-TDS*, 11/4/1970.

[163] 33 people received monetary help at a time. TX 76:56,100th TDS-EC Minutes, February, 1976, 8; TX 73:96.

[164] TX 12:73.83rd TDS-EC Minutes, January, 1973, 2-3.

[165] For a sample see, TX 77:36, 106th TDS-EC Minutes, April, 1977, 3-4.

[166] TX 87: 95,163rd TDS-EC Minutes November, 1987, 2. "A large sum of money was given to the TDS for economic development. A list of recipients was published in the TS minutes. How

called Poor Aid Fund.[167] A well digging project was also started in TDS on 1973.[168] J. Vincent and A.R. Victor Raj got "Gama Delta" scholarship for their entire education.[169] Lot of people received educational loans and study scholarships.[170] The project of sewing machine for Lutheran women was introduced to help them earn money for their livelihood.[171]

In connection with the social and economic backwardness of Luthergiri *Pradesikom* 13th TDS convention (1969) appointed a special study committee under the chairmanship of D. Vedamanikom.[172] Along with the spiritual growth the committee suggested the following development projects. Dairy forms at Vellanad, Chalikonam and Chullimannoor, Rubber plantation in five acres land at Parantodu and Meenankal, Poultry farm at Luthergiri compound, Handloom unit at Chullimannor and shopping complex at Kuttichal, Kallikadu, Vellanad and Parantodu.[173] But these suggestions were not carried out.

Through the IELC Development Department, project consultant R.S. Ernest tried a lot of projects with foresight. The funds were collected through means like LCMS-World Relief grant, Government Aid and Bank loan extended to the beneficiaries. The project had resulted in many socio-economic benefits. The project for the uplift of the poor in the backward circles of Trivandrum was approved and funded by LCMS World Relief during October 1987.[174] The implementation of this project was started with the mini dairy scheme, under which 10 families in the village of Kulathupuzha and Kannur were supplied with milk animals. Drinking water well Project, supply of food grains to the poor families in the congregations as well as to the families of pastors were implemented in TDS during the years 1986-1988 by the socio-economic development committee. The cow for the widow program and a free Computer Training Program in Luthergiri were introduced in Trivandrum Synod with the sponsorship of LCMS, World Relief.[175] Ambur synod of IELC was very much benefitted with projects like, Housing project, construction of community centres, Cows& sheep distribution, poultry units, Bullock carts with bullocks, bullocks with ploughs, petty shops coconut plantation and making hand-fans from Palmyra leaves. The main reason

much of the money is being retuned and what is being done with the amounts returned?" asked the president of IELC, G. Thomas Edward in his letter to TDS Executive Committee, 13 April, 1978.

[167] TX 73: 159, 86th TDS-EC Minutes, July, 1973, 7.

[168] TX 73:191, 87th TDS-EC Minutes, September, 1973, 4.

[169] TX 69:79, 64th TDS-EC Minutes1969, 13.

[170] For a sample of priority list for loan and rank list for scholarship see,73:194, 87th TDS-EC Minutes, September, 1973, 5-6..

[171] TX 65: 124, 46th TDS-EC Minutes, 1965, 27.

[172] TX 69:21, 64th TDS-EC Minutes, 1969, 5.

[173] Working Report of the 14th TDS Convention, 1969, 11-12.

[174] R.S. Ernest, Brief Report of the important work of the IELC Project Department, (nd.)

[175] J. Samuel, President of IELC, Annual Report, 17 July, 2012, 3.

for the almost stagnant status of the projects in the TDS was for want of suitable candidates with sincere involvement to work. The lack of proper persons to put honest effort was and is one of the major reasons for the backwardness in the developments of TDS.

4.6. Trust Association and TDS

IELC Trust Association (IELC-TA) is a registered company,[176] an agency of IELC to hold in trust and to administer the properties of the Church. All congregations/ members who use Trust properties abide by the rules and regulations of the Trust Association and other directives of its Committee of Management.[177] TDS had 164 acres and 31 cents of land in 145 plots throughout Kerala in 1974.[178] The Major compounds were Ponvila (2 Acres) Balaramapuram (4 acres) Concordia UPS compound, Peroorkada (13 acres and 30 cents), Concordia HS compound Peroorkada (9 acres and 59 cents), Alleppey HS compound (8 acres 32 cents), Luthergiri (7 acres 45 cents), Nilamel (10 acres).[179] According to Gentlemen's Agreement, the missionary Bungalows and its surroundings were under the full control of the missionaries.[180] There were a lot of discussions about the use of missionary bungalows' and properties.[181] Separating school compounds from Church compound, a proper order for the collecting compound income, the matters of watchman and gardeners, the development of the properties with income generating projects, the arrangements of taxes were the major concerns on the TDS conventions related to Trust properties.[182] In the 16th TDS Convention (1971) K. Alexander the then Trust Contact man[183] submitted a detailed plan for development and protection of Trust properties. Unfortunately, the convention did not care to implement those suggestions.[184] In the 17th Convention (1972) the Synod President D. Vedamanikom insisted the urgent need of the coordination of missionary rule, Trust rules and TDS administration for the betterment of property

---

176 See the Certificate of Incorporation No.4583 of 1961, Madras on 8 September 1961 under Companies Act, 1956 (No.1 of 1956) by Registrar of Companies, T.J. Gondhalekar.

177 IELC Constitutions and Bye-Laws, VI, 4.

178 But as on 17/11/2004 it was 160 acres 26.1/4cents, Alice Brauer, IELC TA Secretary, 17/ 11/2004.

179 Report of the Trust Contact man, 19th *TDS Convention Minutes*, 1974, 24.

180 IELC-TA Committee on Management Minute, 65/17; Annual Report of IELC-TA, 22 June 1968 IV, 2. But later the major MELIM compounds were handed over to IELC-TA through the "Gentleman Agreement". For the sample for Gentleman Agreement in handing over of two major compounds in Kodaikanal see, Agreement Deed , 7 page stamped document, 28 September, 1975.

181 IX, 66:105, TX 66175,177, 265, TX 67:93, 68;10.

182 14th TDS Convention Working Report, 1969, 2-3.

183 The subcommittee convener and contact man were the TA's synod authorities.

184 16th TDS convention Report, 1971, 5-9.

development.[185] From the beginning of the Synod, there were discussions about developing the mission compound for income production.[186] But creative steps were not taken neither to use nor protect these compounds. The irresponsibility of authorities to protect and use the valuable church properties can be identified through the following examples.

In 1979, A.J. Lutz the then Secretary-Treasurer of IELC-TA let out the lower bungalow in Perurkada to a liquor contractor to produce and supply the liquor to the whole part of Trivandrum district. More than 300 labourers worked there day and night. He had done this by ignoring the protest of the local church. The Concordia High school, synod head quarters also were situated within 100-150 ft. distance in the same compound. This clearly shows the attitudes of the authorities and their visions about the mission.[187]

There were a lot of unauthorised occupants in the mission compounds. There was a court order to evict the 9 families who were unauthorised occupants from the Nilamel compound. The TX observed: "The delay in initiating the process of eviction, in accordance with the court order is viewed as a deliberate action with a view of to weaken the court order as the said order is likely to lapse by time bar."[188] As noticed by the TX, nobody took interest to evict them. Still (August 2012) those families or their dependence continue to stay and enjoy the mission property.[189]

In 5 April 1984, the Executive Engineer of Kerala State Electricity Board (KSEB) send a letter to the then IELC-TA Secretary stating that KSEB wanted 2 acres and 21 cents of land from Peroorkada Vattiyoorkavu compound at the cost of Rs. 22 lakes. The authorities were very much happy to sell it and they asked for postal vote from the members of the Managing Committee to get their approval. Only one member from Trivandrum recorded his negative vote.[190] Meanwhile, Government of Kerala published a gazette notification on 13 May 1985 to acquire this property for KSEB.[191] The legal opinions were for and against to take this

[185] President's Report, 17th TDS Convention Work Reports, 1972. 5.

[186] 4th TDS Convention Working Report, 1959, 1-2. 22, TX,65:74; TX 66:36;TDS Convention Minutes, Nov.21-22, 1978, Resolutions, Appendix Iv, Floor Committee resolutions regarding compound income, trust &property matters, 12-13.

[187] 122th Trivandrum Synod Executive Minutes, TX 80/54, 14/4/80.

[188] TX 85/17, 136 TDS Executive Committee Minutes, 8/2/1983, 1.

[189] TX in 1983 listed 24 families was in need of eviction from the mission compound. In some case church had a favor order from court to evict them. But by playing the politics and communal interests of authorities who won the power time to time nothing were happened.

[190] Letter from Secretary-treasurer IELC-TA to the Members of the Managing body, 2/5/1985. Letter from G. Devadas, Trust member from TDS to the Secretary- Treasurer, IELC-TA, 10 /6/1985.

[191] Acquisition notice served by Government of Kerala, No. LA3- 1906/85 dated 20/9/1985.

issue to the court of law.[192] Since the agitations grew among the common people the then Chairman of IELC-TA made an appeal to the Minister of Kerala.[193] But the negotiations continued and in 3 May 1986 the Chairman of IELC-Trust Association wrote to the Executive Engineer, KSEB stating the willingness of IELC to sell one acre of land from the south-east portion as an alternate to the acquisition project.[194] Once again the local people came forward with protest and after a long process, the government dropped the proposal of acquisition once for all. The Kuttichal pastorate led a fasting protest at the IELC central office due to the mismanagement and partiality of the authorities on 11 February 1991.[195]

About half a kilometre of the Perurkada Concordia UPS compound wall starting from south west corner constructed by granite was completely demolished to a height of 6 to 9 feet and widened by the outside people on 3 November 1996. Formerly 6 feet width road was widened to 15 feet. Trees were destroyed and the electric and telephone posts transplanted into the trespassed area.[196] Still the situation continues worse and taking away the rubbles and other properties. This was started when the IELC officer was living in that compound. A court case was filed against this injustice and prayed for relief. Court appointed a commission and according to the commission report[197] and arguments court directed the accusers to restore the whole compound wall in its original position.[198] But unfortunately the Trust did not move further and the huge 16 acres of land within the capital city of Kerala still continues without the boundaries and the neighboring people are slowly occupying this compound. Nilamel Mission Bungalow slowly slipped to the hands of the anti-social elements of the surrounding society. Just through the middle of the compound, the neighboring community built a public road for their convenience and it was taken by the Panchayat and tarred and made as the public road. The Alleppey Mission bungalow sold to a Hindu Organization and the Shertallay Mission Bungalow had gone into the hands of the rebels. One can cite many such instances of Lutheran property being taken away or exploited by the

---

[192] Advocate Gopalakrishnan Nair (8/10/1985) and Menon and Pai, Ernakulum (17/10/85) advised to move with court against government order. But Trust legal advisor G. A. Jayachandra advised the Trust Association not to legally move against this acquisition notice, 16/2/1985.

[193] D. John Hus, Appeal to the Honorable Minister, KSEB-Kerala, 15/10/1985.

[194] Letter from D. John Hus to the Executive Engineer, KSEB, 3/5/1986; see also letters from KSEB to IELC-TA No. DB.45/PKDA/2006 and 225 dated 17/4/1986 and 25/4/1986.

[195] Kuttichal, Mambally and Thachancode churches, Fasting protest in front of IELC-CBO, Notice dated 23/1/1991.

[196] This was done the outsiders with the silent supports of Church authorities. Interview with K.K. Vasu, the care-taker of the MELIM bungalow in the same compound and he is staying in the same compound, 13 July, 2012.

[197] Commission report filed O.S.No. 712/71.

[198] For the full version of the judgment see, judgment by K. Sasidharan Nair, I Additional District Judge, Thiruvananthapuram Salim Brothers Vs IELC, on A.S. 242/2000; O.S. 1829/1996 on 29/March, 2006.

enemies of the church. The two bungalows at Perurkada High school compound were given out to Keltron Projectors limited company for lease for three years for Rs. 2000 per month.[199] But after signing the agreement the Trust Association ignored the agreement and the Church had a heavy loss.[200] After a long struggle by the Concordia Lutheran Church and local people the property could be regained by the Church. A lot of properties were lost due to unauthorised encroachments and other anti-social activities.[201] The Church made use of this occasion to hand over these properties to outsiders by saying, "Unmanageable, and unprofitable". It became a great loss to the coming generation. These are the clear evidences to prove the negligence and irresponsibility of the Trust Association and Synod authorities.[202] The people who are in power should try at least to protect the properties, if they could not develop it. The Synod and IELC leaders and the Trust authorities conveniently kept aside the Constitution and totally ignored the resolutions and reports. Gradually, a ministry-oriented Church is forced to lose its footing and fell down into its crisis years.

4.7. The Crisis Years (1977-2012)

Issues of financial misappropriation, absence of proper account keeping, misuse of trust properties, punishment transfers and other political revenge measures towards those members of opposition, struggle for power were the order of the day in Trivandrum District Synod. The period from 1977 onwards may be referred to as a period of institutional instability and administrative crisis.[203] The huge amount of court cases and related problems led to administrative stagnation at its highest level. Following is an attempt to analyse this period.

4.7.1. Administrative Stagnation

The administrations of TDS were often in stalemate due to various reasons.[204] In the Trivandrum Synod an effective youth movement was growing with Victor Raj

---

[199] See the lease agreement between IELC-TA and Keltron Projectors, 4 page stamp paper document, 27 December, 1995.

[200] Letter from Prakash Tennyson, Trivandrum Circle President, to A. Sundaram, IELC, Trust Secretary, 2/3/89.

[201] Letter from J. Victor, The former GT-IELC to Alice Brayer, Secretary-Treasurer TA, 26/3/2001. Letter from J. Victor to T. Joy, 29/8/2003.

[202] Concordia Lutheran Church, Perurkada, An appeal to the Secretary- Treasurer of IELC Trust Association, 1 September, 2002.

[203] A.R. Victor Raj, " The IELC after almost 50 years".

[204] In 1960's TDS were caught up with groups', court cases and administrative crisis. IELC executive council appointed a visitation committee to study and propose the remedies to the problems of TDS. As per their report IELC executive council decided to defrock the elected officers of TDS and with held the subsidies to the synod and appoint an IELC level committee to care the institutions. (Letter from B.H. Jackayya, General Secretary, IELC to All workers of TDS, 6 November 1961). The situation weekend the ministry and mission of the church. The

as the youth worker and Paul Pollex a missionary, as advisor.[205] In 1977, many Lutheran youth were physically attacked during the 7th All Kerala Lutheran Youth convention by the ruling group who also destroyed properties.[206] The youth group which was very active and well organised in those days, questioned against the corruption, nepotism and political plays of the ruling group.[207] The allegations made against the Synod officers were on the evidence published by the Synod. Such information was first brought out in the audit report. They published articles, and sent petitions to the IELC and LCMS authorities and government authorities against the corruption prevailed in the church.[208] The then authorities tried to stop this agitation through unchristian means. While the youths from all Kerala assembled at Peroorkada for a residential convention camp on 26 August 1977, the elders of the church including the then Synod authorities created a well-planned confusion and started to beat selected youth leaders and wounded many. As soon as the tragedy occurred in 1977, the then IELC president G. Thomas Edward visited the spot with the other IELC offices, Church Council members and Missionary A.J. Lutz. After getting to know the facts they promised necessary actions against the culprits at special Church Council meeting of 3 September 1977. The IELC accepted that the misappropriation happened and for the name sake they disqualified them from holding any office in the church.[209] This event gradually led to a lot of court cases and administrative stagnation in Synod for several years. A "scheme suit" was filed seeking the secular court's directions to straighten out the IELC's faulty administration, beginning with Trivandrum Synod.[210] IELC also filed a court case for recovery of a big amount

---

ministry among children and youth were made under the control of IELC level committees. The centralization of power paralyzed the ministry. The stalemate was slowly changed from 70's onwards.

205 For more details see 4.4.5.

206 For the full version of the incident see, T. Joy, A.R. Victor Raj, S.D. Jayaprasad and J. Christudas, *Njangal Prathishethikkunnu* (We protest). 4/9/1977. G.E Abraham, Convener, Lutheran Church Action council, Memorandum submitted to the Chief Minister and Home Minister of Kerala, 17/11/1977.

207 The following documents will provide an elaborate treatment of the issue mentioned here. Report of the India Evangelical Lutheran Church renewal conference (Nagercoil: IELC June 26,1982); E.B. Dearman, Business manager, IELC, letter to all pastors and leaders of IELC, 2 October 1985; "Jhangal Pradishedikkunnu" (We protest), *Christiani* magazine, "*Jnan enthu cheyyendu karthave*' (what shall I do, Lord), letter to all members of TDS, 18 August, 1979.

208 *Lutharan Sabhayil Lakshangalude Vettippu, (*Misappropriation of lakes of rupees in Lutheran church) *Thani niram daily news paper,* 1979 February, 4.

209 For more details see letter from Lutheran Action Council to Roger L .Ellison, 6 paged typed document, Palm Sunday 1982.

210 J. Christudas, V. Yesudasan Vs Trivandrum synod of IELC, O.S. Appeal No. 1368 of 78 at the Munsif Court of Trivandrum. 17 October 1980 (OS. 1368 of 78), J. Christudas, V. Yesudasan, G.E. Abraham, Chellappan, I.A. No. 2257/80 in OS no.1 of 1980.

misappropriated by the then TDS authorities.[211] IELC Church Council met at Madurai on 31 January & 1 February, 1979 appointed a Peace Commission.[212] Peace committee appointed an Interim Administrative Council for TS with L.W. Meinzen and H.J. Otten and asked them to take arrangements for the TDS election.[213] But this peace commission and interim committee could not do much to settle the issues. Even though at first IELC tried to take the corrective measures gradually they also became silent with delaying tactics.[214] But no positive measures were taken to correct the Church.[215] The growth and mission of the Church were badly affected. Circles were the primary units for planning the spiritual needs of the congregations. However, they gradually became inactive due to preoccupation with administrative problems.

4.7.2. Peace and Reconciliation Movement

Since the mission and credibility of the Church were lost due to the unending quarrels, it became necessary for the LCMS-BFMS to get involved to restore the life of the Church to its normalcy.[216] Thus from 1980 onwards several reconciliation efforts were carried out.[217] As a result, of these reconciliation efforts, in 1983, the LCMS-BFMS entered into a formal restoration mission with IELC through the Protocol Document as mutually agreed under the direction of Roger L. Ellison. Appointment of a business manager to IELC from LCMS and the formation of Adjudication committee were the two major agreements according to the Protocol

[211] Letter from L Lazar, to E. B. Dearmun copy to all membership of IELC and LCMS officers, not dated; 8 page written statement submitted by l Lazar to the Court of the Subordinate Judge Nagercoil, OS. No. 60 of 1984, 25 September, 1984.

[212] Report of Special Commission meeting for Trivandrum Synod matters, 29 January, 1979; L.W. Meinzen, recording secretary, Special Commission Meeting for Trivandrum Synod matters, 2 paged typed document, 8-9, January 1979. Letter from the officers of Trivandrum synod to the Convener, interim Committee for TS administration, 16 February, 1979.

[213] Letter from G. Thomas Edward, President, IELC to the members of Peace Committee, 5/2/1979.

[214] Letter from the IELC president, G. Thomas Edward to the Officers of TS, 13 April, 1978, Special enquiry Committee Report, 10-11 April, 1978, The Strict Confidential Report of the Auditor, J. Daniel, 15 November, 1977, Letter No. Co/TS/IA/84-78 dated 15 April 1978 to C. Robert.

[215] The agreement was made on 13 August 1986 between the representatives of plaintiffs and the representatives of the defendants in the scheme suit no. O.S. 1 of 80. But unfortunately the both groups were ignored the agreements between them in the later days which they had solemnly entered into and they intended to be bound.

[216] Letter from Edward A. Westcott Executive Secretary-LCMS to the membership of IELC 15, March 1982.

[217] H. Israel and H. Hoefer, Minutes of Peace commission meeting, City Church, Trivandrum, 26 June 1981.The main resource persons were Edward A. Westcott(Executive secretary of BFMS_ LCMS), Louis Y. Nau (Asia secretary, BFMS), Roger L. Ellison (Administrative consultant to IELC from LCMS), Luther W. Meinzen and Herbert E. Hoefer (MELIM Representatives).

Document.[218] In continuation of this, LCMS appointed E.B. Dearmun as the Business Manager in 1982 and he continued till 1985. He was entrusted with the responsibility to simplify, build efficient and corruption free administration for IELC. He also had the duty to introduce and train all departments of IELC in accounts and book keeping, to control and supervise all financial dealings of IELC and hand over the same to the General Treasurer and Comptroller of IELC, once the situation returned to normalcy. The task of the Adjudication committee with legally qualified persons was to act with full authority to enquire, hear, and settle various court cases outside the court.[219] The result of these efforts eventually led to the withdrawal of court cases, bringing normalcy to church life to a certain extent. After a long process of reconciliation TDS election was held and new officers were elected. P.G. Kunju Kunju (President) P.K. George (Vice-President) M.M. Yohannan (Secretary) were elected as the compromise candidates.[220] In a normal IELC Convention, D. John Hus from TDS got elected as the new president of IELC in 1983[221] and he held the office for two terms from 1983-1989. A new Constitution for IELC was formed and approved in a special Constitution Convention of November, 1986 under the leadership of D. John Hus.[222] Following the end of the term of Hus, the IELC election was not conducted on time. There were court cases against the then Vice President I. Abraham to function as the Acting President. The Division Bench of Madras High Court passed a judgment by permitting him to function as the IELC Acting President and conduct the Elections.[223] J. Issac Moon from Ambur District Synod became the next president of IELC.[224] By removing the elected officers of the Synod the Synod Executive appointed J. Sensar as the Acting President and Mary Sheela as the Synod Secretary[225] of TS they got approval from IELC to

[218] Report of the Renewal Conference (Nagercoil: Concordia Seminary, June 24-26, 19820; "Protocol Document" between LCMS and IELC, Nagercoil, 1982; "Mutual Agreement Paper", Between LCMS and IELC, Nagercoil, 1982; code of conduct for members of IELC, 1892 (prepared by H. Hoefer, John Guruswamy, P. David, J.C. Gamaliel, and K. Suseelan); Letter from R.L. Ellison to L.W. Meinzen 30/April 1982; Letter from Edward Westcott to all membership of IELC, 29 April, 1982.

[219] Principal of the Concordia Seminary Nagercoil is the Chairman of this Committee. Rest of the members were appointed by CC in consultation with both parties.

[220] The TS convention was held on 24 and 25, November, 1982.

[221] Letter from E.B. Dearmun, to all pastors and leaders of IELC, 2 October, 1985.

[222] For a detailed account of the IELC Constitutions revisions during various periods, see, Lemuel Anderson," A study of the Constitution of India Evangelical Lutheran Church with reference to select relevant litigation", (Unpublished thesis, UTC, Bangalore, 1999)

[223] Luke Illango Vs IELC, Application nos. 1404 and 405 in C.S. No. 208/89; Judgment from Madras High Court Division Bench on OSA Nos. 125 and 126 /89 dated 26th April 1989.

[224] Minutes of the 13th IELC Triennial Convention, Nagercoil 14-15 July 1989.

[225] TX 4/91; Letter from Paul Titus, chairman of the TX meeting, to all churches, institutions and IELC officers 17/4/1991.

function.[226] Another set of crisis and court cases resulted after Issac Moon's first triennial ended in 1992. The continued disharmony in IELC that deeply worried the partner church LCMS.[227]

4.7.3. Court Cases

Difference of opinion in a church is inevitable and disputes are unavoidable. The Christians and Church believe in the power of the Word in correcting the people. Members of a local church going to court to settle their problems is a mark of spiritual, theological and moral disease. The court cases were common in TDS from its formation.[228] But in 1992, the court cases were aggravated due to the failure of the central payment system. The central payment system was introduced during the first triennial period of Issac Moon. The original purpose behind this was to make sure that all workers of IELC were properly paid. According to this system, each congregation had to pay 75% of its income to Central business office of IELC before the 15th of every month. IELC would pay the salaries of its workers through this contribution called "assessment". But this central pooling system failed miserably as IELC were not able to pay the salaries regularly. Many

---

[226] The Lutheran church at Nilamel complained against Mary Sheela that she was not a member of any Lutheran church. Her father Daniel who was a non Lutheran was nominated to BPLT- IELC. See the letter from the secretary Bethel Lutheran Church, Nilamel to Issac Moon, President IELC, 6/3/ 1992.

[227] Open letter to pastors of the IELC by 19 expatriate MELIM missionaries (nd); An open letter to brothers and sisters in the IELC by Luther W. Meinzen, 23 March 1993 (Luther W. Meinzen was a MELIM missionary born in India, A son of MELIM Missionary and served Indian Lutheran church for more than 40 years); An open letter to IELC congregations, pastors and workers by, A.L. Barry, LCMS President, Glen O'Shoney, Executive Director LCMS world vision, Allan R. Buckmann Director, World Areas LCMS World Vision; David C. Birner, LCMS-Asia Secretary on 21 July 1993.These letters provides a graphic description about various leadership issues and also allege leaders entering into politics for amassing wealth.

[228] The judgement in CC No. 512 of 1960, 30th November 1960 by Smt. A. Chellamma, Sub Magistrate II class, in the court of the sub-magistrate, II class, Kottarakkara remains as a painful memory in the history of TS. A MELIM missionary Wilbur T. May was residing the Nilamel station. While he was away from the bungalow, on 16/4/1960, a theft had happened in his bungalow. A police case was filed and then arrested three people including two Lutherans on 12/5/1960 and the things they stole were also recovered back. Police moved the case to the Magistrate court. One of the chief witnesses Rev. K. Jacob stood for the accusers. Since the witness was contradicting each other the case was judged in favour of the thief. Everybody knew that it was a joint and unchristian play of Lutheran Christians and a pastor against a sincere and dedicated missionary. This shocked the missionary very badly and so he returned to his land in 1960. This was a reward given by church members and a pastor to a missionary and his family for their sincere and dedicated service! For more court cases see, W. Alexander's case against R. T. Keopke O.S. no. 67/3 FC 66/65, 50th TX minutes 1966, 30;Five members from Devicode filed against J. Jesudasan their pastor. OS no 129/66 in Neyyattinkara court. GWC66/12; FC 66/14; TX 66/129; TX 65/89, TX 64/88; Nesamony Benjamin filed a case against TDS (TX 69: 204, 70:75) K. Bhaskaran filed a case against his successor, Manager Rajaian (TX 33:78) 114th TDS-EC minutes, 1978, 5.

congregations stopped paying the assessment and they paid directly to their pastors.[229] Soon, those who failed to pay the assessment forfeited their voting right and their involvement in the election process. Majority of congregations and pastors were declared as ineligible due to failure in paying "Synod Assessment" to IELC.[230] The assessment system had come under severe criticism due to the lack of transparency and unscientific criteria used for estimating assessment without consulting the congregations. The issue of Assessment continues to be a problem causing discontent towards the electoral process. Those congregations who failed to remit the assessed amount every month cannot either nominate or contest in elections. Moreover, they will be treated as the ineligible congregations without voting rights. To illustrate it further, in TS, only 42 congregations out of 137 and 25 pastors out of 65 were eligible for the 2007 elections. Majority of the pastors and congregations were declared to be ineligible due to failure in paying Synod assessment to IELC. It is also assumed to be used to prevent certain congregations and people from election process.[231] The denial of voting right was questioned in the court and the division bench in Madras High Court appointed Jeyasingh Peter, an advocate, as the election officer to conduct elections to the different posts of IELC as well as in the three synods. J. Sensar (President) J. Yovas (Vice President) and K. Stephanose (Secretary) were elected as the TS officers. In the elections conducted for apex body on 14 December 1993, Issac Moon got re-elected. But the final order from the division bench came to be passed only on 8 February1995 and the court asked the president to assume his office with effect from 8/2/1995.[232]

M.S. Poomaniraj the then regional election officer of TDS filed a case against the IELC Election commissioner Daniel Rajagamberam not to allow him to conduct any more elections in IELC, since he proved himself to be a political personality of the church and to avoid further litigations.[233] This led to the re-appointment of Jeyasingh Peter as the Election Officer of IELC by the

---

[229] Minutes of IELC Ad hoc Committee, Madras, 8 June 1993; " Memorandum to Trivandrum Synod Executive" submitted by Congregations denied of voting right in Trivandrum Synod, January, 2003; P.K. Paul Durai, Chief Election Commissioner of IELC, Election notification from the office of the Chief Election Commissioner to all congregations, 24 April, 2007.

[230] In Trivandrum synod only 42 congregations out of 137 and 25 pastors out of 65 were eligible for 2007 elections.

[231] Sam Thompson, "Evolving an Ethical Critique in relation To the leadership crisis of IELC with particular reference to the Trivandrum synod", (Unpublished MTh. Thesis, UTC, Bangalore, 2008), 35.

[232] A. Simon & A. Masillamony Vs IELC, OS Appeal No. 194-196 of 1992 in the division bench of Madras High Court; Court order CMP No. 194-196 of 1992, by Madras High Court, 10/3/ 1993; M.S. Poomaniraj Vs IELC, C.S. No. 674 of 1997 in the Division Bench of Madras High Court.

[233] M.S. Poomaniraj had more than 30 years of ministerial service in Trivandrum Synod and served as president of TDS and also served as Co-treasurer of the Synod and Church Council

Honourable Court vide its order.[234] The court directed the new election officer to prepare the list of eligible voters and publish the same and that the elections shall be completed on or before 30 April 2001.[235] The 12 leading pastors of the TDS representing various caste and groups were assembled at Christian Media Centre – India (CMC-I) on 8th & 9th December 1998 and confessed that they were divided into many groups and had done many things which badly affected the day today administration and growth of the Church. They committed themselves to come under the label Pastor and not under the label of caste movements or groups or any other label which interrupt the spirit of the gospel. A joint statement was submitted before the congregations of TDS with their signatures both in Malayalam and in English.[236] Unfortunately, this unity was short-lived. In the next Synod election, the same group again got divided and fought each other. The next term election was conducted by Jeyasingh Peter, the court appointed election officer.[237] The Synod election was declared to be conducted from 31 May to 3 June 2000. But the then Manager and his companions were able to get a stay order from Madras High Court to prohibit elections until 27/6/2000 due to the fear of losing power. 23 pastors of TS jointly appealed to all the churches against this situation and cooperated with the election process.[238] The election of Synod officers for the next two years was finished on 11/1/2002 and from 21/2/2002 to 23/2/2002. Y. Sukumaran (President) Chacko P. John (Vice President), G. Babu (Secretary) were the elected office bearers of the Synod. These elected officers were split into two groups in connection with the Manager appointment and filed a case at District Munsif court, Kuzhithurai to claim power over the other.[239] Meanwhile, another appeal was filed against this election officer to remove him from the post of election commissioner through the application Nos. 1311 to 1319 of 2002 before Madras high court in C.S No. 674 of 1997 by the various pastorates of TDS. The content of the petition was, due to the non-observance of mandatory provisions of the constitution, the election conducted on 21/2/2002 to23/2/2002 to the Trivandrum Synod should also to be declared as null and void. On 6/5/2003 the High Court of Madras dismissed Jeyasingh Peter and set

member of IELC and was appointed as regional Election officer of Trivandrum Synod from 6/5/ 1995. The appeal no was C S No. 674/97 on 7/11/1977.

[234] O.A. Nos. 688 and 689 of 1997 in C.S. No. 674 of 1997.23/11/1999.

[235] Judgment and order dated 7/2/2001 passed by the Madras High Court Nos.3370 to 3372 of 2000 in C.S. No. 674 of 1997.

[236] M. Soosappan, P. Rajendran, J. Sensar, Mathew P. john, Y. Sukumaran, D.S. Simpson, N. Vasudevan Nair, M.S. Poomaniraj, Gifton E. Joshua, R. Vijayakumar, N. Suraj and P.N. Gopinathan signed in the joint statement submitted before the churches in TDS 9/12/1998.

[237] Jeyasingh Peter was re- appointed as election officer by the Madras High Court in its order dated 23/11/ 1999 passed in O.A. Nos. 688 & 689 0f 1997 in C.S. No. 874/97.

[238] M. Soosappan and 22 others, to the notice of all churches of TDS, 5/6/2000.

[239] O.S.No.244/2002 dated 26/4/2002.

aside the elections conducted by him.[240] A new Election Officer Bharaneedharan was appointed.[241] Meantime on 31/12/2003 Madras High Court passed an order directing fresh elections to be conducted in respect of Trivandrum Synod.[242] Bharaneedharan conducted the elections[243] and placed before the court for confirmation on 23/6/2004. At this time, another issue of the validity of Society registration of IELC was questioned in the court. The division bench of High Court of Madras observed; "Whether the registration of the Apex body of IELC under the provisions of the Societies of the Registration Act, 1860, continues to be in force under the provisions of the new act, viz. Societies Registration Act, 1975, by periodical renewal, as contemplated under law, as in the absence of any such renewal, the Apex body of IELC would itself become defunct. Consequently, the election conducted to the post of office bearers of IELC would become a futile exercise and therefore, it may not be proper for this Court to approve the election of a defunct society, without regulating the registration."[244] The Court directed to regulate the registration of the Synods as well as the Apex body in the manner known to law and asked them to report the matter to the court within eight weeks. At this time P. Kailasam & Girija Alfred who were unsuccessful in the election, filed a CMP nos. 17565 to 17572 of 2004 against the pending case OSA Nos. 265-272 of 2003 to set aside the elections which did not satisfy the provisions of the constitutional by-laws registered under the Societies Registration Act and to conduct fresh elections.[245] The court expressed its concern that having lot of Institutions and vast landed properties to an extent of 440 acres carrying on many socio, religious and charitable activities and transactions with the aid of State and Central Government funds and foreign donations could not be possible and so the court arranged temporal and internal arrangements for administrations. The court directed that the administration, management and financial affairs of the Trivandrum Synod should be controlled by K. Stephanose and V. Jeevaraj as Interim Administrators who should exercise their control over the institutions within the jurisdiction jointly.[246] So, the Court Order dated 22/12/2004 made it

---

[240] Order passed by Madras High Court dated on 6/5/2003 in application Nos. to 1311 to 1319 Of 2002 in C.S. No. 674 Of 1997.

[241] Advocate-commissioner R .Bharanidharan was appointed as election officer to conduct Nagercoil and Trivandrum Synod elections by O.S. No. 265 to 272 /2003, dated 9/9/2003 and 31/12/ 2003. The elected officers of TDS were K. Stephanose (President) N. Vasudevan Nair (Vice president), J. Yovel (Secretary).

[242] Judgment from Madras High Court, OSA Nos. 265-272of 2003 in 31/122/2003.

[243] Trivandrum elections were conducted from 29/4/2004 to 1/5 /2004. See the report filed by the Advocate-commissioner dated 22/12/2004.

[244] Order by High Court of Madras, OSA .No. 265 to 272 of 2003 on 21/7/2004 and CMP Nos. 17563 to 17572 of 2004, 22 December, 2004.

[245] Kailasom & Girija Vs Kallayam Pastorate and others, O.S.A. Nos. 265 of 2003 dated nil.

[246] In the High Court of Judicature at Madras O.S.A. Nos. 265 to 272 of 2003, dated 22/12/2004. K. Stephanose & V. Jeevaraj, Letter to all congregations and institutions in TDS,

clear that an election in the defunct society was not valid so they were advised to regularise the registration first.[247] The interim administrators of IELC were directed to regularise the continuity of registration on or before 31/1/2005 and to finalize the list of qualified members and voters list as per the IELC-Synod constitutions and submit a final report to the Court on or before 28/2/2005. After this administrative paralysis, for one year in 17/8/ 2005, the Court appointed a retired judge of the Madras High Court Justice J. Kanakaraj as the Chief Administrator and Advocate M.S. Palaniswamy as the Associate Administrator to take care of the church and institutions.[248] Meanwhile, the Kallayam pastorate of Trivandrum Synod approached the Supreme Court of India through a Special Leave Petition against the judgement passed by the High Court of Madras in CMP No 17565 of 2004.[249] When this issue was brought before the Supreme Court, New Delhi, the Court over-ruled the High Court judgement in its Order dated 14 September 2006 and declared that IELC was not a defunct Society and declared the elected persons as qualified.[250] The Church Council met on 6th October and resumed its function. Soon after the period of presidentship of S. Rajagambeeram got over on 6th June 2007 Chief Election officer of IELC conducted the elections. D.S. Simpson became the President of TDS and J. Samuel was elected as the president of IELC on 31 August 2007. New cases were filed in various courts. Again Madras High Court appointed Justice A.K. Rajan as an Election Overseer to IELC. The Election Commission of the IELC conducted the elections under the observation of Court appointed Observer. The elections were from the circles to IELC level. M. Robinson got elected as the TDS President D.J. Stanley as Vice President and G. Babu as the Secretary. J. Samuel won the election as the President of IELC for the second term. The report submitted to the High Court by Justice A.K. Rajan, the court appointed Observer, was that the process of election at all levels of IELC was unconstitutional and null and void.[251] Based on this report many cases were filed in Madras High Court Single bench, Division Bench and in Supreme Court of New Delhi by seeking order to prohibit the function of newly elected office bearers. The present administration is still awaiting (as of July, 2012) for the clearance from the Court. Meanwhile, the question of validity of IELC's registration again becomes an issue. Registration Department through

---

27/01/2005.

[247] Kallayam Pastorate vs P. Jeyasing Peter, Election officer, O.S. No. 265-272 of 2003.

[248] Letter from justice J. Kanakaraj and M.S. Palaniswamy, proceedings of Administration, to all congregations and pastorates, 29 October, 2005.

[249] This case was filed through Advocate V.N. Ragupathy on 25/1/2005.

[250] See I Nelson & others Vs Kallayam Pastorate & others, Civil Appeal No. 4124 and 4122 of 2006, by Supreme Court of India at New Delhi, 14/9/2006.

[251] Justice A.K. Rajan Administrator/ overseer, report submitted for the elections in High Court Madras, in connection with the appeals O.A. Nos. 1115 and 1116 of 2010 in C.S. No. 879 Of 2010, 9 February, 2010.

Right of Information Act informed that, no renewal to society registration no. 11/1959 has been done in connection with the constitutional changes of IELC after 1986.[252]

Most of the cases the conversation with the plaintiff and defendant side of the vast majority of the court cases Church will have to agree that there is truth in both the sides. Personal conversations with both sides are convincing to the extent that both parties approach the court wishing the best for their beloved Church.[253] They seem to acknowledge that the present system within the Church as such does not enable the Church to go on with its primary mission. It appears that the Court of law has become the first and the last refuge of the Church's leadership and membership to settle even purely ecclesiastical disputes. Since mutual trust has been lost and they mutually hurt each other the Civil Court becomes their last place of safety, not with the assurance that finally justice will prevail but with an assumption that somehow the opposition would be penalized. Fear and lack of trust of one another dominate the Church's culture. The law-suits at all levels in the IELC had become a constant problem. Going to Court resulted in the blasphemy of God and the Church. God's holiness and the sacred nature of the Church have to be respected and maintained at all levels. So far, we were discussing about the life experience, growth and struggles of the Lutheran Christians as a different community in Kerala. Now the discussions move towards its struggles to keep the identity and mission in an enlarged society.

4.8. State's Partiality

Discrimination of State and Central Governments by denying privileges to Lutheran Christians is another blow against their development. With great expectations, the subalterns of South India embraced Lutheran Christianity. But as Christians they were denied many privileges enjoyed by the non-Christians of the same caste. The State extended various benefits to the weaker sections of the population to realize its declared objectives of integral development of all people. But how much of those benefits were given to the Christian subaltern who actually form the poorest of the poor section of the rural population? A deep and growing sense of frustration prevailed among the Christian subalterns with regard to this matter. They felt that they were being deliberately denied of State benefits for the just crime of being Christians. Benefits for Scheduled Castes and Scheduled Tribes as per the Central Government's policy of 'Protective discrimination' were denied to them.[254] The State Government's benefits earmarked for socio-economically

---

[252] From M. Manikom, District Registrar to S. M. Samlanglin, na, ka, No. 11438/E/2010, 15/12/2010; No. 589/E/2012, 17/2/ 2012.

[253] Interviews with J. Yovel (68), Ex-Comptroller, IELC, and Secretary, TS on 7th July 2012 and Rev. T. Pavithra Singh former BPLT member, on 8th July 2012.

[254] The issue has been clearly explained in the following works, Godwin Shiri. *The Fights of Christian Dalits*(Bangalore: Asian Trading Corporation, 1997), 109-115; John C.B. Webster,

and educationally backward castes and communities were classified as Other Backward Communities (OBC). The Lutherans were excluded from this list and were treated as forward class. Thus, the continued state discrimination in the form of the denial of SC benefits was aggravated further by growing communalization in the socio-political life. All these, in general, had created a deep and serious crisis in their lives. The very fact that if a SC/ST Lutheran has a 'Christian' or 'Biblical' name, he/she is automatically debarred from availing the SC benefits is indeed very alarming. The continued denial of SC benefits to them had eventually led to socio-economic conditions that were extremely pathetic and beyond recovery. It created an unbridgeable gulf between the Christian SC-ST and Hindu SC-ST. There was a deep-rooted communal discrimination behind the unscrupulous denial of SC benefits to Christian Dalits. In brief, change of religion did not bring change in their social positions. In such situations most of them were forced to leave the Church and return to their old religion.

There are some joint Christian movements at the State and Central level for getting SC/ST benefits to the Lutheran Christians also. Nadar Lutherans are also treated as forward class thereby alienated from reservation benefits. Nadar Lutheran Welfare Society[255] was formed and taught for the reservation benefits. Now the Nadar – SIUC and Nadar Hindus are getting some benefits. Therefore, a new trend is growing among the Nadar Lutherans to keep double membership one as Lutheran and other as SIUC Nadar. Since Hindu Ezhavas are getting a high number of reservations, new conversion from this community to Christianity is very low. Moreover, they are struggling much to keep the present generation of Ezhava Lutherans under the Christian fold.

4.9. Setback of Faith

Some of the Lutheran pastor's children have gone back to Hinduism. The TX decided that these pastors should not be elected or appointed to any official posts in TS thereafter.[256] One of the memorials discussed and passed in the 25th Synod Convention was about the reconversion issue of Lutherans. Resolution no. 13 says: "It is seen that many of the church members in TS have converted as Hindus. but such persons are again getting into the committees in congregation, circle and synod levels, and it brings troubles in the congregations so this body resolves: (a) It is welcome to come back as church members those who are converted.(b) but those who have converted, should come back to Christianity with clear proofs and records (Gazette Copy) and they should not get into any committee in the Church, Circle and Synod levels unless and until they do the

---

The Dalit Christians A History (Delhi: ISPCK, 1992), 129-189; I.P. Desai (et.el.), *Caste, Caste Conflict and Reversions* (Delhi: Ajanta Publications, 1985), 124-137; Sunder Raj, *Conversion Called Confusion* (New Delhi: TRACT, 1986).

[255] Register No. T.14/17/2003.

[256] 2nd TDS Convention Report 1958, 6.

above."[257] Therefore, the reversion issue needs more discussion. The great blow from the State to the SC/ST Lutherans was denial of Scheduled Caste benefits to them. In these circumstances they were forced to take an option either to fight for their rights while remaining within the Church or leave the Church and reconvert to Hinduism. In Travancore, attempts for re-conversion dates back to the 1920's. The 1921 Census figures indicated a surprising increase in the number of Christians. This had caused anxiety and tension among the Hindus. The sudden leap in the numerical strength of Christianity was conditioned by forces inherent in the Hindu social order; which had been the irritating causes for mass exodus. The Travancore Temple Entry Proclamation in 1936 was indeed a landmark in the socio-political development of Travancore. It was not because of the zeal for religious reform, but the anxiety to prevent the erosion of the strength of Hinduism. By this, the mass exodus to other faiths ended abruptly and a good number of converts re-converted to their original religion. The All Travancore Hindu Maha Sabha and Kerala Hindu Mission were very active in the re-conversion works.[258] Therefore, one of the main forces behind reversion was Hindu aggressive mission.

It was extensively reported that it had become an almost impossible task for the *SC Lutherans* to avail of any SC benefits like house sites, houses, land for cultivation, loans, scholarships, hostel facilities, and other things. In early years, they somehow managed to get it through either by producing 'false' caste certificates or by begging and pleading with somewhat liberal-minded village leaders/officials. But later on, officials became more rigid in the matter of granting any SC benefits to *SC* Lutherans. A new trend had been started lately to produce a certificate to prove that he/she was a Hindu, in order to get SC benefits.[259] Many of them brought certificates through *Aryasamaj* and Gazette notification.[260] Many *SC* Lutherans hid their 'Christian' identity from census enumerators.

These people were Christians for church purposes but for all other practical purposes they were forced to project themselves as Hindus. Today, because of the miserable situation they are forced to adopt a dual identity, a Hindu identity for the sake of getting some State help which is vital for their very survival, and a

---

[257] TC. 84/08, Resolution and Decisions 13,25th TS General Convention Minutes, 29,30 November, 1994, 4.

[258] V. Sathyanesan, "Temple entry proclamation and Reconversion impulses in Travancore", *ICHR* 26/1 (June, 1992), 5-20.

[259] Through the Gazette notification, K. Staphanose an ordained pastor of TDS became Hindu as Prasannakumar and later he was elected as the President of TDS; 11/11/73E Devadas (Tholoor Gopi) who convert to Hinduism on 6/1/89 later elected as the TX member.

[260] Few examples of Pastors and their families - M.M. Jacob, Mathew P. John, Mathew Soosappan, Y. Sukumaran, K. Stephanose. one of the Lutheran pastor P.K. George and his son were punished by the court for their cheating the government with the false community certificates for getting the medical seats reservation. See Malayala Manorama Daily News Paper, 7 November, 2006, 9. Lay Leaders - Mary Sheela, Tholoor Gopi (Devadas).

Christian identity because of their faint hope of acquiring a social status. While the Church still goes on 'exhorting' them not to backslide but to safeguard their Christian identity, the vital question of survival is forcing them increasingly to assume a Hindu identity. Walter Alexander wrote: "At least half among the SC/ST Lutheran were reverted back to Hinduism for their personal gains and benefits from government. It seems to me that the present administration encourages such SC/ST Lutherans to revert back to Hinduism.[261] I know well that there are even pastors in our District (SC/ST) who encourage their 'Churchmen' to convert back with their help. As you also know there have been at least some pastors who continue as pastors in the IELC at the same time they officially have proclaimed as Hindus through Government Gazettes and receive money and other benefits from the Government."[262]

Further, in a situation where non-Christian religious beliefs and practices continued to hold sway over them on the one side, the essentials of Christian preaching, teaching, sacraments and worship were on the decrease in their congregational life on the other side. Does Christianity still mean anything significant to these people while they hoped for an egalitarian society? Within Christianity they had to face inequality and at the same time the State had promised them Government benefits if they could become Hindus. In such a situation is it possible to rightly judge the reversion issue? Re-conversion was mostly for reasons of Government jobs and other benefits and not due to any kind of preference for Hindu faith. Hence, the Church needs to pay more and active attention towards this reversion issues.

4.10. Rays of Hope

For several years the Synod had been hindered in its mission and ministry as a result of internal problems, weakness in leadership, strife and gradual loss of vision and purpose. Many lay people became discouraged and lost interest in using their talents for the cause of the Kingdom. The training neglected over the years is greatly needed to keep the positive direction. The Lutheran lay training program should be reactivated to equip lay people in key positions in Society to realize vast opportunities for witness and to recognize and utilize resources available for meaningful witness. Many of the local congregations, realizing the failure of the apex body, increasingly assumed responsibility towards worship and to nurture programmes, paying their pastors and developing infrastructure. It has been noted that the last two decades saw the building up of more number of church buildings, parsonages using indigenous funds in the Trivandrum Synod history. Some of the positive signs to recall the Church for mission can be listed as follows:

---

[261] Supreme Court of India declared that even after the conversion of a Scheduled Tribe to another religion their reservation rights will not be loosed.

[262] Letter from Walter Alexander, to Issac Moon, President, IELC, 29 August, 1998, 3-4.

4.10.1. Renewal Program

1985 witnessed some positive changes in the life and ministry of the TDS. First among this was the Renewal program. IELC appointed A.R. Victor Raj as the Renewal Director for IELC and under his leadership once again the TDS went back to its study, worship and evangelical life. There were many study seminars organised at Synod, Circle and congregational levels for worship, wisdom work and witness. They produced study materials, Lenten devotions, liturgies, liturgical calendars, and IELC Diary and so on.[263]

4.10.2. Lutheran Professionals Fellowship

Another Lutheran Fellowship was started in 1985 at Trivandrum for the Lutherans who were employed in government or semi-government offices/institutions. The proposed objectives include providing a common forum for the employed Lutherans in Trivandrum for united action and fellowship. And also it aimed to provide a forum for developing and using their talents and to reach the drop outs and bring them back to the Church. It served the Church and Society in the energetic and productive way. On 24/3/1993 they organized a mass prayer meeting in order to seek God's guidance in the crisis which was prevailing in the Lutheran churches.[264] But later, due to various reasons they were not able to function for many more years. Slowly, this fellowship also became defunct.

4.10.3. Lutheran Prayer Fellowship

Lutheran Prayer Fellowship was started on 27 March 1999 to have fellowship and prayer thereby spiritually strengthening the Church. Till this day this group is continuing its mission actively.[265] Every second Saturday this prayer partners assembled in one centre to intercede for the various needs.

4.10.4. Lutheran Laymen's Fellowship

Lutheran Laymen's Fellowship was functioning from May 2001 at Trivandrum and it stands as a binding force of the local congregations of Trivandrum circle. It carried out as a helping arm for the Lutherans in Trivandrum to continue their mission. In 2003, this fellowship submitted a memorandum to the IELC officers for appropriate action towards the Vattiyoorkavu compound on the following things: 1) Restore the CLUPS compound Perurkada by changing the present pathetic condition. 2) Take suitable and immediate steps to re-construct the boundary wall around this compound, which was demolished by the neighbours. 3) Renovate the two bungalows and other buildings which are getting deteriorated

---

[263] Letter from L.W. Meinzen to A.R. Victor Raj, 25/1/1985; Letter from A.R. Victor Raj to L.W. Meinzen 28 June 1985; Letter from A.R. Victor Raj to all pastors, 2 December, 1985.

[264] See the constitution of Lutheran Employees Fellowship, 26 May, 1985, 1.

[265] T.W. Vijaya Kumar, T. Yesudasan, K. K.Wycliff and Grace Remani Abisai were the former organizers of this fellowship. See their Bulletin, Awake, and Awake for the Church, 12/4/1999.

day by day. 4) Prepare and implement suitable projects for the utilization of the campus for the welfare of the Church after cleaning the campus.[266] LLF-T became a registered Society in 2004 with the reg. No. T. 2070/04.[267] Any Lutheran communicant lay member aged 25 years or above could be a member of this fellowship.[268] The main objectives of this fellowship are:[269] to be a forum for the fellowship and friendship to IELC members in connection with the church growth; To give leadership for mutual growth and united action; To stimulate the spiritual and faith life of its members; to start educational, vocational, technical, medical and charitable institutions and hostels; to be an agency for channelizing government and other voluntary organizations help; To financially help the pastors and others especially the children while they are in need.; To facilitate the members and the Lutheran children for their remarkable achievements; To assist IELC to develop and upkeep the properties and institutions.[270] In its first executive committee meeting, it was resolved to start Bible classes in Lutheran schools, renew the lay training programmes in local churches, clean the CLUPS compound, seek possibilities to start an old age home, build a cellar cemetery and arrange a special prayer for the proper administration in IELC.[271] Their activities comprised volunteers sponsoring the poor students and financially helping poor families,[272] conducting study seminars and Bible classes for all people including youth, women and laymen and families; Distributing study helps and aids to students, conducting Reformation Festivals,[273] Felicitations to the notable laypeople and those who secured high marks in various examinations,[274] arranging family meets,[275] Counselling seminars, Pre-Marital courses, New Evangelism

[266] LLF, Trivandrum, memorandum submitted to IELC on 14/9/2003.

[267] Request for the registration, from the office bearers, 10/8/2004.Registration certificate on order no T.2070 on 11 August, 2004., D. Titus, Annual report of LLF 2004, 30/1/2005, 2.

[268] Constitution of LLF-T, 6, Membership, 2.

[269] Ibid, article 3, 1.

[270] Constitution of LLF-T, Article 3.1.

[271] First Executive Minutes of LLF-T, 20/2/2005, 3.

[272] Annual report of LLFT, 2006, submitted on 18/2/07, 2. Request for the registration, from the office bearers, 10/8/2004. Registration no T.2070 on 11 August, 2004; D. Titus, Annual report of LLF 2004, 30/1/2005, 2.

[273] Secretary, *Announcement for reformation festival celebration, on 25/10/2009* dated 12/10/2009.

[274] Yesudasan, Annual Report of LLFT, 2010, 30/1/2011.2.

[275] Two family meets were arranged one at Calvary Lutheran Church at Peroorkada on 1/May 2008 and next at St John's Lutheran Church Sreekariyam in 2011.

Project,[276] Literary Promotion Project,[277] Production and Promotion of Lutheran Hymns and Albums,[278] publication of News Letter, etc.[279] Through systematic programs and study seminars they are trying to revitalize the Church for action.[280] They were able to form various units at local level to mobilize their ministry. By using the local leadership and indigenous fund, they function as yeast among the Lutheran community in Kerala.

4.10.5. Lutheran Voice

"Lutheran Voice" is another voluntary Lutheran movement in Trivandrum. They mainly focussed on preparing Bible Study Materials, Vacation Bible School study materials, and publication of Christian literatures. Now they have started to prepare, promote and publish a uniform Sunday School Text Book and teachers guide to all Lutheran Churches in Kerala from LKG to 12th standard. Periodic workshops for the Sunday School Teachers, seminars for students, Annual Common Examination and Sunday School students' competitions and festivals were conducted regularly. They also arranged the Residential Summer Camps for three days during the vacation for the children at Concordia Hills, Peroorkada. The program aimed at imparting life skill education to the Lutheran Students with an overall view to enable them to scale greater heights. Emphasis was also given on boosting their emotional abilities to enable them to interact confidently with others. The integral personality development of the individual is targeted. The parents and the participants witness that this camp was very useful to accept life as a blessing, develop a positive outlook and to make their lives as a celebration.

4.10.6. Pastors Fellowships

Another notable development is the regional fellowships for pastors organised by themselves for study, discussions and fellowship except in the Nilamel circle. Pastors have multiple-congregation ministries in pastorates that require much time to serve the varied needs, much travel by bus or two wheelers and even on bicycle, plus meeting personal and family responsibilities with a meagre salary. These factors leave too little time for concentrated continuing education in theology or skills needed for ministry. Also personal libraries are limited. Pastors need opportunity for sharing their experiences and developing more adequate

---

[276] At Pathirapally within the Trivandrum city they started an evangelism centre in 2006 with the local assistance of nearby Lutheran churches and pastors. Now a Seminary graduate is taking care of the work with the partnership of LLF.

[277] Under the initiative of LLF Lutheran literature were sold to the churches and conducted quiz competitions to promote the Lutheran literature.

[278] On 25 October 2009 they released an album produced by themselves with reformation songs.

[279] For more details see the annual reports of LLF, 208- 2012; News Letter, LLF, Trivandrum, August, 2011.

[280] Interview with Sony Lawrence, Secretary, LLF-T, on 14/7/2012.

approaches to meet the increasingly complex needs of ministering in a rapidly changing society. Therefore, the In-Service Training for pastors should be restarted to enable them to carry out effective ministry, faithful to their call and motivated to overcome temptations to institutionalism, while remaining firm in their commitment to mission. In spite of all administrative chaos, litigations, claims counter-claims for "power" in the Church, there are a lot of evidences that God is leading the Church in His grace. New baptisms including the adult baptisms, new evangelistic centres and new congregations are coming up. Congregations are steadily growing in stewardship responsibilities and other ministries.[281]

4.11. Peoples' Movements

As already noted, the Lutheran community in Kerala was and is in a mixed caste situation. The membership of this synod came from dalit, tribal and backward castes and groups from a poor economic background. A majority of the members of MELIM was from the *Sambava* caste, with the next largest representatives coming from the *Nadar* followed by the Ezhavas, Cheramas, Kerala Mudaliyars, *Vellalas, Maravans, Naidus, Reddiars, Artisan castes, Velans,* and some hill tribes like, *Kuravans, Paniyans, Vedars* and *Aryans, etc.* Plurality of caste had caused disturbance, controversy, and offence in the work and growth of TDs. There were often unrest and agitations against others. In Kerala awakening of people according to caste background against others is very common. Whether one belongs to high or low caste, s/he is conscious of his/her origin and feels a loyalty to his/her caste group. In this social situation, the organised sector of backward communities of Lutherans often turned against the administrations when they were not in power. Each group demanded its share in power and resources.[282] Crucial tensions for upward mobility and the inner struggle for self preservation further complicated the issues. The increasing absence of authoritative and paternal influence of missionaries aggravated the tensions.

4.11.1. Movement among the Backward Class Lutherans

The Lutherans from Scheduled Caste showed their unrest in connection with the formation of the Synod. They felt that they may be alienated from the power and others will dominate over them. Against the desire of the missionaries, as a compromise the Sambavars became the officers of TDS in the first Synod

---

[281] However, this positive trend cannot be found in the Tribal churches. Most of these congregations are struggling due to the ministerial and financial crisis.

[282] The crucial tension can be noticed in various reports, minutes, correspondence available during the period. For example see, The General secretaries report in the first General convention Minutes, 2; Report of the president, 18th TDS Convention, Trivandrum 21-23 November 1973, 2-4, and Luther W. Meinzen. *A Church in Mission: Identity and Purpose in India,* 100-101.

election.[283] But later years the most backward communities of Lutherans started their fight against others. The two major movements are discussed below.

4.11.1.1 Led by D. Vedamanikkom

The people who converted from the scheduled caste felt that they were neglected from the mainstream of the Church. They published a notice stating that these Lutherans were not properly cared for and the resources were not proportionally shared, therefore an organised move is inevitable to fight for the rights.[284] Another notice said: "the non Backward Class Lutherans are towering major portion of positions, employments and powers of TDS. If the same situation continues the Backward Class Lutherans will face the same situation which our parents felt with the LMS. In this situation, they questioned the need to continue as Lutherans."[285] With the statistical records they argued the necessity of a new organization for themselves to fight against the situation. Another notice was published by Paul Titus and P.D. Martin for the same cause.[286] In 1972 an association of united Christian Organization was formed under the leadership of two former TDS presidents; namely P.G. Kunju Kunju and K. Manuel.[287] This was a movement intended to seek remedies for their issues within the available provisions of IELC structure. They demanded more job opportunities, separate Trade and Technical Schools for the development of the backward class Lutherans. In 1973, D. Vedamanikkom changed his tone more inclusively and was told that not only for the backward class Lutherans, all caste Lutherans should live and grow together; all should fight for their dignity and rights.[288] After 15 years, he again raised his voice with communal arguments in the name of churches in Luthergiri, against the Synod and IELC officials and he approached the LCMS authorities with his grievances.[289] They demanded to IELC-CC for a separate Synod for the backward communities in Trivandrum Synod. After stating the need for a separate Synod in 31 points, the application concludes with these words; "Since the exploitation, discrimination, victimization, corruption, and maladministration have reached its highest level in Trivandrum synod and IELC, and since all other ways and means had failed, the backward community congregations and circles in Trivandrum

[283] Sukumaran Devadas, On Myself (Autobiography) vol.11, unpublished manuscript, 11.

[284] Action council, *IELC Avasa Christhavarude Avakasa Prakyapanam (Declaration of rights of IELC Backward class Christians) Printed Notice, 6 September, 1971.*

[285] Action council for IELC Backward Churches, *Is it need to us to be continue as the member churches of present TDS administration?* Printed notice, 11 November, 1971.

[286] Paul Titus and P D. Martin, A special notice to the Backward community Lutheran churches of IELC, 3 February, 1972.

[287] UX 72:3, 11. United Christian Organization Executive Minutes. 3 April, 1972.

[288] D. Vedamanikkom, A special notice to undeveloped churches, 11 July, 1973.

[289] D. Vedamanikom, letter to Edward Westcott, Executive secretary, LCMS and Louis Y. Nau Asia secretary BFMS-LCMS on 4 November, 1988.

Synod are are constrained to form a separate Synod at this appropriate time so as to enable to protect the destroying backward congregations and to strengthen the Lutheran confession in backward communities. It is prayed that the Church Council may please take urgent steps to do the needful."[290] The applicants severely criticised the Synod and the IELC administration throughout the petition for injustice, malpractice and corruption. Paul Chirakkarodu argues that, "in 1975 Dalit Christians in Lutheran Church again started their fight for rights."[291] The first three presidents D. Vedamanikom, Paul Titus and K. Manuel; were from the Sambava community. D. Vedamanikom served the TDS as its President for more than 14 years four six terms. In 1975, M.M. Yohannan, a non-Sambavar became the fourth President of TDS the first time on its history. He served about two and a half years as president. The next synod president was also a non Sambavar, J. Yovas.[292] More over D. Vedamanikom was under discipline action by TS and IELC due to his liabilities to the Church and a number of other complaints.[293] In 1973 an action council was started to function to fight for the rights of Nilamel Circle.[294] They tried to organise the people to channelize a considerable amount of fund from IELC for the benefit of the most backward tribal Lutheran Christians. But this action group became inactive in due course.

4.11.1.2. Kerala Lutheran Backward Synod

In 1987, another communal organization was declared: "Kerala Backward Lutherans Welfare Federation."[295] This was an association of the India Evangelical Lutheran Christian Converts from SC/ST.[296] Robinson David a former synod executive and BPLT member was the chief organiser of this association. Along with some other prominent lay leaders some TDS pastors also gave active leadership to this association. The following names of pastors were in the notice; M. Robinson, Y. Sukumaran, J. Sensar, K. Stephanose and A.J. Joseph.[297] They also published a

---

[290] M. Gomez, *Thullal Purayil Ninnu Thudakkam* (Beginning from an Occultist's shed (Nalanchira: Jayamatha, 2011), 204-209.

[291] Paul Chirakkarodu, *Dalith Cristhavar Keralathil* (Mal.) (Dalit Christians in Kerala) (Thiruvalla: CSS, 2000), 194.

[292] According to J. Yovel, the main problem for this agitation were not the caste issues but thirst for power. In order to hide their power mongering they highlighted the communal issues.

[293] TX 74:182, TX 77: 03, TX 77:33.

294 C. Kunju Kunju, Meenkulam, Convenor, action group for Nilamel circle, *Adarsamellam pinnokkakaranum Adayamellam munnokkakaranum* (All dreams to Backward people and All profits to forward people), 9/11/1973.

[295] The declaration of this association was done on 6 August, 1987 and registered under Charitable societies Act XII of 198 with Reg. No. 84/1988. *Evangelical Sabha Pilarnnu* (Evangelical Church had split) *Madhyamam,* daily news paper, 9 January, 1989.

[296] Letter from M. Soosappan, President TS to D. John Hus, President, IELC, 25/7/1988.

[297] Notices published on 2 March1988,& August 1987, 1 November, 1988.

booklet which explained the need of this federation in detail.[298] In 11 December 1988 they declared themselves as a separate synod in IELC and they were able to get favourable judgements from the courts.[299] But IELC Constitution states the procedure for forming new synods.[300] Therefore the then IELC president D. John Hus wrote: "... Hence this unilateral declaration of forming a new synod is unconstitutional, illegal and invalid. IELC cannot countenance any member of IELC having membership in such unlawful organization which will destroy the unity of the church. .. Any one owing allegiance to the so called Kerala Backward Lutheran Synod of IELC cannot be allowed to claim any rights or privileges in IELC or in any of its three synods."[301] But this letter was not able to stop the functioning of Kerala Lutheran Backward Synod. The Neyyattinkara Munsiff Court also passed a decree against the suit by a permanent injunction restraining this group from trespassing into the IELC-TDS property or interfering or causing obstruction to the rights and possessions over the properties of IELC-TA.[302] Thereafter, very many Court cases were filed between congregations of TDS and Kerala Synod and still it continues to be an unending dispute.[303] Kerala Government approved Robinson David as the corporate manager of corporate management schools under IELC Kerala synod.[304] KLBS started to function as a rebel and communal organization from August 1987. Even after 25 years, either the TS or IELC is able to do anything against it. It shows the ability and credibility of the so-called authorities.

4.11.2. Nadar Lutheran Christian Movement

As we had seen earlier, in Kerala over the years, the major mass movements towards Christianity came from the Nadar communities. The Nadars were organised to fight for their rights and equality. After one century MELIM started their work in South Travancore. From the beginnings itself, Nadars actively joined the mission. In later years, members from Nadar community got elected or nominated in

[298] Robinson David, Backward Lutheran churches are on struggle, 34 page Booklet, 24 January, 1988.

[299] O.S. No. 656/2002, OS No. 720/2002; O.S. No. 190/2004, CMA 2/2003, CMA 9/ 2006, AS No. 325/ 2003.

[300] IELC Constitution Article VI A.4,11.

[301] Letter from D. John Hus, President, IELC to The officers of IELC, Church council members of IELC, Election Commission, Synod Officials and unit heads, 15 December, 1988.

[302] Judgment of Additional Munsif of Thiruvananthapuram on O.S.362/1989, 31/1/1992.

[303] Judgment dated 30 September 2003 by the Additional Munsiff, II, Neyyattinkara on the injunction appeal by IELC-TA, TDS and N. Mohan against Kerala synod OS. 720/2002; Judgment by additional Munsiff. I. Neyyattinkara upon the case OS. 656/2002 between Kerala Synod and Mohan dated 31 March 2005. O.S. No. 190/2004, CMA 2/2003, CMA 9/ 2006, A.S. No. 325/ 2003.

[304] Proceedings of the additional Director of Public Instruction (General) Thiruvananthapuram, order no. ET4/ 52533/11/ DPI/ D.Dis. dated 2/3/2012.

the administrative power of the Synod. It was a common phenomenon that whenever a Nadar became an officer of this Church non Nadar communities used the caste card against them to disrupt their function. It was very clear that the persons whom were trained by the missionaries for future leadership of this Church were alienated through the caste politics. The two major issues among the Nadar Lutherans were denial of voting rights and denial of reservation by the Government.

4.11.2.1. Denial of Voting Rights

Denial of voting rights by the majority groups to the minority using the IELC administration was very common in the Trivandrum Synod. Through imposing unjust assessment amount, punishment transfers and other means lot of the Nadar churches and members were purposely throw aside from becoming the part of administrative system. Several appeals and attempts were made to grow together. In 1987, an All IELC Pastors Communion submitted some valuable recommendations for the fruitful and joint functioning of IELC.[305] But no one cared about that. During the 1993 Lent, Ponvila, a Nadar dominated circle of TS analysed the whole situation and it came forward with some valuable suggestions focussing on the fivefold ministry of the church.[306] But that appeal also was thrown away. There were a lot of appeals sent by the Trivandrum circle another Nadar majority membership circle to correct the Church and find the remedies within the existing structure.[307]

One of the oldest members of this Church C. Albert[308] says: "The neglecting attitude or the lack of interest on the part of the LCMS representatives and other dignitaries' happened to be very helpful for the illegitimate leaders and rulers to continue their corrupt practices and to leave the administration in total anarchy. They tried to make others believe that they are trying their level best to solve the existing problems. But we are very sure that they could never agree to any suggestion to get a free and fair election conducted, in a democratic way. They have their own people to file court cases for and against every step. If at all an election is conducted they want to make sure that the result should be favourable to them, and hence they always eliminate the strong and living eligible congregations from

---

[305] PC Document, A R Victor Raj.

[306] From the churches and pastors of Ponvila circle, An open appeal to the members, officials, pastors, Institutions and local churches of IELC, 18 page printed booklet, 22/3/1993.

[307] From Trivandrum Circle, An appeal, 23/9/1997, An appeal on behalf of 10 congregations in Trivandrum Circle who had deliberately denied the right to exercise their franchise, to the IELC and LCMS officials, 24/1/2003; resolution submitted by the churches and pastors of IELC-TS to LCMS officers through Dr. Herbert Hoefer12/6/2004.

[308] C. Albert (87) is a son of Lutheran catechist and served in the local church as President, Secretary and Treasurer for many years and was the TX member and Treasurer of TDS.

the electoral roll, and keep all paper churches promptly included in the list."[309] These show that the confusions were not accidental but were consciously created.

An experienced pastor and administrator Gifton E. Joshua evaluates: "Our congregations had always been willing to accept the responsibility of paying the assessment amount promptly, until recently. But when there was no administration set up and the custodians started raising the amount according to their own will, which is unconstitutional and against all democratic convention, these congregations expressed their displeasure. When we came to know that the assessment money was not used for the purpose for which it was intended, we refused to pay". He continues: "The Synod and some circles do not have any active evangelistic program. But our churches have well arranged evangelistic programs of our own without any assistance from the Synod or IELC. Church buildings are renovated in order to accommodate more people, new parsonages are constructed, new mission fields are opened, and social service projects are run, etc. Our churches are paying to our pastor's slightly better salaries than the outdated IELC scale. If anybody is really interested then let them come and see what is happening among us and asses the situations then let them take decisions. Should we be punished for what we have been doing?"[310]

Active layman D. Titus[311] comments: "the glorious tradition and heritage of this potentially great church has been spoiled by playing dirty politics and ridiculous tricks. Our institutions are in a very pathetic condition, not in a position to serve the purpose for which they were established. The institutions have become a source of taping money for political games and personal gains. Imposing illogical and undemocratic policies and regulations cannot be accepted and tolerate anymore. We want our people, and future generation to grow in Word and in Faith. We want people with moral and spiritual strength to live as dignified Lutheran Christians." He adds: "... The credibility and the mission of the Church are lost. A divided and un-disciplined Church cannot grow. The political favouritism and nepotism have reached their highest level. All most all Courts of Law in South India and even Supreme Court are dealing IELC appeals. The congregations having large membership, educated Lutherans are consciously alienating from administrative process. Through the political arrangements or administrative adjustments we cannot expect a God pleasing solution to our deep

---

[309] Interview with C. Albert on 8 July 2012.

[310] Interview with Gifton E. Joshua (69) Retired pastor of IELC, Former TX member, Chief Editor of *Christiani* and Comptroller of IELC, 12 July 2012. At the time of interview he explained the procedures which he initiated for a fare assessment system while he was the Comptroller of IELC, but due to non co-operation it was not a success.

[311] D. Titus is a retired bank Engineer from bank service and active volunteer of LLF and all evangelistic affairs in the Trivandrum Circle. He also served as the consulting engineer for the church buildings, parsonage and parish halls. Presently he is the president of the Keopke Memorial Lutheran Church, Peroorkada.

rooted issues."[312] These observations show how the Nadars felt the discriminations from the IELC-Synod authorities. Their conclusion is; "If the responsible persons try again to accelerate the speed of present chaos, we will be dragged to seek other ways to safe guard our Christian identity, churches, compounds and institutions for His holy cause," said J. Yovel.[313] Another problem facing the Nadar Lutherans is government discrimination in connection with the reservation.

4.11.2.2. Nadar Lutherans and Reservation Issues

As a secular State, Indian Constitution promised equal privilege to all religions. The special reservation is based on backwardness of the caste and not according to the difference of denominations. The Tamil Nadu Government treated all Nadars as Backward class people. Government of India considers Nadar community as a whole (irrespective of religious affiliations) for recruitment to central Government employment in tune with the findings of the Mandal Commission Report.[314] In Kerala Nadar community is not considered as a whole (irrespective of religious affiliations) for recruitment to State government employment and for purposes of admission to educational institutions, even though the State Order is in force which considers Nadars as a whole.[315] In Kerala, the State reservations were divided to Hindu Nadar, CSI Nadar, and Other Nadar Christians differently on the basis of religious affiliations, which is against the spirit of Indian Constitution. Nadars included in "Other Christians" had been thrown out of the range of reservation through an order of the government of Kerala.[316] The Hindu Nadars and the SIUC Nadars of Kerala included in the classification of communities and Communal Recognition in connected with the reservation issue.[317] In a Special Order, Government included the rest of the Nadar Christians as "Other Christians". by which a rare opportunity were provided other Nadar Christians including the Lutherans.[318] Nettur Damodharan Commission[319] found that SIUC was merged with CSI and ceased to exist from 27 September 1947. Then the government treated Hindu Nadars as a separate class and SIUC as another class including all

[312] Interview with D. Titus, 12 July, 2012.

[313] J. Yovel (76) was the Synod Secretary, TX member, Comptroller of IELC and an active member in Lutheran laymen's fellowship and Lutheran Voice. Interview with him on 14/7/2012.

[314] Gazette notification issued by Government of India, No. 71, 4/4/2000., Nadars are also in OBC list, *Hindu* daily, 17/3/2000, *Mathrubhoom*i Daily, 18/3/ 2000.

[315] G.O. (P)No. 36/2000/SC/ST DD(F)27 May 2000.

[316] Order of the Government of Kerala No. R Dis 26706/57/PD, 14/12/ 1957.

[317] Order from the N. Kunjan Pillai, Chief Secretary to Government to the Public Service Commissioner, Order No. R.Dis. No. 893/General 25 June, 1935.

[318] Order No. S2-15238/50/ CS 17/9/1952.

[319] Nettur P. Damodharan Pillai Commission was appointed by the Government of Kerala for finding the list of socially and educationally Backward Classes of citizens in Kerala for the purpose of Art.15(4) by the Full Bench of High Court direction K.L.T. 266 order No. G.O.Ms. No. 343/ PD17/ 10/ 1967.

other Nadar Christians including the Lutheran, Roman Catholic, Pentecostals, etc. The above position continued till 1979. But the State government without proper study excluded other Nadar Christians from SIUC through an Order.[320] Through another order from Kerala Government in 2009 further divides reservation among Hindu Nadars and SIUC Nadars[321] and thrown out fully the Lutheran Nadars from reservation benefits.[322] Hence, Nadar Lutherans in Kerala became in the forward class.

Since the representations were not heard Nadar Lutherans tried to fight for justice in an organised way. They were actively joined with "*Samvararanam Nastapetta Pinnokka Christian Association*" (SNPCA - Backward Christian Association who were excluded from reservation).[323] But the Nadar Lutherans got a legal advice that it was a clear violation of our Constitution that the discrimination of a community according to faith/denomination. Here it is also worthy to mention that neither the TDS nor IELC take any steps to fight against this age old injustice which was experienced by its members. Therefore, a voluntary movement of its members were moved to form "Nadar Lutheran welfare Society" (NLWS) to fight against the Government discrimination.[324] They were able to make this issue sensational one those days.[325] They approached the Government with various representations but there were of no use.[326] Now the judicial Appeal of Nadar Lutherans is pending with at Supreme Court of India.[327]

---

[320] G.O. R.Dist 26706/57/PD 14/12/1957 G.O. (MS) No. 341/79/GAD 20 June, 1979. The same position was repeated in the notification through the political influence of CSI .G.O. (P) No. 409/ 82/ GAD 13 December 1982.

[321] South India United Church (SIUC) was a denomination of Christianity that ceased to exist on 26th September 1947, merging together with the CSI.

[322] G.O.(MS) 104/2009/SCSTOP, 21/11/2009.

[323] This is a registered Society having the office at Parassala with the membership from Ezhava and Nadar communities from Lutheran, Latin Catholic, Malankara Syrian Catholic Church, Evangelical Church of India and Pentecostals (Reg. No. T797/2003).

[324] For more details about the Nadar Lutheran Welfare Society (Reg. no. 1417/2003) see *Neethikkay Anicheru* (Join for Justice) circular No.1 published by NLWS on 23/7/2003.

[325] For the sample of the daily news in Malayalam news paper see, *Malayala Manorama* Daily, 14 June 2003 2T; 12/8/2003, 13; 22 August 2003, 3; 23 August 2003,11; 8, October 2003, 26, 26 November 2003, 14; 16 January, 2004, 3 March 2004,16, 10, April, 2004, 14; 5 February, 2006, 13; 4/12/2009, etc.

[326] NLWS representation to J.W. Gladstone, CSI, Bishop, 18/8/2003; letter to Vincent Samuel, Bishop of Latin Catholic Diocese; Chief Minister of Kerala, 22/9/2003; representation to Kerala State Commission for Backwards Classes, 15/5/ 2004; W.P (C). No. 7897 of 2004NLWS Vs Kerala State and Others, 23/2/ 2004; Hearing note to KSCBC no. 1232/ 95/ c/ KSCBC, 11/ February 2005.

[327] This sheer injustice and partiality that is being imposed on the Nadar community in Kerala in the manner of reservation has been challenged by Nadar Co-ordination council through the Writ petition (civil) no. 107/2010 before the Supreme Court of India, 29/3/2010. This is a joint

4.11.3. Movements among the Ezhava Lutherans

The Ezhava Lutherans were very active for spreading the gospel in a systematic way by using their own resources. Bethel Evangelism Fellowship (BEF) - The movement mostly among the Ezhava Lutherans was started on 1 November 1985. By seeing failure of the organized church in mission this movement focused to evangelise their own people with their own money, persons and other resources. They published guidelines which narrates the objectives and nature of this fellowship.[328] Bethel Evangelism Fellowship is a voluntary movement for the Chenkavila-Cheruvalloor-Karakonam pastorate of Ponvila Circle, TS. These churches will have their major membership from Ezhava Community. The main objectives of the fellowship are Evangelism, and social service. The first meeting was held at Karakonam on 15 November 1985 and resolved the following objectives: 'Propagate gospel to unreached people through founding Family churches. Start BEF units in various places. Publish a bulletin and small booklets and tracts. Conduct seminars, conferences and conventions.' In order to achieve these goals an Ad Hoc committee was formed under the Presidentship of K. Suseelan with five other members. They met once in three months. They tried to renew the work at Alleppey-Schertallay areas in 1987. The pastors like K. Suseelan, T. Joy, J.C. Gamaliel, N. Vasudevan Nair, K. Alexander, P.K. George and P.K. Parameswarn were in the forefront along with the laymen like G. Madhavan, K. Krishnan and Charals. In 1987 they started the training of voluntary evangelists from the Chenkavila-Cheruvalloor pastorate. In 1991 new units were formed in Trivandrum, Chenkavila, Karakkonam, Cheruvalloor and Keezhroor. On 12 November 1992 BEF was registered under 12th Thiru–Cochi Literary-Science and Charity act of 1952 Reg. No. 722/92.[329]

The aim widened with the hope to build 100 churches in 2000 A.D. and 100 more Evangelists and pastors. BEF also planned to start a printing press, Library, Orphanage-Old age home, and a vocational guidance centre.[330] Bethel Theological Institute (BTI) was started on 5 January 1991.[331] April 2001 BEF board meeting formed seven more sub committees for the future fruitful service. The sub committees were Spiritual Edification, theological Education, New centre Evangelism, Social Service, Publication, Finance, and Care for Sick.[332] The Board of Directors BEF on 12 January 2002 approved a ten year project such as village

---

movement of NLWS, Malankara Nadar Christian Association, *Kerala Nadar Mahajana Sanghom*, Nadar co-ordination council, etc.

[328] Secretary BEF, Easter letter, 25/3/1988.

[329] For more details J.C. Gamaliel, Bethel Evangelism Fellowship- A short history, *BEF Souvenir* 1995 January,1-4; *BEF Bulletin,* 13 March 1993, 6.

[330] *Bethel Evangelism Fellowship Bulletin*, 13 March 1993, 7.

[331] Bethel Theological Institute, K. Sathyaseelan, Registrar, *BEF Souvenir*, January 1995, 29-30.

[332] BELL News Letter of BEF, 5/2001, 2.

Evangelism, Lutheran School of Missiology and Research, Heubner Memorial Library, Bethel Theological Institute and Research Centre, Bethel Tract Mission, Bethel Nursery School, Tailoring Institute, Type writing and computer centre and so on.[333] The Annual General Body meeting of BEF at Chenkavila on 28 October 2009 approved the suggestion for the establishment of James Canjanam Gamaliel Endowment.[334] Majority of Ezhava Lutheran Churches and except a few Pastors from this community joined together in the activities of BEF. The effort for taking the Gospel to the unreached with own resources should be appreciated. In 2010 BEF celebrated its Silver Jubilee. Like the other Lutheran experiments in Kerala, this movement is also slowly loosing the dynamism after the demise of its founder J.C. Gamaliel.[335]

4.11.4. Beyond Caste Consciousness

Nowadays caste awareness among the people in Kerala is quite natural. The caste identity of a person remains even after the conversion to Christianity due to the deep rooted social and cultural factors. Kerala society witnessed the emergence of communal awakening all over the State. The Lutheran Christians who belongs to a particular caste also need to co-operate with such movements to fight for their common rights and to keep their identity. This influence may also initiate the diverse caste groups within the Lutheran fold to organize them. Yet, it did not hinder the mutual growth and life togetherness. For example there are non Nadar pastors working in Nadar[336] congregations, so also in the Sambavars churches the Nadar pastors are well received.[337] The local congregations still have membership from five to six caste Lutherans.[338] Among the ordinary Lutherans there are no caste issues as such. But the Church politicians are using the caste cards for their

---

[333] For more details of the minutes see, *BEF Work Report* 2001-2002, 2-6.

[334] *The Constitution of Rev.Dr. James Kanjanam Gamaliel Endowment,* 13/9/2009; S. Cleatus, *24th Annual Meeting Report of BEF,* 28/10/2009.

[335] J.C. Gamaliel son of Rev. J.C. James was born in 25 December 1925 at Kuttichal. In 1943 he passed ESLC from Concordia High School and got BA from Trivandrum University College in 1947. Next year he started his career as a teacher and then joined the Concordia Seminary for ministerial training. After the ordination on 1952, he worked at Ernakulam and Bombay fields. He upgraded with higher studies at, Leonard Theological College, Jabalpur; Fuller Theological College, California; Concordia Seminary, St. Louis, USA; Erlangen University, Germany; Tubingen university, Germany; Edinburg University, Scotland and got various Masters degrees and three Doctorates. Between these studies he also served Chengavila pastorate and Concordia Seminary, Nagercoil and retired as Principal Concordia Seminary Nagercoil in 1999 and died on 4th October 2005. He was the instrument for the Institution of BEF & BTI; founding many congregations and to publish many books.

[336] For example Ruben Paras (Marayamuttom), M. Gomez (Kalparapotta) and so on.

[337] For examples K. Sathyadas (Tholoor), Valsalaraj (Devicode) and so on.

[338] Few examples are, City Lutheran Church, Calvary Lutheran Church, Mylakkara Lutheran Church, Keopke Memorial Lutheran Church and Concordia Lutheran Church, etc.

own vested interests. The plurality of caste mixture makes Lutheran in Kerala as a unique community of subalterns. Christians are called to transcend the narrow particularities in order to arrive at a higher, wider and deeper level of sharing with all human beings. This demands a transformation of Lutherans in Kerala from within their innermost being, to accept all others as brothers and sisters.

There is a lack of trust and confidence within the pastors and members, and there is unwillingness to forgive and to be reconciled with one another. There is inability or unwillingness of accountability. The political system has divided the Church into parties which fights for power, prestige and money. There is a lack of spiritual leadership and wide spread confusion. Local congregations and pastors are divided into groups, castes and parties. There is political favouritism, and also nepotism in appointments to Church positions and job. Money is used to manipulate people, makes power. Those who have money can even purchase judgments from court. Due to lack of proper Church discipline there are unending litigations and court cases. There are maladministration and misappropriation. The pious Lutherans started leaving the Church and joining other denominations. The Lutheran Christians of Scheduled caste origins are forced to reconvert into Hinduism for reservation benefits from Government. Some of the Lutherans are tempted to have double membership one in Lutheran church and another in one non Lutheran denomination which would provide government special reservation privileges. The member's passive silence and inactiveness is the best opportunities for those who are holding power. The ordinary Lutherans are in big confusion without proper guidance. There is no sign of people's movements for the correction of the erring Church. In this context an emergence of a joint people's movement from grass root level with a Lutheran community conscious becomes an inevitable need. All Lutherans should join together for a common goal. Practice of intermarriage among the sub castes, sharing the resources equally, participatory form of leadership are some of the working models to get rid of the narrow caste feelings.[339]

4.12. Conclusion

Historically, MELIM was the latest mainline Christian denomination to enter the Kerala scene. Unlike many other mission agencies, the MELIM went beyond one caste group and reached out to all subalterns of their fields.[340] People belonging

---

[339] Interview with Advocate Betsy M. Joseph, an activist and leading women worker of TS and was the Chair person of Women desk of UELCI, on 18 July, 2012.

[340] The majority of the mainline Christian denominations in India have a certain specific caste orientation. It stands to reason that as such this subculture functions as an infrastructure that has brought certain stability to those churches institutionally, perhaps based on the homogeneous unit principle. This does not mean that other caste Christians are not included in the membership of any particular denominations. They are, although continuing to remain a minority in terms of headcount. Certain particular castes visibly dominate the entire organization and administration of the Districts, and Dioceses of these churches. Even today there are at least some examples of

to the marginalized communities largely joined together for their upward social mobility which led to the formation of IELC. Lutheran membership of Kerala come from numerous castes sub-castes, the majority of which were deemed outcastes in the out of date but particularly all-pervading Hindu caste system. Plurality of caste in the same Church proved to be both a blessing and a problem. The authoritative, parental and missionary centred leadership style was able to hold together all these diverse communities. The national Church, IELC-TDS was started without competent national leadership. In the formative years this Church started to find the remedies and strength for moving forward with various efforts like Evangelism, Children, Youth, Lay and Women ministries, Literature and Educational ministries and so on. But unfortunately it fell into years of crisis. Peace and reconciliation movements were not able to cure the disease. Administrative stagnation, unending Court cases and State Governments discriminations against the Lutheran Christians weakened the growth and mission of this Church. The issues like maladministration, instability and litigations very badly affected the possibility of collective wisdom and pushed the Church into disunity and failure of vision for mission. Even though there were some positive signs, the present situation necessitates the need of an empirical investigation to find out the various theological, structural and missiological issues behind the situation so that IELC can identify its strengths and weakness to move forward with a guiding vision. But our immediate concern in the following chapter is an enquiry about the existential struggles of these subalterns for life, identity and security in their socio-cultural context. Even after embracing Lutheran Christianity, social and cultural integration had not fully taken place between various Lutheran communities as seen in the first chapter of this study; the beginning of the 20th century witnessed an awakening of caste consciousness without any religious distinction. People of the same caste tried to organize and fight for their rights. So also the Lutherans of different castes had a consciousness of their own separate caste. Therefore, the discussions move to the next chapter towards the significance of Subaltern Studies in Kerala and the emergence of the major Subaltern Movements in their immediate context.

---

congregations that maintain their membership with a particular diocese transcending their geographical locations, particularly on castes grounds.

Chapter 5

Subaltern Solidarity: Cause

5.1. Introduction

The new facilities of historical research and vast treasurers of source materials have come into light in India's post independent era. Along with this new development, the historians' tone of voice has also rightly shifted from the rulers and the ruling dynasties to the people. The earlier trend was a clear undermining of the marginalized. So far the attention had been on the rulers, the elites and the powerful ones. The post independent era witnessed a shift of emphasis to the people and their experiences. This shift has come about largely due to the changing context of India, when people's movements and protest movements started to emerge. This chapter is an enquiry into the significance of subaltern consciousness, subaltern studies and movements in the socio-cultural context of Kerala. Then move towards the major factors which led to the emergence of Lutheran Subaltern Solidarity in Kerala. In order to move forward, firstly we need an understanding of Subaltern consciousness.

5.2. The Significance of Subalternity

5.2.1. Subaltern - Meaning and Significance of the Term

The expression '*Subaltern*' has travelled from Europe to our continent. The word *Subaltern*[1] has a long past. In late medieval English, it was applied to vassals and peasants. By 1700, it denoted lower ranks in the military, suggesting peasant origins.[2] By 1800, authors writing from a subaltern perspective published novels

---

[1] Meaning 'of inferior rank', (commonly used in Malayalam as *Keezhalar/ Adiyalar*).

[2] David Luden, *Reading Subaltern Studies: Critical Histories, Contested Meaning and the Globalization of South Asia* (Delhi: Permanent Black, 2002), 4.

and histories about military campaigns in India.[3] Italian Communist thinker Antonio Gramaci (1891-1937), began to merge ideas about subaltern identity into theories of class struggles.[4] The term 'Subaltern' means non-elite or subordinated social groups.[5] This was to identify the social groups who were excluded from the established structures for political representation in the given society. Subaltern is a term that refers to those groups in society who are subject to the dominion of the ruling classes.[6] Subaltern classes may include peasants, workers and other groups who are denied access to 'hegemonic' power. Since, the history of the ruling classes is realized in the State, history becomes the history of states and dominant groups. Gramsci was interested in the historiography of the subaltern classes. He claimed that the history of the subaltern classes was just as complex as the history of the dominant classes, although the history of the latter is usually that which is accepted as 'official' history.[7] For him, the history of subaltern social groups is necessarily split and periodic, since they are always subject to the activity of ruling groups, even when they rebel. Clearly, they have less access to cultural and social institutions.

In the 1970's, the application of subaltern began to refer to the colonized peoples of the South-Asian sub continent.[8] In the 1980s, the scope of enquiry of "Subaltern Studies" (SS) was applied as an intervention in South Asian historiography, history told from below. The quick applicability of the techniques of the subaltern studies transformed the study into a "vigorous post-colonial critique."[9] The efficiency of the term "Subaltern" eased its adaption and adoption to the methods of investigation in the fields of history, anthropology, sociology, human geography and literature. According to Ranajit Guha, the word 'subaltern'

---

[3] G.R. Gleig (1796-1888), who wrote biographies of Robert Clive, Warren Hastings and Thomas Munro, mastered this genre. For more details see David Luden, Reading Subaltern Studies: Critical Histories, Contested Meaning and the Globalization of South Asia (Delhi: Permanent Black, 2002), 5.

[4] Gyan Prakash, "Subaltern Studies as Postcolonial Criticism," *The American Historical Review*, 99/5, December, 1994), 1475-1490, 1476.

[5] Donna Landry & Gerald Maclean (eds.), *The Spivak Reader* (London: Routledge, 1996), 23.

[6] Geofrry Nowell Smith (Ed.) *Selections from the Prison Note Books of Antonio Gramsci*, (Chennai: Orient Longman, 1988), 52-53.

[7] James Massey, "Subaltern Movements and their Theological Relevance", In: George Keerankeri & V.P. Srivastava (ed.) *Taking Text to Context* (Delhi: ISPCK, 2011), 101.

[8] For more discussion see Vinayak Chadurvedi, ed. *Mapping Subaltern Studies and the Post Colonial* (London: Verso, 2000); David Luden, *Reading Subaltern Studies: Critical Histories, Contested Meaning and the Globalization of South Asia* (Delhi: Permenent Black, 2002); Ranjit Guha, On the Aspect of the Historiography and colonial India", *Subaltern Studies,* R.Guha, ed.vol. 1 (Delhi: Oxford University Press, 1982); Gayathri Chakravarthy Spivak, "Can The Subaltern Speak? In, *Colonial Discourses and Post-Colonial Theory: A Reader",* Patrick Williams and Laura Chrisman (eds.) (New York: Columbia University Press, 1994), 66-111.

[9] P. Sanal Mohan, *Keezhala Patanangalum Dalit Charithravum* (Subaltern Studies and Dalit History), *Malayalam Weekly*, 15/52 (25 May, 2012): 48-58.

stands for the meaning 'of inferior rank'. He has used the term people and the subaltern classes as synonyms throughout his works.[10] For him, the subalternity represents "demographic difference between the total Indian population and all those whom we have described as the 'elite.'[11] Guha recognized that there is some vagueness about these terms, classes, and groups such as smaller rural gentry, poor landlords, rich peasants and upper middle class peasants. For him they are ranked among the people and the subaltern and under certain conditions, they act for the elite.[12]

The philosopher and theoretician Gayatri Spivak advised against a too-broad application of the term, because:

> *. . . subaltern is not just a classy word for "oppressed", for [the] Other, for somebody who's not getting a piece of the pie. . . . In post-colonial terms, everything that has limited or no access to the cultural imperialism is subaltern - a space of difference. Now, who would say that's just the oppressed? The working class is oppressed. Many people want to claim subalternity. They are the least interesting and the most dangerous. I mean, just by being a discriminated-against minority on the university campus; they don't need the word 'subaltern' . . . They should see what the mechanics of the discrimination are. They're within the hegemonic discourse, wanting a piece of the pie, and not being allowed, so let them speak, use the hegemonic discourse. They should not call themselves subaltern.*[13] *Regarding the usage of the term Subaltern James Massey opines, "The subaltern historians like Ranajit Guha take very general view of the Indian society and in doing so they tend to become inaccurate as far as the Indian context is concerned."*[14] In his view Indian psyche can only be understood against the graph of caste system.

The term 'subaltern' specifically denotes the oppressed peoples at the margins of a society who are struggling against hegemonic globalization. Yet, the context, time and place determine who is a subaltern among the peoples at the margins of society. While the subalterns by definition are groups who had their voices silenced, they can speak through their actions as a way to protest

---

[10] Ranajit Guha (ed.), *Subaltern Studies 1: Writings on South Asian History and Society* (Delhi: Oxford University Press, 1982), (Preface vii).

[11] Ranajit Guha (ed.), *Subaltern Studies 1: Writings on South Asian History and Society* (Delhi: Oxford University Press, 1982), 8.

[12] V.V. Thomas, *Subaltern Historiography & Postcolonial Theory: The Case of Dalit Pentecostalism in Kerala,* Paper presented in CHAI Conference, Secunderbad, Oct. 26-29, 2000, 6.

[13] Leon de Kock, "Interview with Gayatri Chakravorty Spivak: New Nation Writers Conference in South Africa." *ARIEL: A Review of International English Literature.* 23 (3) 1992: 29-47. ARIEL http://ariel.synergiesprairies.ca/ariel/index.php/ariel/article/viewFile /2505/2458

[14] James Massey, *Subaltern Movements…op.cit,* 103.

against mainstream development and create their own visions for development.[15] Subaltern groups are creating social movements to keep their identity and develop solidarity. These groups use local knowledge and struggle to create new spaces of opposition and alternative futures.[16]

Subalternity is a situation or the place where the subalterns are. It is a context that has been caused by various factors of this country hard-pressed into. In Kerala, the caste system which prevailed over here is the major thing. The majority of the people of this State considered as the "outcastes" are outside the four 'Varna' system of the Hindu religion. This has pushed them into economic, social, and cultural disabilities.[17]

5.2.2. Background of the Subaltern Studies

As an unending dialogue between the past and the present, history looks forward to the future. In this process, Indian Christian historiography has also gone through a number of perspective shifts. It was deeply rooted in the religious-cultural context of India and in the general Indian historiography. Like other disciplines, history has its own method, which the practitioners of history are expected to follow. The methodological shift in the writing of history in India began in the 19th century. National movement and other Indian situations brought some radical historiographical changes. Colonial experience and nationalism of recent centuries have influenced new methodological shift.

Marxist theory and post-colonial theory[18] were used as tools for the later developments. From the institutional history to people centered approach was a welcome change. The Marxist historiography emerged as a powerful alternative during the post nationalist period. It was the methodological advance than thematic shift. They tend to enlarge the vision of our traditionalist historians.[19] The Marxist method was informed by the theoretical sensitivity, which enabled the conceptualization of the process of social transformation.[20] Marxist perspective emphasizes people's struggles and peasant's movements. A new way of interrogating the historical reality thus came into being. Analysis and explanations in terms of

---

[15] Gayatri Chakravarty Spivak, "Can the Subaltern Speak?" in *Colonial Discourse and Post –Colonial Theory: A Reader,* Patrick Williams and Laura Chrisman (eds.) (New York: Columbia University Press, 1994), 66-111.

[16] Victoria Lawson, *Making Development Geography,* (UK: Hodder Education, 2007).

[17] V.V. Thomas, "Subaltern Historiography and Postcolonial Theory: The Case of Dalit Pentecostalism in Kerala", Religion and Society, 49.2&3, (June –Sep.2004): 127.

[18] Post-colonial theory began to draw larger attention with the appearance of Edward Said's *Orientalism* in 1978. Said's main attempt was to expose the weakness of the ideology of imperialism. It was a challenge to the historical field to remove the guise of ideological discourse on imperialism from the colonial discourse. *Ibid.* 128.

[19] Shankar Goyal, *Recent Historiography of Ancient India* (Jodhpur: Kusumanjali Book World, 1997), 426.

[20] *The Struggling for the Past,* 16.

economic production and social classes have become basic tenets in historical reconstruction in India. It has been particularly strong in exploring the origins of human situations.[21] Marxist approach to the history of India served as a corrective for the over-sentimentalized and over-spiritualized accounts of India. But Marxist historiographers conveniently forget that Marxism is not a substitute for thinking but is a methodology of analysis.[22] Marxism had a stimulating and liberating effect in confirming the manifold problems of history writing. Marx's influence in some manner or the other could be seen in almost everything of importance relating to history published since the late 19th century. The influence of Marxism in modern historiography could be seen in the emphasis it laid on the work of the masses. Large sections of people, hitherto unnoticed, have become legitimate objects of historical inquiry. Along with colonial and National historiography, Marxist historiography is also viewed as elitist in character. Therefore, subaltern history was conceived as an alternative to all other historiographies.

5.2.3. Subaltern Historiography

Indian Subaltern Studies became visible in India after the publication of *Elementary Aspects of Peasant Insurgency in Colonial India* by Ranjit Guha in 1983. Traditional historians addressed the progress of the State, whereas Guha and the other Subalternists wrote about the activities of those peripheralized by the State. If the first used "event history", the other used myth and legend. The former one was homogenized, the other particularized. The traditionalists praised the development of nationalism, but the subalternists found its faults.[23]

The collective SS came out in India in the early eighties. The most significant moment in the development of this school happened when the subaltern study series were published.[24] The SS are collections of monographs on diverse, unconnected topics. SS are fine examples of radical scholarship. It is brings historical enquiry to the foundations of Indian Society. Subaltern historiography[25]

---

[21] E. Sreedharan, *op.cit.*, 487.

[22] Shankar Goyal, *op.cit.*

[23] For an overview by one its American protagonists, Gyan Prakash,"Subaltern Studies as Post-Colonial Criticism," *American Historical Review* (December 1994) 1475-1490. The changing nature of the master concept of subalternity is noted on pp. 1478ff.; The link between Gramsci and the Subaltern Studies group in so far as it can be made appears in David Arnold, "Gramsci and Peasant Subalternity," *The Journal of Peasant Studies* V.11 (July 1984) 155-177. For the de-linking from Gramsci of a number of Indian Subalternists, see the series of articles on Gramsci in *Economic and Political Weekly* (Bombay) of January 30, 1988.

[24] Subaltern studies 1: *Writings on South Asian History and Society* (1982) and Ranajit Guha's pioneering work: *Elementary Aspects of Peasant Insurgency in Colonial India* (1982) were published first. Since then eleven volumes and several other books have appeared representing the school of history. Ranajit Guha edited the first six volumes of Subaltern Studies.

[25] V.V. Thomas' works on understanding subaltern history is an excellent contribution in this line. See V.V. Thomas, *Understanding Subaltern History: Theoretical Tools* (Bangalore: BETSSC/

is digging the innumerable records from their dusty shelves in dark rooms which stand witness to many a story of faith and struggles. Recently, subaltern studies and their methodology have received international academic attention and it is recognized as one of the most unique Asian or Indian contributions to the academia.[26] The subaltern group has come forward to write people's history – the history of the oppressed and the exploited.[27] This was not new in Indian historiography, the concern of the Marxist historians has been precisely that. But now the qualitative change is in its methodology by ushering in the people's history from below.[28] The major marginalized groups in Indian society, Dalits, Tribals and women, hardly appear in Subaltern studies. They are rejected because of the idea that nationalism was predominantly an elite achievement.[29] This is a search to identify the politics of the people that are left out in the "unhistorical historiography."[30] "Maker of his/her own destiny" is the claim by the subaltern school. It opened the possibility of many local, regional and communitarian histories.[31] The subaltern historiography is trying to bring to light the lowest sections of the Indian people who were neglected in the previous histories. The unique contribution of subaltern historiography is to challenge researchers to identify signifiers of these subjectivities in the local area that the researcher is studying. Subaltern methodology is the recognition and restoration of the people who were either silenced or ignored by elite discourses. Here, the subalterns are not just the objects of history but the very subject themselves. The subaltern historians look at the written sources in a different way from other historians. While they use written sources, they use it with caution. Hence, their whole methodology itself is somewhat different from the usual understanding of methodology. From their perspective, the primary source of a subaltern historian is not only what is written, but also the people themselves.[32] Subaltern history is the history of a suffering people of the oppressed and the marginalized. As their history is being

SATHRI, 2006). cf. also Woba James, "Methodological Issues in the Writing of the History of Christianity in the 19th and 20th Centuries with Special Reference to the Post Colonial Theory" *SATHRI journal* 1/1 (January, 2006): 151-168.

[26] George Oommen, "Historiography of Indian Christianity and Challenges of Subaltern methodology" *Journal of Dharma* 28/2 (April-June, 2003): 212-231.

[27] Mathias Mundadan, *Re-writing History*, 161.

[28] K.N. Panikkar, "Alternative Historiographies: Changing Paradigms of Power." *Jeevadhara*, Vol. XXXII (Jan. 2002): 11.

[29] Ranajit Guha, Ed. *Subaltern Studies 1. Writings on South Asian History and Society* (Delhi, 1982), 2.

[30] George Oommen, *op.cit.*, 222.

[31] Francis Thonipara, "St. Thomas Christians: The First Indigenous Church of India." Roger E. Hedlund, (ed.) *Christianity is Indian: The Emergence of an Indigenous Community* (Delhi: ISPCK, 2000), 63.

[32] V.V. Thomas, "Subaltern Historiography and post-Colonial Theory: The case of Dalit Pentecostalism in Kerala", *Religion and Society*, Vol. 49 Nos. 2 & 3, (June & September, 2004): 124.

given attention to, they are moving from the periphery to the centre.[33] Moreover, subaltern studies are the effort to hear the people and their voices which have been silenced in the dominant discourses, it is an effort to make the subaltern people speak in their own language, a language of protest, resistance and negation. Hence, Jesudas M. Athyal argues, "a re-reading of entire socio-cultural process precisely from the perspectives of the subaltern groups is absolutely necessary, to make the Christian service of our people relevant."[34]

5.3. Causes for the Subaltern Solidarity

There were a lot of religious and non religious causes behind the empowerment of the backward class people in Kerala. Following is an analysis of certain factors related to the formation of the Lutheran Subaltern Solidarity in Kerala.

5.3.1. The Initiatives from the Government

The British and Indian administrations who were actuated by liberal impulses in the early decades of the 19th century introduced a series of administrative and social reforms to modernizing the administration and society in Kerala. 'Abolition of slavery (1843) and Castes-disabilities removal (1850) were the earlier ones. 'Breast-Cloth Agitation' by Shannars of South Travancore[35] eventually led to a Royal proclamation on 26 July 1859.[36] The struggle for the upper cloth was not merely a demand for the right to cover the bosom of women, but also to symbolize the aspirations of this people for social equality. In the history of Travancore State, a constant pattern of reform continued during the reigns of Ayilyam Tirunal (1860-1880), Sri Mulam Tirunal Rama Varma (1885-1924), Sethu Lakshmi Bai (1924-1931) and Sri Chithra Tirunal Balavarma (1931-1956). In the above said period, educational conveniences were increased by the opening of more schools and colleges.[37] Transportation facilities improved with the opening of the Varkala Tunnel in 1875 and the rail route to Madras from Trivandrum in 1918. Several development projects were launched with the formation of village Panchayats in

---

[33] V.V. Thomas, *Understanding Subaltern History: Theoretical Tools.* (Bangalore: BETSSC/ SATHRI, 2012) (2006), 7.

[34] Jesudas M. Athyal, Relevant Patterns of Christian Witness in India (Thiruvalla: CSS, 2000), 71.

[35] For more discussions on the Upper Cloth Revolts see, J.W. Gladstone, Christianity and Peoples Movement, 81-92.

[36] This proclamation reads as follows: "His Highness now proposes to abolish all rules prohibiting the covering of the upper parts of the persons of Shanar women, and to grant them perfect liberty to meet the requirements of decency any way they may deem proper, with the simple restriction that they do not imitate the same mode of dress that appertains to the higher castes." No. 895, Letter from T, Madava Rao, Dewan of the Durbar, to Lieutenant General W. Cullen, British resident of Travancore, Trivandrum, 17 May, 1859.

[37] Till the beginning of the 19th century, the formal system of education was unknown to Kerala. Antony Kariyil, *Church and Society in Kerala: A Sociological Study* (New Delhi: Intercultural Publications, 1995), 45.

1925. Setu Lakshmi Bai legally abolished the animal sacrifices in temples and made the *Marumakkathayam*[38] the only legal form of inheritance by a regulation in 1925.[39] It was Sri Mulam Tirunal who inaugurated the Legislative Council in 1888 and the Sri Mulam Assembly in 1904 in an effort to secure for the government the advice of the representatives of the people. Sri Chithra Tirunal reconstructed the legislature[40] and introduced several constructive administrative and social reforms. The Travancore Land Mortgage Bank was established in 1932. A Public Service Commission was appointed in 1935 in order to ensure fair representation for all communities in appointments to the Government service on the basis of a system of communal rotation. Other significant achievements were the Temple Entry Proclamation (1936) and the establishment of the Travancore University (1937). Agricultural Debt Relief Act was (1937) the Governments step towards the relief of the rural debtors'. In order to foster rural development, Travancore Village Union Act (1939) was passed. Number of factories like, Travancore Rubber works, Ceramic Factory the Plywood factory, Fertilizers and Chemicals Travancore, were started to give top priority to industrialization.[41] Prohibition of Untouchability (1950) was another milestone in the people's movements in Kerala. A judicial organization based on western principle was introduced. Corrupt officials were dismissed. Hereditary offices were abolished. Compulsory labour (*uzhiyam*) for the government without payment of remuneration was abolished. The system of service based on payment of wages and salaries was introduced. The restrictions in regard to the use of conveyances, ornaments and dress were gradually removed.[42]

Education, however, brought higher expectations for all.[43] Educated people soon resented living under both, an autocratic form of government and a rigid caste hierarchy. Due to education and liberal ideas, the backward communities

---

[38] *Marumakkathayam*: Matriarchal system. In this tradition which was prevalent among the Nair community in Kerala, lineage is determined from the mother's side and inheritance is given to daughters, and not to sons.

[39] By 1919 changing the law of inheritance became a matter of serious concern among the Nairs. The subject came up for discussion in the Sri Mulam Popuar Assembly in 1920. After many deliberations a regulation in favor of individual partition of the *Marumakkathayam* system was passed in 1925. The Nair regulation of Malabar was passed only in 1933.

[40] This was called as the Legislative Reform Act.

[41] For more details refer A. Sreedhara Menon, *A Survey of Kerala History* (Kottayam: DC Books, 2012) (1967), 273.

[42] For more details refer A. Sreedhara Menon, *A Survey of Kerala History* (Kottayam: DC Books, 2012) (1967), 310.

[43] But Modern mass education given in government- run institutions was not easily available to the subaltern people. Samuel Mateer writes, "To the lower castes, both Christians and heathen is still denied the very essential right to a full share in the education supplied by the state at the public cost…. Illavars, Shannars, Paraiahs, Pulayars and such like, constituting over a third of the population are refused admission into the village or primary school." Samuel Mateer, *Native Life of Travancore*, 346.

became dissent as they were denied entry into temples, schools and public services. Opening of factories in towns increased the migration of people from rural to city areas. The construction of roads, establishment of postal system, and telegraph could be considered as great strides in the field s of travel and communication. Many news papers, periodicals commenced publication with the focus on social problems and even on individual grievances. Rapid expansion of the means of communication also helped to usher in an era of social mobility and migration of traditional evils from Kerala society. The above reforms would show that the Travancore State had an impressive record of enlightened administration to its credit and that it was one of the progressive states of India. All these reforms and development projects proved to be of advantage primarily for the advanced section of the society. The middle class and lower section of the society were touched mostly by the efforts made by the non governmental agencies like Christianity.

5.3.2. Influence of Christianity

Before we take up the depressed castes movements in Kerala, it is appropriate to speak about the social awareness created by the Christian Missionaries among the depressed castes of Kerala such as Nadars, Pulayas, Ezhavas and Sambavars. Christian Missionaries belonging to the LMS and CMS came increasingly into contact with the lower castes. The lower castes that had been under enemy control to various disabilities and social restrictions looked up to the Christian Missionaries for their redemption. Due to systematic Christian teachings and inspiration of human values among the converts from the slave class to Christianity developed a widespread social awareness.[44] This awareness created a feeling that they were in bondage and that they had various rights which it was their duty to fight for. In order to sustain their social, economical and cultural well-being they sought accommodation in the power centers especially in the administrative departments. But, to achieve this goal they had to acquire western education, because English language and education was the basic qualification for gaining employment in the government services, even in the Princely States.[45] In the second half of the 19th century, the changes in the economy of Kerala pushed up the demand for education from the upwardly mobile groups.[46] As we had seen earlier, the role of the Christian missionaries in the spread of western education and liberal ideas deserves special mention in this context.[47] The English education

---

[44] For more discussion see, Clifford G. Hospital, Cloths and Caste in Ninetieth Century Kerala, *ICHR* XIII/2, 1979, 145-156.

[45] M. Nisar& Meena Kandasamy, *Ayyankali: A Dalit Leader of Organic Protest* (Calicut: The Other Books, 2007), 52.

[46] P.R. Abdul Salam, *Educational Developments in India* (New Delhi: 2002), 11. For more details about the educational work of the missionaries see also, J. W. Gladstone, *Protestant Christianity and Peoples Movement in Kerala,* 70-72.

[47] A. Sreedhara Menon, *A Survey of Kerala History,* 369.

offered all castes of people opportunities of learning.[48] Spread of education both in English and vernacular was an integral part of the mission of Christianity.[49] In South their education project grew in a large proportion.[50] For example, in 1827, LMS had 36 schools with 1304 boys and 106 girls in the eastern division and 21 schools with 541 children in the western division.[51] The LMS paved the way for the female education too. They started in 1820 a boarding School for girls in spite of opposition from the caste Hindus.[52] The advent of education transformed the socio-political reality of the subaltern people to a great extent. They tried to make the depressed classes aware of their civil and social rights. R.N. Yesudhas comments: "It opened a new vista of political thought and practice in Travancore along with a realization of a new sense of individuality, dignity, and self respect. On its heels, came an urge for social freedom and equality."[53] Education created awareness and a vision of progress among the people of the lower strata of society. The ideas of enlightenment, such as emphasis on rationalism, right for equality, right for equal opportunity and the concept of freedom influenced the new educated generation.

---

[48] The Kerala Educational Research Centre (KERC) study rightly made the following observation about the involvement of Church in education. "It is hardly necessary to say that a Christian inspired education means essentially education and not proselytization or any type of indoctrination. "*A Study of Christian Colleges in Kerala,* (Trivandrum: KERC, 1892), 17. Christian involvement in education is the extension of the teaching mission of Christ who came to this world to lead people from darkness to light. This is the accepted purpose of any education. Etymologically education is a process of leading (*ducere*) from (e) ignorance (darkness) to knowledge (light). Christian educational institutions reflected this mission of Christ. Antony Kariyil, *Church and Society in Kerala: A Sociological Study* (New Delhi: Intercultural Publications, 1995), 85.

[49] In the beginning the British colonial authorities were not supportive of the missionary activities in Kerala. But later they changed their perspective and soon capitalists considered the missionary and charitable movements as a sophisticated apparatus. Therefore, they allowed missionaries to carry on their charitable and religious mission in Kerala. M. Nisar & Meena Kandasamy, *Ayyankali: A Dalit Leader of Organic Protest*, 52.

[50] British officers such as Colonel Colin Macaulay and Col. John Munro, the British residents in the court of Travancore showed keen interest in the spread of Christianity. By their efforts there were reforms in the field of education. Three important branches of education were introduced, namely, primary, secondary and collegiate. By 1909, the first Director of Public Instruction was appointed. The introduction of education and inspection codes of 1910 marked the inauguration of the new educational policy. William Wilson Hunter, in *The Imperial Gazetteers of India*, says that, since 1887, Trivandrum has been the centre for chief educational institutions. A. Selvaraj, Christianity *and Social Transformation: The Kerala Story,* (Trivandrum: ICRO, 2002), 81.

[51] R.N. Yesudhas, *The History of London Mission Society in Travancore (1806-1985*), (Trivandrum: Kerala Historical Society, 1980), 63. In 1819, when the LMS had 10 congregations in Kerala, they had 12 schools and a plan for extending the number of schools to thirty. J.W. Gladstone, *Protestant Christianity and Peoples Movement in Kerala,* 71.

[52] R.N. Yesudhas, *The History of London Mission Society in Travancore (1806-1985*), Trivandrum: Kerala Historical Society, 1980), 134.

[53] R.N. Yesudhas, *The History of London Mission Society in Travancore (1806-1985*), Trivandrum: Kerala Historical Society, 1980), 154.

The print media introduced by the missionaries in 1820, contributed towards rationalizing and popularizing knowledge, making it available to masses. This generality of the knowledge enabled the participation of the people and it played the key role in the general awakening. The literature which was a distant dream became a reality to thousands. Women were empowered through education. Women hostels and boarding homes were opened in colleges and schools. Thus, mass education sowed the seeds for a new civic consciousness and created a fertile soil for the germination of mass movements.

The evangelical works of the Missionaries among the most backward classes in Hindu society and the large number of conversions from these marginals to Christianity with the hope of social emancipation, created a social atmosphere in favor of radical religious and social reform. There were economic and political reasons which contributed to conversions. As noted by Duncan B. Forrester, "there was hardly a region of India that did not have movement of a depressed caste into Christianity"[54] or "other religions to find remedy for their social ills."[55] "Mass conversions have almost always been forms of social protest against conditions of oppression and discrimination."[56]

The history of the Protestant missionary activities in South Travancore clearly shows that it seriously challenged the religious and cultural domination by the upper caste.[57] Values of individuality, equality, rationality, and liberalism, which propagate by the Protestants, contributed considerably to the emergence of a public awareness.[58] W.S. Hunt quoting Nagam Aiya, "By the unceasing efforts

---

[54] Duncan B. Forrester, "The Depressed Classes and Conversion to Christianity 1860-1960", in G.A. Oddie (ed.), *Religion in South Asia-Religious Conversion and Revival Movements in South Asia in Medieval and Modern Times* (New Delhi: Manohar, 1991), 70.

[55] G.P. Patrick, *Religion and Subaltern Agency* (Chennai: Department of Christian Studies, University of Madras, 2003), 66.

[56] J.R. Nurchison, *Called to Serve – A Profile of the Diocese of Kottar* (Nagercoil: Diocese of Kottar, 1983), 8. For more discussion see, J.W. Gladstone, 19th Century Mass Movement in South Travancore - A result of Social Liberation, *ICHR,* X/1 (June, 1976), 53-66.

[57] For more discussion on this subject, see J.W. Gladstone, 19th century Mass Movements in South Travancore - A result of Social Liberation, ICHR, X/1 (June, 1976): 53-66.

[58] G.P. Patrick, *Religion and Subaltern Agency* (Chennai: Department of Christian Studies, University of Madras, 2003), 68. G. Rajendran, a Hindu writes: "...the role of the Church in providing unity , cohesion, mutual assistance and guidance of its members became a model for the NSS and the SNDP Yogam... The crusade against joint family system, and the impartable *taravad*, made later by Nairs and Ezhavas might have inspiration from the Christian system. An important fact to be remembered in this context is that the Christian Church had played a progressive role in Kerala in contrast to the reactionary role of the Church in Western Europe in the era of feudalism. The Church in the West was a target of attack by the rising middle class while the Church in Kerala was actually accelerating and assisting the emergence of the middle class." G. Rajendran, *The Ezhava Community and Kerala Politics* (Trivandrum: The Kerala Academy of Political Science, 1974), 15. It witnesses how Christianity Served as a model for the other communities in organizing their welfare activities.

and self-denying earnestness of the learned body of the Christian missionaries in the country, the large community of native Christians are rapidly advancing in their moral, intellectual and material condition."[59] The evils in the Hindu social organization also created an atmosphere in favor of radical religious and social reform.[60] Sundararaj Manickam describes the consequences of conversion as this: "There is no denial of the fact that conversion to Christianity was a great blessing at least to a sizable number of the Dalit converts. First of all conversion to Christianity created in them a new awareness and gave them a new identity. They made a rediscovery of themselves. The converts developed an intense feeling of self respect and self reliance that they never had before. They became increasingly alive to the injustice meted out to them for ages together. This new awareness expressed itself in varying degrees of resentment and assertiveness."[61] There is no doubt that the Christian missionaries in South India successfully created an ideological climate which was ideal for the birth of several social justice and social emancipation movements.[62]

5.3.3. Hindu Awakening and Hindu Movements

The 19th and 20th centuries witnessed emergence of a new social order in Kerala under the impact of diverse social, economic and cultural influences. There were Hindu awakening and Hindu movements during this period. Moreover, a lot of Hindu leaders visited Kerala.[63] The awareness of social and religious disabilities led both the higher castes and the lower castes to search for the possibilities of emancipation.[64] The war against caste disabilities and inequalities was being waged by progressive leaders among the affected people groups. Inapproachability and untouchability were looked upon by them as great social evils. They devoted their time for propaganda against these evil systems in the then Kerala society. The caste groups were properly institutionalized and formed into a mass-based movement on those days, because the process of socialization was possible only

---

[59] W.S. Hunt, *The Anglican Church in Travancore and Cochin, 1816-1916*, (Kottayam: CMS, 1968), 230.

[60] A. Sreedhara Menon, *A Survey of Kerala History, op.cit.*, 380.

[61] Sundararaj Manickam, "Origin and History of the Christian Dalits in Kerala and Tamil Nadu", *Religion and Society*, XXXIV/3 (September, 1978): 15.

[62] S. Manickom, *Depressed Class Movements in South India*, in K A Manikumar (ed.) *History & Society* (Madras: FIGA, 1996), 124. For more discussions see, J.W. Gladstone, "*Christian Missionary Work and Socio-Religious Movements in Kerala, 1850-1910*", *ICHR*, XX/1 (June, 1986): 30-42.

[63] C. Rajagopalachari, E.V. Ramaswamy Naicker, Pandit Madan Mohan Malavya, Swamy Vivekananda, Gandhiji etc were a few among them.

[64] J.W. Gladstone, *Protestant Christianity and People's Movement, op.cit.*, 81ff. Vaikkom Sathyagraham and the crusade against untouchability got leadership from the High caste Hindus, the Nairs.

through organizations.[65] Several organizations came into existence towards the decisive phase of people liberation. From that time onwards the lower castes were counted in the affairs of the society and in the administration of the State. The communal feelings became more evident among the people and each caste or community came to represent a pressure group in the political life of Kerala. Organized agitations became a means to demand the justifiable rights of different groups. Similarly, there were social reformers from among the backward class Hindu people. During the period in study, the social settings were determined according to the caste. It was not merely a social or economic order of the society, but a 'religious institution'. After the firm establishment of caste system as a religious institution, it had rigidity which made upward mobility of persons from one caste to another impossible in Kerala. Therefore, conversion of the low caste people to another religion needs special attention. There is a clear relation between conversion and the desire for upward social mobility.[66] These groups wanted a social reform and a rise in the social rank, and not just for some material benefits.

5.4. Mass based Movements and Process of Socialization

5.4.1. Sri Vaikunda Swamikal (1809-1851)

The first and foremost social reformer and a Hindu revivalist from among the backward class was Sri Vaikunda Swamikal also known as Muthukutty Swami (b.1809,[67] at Swamithopu)[68] in the present Kanyakumari District.[69] Like his father he was a Vaishnavite Hindu Nadar. Long before the genesis of popular socio-religious reform movements, he gave the clear call to the oppressed communities to liberate themselves from the clutches of the caste Hindus. He found the "*Samathwa Samajam*' in 1836.[70] The *Samathwa Samajam* had twofold objectives.

---

[65] For a detailed study about Neo-Hindu Socio-Religious Movements in Kerala see, J.W. Gladstone, *Protestant Christianity and Peoples Movement in Kerala,* 205-307.

[66] V.V. Thomas, *Understanding Subaltern History: Theoretical Tools* (Bangalore: BETSSC/ SATHRI, 2006), 44.

[67] There is a difference of opinion about his date of birth. Ayya Vazhi's main religious book *Akhilathiruttu* says, that Muthukutty was 24 years of old in the year 1883 (1008 ME) when he was taken to Tiruchendur. Cf. *Akhilthiruttu* published by T. Balramachandra Nadar, (9th print, 1889), 192; A. Sreedhara Menon, *A Survey of Kerala History*, 313; G. Patrick, *Religion and Subaltern Agency*, 77. Based on the criteria of multiple attestations, the year of birth can be stated as 1809.

[68] Earlier this place was known as *Poovandarthoppu* in *Sasthankovilvilai*, Located in Agastheeswaram Taluk of the South Travancore, a village situated 8miles South East of present Nagercoil. The name Sasthankovilvilai got the new name Swamithoppu after the name of Vaikunda Swamikal.

[69] He was the second child of Ponnumuthan and Veilali who belonged to the social group of the Shannars. His parents gave him the name Mudichoodum Perumal. But the name with suffix 'Perumal' was used by the caste Hindus alone. Due to the opposition from the caste Hindus the parents were forced to adopt a new name for their son - Muthukutti.

[70] R.N. Yesudhas, *A People's Revolt in Travancore* (Trivandrum, 1974), 80.

One was to address the grievances of the *Avarnas* and the other was to fight against the short comings and lapses in the State administration.[71] This Samajam seems to be the earliest social organization in Kerala. He organized frequent joint inter dining (*Sama panthi Phojanam*)[72] in order to unify the subaltern people together and eradicate untouchability. He was able to organize the Nadars of South Travancore for fighting for their rights. He was very critical of the oppressive and exploits tax system of the Travancore Government for which he suffered even rigorous imprisonment.[73] He was opposed to Brahmanism and Brahmanical from of Hinduism which he considered to be the prime cause for the over-all depravity of the depressed castes.

He was arrested in 1837 during the reign of Swathi Thirunal and lodged in the Singarathopu jail in Trivandrum.[74] *Ayyaguru* who was the jailor at the time accepted Vaikunda Swamy as his guru. The work of the Vaikunda Swamy in the cause of social equality was one of the primary causes behind the "Upper Cloth Revolt"[75] which is referred earlier. He died in the year 1851, (ME 21 Vaikasi 1025) at the age of 42.[76] He was against conversion to Christianity.[77] The LMS report by missionaries about his unfavorable characters proves the historical impact Muthukutty had as a popular religious and social activist in his time.[78]

---

[71] A. Sreedhara Menon, *A Survey of Kerala History* (Kottayam: DC Books, 2012) (1967), 313.

[72] Even among the Sudras inter dining was not in practice. He instructed his followers, irrespective of caste and creed/community, to cook food by taking water from the well at Swamithoppu and asked them to eat along with him. He also sent his disciples to the houses of the tribal people in order to encourage inter-dining. For more details see, C. Umaithanu and P. Kasi Udayan, *Bhagavan Vaikunda Swamikal Varalaru* (Tamil), (Nagercoil: 1966),18.

[73] When Maharaja Swathi Thirunal visited Suchindrum, the caste Hindus informed him, a man from the untouchable Shannar claims himself as Vaikunda Swamikal and he wants to abolish all castes and tribes to unite all low caste people. Acting on this, the king ordered an enquiry in to his activities. On the basis of enquiry reports, the king ordered the immediate arrest.

[74] He spent 110 days in jail. His stay in Jail made him a more influential person among the people. Later the king relased him unconditionally. N.K. Jose, *Vaikunda Swamikal: Kerala Samuhya Navodhanathinte Margadarsi* (Mal.) (Vaikunda Swamikal: Forerunner of Kerala Social Reformation) (Thiruvananthapuram: Bahujana Vartha, 2008), 77.

[75] These struggles took place in three Phases, during the years 1822-23, 1828-30, and 1855-59.For a detailed account of this struggles see, D.H. George, *Kumari Mavatta Penurimai Porattam* (Struggles for women's right in Kanyakumary District) (Chennai: Pavai Printers, 1982).

[76] *Akhilathiruttu*, 362. But Samuel Matteer record the year of death of Muthukutti as 1848. Samuel Matteer, *The Land of Charity*, 222.

[77] N.K. Jose, *Vaikunda Swamikal:Kerala Samuhya Navodhanathinte Margadarsi* (Mal.) (Vaikunda Swamikal: Forerunner of Kerala Social Reformation) (Thiruvananthapuram: Bahujana Vartha, 2008), 121.

[78] LMS missionaries felt Muthukutty as a threat to their mission. From their negative predisposition, they characterized him variously as a 'religious pretender', a person of 'deranged mind', an agent of Satan', 'imposter', 'false prophet', etc. *LMS report for the year1843*, 75, *LMS report for the year* 1843, 75, 78-79 cited by G. Patrick, *Religion and Subaltern Agency*, *op.cit*, 84.

His shamanic activities, his instructions, his ordeals and most importantly, his claim as an incarnation- all had contributed to his emergence as a popular social and religious leader.[79] The written works (*Akilathiruttu* and *Arulnul*), most of the doctrines and claims of *Ayya Vazhi* were the later development, by his later-day biographers. In any case, the life and mission of Sri Vaikunda Swamikal constitute an important landmark in the history of the subaltern people's movements. Sri Vaikunda Swamikal became a forerunner to the later gurus who were influenced by him consciously or otherwise. The other Ezhava social reform movement that directly influenced and interfered in the public sphere has to be analyzed in this context.

5.4.2. Sri Narayana Guru

Ezhavas had enjoyed a little bit of freedom and a separate identity even in the rigid *jati* hierarchy of the pre–colonial period. Even though their material status was prosperous in the changed colonial milieu, their social status was still at the lowest level. The awakening of the Ezhava community began with the life and work of Sri Narayana Guru (1854-1928) from South Travancore.[80] He was an *Ezhava sannyasi* who made solid contributions towards the social change and Hindu religious reforms from the age of long slumber. Unity of mankind, oneness of god and justice were his prime teachings. He established an ashram in 1887 with his unifying creed of 'one caste, one religion and one god.'[81] He became an influential figure locally.[82] In 1888, he performed a bold and revolutionary act by consecrating the "Ezhava siva"at Aruvipuram. By this action, he questioned the religious domination of Brahmins and indicated that Ezhavas, like Nairs and

[79] For a detail study of Muthukutty Swamy, see, G. Patrick, *Religion and Subaltern Agency* (Chennai: University of Madras, 2003).

[80] Though many of his biographies agree that the guru was born at Chathayam star relating to Onam festival, there is no unanimity among the authors regarding the year. Kumaran Asan gives the year as 1856 (1032 Chingom), Mahakavi Kumaran Asan, *Brahmasree Narayana Guru*, (Kottayam: Lalu Books, 1997), 9. Narayana Guru himself is said to have stated that his year of birth was 1854 (1030 *Chingom*). Mukorth Kumaran, *Sree Narayana Swamikalude Jeeva Charithram*, (Talassery: Saraswathy Vijayam Press, 1930), 72-73. Nataraja Guru and M.K. Kumaran says, Narayana Guru was born on 20 August 1854. Nataraja Guru, *The Word of the Guru* (Ernakulam: Pai & Co., 1968), 254. M.K. Kumaran (ed) *Sree Narayanayugapraphavam* (Varkala: International Sree Narayana Guru year Commemoration committee, 1978), John Dharmatheeram, K.K. Panikkar, P.S. Velayudhan and others also consider 1854 as the year. John Dharmatheeram, *Sree Narayana Guru Devan* (Trivandrum: St. Joseph's Press, 1965), 1; K.K. Panikkar, *Sree Narayana Paramahamsan* (Alleppey: Vidyarambam Press, 1985), 71; Scholars like M.S.A. Rao, K.R. Achuthan and Vijayalayam Jeyakumar treat 28 August 1855 as Guru's birth day. Vijayalayam Jeyakumar, *Sree Narayana Guru Oru Samagra Ptanam* (Kottayam: NBS, 1995) (1993), 60.

[81] For an analysis of the religious thought of Narayana Guru see, Joshua Siromony, *Comprehensive Vision and Transforming Mission: the Evolution of the Religious thought of Sree Narayana Guru and its Practical Implications* (Delhi: ISPCK, 2005). 83-108.

[82] T.J. Nossitier, *Communism in Kerala: A Study in Political Adaption* (Bombay: OUP, 1982), 30.

Brahmins, have equal rights to own temples and to worship the Sanscritic deities. In addition to the consecrations of temples in the different parts of Kerala, he advocated several reforms among the Ezhavas to give them greater respect within the larger Society. His reforms were based on religion. He rejected the caste distinctions. He associated with people of the untouchable caste and inter-dined with them. He also took a few untouchable boys to his Ashram at Varkala.[83] He was concerned about people, rather than religion. One of his famous statements runs as follows:" whatever be the religion it is enough if the people could be improved'. Narayana Guru had the support of other Ezhava leaders like Palpu, and Kumaranasan in the propagation of the reforms he initiated and in organizing the Ezhavas at the State level. After a series of unsuccessful petitions, ten wealthy Ezhavas established in 1903 the first caste association in Kerala, named *Sree Narayana Dharma Paripalana* (SNDP) *Yogam*. It aims "to promote religious and secular education and industrious habits among the Ezhava community."[84]

The Ezhava movement posed a serious problem and their inclination towards group conversion to the Lutheran Church created a novel situation.[85] It is very clear that the guru was influenced much by the teachings of Christianity.[86] The Lutheran missionaries met Narayana Guru every week at Varkala to exploit the trend for conversion.[87] Once MELIM missionary Zukker read Bible for him, Guru turned to his disciples and said: "what he said is true and logical."[88] One Krishnan a notable Ezhava chief got converted to Christianity with his family. The Yogam chief declared that it was not a surprise to him and added that "undoubtedly many more will follow their examples."[89] Since then requests to establish Lutheran churches among Ezhavas increased. By 1927, it became evident that the whole Ezhava community of approximately seven lakhs preferred to join Lutheran Christianity.[90] But at that time, the Church was unprepared to face the situation effectively. In spite of repeated requests, no missionary was

---

[83] V. Bhargavan Vaidiyan, '*Ente Gurudeva Smaranakal*' (Mal.) (*My Memories About Gurudev*) (Quilon: Sree Narayana Guruvarsham Smaraka Grandham, n.d.), 9.

[84] For more discussions see, P.K. Balakrishnan, *Narayana Guru* (Kottayam: NBS,1963); C.R. Kesavan Vaidyar, *Sree Narayana Chinthakal* (Kottayam: NBS, 1972); V. Bhargavan Vaidyar, 'Ente Gurudeva Smaranakal (Mal.) (Quilon: Sree Ramavilasom Press, n.d.); T.J. Nossitier, *Communism in Kerala: A Study in Political Adaption* (Bombay: OUP, 1982), 30.

[85] V. Sathyanesan, "Temple Entry Proclamation and Reconversion Impulse in Travancore," *ICHR* XXVI/1, 1992, 11.

[86] V.V. Thomas, *Dalit Pentecostalism* (Bangalore: Asia Trading Corporation, 2008), 120.

[87] F.R. Zukker, *Ezhava Movement: Ezhava Report No.2,* Trivandrum, 27 June 1927. Concordia Seminary Nagercoil, Archives.

[88] V. Sathyanesan, "Temple Entry Proclamation and Reconversion Impulse in Travancore," *ICHR* XXVI/1, 1992, 12.

[89] *Ezhava Report*, ibid.

[90] V. Sathyanesan, *opcit*, 12. See also, A. Selvaraj, Christianity *and Social Transformation: The Kerala Story* (Trivandrum: ICRO, 2002), 68.

sent to this area between 1921 and 1926. Zukker reported that if there were fifty men in Trivandrum side, he would have found it very easy to allocate them to all centers.[91] The historic Temple Entry Proclamation[92] on 12 November 1936 by Raja Chitra Thirunal (1931-1948) achieved the desired results. Mass exodus to other faiths from Ezhavas ended abruptly.[93] In later days Guru declared that Hinduism contains the basics for salvation.[94] Therefore, conversion of Ezhavas to other religion was not encouraged. He opened separate temples for his brethren. He gave utmost importance to education as well as economic development of the community.[95] Within a period of less than fifty years (1888-1928), Sri Narayana Guru elevated the Ezhava community from dust into people who could stand on their own legs as self respecting human beings. By the turn of this century, they had attained a sufficient level of social consciousness, identity and ambition, that they could launch large scale agitations for the removal of inequalities.[96] The continuous effort of the elite members of this community over the following decades eventually brought them the status that they now have in Kerala society. Today, the Ezhavas, have a significant role in the politics of Kerala.

Most of the time, the speeches and activities of the leaders of Ezhava social reform movement including the Guru addressed only Ezhavas. They concentrated on the economic as well as social well being of their caste/community. Even the influence of Guru did not reduce the caste consciousness of Ezhavas instead it strengthened the feelings of 'Ezhavaness' in their minds.[97] When the Ezhavas became organized and obtained access to the public sphere of Kerala they tried their best to absorb every available opportunity for their community. Though the organization behind the social reform movement shouted slogans against the caste system, in practice they were trying to strengthen the *jati* consciousness in

---

[91] *Ezhava Report*, Ibid.

[92] Socially marginalized and ritually discriminated people of the lower strata of the society were forbidden to use the Temple Tanks, walking on temple roads, roaming around temple premises etc. with the claim of pollution. But by this Order Government opened the roads, wells, tanks, *inns*, schools etc to all class of peoples.

[93] Gandhiji also took interest for this Temple Entry Proclamation. It is not because of his love towards the untouchables but the unusual interest of Gandhi in Kerala was to prohibit the mass conversion of dalits to Christianity. Ref. Gladstone, *Protestant Christianity*, 403, 408; A.Selvaraj, Christianity *and Social Transformation: The Kerala Story*, (Trivandrum: ICRO, 2002), 69.

[94] J.W. Gladstone, *Protestant Christianity and People's Movement in Kerala,* 251.

[95] A. Sreedhara Menon, *A Survey of Kerala History*, 371.

[96] Mukort Kunhappa comments "It was a bloodless revolution which he achieved. Wherever the downtrodden, under privileged groups in the world, message of Sree Narayana Guru ; ' educate-that you may be free, organize that you may be strong, industrialize that your financial status may improve' – has relevance at all times "Murkot Kunhappa, *Sree Narayana Guru* (New Delhi: National Book Trust, 1988), vii.

[97] The Ezhavas attacked the Pulayars and Parayars and other slave caste groups in several part of Travancore.

the minds of people through various methods. Indirectly, this condition denied opportunities to the people of the lower strata of society who were far away from the periphery of the public sphere. They neglected the problems of the most downtrodden groups, the slave communities other than Ezhavas. Therefore, SNDP did not reach out in the wider sense of social reform. Dalits were excluded from the main stream and denied even human rights in a society dominated by those who prepared and rallied themselves under the banners of their respective caste. This was the social setting where the dalits asserted themselves under the leadership of Ayyankali.

5.4.3. Sri. Ayyankali

Sri. Ayyankali[98] (1863-1941) another social reformer was born at Venganoor,[99] Neyyattinkara.[100] A Pulaya by caste, Ayyan Kali dedicated his life for the emancipation and liberation of his community by remaining within the Hindu fold itself without opting for conversion to either Christianity or Islam. He had not received any formal education. He was physically strong and well versed in martial art. Ayyankali behaved like a rebel. He organized a group of Pulayar young men and wandered about with them. He gave martial training to his men.[101] Whenever they got a chance to attack, challenge or threaten the Upper caste Nairs they did it well. They were popularly known as the *Ayyankali pada*.[102] At first he sought to regain the right to walk along the streets - entry into the public roads and streets that were reserved for the upper castes.[103] In 1893, Ayyankali willfully violated this command by travelling through a public road in a *villuvandi* (Bullack cart) that was used only by the upper castes.[104] He dressed like a Nair. This irritated the Nairs who tried to block him but failed. His historical journey through the forbidden roads gave a wide spread welcome and success among the downtrodden

---

[98] Ayyankali was born to Ayyan and Mala on 28 August, 1863. He was the eldest of 8 children. Friends called him *Urpillai* or *Moothapillai* with respect. In 1888, Ayyankali married Chellamma, with whom he had 7 children.

[99] A small village 13 km north of Thiruvananthapuram.

[100] For the full version of the biography of Ayyankali see, T.H.P. Chentharassery, *Ayyankali-Jeeva Charitram*, (Mal.) (Trivandrum; 1987); *Sree Ayyankali Smaraka Puthuvalvilakom L.P.S. Platinum Jubilee Souvenir*, Vengannoor, 1980.

[101] T.P.H. Chentharassery, *Ayyankali* (Trivandrum: Prakasam Printing Co., 1979), 19.

[102] M. Nissar & Meena Kandaswamy, *op.cit.*, 69.

[103] If any lower caste violates this caste code (*Jati Maryada*) he/she would be punished severely.

[104] The act of a Pulayan buying a *villuvandi* was itself a violation of the social codes of his time. Only the upper caste people were permitted to use ox-carts in those days for travel. For more discussion on this see, *Abhimanyu, Ayyankali (*Mal.) (Trivandrum: Kerala Samskarika Vakuppu, 1990), 59; Appan Vanchiyoor, *Ayyankali Padathalavan (Mal.)* (Ayyankali the Captain) (Trivandrum: Kerala Harijan Sahithya Pravarthaka Co-operative Society, 1984), 8.

masses.[105] Then he led a successful strike against their oppressive caste masters for the untouchable agricultural laborers' equality in 1904. Ayyankali and his people began to pay violence with violence.[106] Ayyankali was deeply aware of the extreme illiteracy which prevailed among his people. In 1904, he started a primary school with two *Pulaya* students at Katakala, Vengannoor.[107] In 1907, he founded *Sadhu Jana Paripalana Sangom* (SJPS), Association for the welfare of the poor)an organization of the Pulayas with the socio-economic development of his people as its prime objective.[108] It was evident that the Pulaya Movement and the SJPS were directly influenced by the Christian experience, especially on education.[109] The Maharaja nominated him as a member of the *Sri Moolam Praja Sabha* on 5th December 1911 to present various needs of the people whom he represented.[110] He used this forum for his constant fight for the rights of his people.[111] He was the Secretary of the All Travancore *Pulaya Maha Sabha,* an organization founded in 1938 at Trivandrum under the presidentship of T.T. Kesavan Sastry. It contributed to a great extent to the economic and political

[105] J. Prabhash, *Affirmative Action and Social Change – Social Mobility of Dalits* (New Delhi: 2001), 47.

[106] T.H.P Chentharassery, *op.cit,* 61-62.

[107] The Government legislation of 1904 entitled him to total reimbursement of the costs incurred for the school for the Pulayas from the government. However, this school did not function Properly and it was closed down soon.

[108] J.W. Gladstone, *op.cit.,* 263-68. Ayyankali's fight in the Assembly for the equal right of the Pulaya students in the government public school can be found in the *Proceedings of the Sree Mulam popular Assembly,* 1912, 82; 1914, 58; 1916, 105; 1921, 127; 1922, 163; 1924, 211; 1927, 114; 1930, 85.

[109] Two Pulaya Christians in South Travancore, V.J. Thomas Vadiyar and Harris Vadiyar, was instrumental in the formation of the SJPS itself. George Oommen, *Dalit Liberative Identity as Amalgam: Pulaya Christians, Missionaries, Caste Associations and Labour Union Movements in the 20th Century,* A paper presented at the International seminar on Missionary Foundations of Indian Renaisance, at Vasco Da Gama Research Institute of Cochin (VGRI), 22-24 (September, 2011): 6.

[110] The Travancore Government began to nominate representatives to the Sree Mulam Popular Assembly from the lower castes in 1907. In that year N. Kumaran Asan was nominated from SNDP, the Ezhava organization. During the Dewanship of P. Rajagoplachari, unrepresented lowest castes were given representation. *Proceedings of the Sree Mulam Popular Assembly,* 1912, 82.

[111] The presence of educated Pulaya Christian's representative in this Assembly added new dimensions to the Pulaya movement and also helped to improve the Pulayas' socio-economic situation. Pulaya Christians were very visible in the Assembly during the 1920s and 1930s. Prominant Pulaya representatives such as Charthan Solomon, Vellikara Mathai (Choti), Paradi Isaac, N.J. Joshua and J. Joseph was all Christians and constituted almost half of the Pulaya members in the Assembly. Proceedings of the 19th session of the Sree Moolam Assembly, 1923, 176; Proceedings of the 20th session of the Sree Moolam Popular Assembly, 1924, 176. Proceedings of the 23rd session of the Sree Moolam Assembly, 1927, 266-267. Proceedings of the 24th session of the Sree Moolam Popular Assembly, 1928, 145. Proceedings of the Sree Moolam Assembly, Vol. III, 1935, 137.

uplift of Pulayas.[112] As a result of his efforts and also due to the liberal policies of the Travancore government in the 1930's, Ayyan Kali was able to secure full fee concession, exemption from examination fee, priority to Pulayas in government employment, house sites and small-scale farm land for Pulayas.[113] Ayyankali's brave efforts were powerful enough to break the silence about the Dalit condition that prevailed in the public sphere.[114] Thus, Ayyan Kali and Pulaya movement occupy a significant place in the social history of Kerala.[115] Poikail Yohannan was the one who developed another critique against caste hierarchy from Christian Dalit Perspective.

5.4.4. Poikayil Yohannan

Poikayil Yohannan (1879-1939)[116] was a Mar Thoma Christian, a man belonging to Paraya caste. His parents and fore fathers were agricultural labours of a dominant Mar Thoma Syrian Christian family. He was baptized at the age of five with a new name Yohannan.[117] He became an Evangelist in the Mar Thoma Church. He saw that the untouchable converts were not treated equally with the other Christians. He left Mar Thoma Syrian Church and joined CMS and there also he felt terrible caste prejudices. Then he left CMS and joined the Brethren Mission.[118] But he could not continue there. He, therefore, rejected Christianity and Hinduism and founded a new faith named *Prathyaksha Reksha Deiva Sabha* (PRDS - the Church of God for visible salvation) in the year 1910. The spirituality he advocates was of this world; the salvation and heaven must be

---

[112] R.K. Kshirsagar, *Dalit Movements in India and its Leaders, 1857-1956* (New Delhi: MDP, 1994), 101.

[113] J.W. Gladstone, *Protestant Christianity and People's Movement, 275*-84.

[114] In order to change the disgraceful name '*Pulaya*' as it denoted pollution, on 4th January 1921 Pampady John Joseph (1887-1940) started *Cheramar Maha Jan Sabha.* He was a Catholic Christian from *Pulaya* untouchable caste. He changed the name '*Pulaya* caste' to '*Cheramar*' which means 'Sons of the soil'. He started one magazine '*Sadhu Jan Dootan*' in order to awaken his brethren. On 8 June 1931, he was appointed as a member of Sri Moolam Legislative Assembly, Travancore. When he observed that his brethren were not getting equal treatment in the Church, he advised them to build their own churches and temples. He died in July 1940 at the age of 56. For more details see, T.H.P. Chentharassery, *Pampady John Joseph* (mal.) (Thiruvalla: Backward Peoples' Development Corporation, 1989).

[115] R.K. Kshirsagar, *op.cit.,* 72.

[116] Even though this liberation attempts did not happen in South Travancore, this had made an effective impact among the Paraya Christians throughout Kerala.

[117] He was born at Eraviperoor, in North Travancore. Before his conversion to Christianity his name was Kumaran. Vijayan Kangazha, *Sree Kumara Guru Devan: Biography* (Trichur: 1978), 8.

[118] For more discussion on the influence of Poikayil Yohannan and PRDS Movement among the Brethrens see, T.S. Samkutty, *The Place and Contributions of Dalits in Select Pentecostal Churches in Central Kerala from 1922-1972* (Delhi: ISPCK, 2000), 74-79.

realized on this earth.[119] He insisted his followers to believe in liberty, equality and fraternity. He explained his vocation as to uplift the lowest castes who had been degraded for centuries.[120] Later he declared himself as an incarnation of god to uplift the slave castes and he was renamed as '*Poikayil Sree Kumara Guru Devan*'. Having considered his leadership, caliber, zeal for social reform and strength of his followers, Yohannan was twice nominated to the Legislative Council of the Princely State of Travancore in the years 1921 and 1931. He started schools with the assistance from the Government to spread education among untouchables.[121]

The evils of caste system that prevailed in Kerala society were gradually challenged. Assumed superiority based on colour, race, caste, culture, language and religion was seriously questioned. A new sense of social awakening, self respect, and vision of a new society was emerging in the minds of enlightened leaders.[122] Gladstone writes," As a result of these movements, the whole of society became more open to and aware of the needs of each other, though reactionary elements cannot be excluded. This openness and awareness led the people towards new realities and challenges in society."[123] But the world views of these reformers/ movements were not successful enough to unify all the sub-castes and lead them into an all embracing movement. The subalterns both within and outside the Church stood on the doorstep of a hope, longing for a better life. There the Christian Gospel also played its role to find meaning and strength for many towards a common perception in this new movement.

5.5. The Gospel Experience

MELIM missionaries passionately arrived into this chaotic atmosphere and earnestly kindled the burning torch, a light of salvation. Gospel entered through MELIM missionaries into socially-biased and culturally prejudiced people groups. While this researcher interviewed senior members of both the lay and ordained of TDS among the several caste groups, they explained how the Christian Gospel influenced their life style.[124] Jesus dismantled the wall that segregated

[119] P.C. Joseph, *Poikayil Sree Kumara Guru: Jeevithavum Darsanavum* (Mal.) (Life and Vision of Sree Poikayil Sree Kumara Guru), (Thiruvalla: np. 1994), 62.

[120] In 1918 the *Adi Dravida Mahajan Sabha* appealed to Government to abandon their disgraceful name '*paraiah*' and to give them the respectable name 'Adi Dravida'.

[121] For more discussions see, T.H.P. Chentharassery, *Poikayil Sree Kumara Guru Devan* (Mal.) (Trivandrum: Navodhanam Publications, 1979).

[122] V.V. Thomas, *Dalit Pentecostalism,* 130.

[123] J.W. Gladstone, *Protestant Christianity and People's Movement, 308.*

[124] Interviews with Y Ambrose (83), St Paul's Lutheran Church, Ponvila, 12 August, 2012; Rev. K. Suseelan (86) Bethel Lutheran Church, Chenkavila, 12 August, 2012; Krishnapanikkar (86) and Rev. P.K. Parameswaran, Immanuel Lutheran Church, Cheruvallooor, 12 August, 2012; Adv.Y. Silvanose (76), St. Luke Lutheran Church, Medical College Jn. Trivandrum, 13 August, 2012, K.M. Justus (81) S/o late Rev. K.P. Masillamony, and Rev. Gifton E. Joshua (70) Former Comptroller, IELC, St. John's Lutheran Church, Sreekariyam, 13 August, 2012.

common people on the basis of class, caste and gender. This was a great reverse and radical act of the gospel that overturned a terrible practice based on 'pure' and 'impure', 'touchable' and 'untouchable'. The social psyches of this subaltern were increasingly being conditioned by fear about the cruel punishment for 'caste violations'. Ignorance on the part of the subaltern was another cause of fear. The century old illiteracy, the lack of opportunities and facilities to know matters of civic life and physical iniquities had rendered the social psyche of the people nervous and fear stricken. Gospel gave a call from a state of subhuman to human, from non-entity to personhood. Gospel has always created the desire for a new life and the power to bring a new awareness, and new culture. The poorest section of the Society imbibed a new spirituality, a new humanity, and a new personality instead of their old frigidity, fear, and slavery. The uplifting power of the gospel served to raise the most backward people from their lowest stair of social and moral humiliation to the heights of vitality, self respect and dignity. Lutheran Christianity transformed them in such a way that they could become real and valuable citizens of India. The power of the Gospel liberated them from cultural bondage and ethno-centrism.[125] That led to the creation of caste cohesion and unity despite the divisions among them.

5.6. Solidarity as Mission Principle

Solidarity is a bond which welds together living, especially human beings, when they belong to the same whole or are commonly dependent upon each other. According to Gnana Robinson the present missionary principle should be solidarity.[126] God's as well as Christ's way of doing mission is the way of solidarity. The concrete example of God's solidarity with the suffering humanity is evident in the incarnation of God in Christ. (Jn. 3: 16-17) God stepped in human history to provide abundant life (Jn. 10:10) to all those who are denied opportunities to give fuller expression to their life in this world. Suffering death of Christ on the cross is another sign of God's solidarity with dehumanized and suffering people.[127] Thus, solidarity is the missionary principle of God.[128] Christ also lost His identity for the sake of the lost, publicans and sinners.[129] Jesus' identification with the suffering people was not pretence. It was genuine. The identity of Christ

---

[125] Ideas compiled through the interviews with the selected Lutheran Christian leaders of TDS. See, Foot note no. 161. According to them, the major cause for conversion is not desire for upward social mobility but the major thing was the gospel inspiration. See also, J. Jesudasan (b.23-2-1911), *Biography*, 98; Sukumaran Devadas (15 July, 1916 to 6 Sept. 2001), *On Myself* (biography) vol. 2, 92.

[126] Gnana Robinson, "Solidarity as Missionary Principle", in W.S. Milton Jeganathan (ed,) *Mission Paradigm in New Millennium* (Delhi: ISPCK, 2000), 58-93.

[127] Anthoniraj Thumme, *Springs from the Subalterns: Patterns and Perspectives in People Theology* (Delhi: ISPCK, 1999), 26.

[128] Kim Young Bock, "Peoples Solidarity in the Global Market", in M.P. Joseph (ed.) *Mission and Solidarity* (Bombay: Urban Industrial League for Development, 1995), 93.

[129] Ref. Lk. 19:10, Mt. 9: 12-13, Phil. 2:7, Lk. 5:30, 15: 1-2.

is mocked, spat upon, beaten and to the extent of death identity.[130] Thus Christ's way of salvation is the way of solidarity, not the way of superiority, dominion and authority.[131] The followers of Christ are called to select the narrow way of solidarity with suffering people, in order to carry out the great commission for mission. This is the identity from below, the identity of the people with whom they solidarize. How the MELIM missionaries followed this perspective for their mission is dealt with in the following discussion.

5.7. The Missiological and Doctrinal Approaches of MELIM Missionaries

The MELIM missionary thinking, service and interactions in Kerala were influenced by doctrines and theology of LCMS which gradually led to formation of a subaltern Lutheran solidarity[132] in this state. They had no previous exposure to people of other culture, creed and caste. They never had any specialized training to minister in a cross-cultural setting. The context in which they were called to serve shaped their thinking and strategy. In a land marked by caste divisions, special effort and determination were needed to produce the Church becoming another collection of endogamous 'caste' (Denominations), thereby clouding the image of healing, reconciling with the savior.[133] When the MELIM pursued its evangelistic work, it proceeded on the principle that God intends His Good News for "all peoples" (Mt. 28:19) because of His desire that "all be saved" (1 Tim. 2:4).[134] On this scriptural authorization, MELIM began its work in several different regions of South India and among several different people groups. By the power of the Holy Spirit at work through His Word, people responded from various caste and religious backgrounds.[135] Missionaries made quantitative contributions by planting the churches, institutions and by increasing the number of members and workers. Also they made qualitative contribution by making a unique subaltern solidarity in an entirely different Western culture. Lutheran's gospel/mission perspectives can be summarized as follows.

---

[130] Is. 53:2-3; Mt. 8:17; Mk.9: 12, 15:19; Lk.23:36, Jn. 19:3 Rom.4:25; 1Pet. 2:24.

[131] Gnana Robinson, *op.cit*, 65.

[132] Solidarity is the integration, union or fellowship arising from common responsibilities and interests, between people who have the same interests, goals, etc.

[133] M.L. Kretzmann, The Mission and His Theology, Essay-1, General Conference MELIM.1962.

[134] A.G Huebner, *Some Information's Regarding the False Idea about the Caste System,* (5 page German document, nd.) 4. Concordia Archives.

[135] Herbert Hoefer, "But it work? Unintended Social Consequences of a Perfectly Good Theology", *Missio Apostallica Journal of the Lutheran Society for Missiology*, XI/1/23 (May, 2004), 49.

5.7.1. Luther and Mission

Luther exposed with radical sharpness and strongly the Theo-centric and eschatological dimension of *Missio Dei* in the Bible.[136] He fought against the distortion of the gospel message which had led to the degeneration of mission into ecclesiastical propaganda, forced conversions, crusades, and non-evangelical methods. While describing the approach of Luther to missions, James A. Scherer summarizes: "Luther's obedience to the mission command meant reestablishing the church on its one true foundation of Jesus Christ and Gospel. For Luther, mission was the essential task of the Church in every age, but only a Church itself grounded in the Gospel could do mission. Luther was the father of Church-centered mission work based on the Gospel."[137] *Missio Dei* contrasts sharply with the humanistic missionary attitudes of later periods, flooded in personal piety and weak to pressures of cultural imperialism and western expansion. The 19th century neo-pietistic groups challenged the more society-oriented horizontal view of mission. German origin MELIM missionaries were the product of pietism with a definite evangelistic zeal. They stood for the mission of "seeking and saving the lost" from the lost and dying world.[138]

K. Suseelan, one of the senior most retired pastors of TDS comments about the missionaries' approach as this; "*Gospels reveal how Jesus openly identified with the social out castes, the people who were ceremonially and morally beyond the pale of the then Pharisaic (Brahmanic) teaching. The socially disinherited classes of India had been considered for generations by the upper classes and castes to be slaves, and polluted. The outcastes' search for a reputable place in the social order was met by the thrilling touch of Jesus. The Lutheran missionaries took this truth as their principle in ministry and brought a message of emancipation to those who were suffering under socio- economic and political deficiency.*"[139] With this definite Gospel understanding, MELIM missionaries did their mission in this land.

5.7.2. Lutheran Confessions

The word 'Evangelical' in MELIM and IELC clearly shows the outlook of the then missionaries and later the Church. The Lutheran Confessions present distinctive strategies that are appropriate to missiology for the Lutherans. This pertains to the theory and practice of gospel-centered mission work. The Lutherans in Kerala maintain the same theology of its mother Church-LCMS. Some Lutheran

[136] James A. Scherer, "Luther and mission: A Rich but Untested Potential", in Eugene W. Bunkowske (ed.) *The Lutherans In Mission* (Fort Wayne: Lutheran Society for Missiology Book Series, 2000), 5.

[137] *Ibid.*, 2.

[138] Comments by Rev. T. Joy (74), Former Principal CTS, Nagercoil and a Member of Bethel Lutheran Church, Chengavila, Interview on 14 August 2012.

[139] Interview with Rev. K. Suseelan (86), Bethel Lutheran Church, Chengavila, 14 August, 2012.

doctrinal approach to the cross-cultural communication of the Gospel is outlined below.

5.7.2.1. Justification by Faith

The most important theological principle of Lutherans is Salvation by grace alone. Lutherans are highly sensitive to any work through righteousness. Justification by faith is the doctrine by which any Church stands or falls. The teaching of *objective* and *unconditiona*l justification declared to the whole world of sinner's righteousness on account of the perfect vicarious atonement by Jesus Christ. This constitutes the fundamental *basis* for all missionary activities. The doctrine of *subjective* justification in turn provides the essential motivation for mission work because the blessings of the forgiveness of sins and other added blessings must be received by each and every receptor through faith in the divine giver.[140]

5.7.2.2. Lutheran Ecclesiology

Lutheranism, originally stemming from one single culture, has branched out and developed into a multicultural scenario, which stays together as a communion because of the Lutheran heritage it holds. This multicultural context entails ethnic and national identities, which significantly shape the particular ecclesiological understanding of Lutheran Churches in the different contexts. Ethnicity and nationality as sociological realities deeply affect their theological and ecclesiological formation and understandings, and in turn, their relation to others and service to the world.

MELIM were aware of Luther's notions of the Church as a communion of justified sinners gathered around the Word and Sacrament. The Church, as a gathering of people, is bare to the dynamics and orientations of social, political, and economic processes. It is expected to be different from other social units. The concept of community crosses beyond the limit of any particular caste. Therefore, the challenge was to build an alternate community, one that is inclusive, participatory and sensitive to justice and equality.[141] The LCMS has a congregation-based polity. M.H. Grum says: "the power of the keys lies in the body of believers gathered around Word and Sacraments. The sovereignty is in the local congregation. The Church/the Synod are merely the grouping of these units for the common work of the Church."[142] People are to consult each other, but there is

---

[140] For more discussions about the objective and subjective justification see, Ernst R. Wendland, "Cultural and Theological Specificity in Lutheran missiology", in Eugene W. Bunkowske (ed.) *The Lutherans in Mission* (Fort Wayne: Lutheran Society for Missiology Book series, 2000), 115. A.R.Victor Raj, "Justification only through faith", Doctrinal Essay presented at 21st TDS Convention, 1977, *Christiani*, 52/11, (Trivandrum, 1977), 61-66.

[141] J.W. Mayer, "The Church as the People of god United in the word of God", General Conference Doctrinal Essays-Trivandrum, 1960, 19-27.

[142] M.H. Grum, "The Church and Social service", a paper presented in the IELC Convention, Pernambut, IX 61/ 172 (June, 1961): 7.

no central figure or board that controls everything. Therefore, individual LCMS Missionaries were expected to consult with colleagues but were free to reach out to whomever they felt to be called to reach. It resulted in different missionaries working among different caste groups and an IELC church is composed of many different caste groups. These groups are socially quite distinct, and they were clearly uncomfortable and distrust each other. Yet, Missionaries gathered them into one Church body, told them they are fellow Christians, and expected them to socialize, meet, eat and organize together.[143]

5.7.2.3. Priesthood of all Believers

This doctrine highlights the facts that every Christian can and must be engaged in missionary activities. All believers in Christ have the divine call to bear witness to the Gospel across socio-cultural boundaries. M. M. Jacob one of the senior-most retired pastors and a close associate with the missionaries of TDS explained it like this: "On those days religion, culture and society told to our forefathers that they are only slaves and polluted untouchables and outcastes. But the beloved missionaries told them that they are also very special people and very valuables in the sight of God. Following the example of Jesus, the missionaries mingled freely with all kinds of people. They did not hesitate before the obstacle of dirt, poverty, injustice and custom to bring the message of Christ to the marginalized. They served Christ selflessly and in doing so set an example to be followed. The love of God provided the Missionaries with a deep-seated affection for the most backward communities. This is evinced in the hospitals, Schools, Boarding homes, Economic development projects and relief funds which were provided by the missionaries as the expression of Christian love. The outcome result was that the slaves became free citizens of the land and they came out from age old superstitions and inferiority complex. People found new dignity and honor in being a Christian, because the missionaries taught them that they are also the divine people and children of God just as the Brahmins."[144] This gave a new hope and dignity for the people who were under the age-old slumber and they came under the umbrella of Lutheranism.[145] The people who were once nobody have begun to realize their worth.

[143] Herbert Hoefer, "But Does it works? Unintended Social Consequences of a Perfectly Good Theology" *in Mission Apostolica, Journal of the Lutheran Society for Missiology, XII*/1/23 (May, 2004), 49.

[144] Interview with Rev. M.M. Jacob (86), Former Secretary of TDS, 15 August, 2012.

[145] Cf. K.Suseelan, "*Royal Priesthood and Lutheran Confessions*", Essay presented in 9th Triennial Convention of IELC, Ernakulam, 26-28 February, 1976.

5.7.2.4. Law and Gospel

Another theological theme is the distinction between Law and Gospel, the understanding that sanctification is the work of the Gospel, not of the Law. Without mixing the law and Gospel, MELIM missionaries worked with a clear gospel motivation.[146] One cannot and should not legalize morality in the Church. Rather, the Gospel should be preached with the conviction that the Holy Spirit will change hearts. That change will then be solid and lasting. The pressures toward caste animosity with the society are immense, so sanctification will be a long and complex process. But the Holy Spirit will bring the change if one keeps on preaching God's Gospel call. Hence, the clear law – gospel distinction lead them to create an amalgamation of caste solidarity.

5.7.2.5. Sinners' and Saints

The next governing theological theme is that of paradox. In this fallen world, we recognize that we must deal with realities while also standing for principles. People are both sinners and saints. Christians are not perfect, but they recognize their sinfulness and strive to overcome by the power of the Holy Spirit. They accept each other as fellow pilgrims struggling to gain maturity in the faith, across caste lines. The Community of Christ is not a perfect community of saints, the sinless holy people. This is also a community of sinners, the community of those who are in need of fuller life; one that leads to saintliness. It is not only the fellowship of the saved ones, but it is a fellowship that affects salvation. Since Christians are waiting for the final glory in its fullness, the caste differences among the Christians were not viewed as a serious one in this present world.

Finally, the theological themes of Two Kingdoms and Orders of Creation caused Lutherans to recognize that God uses caste also for earthly good. People need support networks and accountability in life and God provides that not only through the church but also through family, caste members, courts, government'. Christians are not to strip these controls and support away as they follow evangelism. Chaos and instability were viewed as the natural result in the fallen world. Changing political and social structures were not counted as part of mission. Individual conversions were their main mission motto. When individuals change, structures will also change and through them peace and justice will be established.[147] Therefore, Missionaries never tried any direct effort for the structural change.

The understanding of MELIM can be summarized in the word of Henry J. Otten, former MELIM missionary. According to him; "Ethnicity is good. Ethnicity is a part of God's creation. Diversity is a part of creation and a part of

---

146 Herbert Hoeffer, "But Does it work? Unintended Social Consequences of a Perfectly Good Theology" *in Mission Apostolica, Journal of the Lutheran Society for Missiology,* XII/1/23 (May 2004): 50.

147 M.L. Kretzmann, *The India Mission, 1947-1950*, 3.

God's plan for salvation. If God desire to save all nations, why God choose one particular nation (*ethnose*), the Jews? There is only one possible answer: Grace. This one *ethnose* becomes a model for how God will treat all *ethnoi.*" No one ethnic group has all knowledge, all talent, all of God's salvation. God's plan for salvation began in a multi-ethnic setting, continued there, and will end there. (Rev. 7:9).[148]

5.8. MELIM's Approach to Caste

Churches in India followed different approaches to caste. The earliest of the protestant mission in India, the Danish Halle Mission, had permitted its Christians to retain caste distinctions.[149] Rajarigam reports Tranquabar missionaries' approach as thus: "Winked at the distinction of caste, although not at its sinfulness, in the hope that by patiently bearing with it for a while, it would gradually be dispelled by the strong light of the gospel shining upon their hearts."[150] This attitude left a heritage to subsequent missionaries.[151] Thus, Lutheran missionaries normally took a moderate step to abolish it. But the MELIM missionaries moved beyond this policy.

E. Griesse identifies five aspects of the caste question as the MELIM confronted it in the early 1930's. They are; a) The matter of exclusion b) separate worship for separate castes; c) Caste customs; d) Yielding to a demand and e) The matter of inclusion.[152] Most of the Lutheran local congregations were in a pluralistic social make up. E.H. Meinzen explains: "*As long as our congregations consisted of people belonging to the same caste, with intermarriage already practiced or at least possible under Indian customs, it was not a big problem to cultivate the feeling of belonging together. The problem became more difficult when the spiritual relationship and the physical were no longer identical, i.e. when work was begun among another*

---

[148] Content of the Bible Study conducted by Rev. Henry J. Otten, in the 6th All Kerala Lutheran Youth Convention, Perurkada, on 4 September 1977. For the full version of the lesson see, H.J.Otten, *Aathmika unarvinte Anugrahangal* (Blessings of Spiritual Renewal), Christiani, 52/10 (October, 1977) 14-17, (16).

[149] The first protestant missionary to India, Zeigenbalg, had the opinion of toleration of caste to considerable extent. M.D. David, Social Background of Basil Mission Christians: The Problem of Caste, *ICHR* XVIII /2, (December, 1984), 141.

[150] D. Rajarigam, "Tamil Churches and Caste, A Historical Sketch", *Religion and Society*, XV (September, 1968), 20-21.

[151] But other Protestant missions took more drastic measures. According to Rajarigram, "To discourage, repress, and eradicate the evil of caste. Wherever it existed caste was to be treated as a great evil, and appeals made to all Indian Christians to use all lawful means to eradicate so unchristian system."*Ibid.,* 22. Engish and American missionaries of the South India Missionary Conference after 1847 imposed the penalty of suspension from the mission service on all who did not dine together. In Madurai 72 persons, 38 of them catechists were suspended for refusing to obey the compulsory dining law.Luther W. Meinzen, *A Church In Mission*, *op.cit*, 48.

[152] Elmer Griesse, *Lutheran India Missions*, (St. Louis: Unpublished M.A. Thesis-Washington University, 1945).

caste."[153] Another MELIM missionary E Griesse reports: "Lutheran churches no doubt recognized the breaking down of caste distinction as an ideal, but did not necessarily favor an abrupt setting aside of these local distinctions. In any case, they did not favor a forcible disruption of the method of living that had through the centuries become crystallized in the caste system."[154] "Lengthening the cords" was the planning document in 1953. It recognized the caste complications as both obstacle and challenge to growth. With regard to the extension of work among new castes, the document says: "*The Church tends to be identified in a given geographical area with the caste in which it has had the most fruit.... In our own area we have several pockets in which the Church's membership is drawn almost exclusively from one caste. If that situation obtains for a longer period of time the Church is "labeled" by the name of that caste and accessions from other castes are well nigh impossible.*"[155] L.W. Meinzen writes: "*In a particular geographical area, the expansion of the church was limited to tribes or castes of similar status, and others were not attracted to the fold of the church. The expansion of the church was steady, but in different tribes or caste groups. When all mission stations were viewed together as one unit, there emerged a new society composed of different caste or Tribal groups, accepting Christ, but not rejecting caste or tribe.*"[156] This statement in a report about the structure of the congregation shows how the low caste maintained solidarity. It is also very clear that the inclusivism was the general agreed strategy of MELIM mission in India. And they handed over to the following generations to carry out this legacy.

5.9. Formation of a Lutheran Subaltern Solidarity

Even though the Sambavars and Ezhavas were the main instruments for the arrival of MELIM in Kerala, MELIM was not restricting their mission work within these two people groups. They like to build a community with all who suffered due to caste discrimination. The Mission records identified each congregation on caste basis. That shows their inclusive approach to this mission. They were very conscious about their mission to form a subaltern solidarity even in their age. This can be described under the following headings.

---

[153] E.H. Meinzen, *Fifty Years,* Unpublished History of Nagercoil District Conference 1907-1957, 26.

[154] Elmer Griesse, *Lutheran India Missions,* (St. Louis: Unpublished M.A, Thesis-Washington University, 1945), 7.

[155] Martin L. Kretzmann, *Lengthening the Cords, A Survey of Expansion Plans in the MELIM for the Next Five Years,* Nagercoil: MELIM, 1953), 3.

[156] Luther W. Meinzen, "The Structure of the Congregation in Mission", *The Gospel Witness,* LXV/1-3 (January-March, 1970): 6.

5.9.1. Efforts through the Literature

The 17th Trivandrum District Church's representative council met during 27-28 June 1928 at Vattiyoorkavu School. One of the paper presentations by W. Alexander was about *Caste Distinction among Christians.*[157]

Against the caste discriminations among Christians, *Christiani* criticized it through its articles.[158] The examples of such articles are: *Jathi spardha, There is caste among the Christians but there is no caste in Christianity, Caste is a religious matter. After entering in to the Christianity the caste identity must be forgotten,*[159] *Jathi Bhodam Anavasyam (Caste conscious not needed), Christiani editorial,*[160] *Jyathi Vyathyasam (caste Distinction), Thottukoodaymayum Christhianikalum (Untouchability and Christians) so on.*[161] The 19th volume of *Christiani* spent many pages to fight against the caste differences among the Lutheran Christians.

5.9.2. A Church for all Caste People

TDCM resolved to take necessary steps to deal with the congregations of Vattiyoorkavu and Concordia in Peroorkada, with the hope that they might eventually be amalgamated into one congregation under one pastor.[162] In order to form a common casteless church at Peroorkada (Central Church) a formation committee was organized with missionaries Wynakon, Chuvala and local pastors P.V. David, N.A. Ponnan.[163] TDCM reports: "By amalgamating the two churches in Peroorkada, we would have the one and only church in the Trivandrum District where all the castes among whom we work are gathered in one congregation. This would be a good opportunity to show that all castes can worship together as Christians."[164] A well constructed Lutheran Church building was dedicated on 18 Aug. 1957. Missionary Wilber May wrote "This is a congregation in Trivandrum District where Lutherans of all castes will worship together. It is a living demonstration that Christians can forget their Hindu caste animosities and worship together."[165]

---

[157] *Christiani,* 4/7, 1928, 201. *Christhyanikalkidayile Jathi bhedam.*

[158] *Christiani,* 5/5, 1929. 102-103. *Christiani,* 19/5, 1943, 253-54; 19/7, 1943, 280-282.

[159] *Christiani,* 5/5, 1929, 125.

[160] *Christiani,* 5/10, 1929, 218.

[161] *Christiani,* 6/1, 1930, 19.

[162] *TCDM* March, 1949, 15. See the enthusiasm of the board in this matter, Board letter, *TDCM* 1951, 17.

[163] *TDCM* 1950, 36, & 93.

[164] *132 TDCM* 1954, 65. *133 TDCM,* 1955, 12.

[165] *Lutheran Witness,* 5/10, 1957, 543.

5.9.3. Cheramar's Pettiton

A complaint in 1931 was sent to TDC by Cheramar for a special package for them in mission and TDC immediately appointed Rasch and Lutz to enquire in to the matter.[166] According to the subcommittee report the TDC resolved to ignore the petition since the MELIM has a vision to do mission among all the alienated and marginalized people of this area without special favor to any particular community.

5.9.4. Ezhava Lutheran Christian Society

Lutheran Christians from the Eazhava caste organized a society of their own with the help of their missionary Jank, *The Irava Lutheran Christian Society*.[167] This was an organization of the Ezhava workers within Lutheran Mission for the purpose of publishing tracts, and through other ways to be active in encouraging non Christians, in particular the Ezhavas, because of their present political, social and religious unrest, to join the Lutheran Church. A subcommittee was appointed to study the matter in detail. Its report was discussed by the TDC and GC of MELIM in detail at various times and finally they decided not to approve this society. They felt that it might create faction and strengthen communal feelings within the Travancore Lutherans, leading to the establishment of an 'Irava Lutheran Church' in India.[168] Therefore, the GC considered this organization as a weakness in TDC, unadvisable and not to encourage. They suggested that if they wished to proceed they could use the title "Lutheran Christian Gospel Society."[169] 70th TDC also discussed this matter and found that the members of this society were only *patcha* (real) Iravas. They felt that it might be a real issue in the future MELIM mission. Because MELIM wanted to do their mission in an inclusive perspective, therefore they were not allowed to proceed with the activities of this society.[170]

5.9.5. Private Properties at Luthergiri

Missionary Lutz had a special love towards the Sambavas. He purchased some private property at Luthergiri area, in Vallimangalam, Kuttara, Mandikalam, Poovachal and so on exclusively for the future use of the Sambava people. The money was paid through a private fund. But the TDC discussed this matter at length and found that it might cause unrest and division among other caste

---

[166] *TDCM,* 1949, 31.

[167] The *Irava* was an alternate word used for the *Ezhavas* on those days.

[168] See a notice about "Chengavila Bethel Ezhava Lutheran Church" by K. Suseelan, *Christiani*, 23/11 November, 1947, 125.

[169] *69th TDC Minutes* Nov. 18-25, 1935, 6-7, & 70th *TDC minutes* March 16-21, 1936, 1-2, F.R. Zucker, notes on Ezhava movements, Concordia Archives.

[170] *70th TDC Minutes*, 16-21 March 1936, 1.

Lutherans who had become members. Later these properties were added to TDC as the MELIM's property.[171]

5.9.6. Appointment and Transfers of Workers on Inter-Caste Basis

Through literature work, the MELM had encouraged Thiyas/Ehzavas to convert to Lutheran Christianity.[172] Mannoorkonam church in Luthergiri station was started in 1911 itself among the Nadars and Aryanad church among the Nadars was started in 1912.[173] To have people of different castes in one congregation was a unique feature of Lutheran church in Kerala in those days. It is reported that one of the first MELIM churches in Kuttichal had members from Paraiah, Pulaya, and Nadar and Ezhava castes.[174] That means that from the beginning itself, the Lutheran mission in Kerala was an inclusive mission for all subaltern communities. The workers' list clearly shows that in the early period the workers were not posted according to their community basis in the different churches. Puliyoorkonam church led a protest in connection with the appointment of R. Benjamin, a non-Sambava as a catechist there. But the Conference ignored the agitations and again a Nadar caste worker Masillamony of Kanacode was asked to conduct the services there.[175] A Paraiah catechist S. Johnson was appointed at Manninthala a Nadar church, but he hesitated to take over the charge. Therefore, the conference rejected his appointments.[176] Most of the Lutheran congregations on those days gladly accepted the services of other caste workers without any hesitation. The appointment and transfer list and the worker's list clearly shows that during the period of the Missionaries, people of all caste worked, mingled and grew together as a common community, yet kept their own identity. The commonness among them was Lutheranism.

5.9.7. Petition from Syrians at Thiruvalla

A group of Syrian Christians had separated from the Jacobite Church due to a quarrel and conducted separate services at Thiruvalla for about three years. They approached the MELIM with a request to start their work among them. Missionary Oberheu studied the matter and reported it to the Trivandrum District Conference. MELIM missionaries objected seriously to the policy of Syrians keeping low caste people out of the Church. Since the Syrian Christians attitude was against the policy of the MELIM missionaries, TDC rejected their appeal.[177]

---

[171] *TDCM,* 1950, 58, *TDCM* 1950, 69.

[172] *Thiyarodu randu vaakku* (Two words to Thiyas) *Christiani* 10/10, 1934, 153-55.

[173] Wiber May, *Congregation report,* 1951. Concordia Archives.

[174] *Christiani,* November 1951, 240.

[175] *62 TDCM,* 1933, 219.

[176] *62 TDCM*, 1933, 16, *63 TDCM,* 1934, 17-18, 64 *TDCM*, 1934, March, 18.

[177] *59th TDCM,* Sep. 5-9, 1932, 27.

5.9.8. Conference's Resolutions

The GM minutes witnessed the bold vision of MELIM missionaries to form a subaltern solidarity. MELIM General Conference went on record as follows:

"*Since the British government has definitely stated that caste is not a part of its system and since the native government also, besides being under the British government, and thus not the final authority in the land, does not recognize the caste as a part of its system, we cannot recognize caste as the form of government ordained by God in this land, even though these government at times make use of influential members of castes for having their orders carried out; we therefore consider caste a manmade organization without divine authority, either expressed or implied, which may, however, enjoy delegated authority as any other organization, though we know of no case on record.*"[178] In 1927 itself GC of MELIM discussed to expand its mission among more Shanars, Brahmins and Eazhavas.[179] General Secretary of missions and foreign mission reports that MELIM's work focused not only among Pariahs but it has always been done wherever an opportunity seemed to present itself.[180] *Work among Castes* document clearly shows that the missionaries of Trivandrum really wanted to overcome the old name Paraiah mission for MELIM mission.[181] General Conference wrote a detailed 7 page letter to G. Jesudasan against his complaint for working among the non-Sambavars. In that, the missionaries clearly explained that they won't restrict their work only with Sambavars, and that it would not be a Paraiah mission. They were very particular about reaching out among all the depressed Panchamas.[182] The first missionaries were convinced that they should work among various backward class people, even though the Pariahs might not like it.[183] In order to show that there was no place for the caste disparities among the Evangelical Lutheran Christians in Kerala they arranged a common feast for all communities to mix together.[184] This became a common practice in almost all *Pradhinithi Sangams*, and it continued. TDC also encouraged inter-dining and intermarriage to promote Christian fraternity.[185]

Joint Travancore Conferences realized the cause of the slow progress of their mission as follows: "*There are different classes of people to work with. The slow progress in mission work in India is due, to a great extent, to the fact that most*

---

[178] *15th GCM of MELIM,* Nov-24-Dec. 4, 1926, 10.

[179] *Minutes of the 17th GM of MELIM* 29 June 1927, 21.

[180] F Foster, *Report of the General Secretary of Foreign Missions,* 2-3. Concordia Archives.

[181] Schulz and Yank, *Work among Castes,* 3 pages typed document. Concordia Archives.

[182] Letter from G. Jesudasan to R.M. Zorn 5 Dec. 1941, Letter from G Jesudasan to R.M. Zorn on 3 Feb. 1942; Letter to G. Jesudason from General Conference April, 1942.

[183] A.G. Huebner, *Some information regarding the false idea of caste system,* 4 page German Document - got translated. Concordia Archives.

[184] *Christiani,* 4/4, 1928, 116.

[185] *63 TDCM,* Jan 8-16 & 25-26, 1934, 2.

of the mission work is being carried on among the outcastes. Even this fact makes through training more imperative. But the cause of this slow progress may be found in us to certain extent. We lack the proper fire."[186] Wyneken reports, "*Trivandrum district has congregations made up of members from no less than eight chief castes. Although most of the congregations are made up of one of these eight castes we have congregations in which several different castes are represented. The fact that we have so many different casts among our Christians makes each congregation and each section of our work in the Trivandrum District differs greatly from the congregations and work of other sections.*"[187]

A sub-committee appointed by TDC to work out a five year plan[188] suggested as the first priority to work among castes other than those now worked among. Their motto was by entering new fields without caste bias which help to make Christianity a religion embracing all castes. MELIM schools especially the five middle schools had large enrolments of various caste people including the Nairs. Very little follow up work had been done in the homes of these people. In order to get the other castes, TDC needed to take advantage of this readymade opportunity by the introduction of a planned program of follow up work in the homes of other castes from which children had come. The committee urged the conference that the entire Indian staff should participate and the Missionaries also need to furnish the spark by their own example in this program.[189] The LCMS visitor reported that MELIM had a tremendous growth among the most depressed class people throughout the field.[190]

5.9.9. A.J. Lutz Study on Christianity and Caste

Files show the concerns of MELIM about the caste issue. A.J. Lutz was one who studied this issue in detail. His essays were discussed in the GC in detail.[191] Can one be a Christian without losing one's caste identity was the main question. A.J. Lutz said "*The caste system is indeed man-made, even like the outward form of civil government, and like customs and usages, but punished by god for sin, from which a man need not separate himself if he feels that he will fare better within his community than among strangers, provided he does not deny his faith and Christian love in order to remain in caste.*"[192] He argued that Caste is a social evil which should be corrected. But Church's major mission is to save the whole humanity. A.J. Lutz opined that Gospel can change the attitudes of heart. Gradually through

---

[186] Minutes of the Travancore joint Conference, Trivandrum, August 21-22, 1928.

[187] Wyneken, *Write up to the delegate meeting,* 1942, 3. Concordia Archives.

[188] *TDCM* 1952, 26, 54.

[189] Wyneken, *Report of five year plan committee of TDC,* 17, Oct. 1952, 1.

[190] See the Malayalam version of the Letter from O H Shmidt secretary BFMS-LCMS to Herbert Zorn in *Christiani,* January, 1954, 8-10.

[191] *Essay read by A.J. Lutz at the 23rd GC, 22-29 January, 1941. Discussion on Church and Caste.*

[192] *5th GCM of MELIM,* Nov. 23-Dec. 4, 1926, 10.

the power of the Gospel and Christian Love the Society could overcome this issue. Mission accepted caste as a social reality. This was not to justify the caste conflicts but to accommodate others by accepting their identity.

5.9.10. Inter-Caste Marriages

MELIM missionaries conducted several inter caste marriages among the Lutherans to eradicate the stiffness of the evil caste system. The first convert to MELIM from Ernakulam by Harry D. Smith was K.K. Vasu from an Ezhava caste.[193] Later missionaries found Baby Sarojam from Kallayam a Nadar girl as the bride for Vasu.[194] Lot of marriages of the servants in the missionary bungalow was arranged by the missionaries in this way.[195] Missionary Huebner's correspondence shows that they viewed as a policy to overcome caste differences among the Lutherans.[196] Missionaries did not allow any caste distinction to be observed in the boarding schools in MELIM. All the children were fed and clothed and treated alike. They mingled in every respect on equal terms.[197] Its distinctiveness is its one century life as a unique Christian subaltern solidarity.[198]

5.10. A Unique Subaltern Solidarity

This oldest of the LCMS' daughter-sister-partner church, initially began with converts directly from the Hindu (out) castes. Over the years, people from other castes who had got converted to Christianity and since had become members of other Christian denominations have also joined this Church. In the midst of awakening among separate caste movements, different marginalized communities formed a Christian solidarity under Lutheran Mission.[199]

---

193 K.K. Vasu was baptized on 26 October1952 at the Ernakulum Station. See, Martin Wynekan, *Significant dates in Trivandrum Station in 1952,* 18 December, 1952, Concordia Archives.

194 The marriage took placed at The MELIM Conference Hall Peroorkada on 18/April/1959. Missionaries made all the arrangements for the marriage.

195 Interview with K.K. Vasu, the first convert from Ernakulam field; now staying at Concordia UPS Compound Peroorkada, on 4 Feb. 2012.

196 A.G. Huebner, *Some information's regarding the false idea about the caste system, (5 page German document, nd. got translated)* 4. Concordia Archives.

197 Interview with Rev. M.M. Jacob (86), Former secretary of TDS, and a member of Karode Lutheran Church, Vilappilsala, 15 August, 2012 .

198 For more details about the MELIM's approach towards this subaltern solidarity see, 3.12. *Bold vision.*

199 About the amalgamation of caste among the Lutherans in Kerala, E.E.Gresse writes, "Chenamcode has a congregation of Paraiahs, Pulayas, and vedas, Kalathukal consists largely of Paraiahs. Karuvallam largely with Ezhavas but a mixed caste group including several of the Nayar persuasion". E.E. Greesse, *Lutheran India Missions, op.cit.*, 31. "The following are the stations in the Luthergiri field and the caste or out caste groups among whom work has been conducted; Chalikonam-Paraiah, Kurungalloor-Paraiah, Konni- Pulayas, Luthetgiri- Parayas, Aryanad- nadars, Tholoor- Parayas, Kuttichal- Parayas, Thachancode- Nadars, Kannankonam- Vedas and Pulayas,

Lutheran missionaries realized that the power of the Christian gospel would be the main source for the freedom of the most downtrodden people. The Lutheran missionaries concentrated among the various people groups of those areas like Sambavars, Nadars, Vellalas, Ezhavas, Pulayas, Barbers, Mannans, Panans and many tribal peoples.[200] They loved them as brothers and sisters and taught them that they were as valuable and acceptable to God just as Brahmins. The parenthood of God and Christian love opened the said group's eyes which helped to build up their self esteem.[201] The socially alienated people groups were attracted by MELIM missionaries and so joined to the Lutheran church. In this view, Lutheran Christian community in Kerala is a graphic design of a united people who came from very distinctively different caste as well as socio-economic background. Over half of the membership today is deprived of their caste rights and privileges in independent India simply because they are Christian, and worse, the government considers them 'forward' because they identify themselves as Lutheran.[202]

By the systematic and conscious efforts of the Missionaries, slowly the people of the land were able to attain the social dignity along with the spiritual salvation. Lutheranism became a liberating force for the socially alienated people from their age old slumber. Lutheran Church in Kerala has 98% of her membership with subaltern Christians. It is a unique subaltern solidarity which brought together about 18 Backward & Other Backward Class and tribal people groups into the Lutheran Christian fold. The slaves of the land became the people of the land and a community of equals. They were able to come out of seclusion and fought for their equality in society. The liberated people from different ethnic groups, once oppressed human beings, formed a unique Christian subaltern solidarity under the Lutheran Christian fold.

5.11. Conclusion

Subaltern Studies and Subaltern movements paved the way for new perspectives in historiography. The conception of subaltern locates the humans in a social position of subordination and makes them as historical subjects capable of active agency. Subaltern people in Kerala were kept under the yoke of the political and hierarchical exploitative social system. While the denial of rights to public space excluded the subaltern subject from participating in the social psyche, fear weakened the process of emergence of the subaltern subjects in history. Administrative reforms, modern education and Christian Mission, etc., were the

---

Valiyamangalam-Pulayas, Mylakkara- Nadars, ...(*Survey of the Luthergiri Report*, MS, missionary report, 1-2.CTS Archives).

[200] See *Lengthening the Cords,* A survey of Expansion Plans in the MELIM (January, 1953).

[201] Letter from P.V. David,to the missionary Council, 9/7/1962.

[202] Wilbert Rosin, *A Report on Mission in India, Based on A brief visit to IELC Missions,* January 1964, 13 pages document, CTS Archives, Nagercoil, 10.

guiding force for finding a social space to the subalterns. Kerala society witnessed a lot of mass based social awakenings and movements at the end of nineteenth and beginning of twentieth centuries. These movements were the form of protest towards self affirmation. The communal feelings became more evident among people and each caste or community came to represent a pressure group in the political life of Kerala. However, the subaltern subjects gradually began to affirm their social self.

As one of the latest Christian mission agency, MELIM planted churches in Kerala as an ongoing experiment. Unlike most other Christian denominations in India, a multitude of castes co-exist in this Church of a hundred years. The organizational structures of the majority of the mainline Christian denominations in India have a certain specific caste orientation. It stands to reason that as such this subculture functions as an infrastructure that has brought certain stability to these churches institutionally, perhaps based on the homogeneous unit principle. This does not mean that other caste Christians are not included in the membership of any particular denomination. They continue to remain a minority in terms of headcount. Certain particular castes visibly dominate the entire organization and administration of the districts and dioceses of these Churches. Even today, there are at least some examples of congregations that maintain their membership with a particular diocese transcending their geographical locations, practically on caste grounds. But Lutheran Church in Kerala has in its membership a multitude of castes, being a textbook example for all mission Churches of the 21st century. Because, for a Church of her size, TDS membership has come from numerous castes and sub-castes, the majority of which were deemed outcaste in the antiquated but practically omnipresent Hindu caste system.

MELIM missionaries accepted the caste system as evil and also as a social reality. Of course, they had not done much to eradicate the caste practices among the converted Lutheran Christians. They thought that a casteless Christianity was not possible and practical in the then Indian context. They permitted them to keep their own caste identity and practices. Along with that, put them to live and stay together with many other caste people as the children of the one living God. This was a unique effort in those days. To belong to a 'community' is to be able to share its resources and communicate with its participants, though this does not mean necessarily accepting all the values and wisdom of those communities.[203] Lutheranism became a locus for the upward social mobility to the subalterns in Kerala. Christian gospel gave this people a sense of freedom and self respect. By ignoring their caste and sub caste barriers, an all embracing movement of different people group was possible in history. People from the bottom got identity and history. Even though this people have

[203] Erric J. Lott, Issues in the Philosophy of Research, in Wati Longchar, (ed.) *Issues in Theological Research: A Methodological Exploration* (Bangalore: BTESSC/SATHRI, 2010), 5.

a century unwritten history, they were ignored in the pages of both secular and Christian historians. In this context, it is highly important to search why this unique history of the Christian Lutherans in Kerala was forgotten in the common history of Christianity. The next chapter discusses the unacknowledged situation of Lutherans in Kerala.

Chapter 6

Lutherans in Kerala: An Unacknowledged Subaltern History

6.1. Introduction

The Bible is supposed to be the most egalitarian faith that opposes any kind of discrimination on the basis of race, sex or otherwise.[1] But the problem of caste among Christianity started soon after Christianity got rooted in a caste-ridden Indian Soil. The Christians in India are divided into two main groups: about 70% of them are subaltern Christians and the rest 30% upper caste and Christians from various indigenous communities.[2] This chapter firstly tries to describe shortly about the major protestant churches in South Kerala and then to analyse the caste practices in Kerala Churches. Then it tries to describe how far Lutheranism in Kerala has become a Subaltern quest for empowerment. It follows an attempt to evaluate the major features behind the un-acknowledgement of this unique Lutheran solidarity.

6.2. Major Protestant Christian Denominations in Kerala

The Christians form the most important part of the population in Kerala State as the second largest community in Kerala State next to Hindus. The ancient Christian community in Kerala is known as the Syrian Christians / St. Thomas Christians.

---

[1] The magna carta of the Christian concept of equality is found in the letter of Paul to Galatians in these words, "*There is no longer Jew or Greek, there is no longer slave or free, there is no longer male or female, for all of you are one in Christ Jesus.*"(3:28)

[2] Kuncharia Pathil, *Indian Churches at the Cross Roads* (Bangalore: CIIS & Dharma), 116-128.

6.2.1. The Syrian Christians

Jacobite Church[3] and Syrian Orthodox Church[4] are the two major non-Catholic denominations in Kerala. This community, under the titles '*Bava*' group[5] and '*Methran*' group has a long history of internal split. Geographically speaking, the northern regions of Kerala by and large back the '*Bava* group' while the central and southern regions of the State extend support to the '*Methran* group.'[6]

6.2.2. The Protestants

The CMS missionaries started to serve as a 'Mission of Help' among the Syrian Christians of Malabar. In 1835, a schism took place as a result of differences between the Eastern and Protestant interpretations of Christianity and the failure of the attempts to reconcile the tensions between the missionaries and local leaders. A group of Syrian Christians left their Church, and formed a new protestant Christian community within the Anglican Communion with the help of CMS.

Marthoma Syrian Church had their origin from the excommunication of a Jacobite bishop, Mathews Mar Athanasius, in 1875. They are 'Protestant' in doctrines and 'Syrians' in externals.[7] They engaged themselves very actively in evangelistic and educational work.

The LMS and CMS worked in Travancore for a very long time and had great influence on society and government policies.[8] The CSI[9] in Kerala is divided into

---

[3] In 1665, a Jacobite bishop, Gregorios from Jerusalem, on the invitation of the local people, came to Kerala. The group which rejected the supremacy of the Roman Pope after the 'Coonan Cross Oath' followed Mar Gregarious. The Church was there after known as 'Jacobite Church'. The title 'Jacobite 'is associated with the name of Jacob Bardai who had organized a faction within the Church of Syria during the sixth century.

[4] This is the '*Methran* group' of the Jacobites. Today they have adopted the name 'Syrian Orthodox Church' based on the assumption that it is this Church that has preserved the true Christian faith.

[5] Group/party in Malayalam it calls as *Kakshsi*.

[6] Normally the term 'Patriarch group' and 'Catholic's group' are used in history of Christianity Indian text books.

[7] The Mar Thoma Church suffered division in 1961, a section of Syrian Christians forming themselves into the new St. Thomas Evangelical Church of India.

[8] The LMS was established in London in 1795 by members from various denominations such as the Congregationalists, the Presbyterians and the Methodists. The first LMS missionary to Travancore was W.T. Ringaltaube, a German Lutheran, who commenced his work in 1806.The CMS was formed by the Evangelicals in the Church of England in 1799 and started its work in North Travancore in 1816. Dick Kooiman, *Conversion and Social Equality in India* (New Delhi: Manohar, 1989), 33-35.

[9] The CSI was inaugurated in 1947, after 30 years of union negotiations between the South India United Church-the combined body of Presbyterians and Congregationalists- the Anglican Diocese in South India and the South Indian districts of the Methodist Church. Out of 22 dioceses of the CSI one is in Jaffna, Sri Lanka. The basis of the constitution is the Lambeth Quadrilateral,

four dioceses: East Kerala, South Kerala, Madhya Kerala and North Kerala. Each diocese is under a bishop residing at Melukavumattom, Trivandrum, Kottayam, and Shoranur respectively. CSI-SKD is situated closely within the geographical areas of Lutheran Church in South Kerala.

Besides these Churches, there were a few more protestant missions, though they were relatively new and smaller in size.[10] The Salvation Army[11] started their work in Travancore in 1889. They secured a firm footing and established its head quarters at Nagercoil in 1892.[12] Salvation Army work commenced in the old Travancore State on 18 March 1894 by Captain Yesudasan Sanjivi, who was a Namboothiri (high-caste Brahmin) before his conversion. When the founder of the Salvation Army, General William Booth, visited Nagercoil, he was impressed by the enthusiasm of Captain Yesudasan (later Colonel) and the General appointed him on the spot to start the Army's work in Kerala State. He was called Namboori Ayyah by the members of the Church. The visit produced a great impression on the converts. His son, Colonel Donald A. Sanjivi, became the first territorial commander from Kerala. The work was spread to other parts of the State through the dedication of pioneer officers-Commanders. Many officers who had worked for the poor and the oppressed had been banned from many villages and cities. They were even beaten up mercilessly. The Army extended its activities. In 1924, Trivandrum was made the headquarters of the South Indian districts. The divisional centres were established at Neyyattinkara, Nedumangadu, Kattakada, Trivandrum, Kottarakkara, Adoor, Mavelikkara Ranni and Thiruvalla. Each division was under the charge of a Divisional Commander. The India South Western Territory came into being on 1 October 1970 when the Southern India Territory was divided into two. The territory has its headquarters at Thiruvananthapuram and comprises the entire Malayalam-speaking area known as Kerala State.

The Brethren mission started its work in 1898; and the Lutheran mission in 1907.[13] Bible Faith Mission (BFM),[14] was begun in 1913 by an Indian evangelist

---

the historical episcopate being accepted in a constitutional form. These Churches were brought to Kerala by the British towards the beginning of the 19th century.

[10] Koji Kawashima, *Missionaries and a Hindu State Travancore, 1858-1936* (Delhi: OUP, 1998) 55.

[11] *Raksha Sainyam* is the Malayalam term used for the Salvation Army in Kerala, India. *Ratchannya Senai* (Tamil) and *Mukthi Fouj* (Hindi) are other names for the same organization. *Raksha Sainyam* is a Christian Charity and Social Services organization. It's also a Church with Territorial Head Quarters at Kowdiar, Thiruvananthapuram. Salvation Army is an international organisation and it is working in 121 countries. General William Booth is the founder and first General of the Salvation Army.

[12] T.K. Velupillai, *Travancore State Manuel, op.cit*, 781.

[13] *Census of India, 1931, Vol. XXVIII, Travancore, Part1, Report* (Trivandrum: Government Press, 1932), 341.

[14] The Bible Faith Mission was originally founded and registered in The Maine State of America in 1911 by Sara K. Tailor. Its main motto was: "to engage and unite the efforts of Christian men

who was burdened to reach the Dalits (or 'Untouchables') in Kerala, South India. A Brahmin convert Charles young Vethanthachari[15] who married a pariah orphan girl became the instrument to start BFM work in Kerala in 1913. From 1913 to 1937, he was able to found about 120 churches and 45 schools in South Travancore with the generous help of *Dewan* C.P. Ramaswamy Ayyar.[16] The Parayars, the Ayyanavars and the Nadars were the major sub castes, who had become members of BFM.[17] Under the leadership of Moses Swamidas, this Church runs a church-planting ministry among the Dalits. Now the mission has its headquarters at Parasuvakkal, in Trivandrum District, South India.[18] While maintaining amicable relations with other denominations, the BFM has determined to limit its ministry in practice to the Dalit communities. BFM's motto is to "seek the lost and reach the unreached."[19] BFM operates India's only registered school for Dalit children who provide a unique life-changing opportunity through education and for future accomplishment. Today, BFM's vision is to bring economic, social and spiritual transformation to the Dalits and it is stronger than ever.

The trouble of caste tradition continues as an awkward block in the evangelistic path of the Churches in Kerala. The upholding of caste structures within the Church visibly is a contradiction of the Church as a redeemed community. Demands for complete separation on caste basis, separate administration within the Church, have been increasingly made by many sections of the backward classes. In this context, the history of Lutherans in Kerala need special attention.

As discussed earlier, Lutheran Mission entered in the present day Kerala in 1912. Lutheranism penetrated among all the socially marginalised communities in South Kerala. J.W. Gladstone has argued that the conversion movements of the lower castes in Kerala were a 'part of the struggle of the oppressed sections

---

and women in sending of the 'Gospel of the kingdom' throughout the world." Moses Swamidas, *Conversion and Reconversion in India: A Study of the Experience of Dalit Christians in the Context of the Ministry of the Bible Faith Mission* (Parasuvakkal: Bible Faith Mission Publication Series, 2001), 55.

15 Born on 18 September 1885, in Bangalore and died on 28 October 1937 at Madras.

16 Sarosh T. Jacob (ed.), *Kerala Sabha Chratithra Nigandu* (Mal.) (Dictionary of Kerala Christian Church history), (Pathanapuram: Spiritual India Publications, 1999), 121.

17 Moses Swamidas, *Conversion and Reconversion in India: A Study of the Experience of Dalit Christians in the Context of the Ministry of the Bible Faith Mission,* (Parasuvakkal: Bible Faith Mission Publication Series, 2001, 56.

18 To see more details of the history of BFM in Kerala see, "our Journey from darkness to light", BFM Platinum jubilee Souvenir, released on 13) October 1988, 15f.; J. Divakaran, BFM Charithravum Velluvilikalum (Mal) (BFM - History and Challenges) P*rayanam* of a persecuted Community, BFM Souvenir, Published in connection with the consecration of the first bishop Moses Swamidas, 13 March, 2006, 46-48.

19 Interview with Moses Swamidas (BFM Bishop) on 4th January 2013.

of the society for their emancipation.'[20] However, it is difficult to accept that all cases of conversion could be treated as struggles for emancipation. There was no mass conversion towards Lutheranism as such.[21] Most of them were only small groups or families. The conversion due to the persecution by their masters and employers were also reported. The Lutheran missionaries used to hire Nadar Christians who were well versed in martial arts to protect the Sambava converts from the persecutions of Nairs. Later, these Nadar Christians became Lutherans. Some of them were converted by the teaching of missionaries. Some of them became Lutherans for financial help, since they were in extreme poor situation. T.K. Velupillai noted that, "The Lutheran Mission differs from other protestant denominations by its adherence to the Confessional principal."[22] Now this Church had more than a century of life and history. There is quite a few writings about the Christian Churches in Kerala by both Church historians and other secular historians.

6.3. The Occurrence of Caste among the Kerala Churches

The low caste people were subjected to severe indignities, disabilities and inhuman treatment throughout the years. It is quite natural that they were attracted to the religions like Buddhism, Christianity, Islam and Sikhism. Christianity gave them shelter, education, better living condition and a better quality of life. But unfortunately, the Christian social order remained more or less same as the Hindu social order. The caste practice continued to affect faultily in the convert's life. Normally, a convert follows the caste customs and ceremonies in his/her life cycle celebrations such as birth, marriage, funeral and food and dress habits. Over the centuries, the caste consciousness has become part and parcel of the Christian's psyche.

6.3.1. St. Thomas Christians

During the early Christian era in Kerala, St. Thomas Christians followed caste system as the Hindu religionists followed. They did not baptize the low castes; for fear that they should lose their social position.[23] Like the high caste Hindus of that time, they strictly followed the caste laws pertaining untouchability and unapproachability in their relations to with other lower caste people.[24] Syrian

---

[20] J.W. Gladstone, *The Protestant Christianity and People's Movements in Kerala, op.cit.* 137-138.

[21] Rajasekhar argues that: "from the beginning of the dalit conversion missionaries helped to bring the dalits in a collective form of religion which was a threat to the religion of the upper caste." (V.T. Rajasekhar, *Aggression on Indian Culture* (Bangalore: Dalit Sahithya Acadamy, 1998), 14.

[22] T.K Velupillai, *The Travancore State Manuel, Vol. I*, (Trivandrum: Kerala Gazetteers Department, 1996) (1940), 792.

[23] Joseph Thekkedath, *History of Christianity in India*, Vol.II, (Bangalore: TPI, 1984), 22.

[24] George Varughese observes, "In practice the Indian Orthodox Church continues to consider Dalit Christians as the "other", demonstrating that it is a foreclosed system in spite of its self-perception

Christians were regarded as a caste and had a recognised place in the caste hierarchy. [25]

6.3.2. Protestant Mission in India

The problem of caste was a big issue from the very beginning among the Protestants too.[26] Even after conversion, the lower caste converts were continued to be treated as *Harijan*[27] Christians to whatever denominations they changed into. The missionaries addressed the Christian converts from low castes as "Mass Movement Christians" or as 'Christians'. Whereas, the title 'convert' they would use only to the upper caste Christians.[28] In many places, there were separate Churches or separate seating during the worship, separate communion vessels, separate cemeteries and burial places with in a common cemetery.[29] In some parishes, the low castes were not allowed to assist the sacraments and they were given sacraments only after upper caste Christians had been administered.[30] A problem like the caste system was viewed as an affair of this world and not a contrary factor for salvation, so it did not matter if it was followed or not. Some missionaries like Joseph Peet, thought that the addition of low caste people may become a stumbling block to the reception of Gospel by the higher caste. He

to the contrary." George Varughese, "The Foreclosed system of the Orthodox Church's Caste Identity: A Christian ministry Perspective", Unpublished paper, presented in Staff-student Seminar at Gurukul Lutheran theological College and research Institute, Chennai, (18 July, 2012), 9.

[25] Duncan B. Forrester, *Caste and Christianity* (Briton: Cruzan Press, 1979), 99. The Syrian Christians had kept a distance from newly converted from the very beginning even in the Dutch periods. "They do not mix or intermarry with newly converted Christians of lower castes or class. The majority of the people belong to the Nair castes of class of nobles. And for this reason, they like the Nairs, carried a sword in the hand as a token of their dignity." George Vargees, *Malankara Nasranikalude Jathyaulkristyavum Rajayasevana Nirathayum* (mal.), [The Civil Service and Caste Nobility of Malankara Nasraniees] (Kottayam: MOC Publications, 1988), 130.

[26] For more discussion on Christian Mission and their attitude to the observance of caste, see, Louis Dunmont, *Religion/Politics and History of India* (Paris: Mouton Publishers, 1970), 190; S. Manikam, *Studies in Missionary History: Reflections on a Culture –Contact* (Madras: CLS, 1983), 43; Pramod Rao, *Religio-Cultural Changes and Communities* (Delhi: ISPCK, 2012), 242; Arthur Jeyakumar, *History of Christianity in India, Selected Themes* (Madurai, TTS, 2007), 55-68. See also Richter Julius, *A History of Missions in India* (New York: Fleming H. Revell, 1908), 108; C.B. Firth, *op.cit*, 137: M.K. Kuriakose, *History of Christianity in India: Source Materials* (Banglore: CLS, 1982), 57-59.

[27] The word *Harijan* popularized by M.K. Gandhi referring to the low castes are the sons/daughters of the lord *Hari* (God). Later this term became an offence for low caste groups. But today the term is officially banned by the government through the Ordinance. Fr. Shouri, "Dalit Christians Threat to Walk Out of 'Hindu' Church", *Dalit Voice*, 10/19 (August 16-31, 1991), 16; V.T. Rajasekhar, *Christians and Dalit Liberations* (Bangalore: Dalit Sahithya Accadamy, 1987), 16.

[28] James Massey, "Christian Dalits: A Historical Perspective", *Religion and Society XXII/*2 (July, 1990): 56.

[29] M.E. Prabhakar, "Christian Dalits", *Religion and Society 34/3* (September, 1987): 3.

[30] Joseph Thekkedath, *op.cit.*, 22.

commented, "We have rushed needlessly into the arms of the lower classes... fraternizing with a despised race is just the way to raise prejudices and prevent the extension of our influence upward."[31] Though Christianity does not recognize caste system, they were having upper and lower caste among Christians.[32] According to Duncan B. Forrester, "The caste system seems to have made possible for Christianity to survive in Kerala."[33] The pathos and problems of the subalterns were ignored conveniently for centuries, even in the churches and theologies. Christianity buried its egalitarian principles beneath the caste system.

6.3.2.1. The South Kerala Diocese of CSI

CSI-SKD has a membership consisting of different people groups mostly from the B C and SC&ST groups along with the majority of Nadars. The diocese has accepted the principle of appointing workers of the same caste group as that of the parish members as far as possible and this has been welcomed on the whole as a satisfactory arrangement.[34] In order to satisfy the discontent among backward class Christians, attempts were made for a regrouping of parishes providing a kind of limited type of separate administration.[35] Later they formed eight Dalit districts to give more administrative participation and care for the most oppressed section. Bishop Sam Amirtham started a Dalit Development Department. Dalit CSI Christian's reservation is another major concern.[36] Now the move for the bifurcation of dioceses on the basis of caste is officially on the process.[37] Synod secretariat resolved to divide South Kerala Diocese into the major two centres namely Trivandrum and Kottarakkara. Proposed new diocese will be among the most backward CSI Christians and the program is on the process.[38]

6.3.2.2. Mar Thoma Church

Mar Thoma Church is the result of a reformation movement in the old Syrian Church and was inspired to a great extent by the work of the Church Missionary Society. Work among the backward classes and conversion to Marthomite

[31] Robin Jeffrey, *The Decline of Nair Dominance in Society*, 36.

[32] A study undertaken by the Jesuits in Tamil Nadu in 90's reveals that the dalit Christian's constitute 70% of the total Christians in Tamil Nadu. There was one dalit bishop among the Catholics and mere 3.8% of the priests were dalits at that time. Brojendra Nath Banerjee, *Struggle for Justice to Dalits Christians* (New Delhi: New Age International (p) limited, 1997), 63.

[33] Duncan B. Forrester, *Caste and Christianity* (London: Orson Press, 1980), 99.

[34] Ninan Koshy, *Caste in the Kerala Churches* (Bangalore: CISRS, 1968), 23.

[35] The following SK minutes witness the issues connected with Kottarakkara Area. SK 33/98,359/99, 952/96, 974/03.

[36] SK 949/96,980/97, 1831/98, 798/99, 1032/03, 453/2005, 690/2005, 1055/2005, 1249/2005.

[37] SK.286/02,1035/03,1481/2004, 1046/2005, 1537/2006, 1778/06, 2295/2007.

[38] Interview with Bhanu Samuel, Co-coordinator, New Diocesan Formation Council of CSI-SK Diocese on 4 January, 2013.

Christianity have been under the auspicious of the evangelistic Association founded in 1888.[39] The converts were organised into '*Sabhas*', a name for the congregations of the backward caste people as against the '*Idavakas*' which is the name for the parishes of the Mar Thoma Syrians. In 1980, a few of the churches in the mission fields had been upgraded into *Idavakas*.[40] *Idavakas* can send official and elected representatives to the Church Councils. *Sabhas* are represented by a limited number of nominated members. Therefore, the share in the administrations of this section is very limited. The situation has brought about a sense of grievance in the minds of the members of the low caste against the Syrians of this Christian community.[41] The Church has established Christian Agency for Rural Development (CARD) and Backward Peoples Development Commission (BPDC)[42] for the uplift of Dalit Christian Converts in the Mar Thoma Church. The problem of caste discrimination in Mar Thomite Church had been brought out by the study of Alex Thomas.[43]

6.3.2.3. Salvation Army

There is not much caste issues in the Salvation Army Cores in Kerala. One of the main reason is that though this Christian mission started in Kerala with the Syrians and Brahmin converts, later its major adherents were from Pulayas, Parayas and Kuravas. Since they all belong to the Dalit group there is no much caste disputes as such. Another reason may be the Army discipline of this Group.[44]

Bible Faith Mission declared themselves as the Dalit church with only the dalit members. Since most of this type of Churches is chiefly made up of the backward classes and they have here apparently greater opportunities for self expression, the caste conflict is not openly evident. Therefore, the caste oppression is not a big problem among them.

6.3.2.4. Pentecostal Movements and Caste

Pentecostal influence among the lower castes began with the arrival of foreign missionaries especially with the arrival of R.F. Cook. The early missionaries freely

---

[39] For more details see Babu Kodemvelil (ed.), *K.M. Chacko: A Lightening Face for the Search of Dalit Christian Identity* (Mal.) (Thiruvalla: CSS, 2002), 38.

[40] Babu Kodemvelil (ed.), *K.M. Chacko: A Lightening Face for the Search of Dalit Christian Identity* (Mal.) (Thiruvalla: CSS, 2002), 78.

[41] Now Mar Thoma Syrian Church has more than 100 *Idavakas* from the Backward Caste converts.

[42] Later the name changed into Backward Peoples Development Corporation (BPDC).

[43] Alex Thomas, "Problems and Prospects of Dalit Mar Thoma Christians: A Socio- Historical Survey since, 1888". An un published MTh thesis, Senate of Serampore (March, 1997): 92-112.

[44] Interviews with John Susil Kumar, (Editor, SA, Publications), Pakiya Das, (Asst. Editor, S.A. Publications), Roy Joseph, (Social Secretary), and George Jacob (Evangelism Secretary) Salvation Army Headquarters, Kowdiyar Trivandrum on 4 December, 2012.

mingled with the untouchables in the society. The conditions of the poor low castes were well narrated by Cook as follows:

"*Our main work here is mostly among the low castes, those called the untouchables or the neglected; such respond readily to the Gospel and became sincere worshippers of the supernatural. The Lord blesses them abundantly in the spirit of ignorance. A good number of the so called Syrian Christians do not come far behind spirituality.*"[45] He also says that, the Syrians and high caste Hindus treated these low castes as inferiors.[46] Samuel Kutty says, Dalits in Pentecostal churches from the second half of the 20th century have seen not only discrimination in general but also more specifically in their ministry and leadership.[47] Discrimination of dalits in Church of God (Full Gospel) in India led to the division in 1970.[48] Overall, Pentecostal churches in Kerala especially Indian Pentecostal Churches, have sidelined the role and involvement of dalits Pentecostals in administration and ministry.[49]

The above fact clearly shows that caste practices prevailed among various Churches in Kerala. The Dalits are naturally unsatisfied with the small efforts for their liberation and developments made by the leadership of the Church which is mainly non-Dalit. Dalits now take up themselves the task of their liberation. Dalit Christian's organizations were formed- most of them are action groups. It can be observed that caste conflicts and problem faced among the Lutherans in Kerala is not an isolated one but it had similarities in other churches too.

6.4. Government Commissions Identified Castes in the Church

The various Commissions appointed by the Government to study the plight of the subalterns, reported that the converts from low caste to Christianity suffer from the same caste practise by their non convert counterparts. There are considerable evidences available from various Governments appointed Commissions identifying caste system being practised in the Kerala Churches. The first Backward Commission was appointed by the Indian President on 29 January 1953 with Kaka Saheb Khalelkar as its chairman.[50] The commission report (1955) made the following observation that: *"Even a change of religion does not*

---

[45] Robert E. Cook, *Half a century of Divine leadings and 37 Years of Apostolic Achievements in South India*, (Cleveland: Church of God Foreign Department, 1955), 27-28.

[46] Ibid., 98.

[47] T.S. Samuel Kutty, *The Place and Contribution of Dalits in Select Pentecostal Churches in Kerala from 1922-1972*. (Delhi: ISPCK, 2000), 116.

[48] Saju Thomas, *Kerala Pentacostal Charitram* (Mal.) [The History of Pentecostals in Kerala], (Kottayam: Good News Publications, 1994), 266-267.

[49] T. Sunil, "Changes in the understanding of mission among Pentecostals in Kerala with a Special Reference to the Indian Pentecostal Church of God since, 1934". An unpublished MTh. Thesis, (Senate of Serampore, March, 2008), 92.

[50] This presidential order was based on Article 340 of the Constitution. He submitted the report on 30 March 1955 and the Commission identified 2399 Backward Communities/ Castes in India.

destroy caste. For instance, converts to Christianity sometimes carry caste practices with them though their religion does not recognize it. A. large number of people belonging to lower castes, and in particular, from among the untouchables become converts to these religions to escape the rigour and humiliation of the Hindu caste system. It is sad to note, however, that, even these converts could not easily shake off their old caste disabilities."[51] Further the report states: "We discovered with deep pain and sorrow that untouchability did remain in the extreme south among Indian Christians."[52] The report of the Backward Classes Commission (1955 and 1980), made it clear that this 'unfortunate aspect' continues to dominate the life of Kerala Christians, because of which the Christians of low caste continue to suffer various disabilities in the Church and Society.[53] The Kumara Pillai committee report submitted to the Kerala Government in 1965 too states that : "... the evidence is that the degrees of segregation of the new convert from Scheduled Castes is almost as high as before his(sic) conversion...We are convinced that in practice converts to Christianity from scheduled castes are treated as socially backward."[54] The Santhanam Sathyanathan Committee Report of 1970 admitted that "the same spirit of renaissance which animate the Indian Scheduled Castes had not spread to the Christian section and that due to the absence of employment opportunities similar to those reserved for Scheduled Castes, there was no temptation for the converts to go into higher education. Dalits are ill treated by the upper caste Christians."[55] The Chidambaram report said, "...that casteism is practised widely among the members of the Christian fold as judged by the characteristics of caste system and going by the economic status of the Harijan(sic) Christians. It is evident that they are a poverty stricken lot."[56]

Mandal Commission[57] also affirmed that "*Though caste system is peculiar to Hindu society, yet in actual practice it also pervades to non-Hindu communities in India in varying degrees. There are two reasons for this phenomenon: first, caste system is a great conditioner for the mind and leaves an indelible mark on a person's social*

[51] Kaka Saheb Khalelker Commission Report, 1955, quoted in Antony Raj, *Discrimination Against Dalit Christians in Tamilnadu* (Madurai: Ideas Centre, 1992), 19.

[52] James Massey, *Dalits in India-Religion as a Source of bondage or liberation with Special Reference to Christians* (New Delhi: Manohar, 1995), 81.

[53] M.K. Kuriakose, *History of Christianity in India: Source Materials* (Delhi: ISPCK, 1999), 14.

[54] Kumara Pillai Commission Report (Kerala Government, 1965), quoted in Brojendra Nath Banerjee, *Struggle for Justice to Dalits Christians* (New Delhi: New Age International (p) limited, 1997), 62.

[55] Ibid, 63.

[56] Kumara Pillai Commission Report, 63.

[57] The second Backward Classes Commission, Known as Mandal Commission in 1980 under the chairmanship of the late B.P. Mandal, was officially appointed on 1 January 1979 by Morarji Desai the then Prime Minister and given two extensions by Indira Gandhi. The six Commission members including the later joined I.R. Naik were from the OBC's. The report of the commission was submitted on 31 December, 1980.

consciousness and cultural moves. Consequently, even after conversion, the ex-Hindus carried with them their deeply ingrained ideas of social hierarchy and stratification... non-Hindu minorities living in a predominantly Hindu India could not escape from its dominant cultural influences. Thus both from within and without, castes amongst non-Hindu communities receive continuous sustenance and stimulus."[58] Further the Mandal Commission observed, "... even after conversion, the lower caste converts continued to be treated as *Harijans* by all sections of the society..."[59] The above mentioned commission reports are the clear references to prove that the unchristian caste practices extremely prevailed over the Christian Churches. The pre Christian culture was carried out along with their Christian faith. This is one of the major areas where Christian community have to seriously examine. In this context Lutherans in Kerala remains as a mixture of different socially backward communities and formed a unique subaltern solidarity.

6.5. Lutheran Christianity as a Subaltern quest for Solidarity and Empowerment

Christianity became a locus for the upward social mobility to the subalterns in India. In Kerala, Lutheranism gave the people an initial source of freedom and self respect. It is a convergence of alliance and amalgamation of outcastes for dignity. Christianity through Lutheran mission worked as a catalyst to modernity for the subalterns.

6.5.1. Missionary Foundations

In a letter to his sister, Robert Caldwell (1814-1891) highlighted the differences between the German missionaries and the missionaries of the LMS: "All the missionaries of London Society in this country... are in large towns and European settlements ... All the German missionaries whose names are so celebrated and who produced such result in India, lived nearly on a level with the natives and among the natives..."[60] The German origin MELIM missionaries also lived in the villages along with the natives.

The MELIM missionaries were the by-products of German pietism. Their evangelical zeal motivated them to suffer for Christ and bear witnesses with all urgency to redeem the souls. When MELIM missionaries reached South Travancore, their main aim was to preach the 'pure Gospel' and thereby convert

---

[58] *Mandal Commission Report of the Back Ward Classes Commission, 1980: Reservations for Backward Classes* (New Delhi: Akalank Publications 1991), 60; Dominic George , " Mandal Commission and the future of Dalits", *Religion and Society* , XLI/1 (March, 1994): 61.

[59] *Mandal Commission Report of the Back Ward classes Commission, 1980: Reservations for Backward Classes* (New Delhi: Akalank Publications, 1991), 55.

[60] J.L.Wyatt (ed.), *Reminiscences of Bishop Caldwell* (Madras: Addition & Co, 1894) in Y. Vincent *Kumaradoss, Robert Caldwell: A Scholar-missionary in Colonial South India* (Delhi: ISPCK, 2007), 23.

the '*heathens*' to Christian faith. They taught and preached the Gospel of Christ as the redemptive force. Even though it was against the then comity arrangements, MELIM took bold steps to uplift this poor people.[61] They loved them as people. M.M. Jacob said, "*We were nothing on a caste-ridden society on those days. MELIM missionaries came to us as the angels from God and they were ready to accept and treat us as human beings. Once the people who rejected us now started to accept us. We all are deeply thankful to the MELIM missionaries for this unique mission.*"[62] This acceptance gave them hope to trust these missionaries for all the developments.

Lutheran Missionaries were tolerant of the caste system.[63] They never planned for the abolition of caste system in the society. They hoped that by patiently bearing with it for a while, it would gradually be dispelled by the strong light of the Gospel shining upon their hearts. Thus they accepted caste as a reality. MELIM tried to use caste differences as a way for evangelistic work among each and specified ethnical group. In other words, caste distinction was viewed by the MELIM missionaries only as a chance for evangelism.[64] Missionaries also silently approved a kind of caste separation. In almost all missionary records, the local congregations, members, teachers, Catechists and pastors were referred to with caste appellations.[65] That was good for identification on those days, the missionaries who maintained caste system could not be totally blamed, as it was a common practice in those days even in all other Christian denominations. Moreover as Dumont observed, "… a sect cannot survive on Indian soil if it denies caste."[66] Today, people from all castes live together in the society. Most of the villages were separated by caste people and non-caste people. When missionaries entered into a village with the Gospel, some family and their relatives reacted favorably. Slowly,

---

[61] EHELM, *op.cit*, 20-22.

[62] M.M. Jacob, *Christiani*, 21 TDS Synod Convention Special (November, 1976).

[63] Arno E Lehmann, *It Began at Tranquebar,* (Madras: CLS, 1956), 62-66; For more details about the caste tolerance in Christianity see also M.D. David, "the Problem of Caste", *ICHR* 18/2 (December, 1984): 141-153.

[64] MELIM missionaries' attitude towards caste issues was often a subject of abuse. A journal of Christian and social progress, *The Christian Patriot* vehemently criticized the MELIM's approach to caste. It says:

"The eagle is from America under the name of Missouri Evangelical Lutheran Mission and has clouded the LMS with its wing with the result that the worth of the LMS for more than a century has been shattered to the foundation. The Lutheran Mission is worshipping caste instead of treading it. Down this caste or color is the cry in India but not in Missouri". Janaka, " The Introduction of Untouchability into Christianity", *Christian Patriot,*37/13 (September, 1928): 6-9.

[65] The Statistics and early MELIM records kept at Concordia Seminary, Nagercoil Archives prove this fact.

[66] L. Dumont, *The Caste System and its Implication* (Delhi: Vikas Publishing House, 1970).

the congregations of the same caste were formed. It closed the door to other caste people to be members of that particular congregation.[67]

The majority of members of MELIM was from the *Sambava* caste, with the next largest representatives coming from the *Nadar* followed by the *Vellalas, Maravans, Naidus, Ezhavas, Reddiars,* Muthaliyars, Artisan castes, *Cheramars* and some hill tribes like *Vedars, Kuravas, Paniyans* and *Aryans.* Plurality of caste in the same church proved to be both a blessing and a problem. The former LCMS missionary Elmer Griesse described the nature of the problem as follows: "*Caste had always been a debatable question even for the earlier missionaries of the Missouri Mission. There had always been an attempt to gain the confidence of higher castes but with little success. On the one hand, there were fewer high caste groups in the Southern portion of India than in any other part and on the other hand, the high caste groups that did exist there tended to be more fanatical supporters of Hindu beliefs than ever. The outcaste groups, being the greater majority, had in certain areas learned to assert themselves more than formerly. With continued political agitation for greater freedom among out castes, the situation became tense.*"[68]

It is also notable that the MELIM missionaries tried to hammer the uselessness of observing caste differences through their institutions. Students in the educational institutions were seated together irrespective of their caste. The students from different caste were put together in boarding homes. Patients who came to missionary medical and health-care centers were given treatment alike, and beds for inpatients had no distinction. By systematic and conscious efforts the MELIM missionaries were able to eradicate many blind beliefs and customs of these people. They helped them to be clean and healthy and assisted them to receive good medical treatment. They insisted them to dress neatly and speak decent language as the caste people do. Slowly they attained financial stability and job security, which liberated them from the age-old slavery under their landlords. Missionaries always exhorted them to take care of the education of their children. While they became Christians, the landlords and the moneylenders joined together in persecuting them. The caste Hindus could not tolerate this poor people asserting their human hood and dignity. But in those days, the presence of a missionary in the background symbolized the existence of a rival power against such persecutions. On those occasions missionaries used their influence as the agents of the British Government to protect them.[69] Once they were considered as 'polluted' and 'untouchables', but later on, they slowly entered into the mainstream of the society. Missionaries occasionally arranged local and district festivals for

[67] Statistical data of 1951 May to 1952 May reveal that there were 26 *Nadar*, 24 *Paraiah*, 21 *Pulaya* and 8 *Ezhava* churches in Trivandrum District. Among the workers included pastors, evangelists, catechists and teachers. According to the list *Nadar* workers were 81 (312%), *Paraiahs* 40 (147%) and *Pulayas* 14 (67%), whereas the *Ezhavas* were 42 (525%).

[68] Elmer Griesse, *Lutheran India Missions* (unpublished Master Thesis, St. Louis: 1945), 37.

[69] Interview with Thimotheos (89) on 5 January, 2013.

them. The well-dressed Lutherans along with their wives and children carrying their traditional trumpets assembled together, sang together, and ate together and made processions in the streets. Thus, the Lutherans proclaimed to the public that they were no more slaves but people of the gracious and loving God.[70] Hence, the slaves of the land became the people of the land. Missionaries could open the eyes of this oppressed section to their deplorable conditions and they were made aware of the necessity to better themselves through education, social and financial uplift and social dignity.

As seen earlier, the beginning of the 20th century witnessed an awakening of caste consciousness without any religious distinction. People of the same caste tried to organize and fight for their rights. So, also the Lutherans of different castes had a consciousness of their own separate caste. Moreover, caste conflicts were common in different ways in almost all multi caste denominations. Even after embracing Lutheran Christianity, social and cultural integration had not fully taken place between various Lutheran communities. Although the struggle between different caste congregations was not recorded in early years, there were complaints against caste discriminations within the Lutheran community. But compared to other denominations, Lutheran Church in Kerala seems to be more inclusive community and a community of equals.

6.5.2. Conversion to Lutheranism as a quest for New Identity

The whole question of identity is a major issue that is part of the experience of anybody belonging to a community. Identity is socially constructed and legitimized through representation.[71] The term identity is the degree of capacity and power to determine one's own life in a given social system in terms of self respect, feelings, practices or beliefs that affirm representation. It is very crucial with regard to the dalit community as a quest for subjectivity. The experience of these oppressed people was that their culture was dominated and suppressed by the upper caste. Mohan Larbeer mourns: "The caste Hindus have wiped out our history, distorted our self esteem and made us feel ashamed."[72] The term Lutheran itself created a historical consciousness which generates a new sense of self worth and dignity, a sense of oneness and unity. It is the experience of joy at having found a new identity in Christ and joy of the Spirit that comes out of having a new identity through the witness activity of Lutheran Church.[73]

---

[70] *Christiani*, 21 TDS Synod Convention Special (November, 1976), 48-49.

[71] Pramod K.Nayar, *An Introduction to Cultural Studies* (New Delhi: Viva Books, 2008), 27.

[72] Mohan Larbeer, " Dalit identity: A theological Reflection" in *Frontiers of Dalit Theology*, V. Devasahayam (ed.) (Madras: Gurukul & ISPCK, 1997), 377.

[73] Interview with Rev. K. Suseelan (89) on 6 February, 2013.

Conversion is a liberative experience of oppressed people coming out from a system of domination and subjugation.[74] The social, cultural and religious aspects of people happen tobe important in conversion. As stated by J.W. Gladstone, the factors such as dignity, self respect, patrons who will treat one as equals, the ability to choose one's own destiny inclined people to opt for religious conversion.[75] According to the Subaltern historians, these conversions were clear protest movements against the dominant castes on the basis of their autonomous subjectivity.[76] Studies made it clear that, Conversion to Christianity was able to facilitate structural change, caste mobility, and realization of a common identity.[77] Geoffrey Oddie argues that though the Hindu customs clearly remained in the day today life of the people in India, they responded to the modernity offered by the Christianity.[78] When we look into the conversion activities in India, one of the motivating factors behind it was the resistance of the common people against the socio-economic and religio-political conditions of India in order to construct a new identity.[79]

It was also an expression of communal caste resentment against certain disabilities and struggles as they had been unjustly subjected to for long or short periods of time. Therefore, the role of secular factors in the process of conversion of the backward people to Lutheranism should be noticed. Mission offered to this subaltern not only the Gospel of a new religion but also the possibility of secular salvation from the clutches of the tradition which had for centuries burdened them with social disabilities and economic dependence. It is quite clear "a new religion" is not only 'imposed' by an outside agency, but also consciously 'adopted' by certain groups of people who have their reasons for accepting a new religious tradition. They were united as one body purely on the merits of the grace of God bestowed upon them in Jesus Christ. The faith in Christ liberated everyone from all bondage and through re-birth they all were united in one confession, one

---

[74] Geevargees Coorilose Nalunnakkal, *Ethical Issues: Subaltern Perspectives* (Thiruvalla: CSS, 2007), 47.

[75] J.W. Gladstone, *Protestant Christianity and People's Movement In Kerala*, 16.

[76] George Oommen, " Historiography of Indian Christianity and Challenges of Subaltern methodology". In *Journal of Dharma*, 28/2 (April-June, 2003): 230-231. We know that Ambedkar and one million Dalits became neo-Buddhists in protest against the religiously sanctioned practice of Untouchability. Dhayanandan Carr, *God's Mission towards a Community of Communities*, (Thiruvalla: CSS, 2002), 83.

[77] Sebastian C.H. Kim, *In Search of Identity: Debates on Religious Conversion in India* (Oxford University Press, 2003), 2.

[78] Geoffrey Oddie A, "India, Missionaries, Conversion and Change", in *The Church Mission Society and World Christianity, 1799-1999* (Madras: Gurukul Lutheran Theological College and Research Institute, 1994), 15.

[79] For more discussion on this see, Joy Gnanadason, *Forgotten History*, 15; J.W. Gladstone, "Mission and Evangelism in India - A Historical Perspective" in W.S. Milton Jeganathan (ed.) *Paradigm in the New Millennium*, (Delhi: ISPCK, 2000), 84.

body and one spirit; breaking every barrier and crossing all boundaries. Some got self respect, developed organized skills, confidence in group, social acceptance. For some people the regular gathering, prayer meeting, participation in worship, *Sabha yogam,* and organizational meetings brought self-confidence and worth in their life. By such experiences they were able to employ in any kind of public engagement in the civil society like, *Ayalkoottam, Grama sabha, Panchayat* etc. They proved themselves capable for free and easy interaction with various peoples and issues. But the historians in Kerala knowingly or unknowingly have ignored this unique history. The following section describes it in detail.

6.6. An Ignored History

A lot of books had been published about the history of Christian Churches in Kerala. There were histories written by Church historians, Christians but written for non-Christian purposes and by the non Christians.[80] An analysis of the existing work will help us to evaluate their approach to the history of Lutherans in Kerala. Ninan Koshy's book titled, "*Caste in the Kerala Churches"* was published in 1968. In this work, the author has mentioned about the Lutheran Mission in Kerala but the details and distinctive features of this mission were not given.[81] While describing the Backward Class Christians in the Churches he forgot about the Lutheran Christians who belongs to from the most backward section of the then society.[82] C.V. Cherian's book *A History of Christianity in Kerala* was published in 1973. Even though the title talks about all the churches in Kerala, it dealt only with the history from the mission of St. Thomas to the Arrival of Vasco da Gama, AD 52-1498.[83] M. George in his book, *Christianity in India through the Centuries* tried to summarize the Churches in Kerala. But he forgot to mention anything about the Lutheran Churches in Kerala.[84] Susan Viswanathan's work, *The Christians of Kerala,* only dealt with the history, belief and ritual among the Yakoba Christians of Kerala.[85] Koji Kawashima seeks to show how, during the second half of the 19th and early 20th centuries, a self-declared Hindu State changed itself into a modern State, how the State used Christian missionaries, who had a completely different religious position from itself, during the process of state building. The title of his book is, "*Missionaries and a Hindu State Travancore 1858-1936*." In this book, he only mentioned two things about Lutheranism one is about the Christian

[80] K.J. John (ed,), *Christian Heritage of Kerala* (Cochin: L.M. Pylee Felicitations, 1981); Placid Podipara, *The Thomas Christians* (Bombay: St. Paul Publications, 1944); S.G. Pothen, *The Syrian Christians of Kerala* (Bombay: Asia Publishing House, 1963).

[81] Ninan Koshy, *Caste in the Kerala Churches* (Bangalore: CISRS, 1968), 14.

[82] Ninan Koshy, *Caste in the Kerala Churches* (Bangalore: CISRS, 1968), 23-25.

[83] C.V. Cherian, *A History of Christianity in Kerala* (Kottayam: CMS Press, 1973).

[84] K. M. George, *Christianity in India through the Centuries* (Hyderbad: Authentic, 2009) (2007), 176-184.

[85] Susan Viswanathan, *The Christians of Kerala* (Delhi: OUP, 1999).

Background of First protestant missionary Ringaltaube as Lutheran and another is about the entrance year of Lutheran mission at Travancore as on 1906.[86] Mar Aprem compiled an *Indian Christian Directory - Who is Who* and later an enlarged revised edition of this was also published. But in these books the author not even mentioned about the Lutherans in Kerala.[87] An edited work by B. Sobhanam on the title "*A History of the Christian Missions in South India*" published on 1996.[88] It analysed the establishment and growth of the Christian Churches and missions with particular reference to the South Indian Context. A. Devanesan's article in this book on the "Lutheran mission" is a valuable contribution. It depicts the different facets of the Lutheran Mission in South India which exhibited a spirit of dedication to the spread of the Lutheran ideas even to the then Travancore. He tried to narrate the context of the arrival of MELIM in Trivandrum, the Malayalam speaking area with a very few words.[89] It does not cover the unique features of this Mission's endeavour. Antony Kariyil did a sociological study about the "*Church and Society in Kerala.*"[90] In this book, the first chapter is about the brief history of Churches in Kerala. Here, he summarized the catholic and non catholic churches in Kerala including the major protestant churches like, CSI, Marthoma Churches. The last section of this chapter is about the other Christian denominations like, Church of Brethren, Pentecostal Churches, Salvation Army, Seventh Day Adventists, The Church of Vidwankutty, The Cheramar Daiva Sabha, PRDS, and then the Lutheran Churches. After mentioning how Lutheran Church originated in Germany in two sentences, he wrote one sentence about the Lutheran Church in Kerala as this: "This Church Started its work at Peroorkada near Trivandrum in 1911."[91] *Protestant Christianity and People's Movement in Kerala* by J.W. Gladstone was a study of Christian mass movements in relation to neo-Hindu socio-religious movements in Kerala.[92] This was a pioneer and excellent study about the history of Christianity in people's perspective. The period of this study extend from 1856-1936 and the Lutheran mission started their work in Kerala in 1911. Since this study focused only the mass movements

[86] Koji Kawashima, *Missionaries and a Hindu State Travancore, 1858-1936* (Delhi: OUP, 1998), 55.

[87] Mar Aprem, *Indian Christian Who is Who* (Bombay: Parish Church of the East, 1983); Mar Aprem, *Indian Christian Directory: A Companion to the Indian Christian Who is Who* (Bangalore: Parish Church of the East, 1984).

[88] B. Sobhanam, *A History of the Christian Missions in South India* (Thiruvananthapuram: Kerala Historical Society, 1996).

[89] A. Devanesan, "The Lutheran Mission", in B. Sobhanam, *A History of the Christian Missions in South India* (Thiruvananthapuram: Kerala Historical Society, 1996), 160-169.

[90] Anthony Kariyal, *Church and Society in Kerala: A Sociological Study* (New Delhi: Intercultural Publications, 1995).

[91] Anthony Kariyal, *Church and Society in Kerala: A Sociological Study* (New Delhi: Intercultural Publications, 1995), 42.

[92] J.W. Gladstone, *Protestant Christianity and People's Movements in Kerala, op.cit.*

resulted by the work of LMS and CMS, it has left out the MELIM mission in Kerala. "*The Christian Church History Dictionary of Kerala*" was published in 1998, and it just mentioned about the Lutheran Mission in Kerala whereas gave many details about other Churches even Christian Sects.[93] Sadasyatilaka T.K. Velupillai's *The Travancore State Manual in* its first volume listed the protestant churches in Travancore.[94] Among other missions the author specially mentioned that the Lutheran Mission opened schools in many places and carried on much beneficial work among the backward communities.[95] By the above facts, it is evident that, the history of Lutherans in Kerala as a unique Subaltern solidarity were not recognised properly. Before searching the major reason behind this, a closer look towards caste system in Kerala Churches will help us to realize the unique characteristics of Lutheran mission in Kerala.

6.7. Findings of Empirical Study

Why this unique Lutheran Subaltern solidarity still remains unacknowledged is one of the central questions of this research. Since the nature of study demanded descriptive and empirical aspects of the issues, the qualitative method was followed along the quantitative method for this study. Since human experiences and realities are often difficult to be measured by statistical analysis, it needs descriptions and details from all the related areas. The qualitative method is concerned specifically with subjective assessment of attitudes, opinions and behaviour as it permits broad understanding and deeper insight into the complex aspects of human behaviour. The researcher gathered information from the respondents through various research methods like, questionnaires, personal and structured interviews, and focus group discussions to explore and analyse the real situation. A questionnaire was framed with both open ended and closed questions. By the free open-ended questions, the respondent is able to give subjective and qualitative reflections of his/her attitudes and opinions. By 'closed' questions the answers of the researcher's respondents provide the researcher with information, which is of uniform length and that in a form that lends itself to being quantified and compared. The study is also explanatory in nature as it attempts to gain familiarity with the phenomenon or to achieve new insights into it. Questionnaire helps to evaluate positions and responses for cross verification and re-confirmation of the data. The data obtained from the various respondents were separately analysed for comparative purposes. The analysis and interpretation of the data are presented in following pages.

---

[93] Sarosh T. Jacob (ed.), *Kerala Sabha Chratithra Nigandu* (Mal.) (Dictionary of Kerala Christian Church History), (Pathanapuram: Spiritual India Publications, 1999), 216.

[94] T.K. Velupillai, The *Travancore State Manuel, Vol.I,* (Trivandrum: Kerala Gazetteers Department, 1996) (1940), 769-799.

[95] Ibid, 782.

6.7.1. Demographic Explanations of the Respondents

The percentages of respondents are given below.

Table-1 Sex-ratio and marital status of respondents

Gender of Respondents			
	Frequency	Percent	Valid Percent
Male	207	69.0	69.0
Female	93	31.0	31.0
Total	300	100.0	100.0

The above tables indicates 69% of the respondents were male the rest of 31% women.

Table 2 Marital status of respondents

	Frequency	Percent	Valid Percent
0	5	1.7	1.7
Unmarried	188	62.7	62.7
Married	104	34.7	34.7
Others	1	.3	.3
5	2	.7	.7
Total	300	100.0	100.0

62.7 of the respondents are married and 34.7 % are single.

Table 3-Caste background

	Frequency	Percent	Valid Percent
SC	25	8.3	8.3
ST	27	9.0	9.0
OBC	207	69.0	69.0
General	41	13.7	13.7
Total	300	100.0	100.0

The above table shows among the 300 respondents 207(69%) was from OBC and from SC & ST background is 17.3%. 41 persons are from forward class.

Table 4-Eductional status of the respondents

	Frequency	Percent	Valid Percent
Illiterate	6	2.0	2.0
Primary (Class 1-7)	7	2.3	2.3
High school (Class 8-10)	63	21.0	21.0
Higher secondary (11-12)	75	25.0	25.0
Graduate	82	27.3	27.3
Post graduate	32	10.7	10.7
Theological	35	11.7	11.7
Total	300	100.0	100.0

As the figure above exposes, the respondents represent various educational levels reflecting the general condition of Lutheran Christians in Kerala

Table 5. Occupational position of the respondents

	Frequency	Percent	Valid Percent
No job	116	38.7	38.7
Govt. job	23	7.7	7.7
Private Job	25	5.0	5.0
Retired	28	9.3	9.3
Agriculture	4	1.3	1.3
Others	81	27.0	27.0
Church worker/Pastor	33	11.0	11.0
Total	300	100.0	100.0

The overwhelming majority of the respondents are unemployed. 33 of them are church workers or pastors. 28 (9.3%) are retired persons and only 23 (7.7%) are having a government job. Others (33) may include daily wages or unemployed.

The above table show that three hundred Lutherans from both genders, of different age groups, and of various educational standards, with a mixture of economic and job backgrounds and diverse castes actively participated in this study project.

6.7.2. Reasons for Un-acknowledgement

The empirical study was conducted through questionnaire and interviews. The questionnaire was prepared with care, with a view to secure relevant data in maximum quantity. The questionnaire was translated into Malayalam and was used as one of the instruments in collecting data's from the local people.

One of the major queries was; 'in your opinion, why the one century history of Lutherans in Kerala was not noticed so far?' The option of answers was given as follows: to number on the priority basis, viz Lutherans ignored of its importance; the other historians ignored this history; Lutherans may not provide the details about themselves to others; Due to lack of social/political involvement and Specify if any other reason.

Table-6. In your opinion, why the one century history of Lutherans in Kerala was not noticed so far?

	Frequency	Percent	Valid Percent
0	29	9.7	9.7
1	55	18.3	18.3
2	68	22.7	22.7
3	65	21.7	21.7
4	76	25.3	25.3
5	5	1.7	1.7
6	2	.7	.7
Total	3	100.0	100.0

Code: 0-non=answered; 1=Lutherans ignored its importance; 2=other historians ignored this history; 3= Lutherans may not provide the details about themselves; 4=due to lack of social/political involvement; 5=Lutheran teachings; 6= specify if any other.

As the above table indicates 29 people out of 300 (9.7%) did not respond to this question. The following description will give an overall picture of the respondent's opinion on this issue according to their priority.

6.7.2.1. Lutherans Ignored its Importance

18.3% of the respondents believe that the Lutherans in Kerala lack a sense of their history. They opined that the major reason behind the non recognition of the history of Lutherans was because they themselves forget and ignored their past history. Those who visit the head quarters of TDS will support this comment. The office is not functioning properly and moreover they miserably failed to keep the records and minutes. 21.7% of people find the reason as 'the Lutherans may not provide the needed details to the other researchers and historians'. Even though this Church had one century life in Kerala, until this time there is no written and published history of them.

6.7.2.2. Ignored by the other Historians[96]

As the above table shows, 22.7% of the respondents found the reason as 'the other secular and church historians ignored the history of this church'. As mentioned earlier, in the most of the available histories about Kerala Churches, the Lutheran Church's history is either mentioned properly or not even mentioned. The present

[96] For more details see, 6.7.

researcher had a personal conversation with Bishop Mar Aprem, the author of *The Directory of Churches in Kerala.* As the answer to the question, Why his book had left out mentioning of Lutheran Church in Kerala, He said that even after repeated appeals, no one ever provided him the needed information about the Lutherans in.[97] Since the gulf between socially higher–ups and those placed at the bottom of the social pyramid still continues, the negation of the non-elite's history is quite natural.

6.7.2.3. Due to Lack of Social/Political Involvement

According to the above Table No.6, most of the Lutherans (25.3%) gave first priority to the history of Lutherans in India which had not been noticed so far because of lack of social and political involvement. Politically, the Lutherans in Kerala were unstable in the secular State. Since Lutherans in Kerala have a multi-caste nature and each caste is a microscopic minority, and belong to the economically weaker section, they were ignored by the State politicians. There is no common effort or a charismatic leader to unite the Lutherans politically in order to show their strength at least at the time of State election. So, the Lutherans failed to exercise their secular political power. They were not able to unite together to the level of a political bargaining force. Now they are nothing in the political scenario. Some pointed out that due to the in discipline and disunity among Lutherans in Kerala they are not able to project themselves before the politicians and State leaders as a solid vote bank. They were not able to produce a strong political leader from among them. So nobody is to demand their rights and justice. They have became an abused group by the politicians who had their own vested interests. It is caste that plays a major role in the political power. Lack of socio-political involvement by Lutherans in Kerala is another reason for the un-acknowledgement of their history. At the level of sharing political power, the economically and socially high caste Christians assume dominant position and evolve effective mechanisms to control others. Economic instability may be for pulling them back to have any political power. Socially backward, economically impoverished, politically powerless and as a corollary to others, have a low self image. They were skillfully injected with fear through socio-economic discrimination. Thus they experience hopelessness, despair and inferiority complexes. It may gradually make them to withdraw from active socio-political involvement.

6.7.2.4. Lutheran Teachings

1.7% of people note that the Lutheran teaching is an important reason for pulling them back and the Lutheran Christians are among the flourished comprised to Christian and non-Christian communities. The focus group of Luthergiri view this as follows: "Luther believed that each individual has the right to reach God

[97] Interview with Most Rev. Mar Aprem at Chaldaya Syrian Church at Koyambedu on 4 March, 2012.

through Scripture with responsibility to God alone. It is not necessary for a priest to mediate. Therefore, every individual can have a direct access to God through faith. Lutherans teach that salvation comes by grace through faith alone; not by works and sacraments. Salvation is available to all humans through the redeeming work of Christ and the Scriptures contained the one necessary guide to truth." With this basic understanding today an average Lutheran Christian belongs to the Evangelical faith. The idea of 'Other world' has become part of their blood and life, which was infused in them by the Lutheran doctrine. For them caste is a social and cultural reality." Therefore, MELIM missionaries were very patient to caste system and they did nothing to eradicate this evil among the Indian Lutherans. The Lutheran Church in Kerala seems to be a church for the most backward peoples. This closed the possibility of conversion of the high caste people to Lutheranism. Thus, this church lost its significance and popularity among the caste ridden society.

6.7.2.5. Other Comments

It is also worthy to note that even today 9.75% people were not interested to respond to this question may be due to ignorance or disinterest. Those who try to specify other reasons than given options (0.7%) suggested that the reason behind this non-recognition may be due to the non bishopric Church structure. Some noted that the administrative headquarters at Peroorkada stopped function and shifted the offices to the residences of the officers which blocked the free access to the public. It is not easy to list the reasons for the un-acknowledgement of one century history of Lutherans in Kerala. Not one, but all the above reasons may play its role for their non admiration.

6.8. Conclusion

The salvific plan of God embraces all humanity and the whole creation. Any attempt of exclusion in the fellowship in the name of caste or colour challenges the basic Christian principle of universal salvation. In this sense caste discrimination in the Church is a wound in the body of Christ. Any kind of divisions, also the transmission of the caste structure in the Church challenges the ecclesiastical life of the Church as depicted in the New Testament. The marginals are the bearers of alternative society inaugurated by the divine intervention. The converts to Christianity carried out their pre-Christian culture along with their Christian faith. Most of the Churches in Kerala have failed to live the life of fellowship to which it is called. Unpleasant distinctions are made on the score of one's birth, position and level of culture. All churches in South Kerala have caste conflicts among their members. It is quite natural to have caste differences and tendency to keep their own caste consciousness in a multi caste Church which exists in a caste ridden society.

Among all Christian Missions, the MELIM's role in Kerala is remarkable. This was a subaltern's quest for dignity, identity and social empowerment. The idea of a closely-knit fellowship of persons with a sense of belonging together must concord a central place in the life of congregations. Men and women must find security in belonging to one body, become conscious of their worth and realize their interdependence. It is only when the Church, the people of God, can grow into such a oneness that it becomes an effective witness.[98] The hundred years of pilgrim journey as a unique subaltern solidarity has remained as unrecognised one. The reasons for this rejection may be found within and outside this community. The findings of empirical study and interviews reveal that even though this Church has a unique history to share, they are facing many challenges to move forward with their uniqueness. The next chapter is about the problem and prospects of this unique solidarity.

[98] Ninan Koshy, *Caste in the Kerala Churches* (Bangalore: CISRS, 1968), 85.

Chapter 7

Lutheran Subalterns in Kerala: Challenges and Hopes

7.1. Introduction

Identifying the problem is the beginning of its solution. The dominant discourses define civilization as that which defines 'who you are' as in where you-belong-which tends to seed conflict.[1] As we all see around us, caste and racial discrimination continue very badly. Although, we refer to our world as a global village, it is a world sadly lacking in the sense of closeness towards neighbor and community, which the world village implies. In each region, and within all smaller communities, there are problems stemming from either a lack of respect for, or lack of acceptance of the inherent dignity and equality of all human beings. Our world witnesses serious ethnic conflicts, caste discriminations, denial of rights to the minorities. In this context, amalgamation of different under-privileged people groups into Lutheran Church in Kerala in the beginning of the 20th century catch our deep attention and appreciation. The historical sketch of the first period in the history of missionary work that led to the formation of the TDS had demonstrated areas of strength and weakness. The developments, struggles, tensions and progress of the TDS in its formative years were directly related to its heritage and with its early Missionaries. Their ecclesiastical and structural forms were mostly an imitation of the West. The impact of the Gospel on the lives of people was in diverse type in relation to the complex nature of our society. As we look into the historical background of the context, an analysis of missionary polity and method may help to understand present situation and provide thought for constructive planning for the future. In this chapter, the first attempt is to

[1] Rajni Bakshi, "Gandhi and the Clash of Cultures." *The Hindu Talking Point Magazine,* 7 October, 2012, 3.

search whether the multi caste (Subaltern) nature of this Church is a blessing or a problem. In the second place, we will undertake an analysis of some pertinent issues which badly affects the present Church and then moves on to bring out the major challenge in their life and their pilgrimage as a subaltern solidarity. Finally, we will try to find out some urgent needs and bring out the major proposals and shared hopes for its further journey.

7.2. Multi Caste Nature: A Blessing

Conversion to Lutheranism in Kerala by the socially backward and slave class can be understood as a quest for a new social identity. It was a marginalized people's movement. Harmonious co existence of various depressed caste people is a unique feature among the Lutherans in Kerala. One question asked to the respondents at the time of interview is, whether they are proud of being a Lutheran Christian. It was to evaluate how the present day Lutheran Christians view the Lutheran enterprises in Kerala. Whether this mission a success or a failure? How they evaluate themselves as Lutherans? The response is as follows:

Table -7. Question: Are you proud of being a Lutheran Christian? Yes/No

	Frequency	Percent	Valid Percent
Yes	277	92.3	92.3
No	23	7.7	7.7
Total	300	100	100.0

Only a very few (7.7%) answered in the negative. That means, among the other flourished Christian denominations they might have felt humiliated to call them as Lutherans. But irrespective of their caste/ gender/ educational status to which they belong, the majority (92.3%) who had responded to this question very positively. They are very proud of being a Lutheran Christian and to keep the Lutheran heritage for the coming generations. This means the mission was a success and still it has a definite role to play.

Another question was about the multi caste character of the congregations. The following extract gives an overall picture of the Lutheran Church in Kerala as a fellowship of different castes.

Table-8. Is your local congregation a multi-caste community? Yes/no

	Frequency	Percent	Valid Percent
Yes	199	66.3	66.3
No	101	33.7	33.7
Total	300	100	100

66.3 percent of congregations of TDS are in the status of multi-caste situation. This is very unique in Kerala culture and in the history of other Christian denominations in Kerala.

Table-9. How many caste people are in your church?

	Frequency	Percent	Valid Percent
0	10	3.3	3.3
<3	210	70.0	70.3
4-6	60	20.0	20.0
>5	20	6.7	6.7
Total	300	100	100

a) *Below 3* b) *4-5 Casts* c) *above five*

The above table shows more than 70% of congregations have members from more than three castes. 20% of the congregations have five to six communities in their local church whereas, 6.7% of the local churches have the membership from more than five castes. It proves that the Lutheran congregations in Kerala are multi-caste in nature.

Naturally, the majority of the members of a local congregation like to have a pastor from their own caste background. Appointing pastors in the local congregations from the same caste is the procedure used by the authorities to avoid caste struggles in almost all multi caste Christian denominations. So, Lutherans practice 'call system' in their churches. But the following table shows that 85% of people like to have a pastor from other caste in their local church.

Table-10. Do you like to have a pastor from other caste to your Church? Yes/No.

	Frequency	Percent	Valid Percent
Yes	255	85.0	85.0
No	45	15.0	15.0
Total	300	100.0	100.0

The above table clearly exposes that the local membership of the Lutheran Church thinks beyond the rigid caste limit and they are very much open for an inclusive community. In order to search the attitudes of Lutherans towards the caste conflicts in the churches, asked to them the following question for finding the possible answer were calculated. The respondents were asked to tick the appropriate answer to find out the main causes for caste crisis among the Lutherans in Kerala, what will be main causes?

Table-11. How do you view caste crisis among the Christians?

	Frequency	Percent	Valid Percent
0	33	11.0	11.0
A	49	16.3	16.3
B	62	20.7	20.7
C	64	21.3	21.3
D	63	21.0	21.0
E	29	9.7	9.7
Total	300	100	100

Lack of understanding of Christian doctrine. B) Failure in practicing the Christian faith, C) Due to Church politics and secular factors, D) Due to natural, socio-cultural phenomena, E) Due to satisfy the financial interests. It is clear that faith and secular factors are jointly playing the caste crisis in the Church.

About half of the people (47%) felt that the first priority to the first two options are the main reasons. It means the problem of caste in the Churches is mainly due to the lack of faith and praxis of faith. 16.3% people said it was due to the lack of understanding of Christian doctrine. For 20.7% it is because of the failure of practicing Christian faith. 42.6% respondents opine that it happens because of Church politics and secular factors (21.3%) and also due to satisfy the financial interest of the few (21%). 33 people did not properly respond to this question.

Table-12. Do you think TDS needs a bifurcation according to the caste basis? Yes/No

	Frequency	Percent	Valid Percent
Yes	52	17.3	17.3
No	248	82.7	82.7
Total	300	100	100

Among the 300 respondents 52 people (17.3%) favoured bifurcation of TDS according to caste basis. That means the caste consciousness in the society is also influencing the thinking of the members of the churches. Church exists in a larger society. It is quite normal to reflect the social issues within the church. Church politicians also use caste tag in the elections. But one must note that 248 respondents (82.7%) were against any division in the Church on the basis of caste. Groupism and division in the Church is a contradiction to the kingdom of God. But here another question needs an answer is whether one can be a good Christian along with keeping his/her caste identities. The next question focused on this issue.

7.3. Keeping Caste Identity along with the Christian Faith

The social prejudices and practices which prevail in our secular society at large have crept into the Church also.[2] It is so deep-rooted and so common that caste distinctions among the Christians are taken to be normal and unobjectionable.[3] It is surpassing how caste and Christianity could move together. To find out the ordinary people's feelings the following questions were asked.

Table 13 shows how one can be a Christian along with keeping his/her own caste identity?

	Frequency	Percent	Valid Percent
Yes	255	85.0	85.0
No	45	15.0	15.0
Total	300	100	100

85% of Lutherans in Kerala think that one can be a faithful Christian along with their own caste identity. Only a few respondents, 45 (15%) recorded the answer as to state caste that system and Christian faith cannot move together. Then how do they estimate this plurality of caste among the same church, is it a blessing or a dilemma? It is interesting to note that the plurality of caste among the same Church a blessing or a dilemma.

Table 14 shows the evaluation of the multi-caste nature of Lutheran Church in Kerala, a blessing or a problem.

	Frequency	Percent	Valid Percent
A blessing	251	83.7	83.7
A problem	49	16.3	16.3
Total	300	100	100

A vast majority (83.7%) of the respondents look to the multi caste nature of Lutheran community as a blessing from God. Only a few (16.3) view it as a problem or confusion. This judgment leads to seek their basic mind-set towards caste. For that the following two questions were asked.

[2] See the table 11. There 21% of people think that the secular factors are creating caste conflicts in the Church.

[3] Masillamani Azariah, *A Pastors Search for Dalit Theology* (Delhi: ISPCK, 2000), 24.

Table 15 shows how the members of MELIM in Kerala consider its attempt a unique one compared with other Protestant missions.

	Frequency	Percent	Valid Percent
0	4	1.3	1.3
Yes	233	77.7	77.7
No	63	21.0	21.0
Total	300	100	100

77.7% Lutherans in Kerala view MELIM's attempts in Kerala as an exceptional mission. The above tables clearly support the hypothesis of the present researcher about the Lutheran community in Kerala. The vast majority who participated in this study agreed that this was a unique mission effort and the members are very proud of being Lutherans. They were not hesitant to accept pastors/ Church workers other than from their caste. Almost all congregations have membership from different caste backgrounds. And they felt this mixed caste congregation as a blessing and not a confusion. And also it is important to note that 85% of Lutherans in Kerala opined that one can be a faithful Christian along with keeping his/her caste identity.

As a Christian, how one views the problems of caste is another question. This question was asked to the cross section of Lutheran members in Kerala with the direction to tick the appropriate answer which they choose as very apt. *A-Caste is a sin; B-Caste is a social and cultural reality, C-The caste system is an affair of this world and not a contrary factor for salvation, D-for the time being we must be patient with caste system.* These are the answers given to them and asked to select any one of them which they think as the most appropriate answer.

Table 16: As a Christian, how do you view the problem of caste?

	Frequency	Percent	Valid Percent
0	24	8.0	8.0
A	103	34.3	34.3
B	81	27.0	27.0
C	59	19.7	19.7
D	33	11.0	11.0
Total	300	100.0	100.0

The above table clearly shows that the majority of Lutherans believe caste as sin and social evil. (103 = 34.3%). Next to it, they also accept caste as the socio-cultural reality of this age (81 = 27%). 59 people think that the caste system is an affair of this society and not a contrary factor for salvation.[4] For them, caste is not a sin which alienates them from eternity. 11% (33) had an opinion

[4] This was the common understanding of Lutherans about the caste system. See for more discussions, 5.9.

that for the time being we must be patient with caste system. It also needs to be mentioned that 24 people out of 300 had not responded to this question. It may be because of confusion or ignorance. The politicians often tried to make use of caste for their vested interests. It is very evident that the ordinary members of this Church understand merger of different caste group people in this church as unique and as a blessing. Church politicians for their vested interests use divide and rule policy for their own sake. Ultimately, it affects the holistic growth and total liberation.

Generally speaking, caste has split us at all levels. No Indian can claim a mind which is hundred percent free of caste prejudices. As per our present situation caste will remain till one's death.[5] Christians are unable to testify to the oneness of life as members of the body of Christ. In this context, this type of Christian subaltern solidarity must properly be acknowledged. Therefore, conscious effort must be taken not to develop any kind of unrest and caste-based agitation in this Church. If it happened, this may adversely affect the uniqueness and the life and growth of the Lutheran Community in Kerala.

7.4. Challenges of this Solidarity

As stated above, this study follows people's perspective. When we say "people", it is in subaltern perspective. The primary source would not only include what is written, but also the experiences and sharing of the people. So, here onwards this study will take the oral dimensions of their lives seriously to build their past history for a meaningful future.

7.4.1. Discrimination by State

The State Government's benefits earmarked for socio-economically and educationally backward castes and communities were classified as Other Backward Communities (OBC). As Lutheran Christians, they were denied of many privileges enjoyed by the non-converted people from their own caste. It was widely reported that it had become an almost impossible task for the *Lutherans* to gain any State benefits like house sites, houses, land for cultivation, loans, scholarships, hostel facilities and other benefits. In early years, they somehow managed to get it through either by producing 'false' caste certificates or by begging and pleading with somewhat liberal minded village leaders/officials. But, later on, officials have become more unyielding in the matter of granting any reservation benefits to *Lutherans*. Indian Constitution guarantees to all citizens the fundamental rights of equality and equal protection under the law. Article14 of the Indian Constitution reads as follows: "The State shall not deny to any person equality before the law

[5] Max Muller rightly said, "caste cannot abolished in India, and to attempt it would be one of the most hazardous operations that was ever performed in a political body. As a religious institution cast will die; as a social institution, it will live and improve." Max Muller, *Chips from a German Workshop*, Volume 11 (New York: Charles Scribner and Company, 1869), 353.

or the equal protection of the laws within the territory of India". The State shall not discriminate against any citizen on the grounds only of religion, race, caste, sex, place of birth or any of them (Article 15). Further, more specifically, Article 16 asserts that, "(t) here shall be equality of opportunity for all citizens in matters relating to appointment to employment to any office under the State." At the same time, it throws a responsibility upon the State to give special protection to certain classes of citizens in order to improve their status. Clause 4 of the same Article contains this provision. "Special provision for the advancement of any socially and educationally backward classes of citizens or for the Scheduled Castes and Tribes, which in the opinion of the State, is not adequately represented in the services under the State." As per the order of the President of India 1950,[6] the Indian Constitution does not give the equal rights to Christian Subalterns as it gives to other Indian Subaltern in general.[7] Moreover Government encourages the Dalit Christians to reconvert to Hinduism by giving attractive benefits. "…*The Government of India have recently had the occasion to consider the question whether a person belonging to a Scheduled Caste who had renounced Hinduism by converting himself (sic.) to another religion, will revert to his(sic.) original Scheduled Caste, if he(sic.) becomes a Hindu again. After examination, the Government of India advised that such reconverts who originally belonged to a Scheduled Caste should be deemed reverted to his (sic.) original caste and would be eligible for the privileges and assistance provided for the members of the Scheduled Caste.*"[8] It clearly shows religion is the basis for including a person into the SC list. It is against the interest of Indian Constitution and her secular interest. Rules are in favor of backward class Hindus. Since they felt that they were being blatantly denied of state benefits for the just crime of being Christians.[9] Benefits for Scheduled Castes and Scheduled Tribes as per the Central Government's policy of 'Protective discrimination' were denied to them.[10] Denial of constitutional rights is a grave injustice to this community.[11]

---

[6] Amended in 1956.

[7] James Massey, "Christian Dalits: A Historical Perspective"; *Religion and Society, XLI/1* (March 1954), 58; James Massey, *Towards Dalit Hermeneutics* (New Delhi: Centre for Dalit Studies, 2002), 43.

[8] Letter No.18/4/58-SCT-IV from the Deputy Secretary of the Government of India Home Affairs, New Delhi, 23 July, 1959 to all State Governments and Union Administrations. S. Arputharaj," Christian Minority in India", in V. Devasahayam, ed., *Dalits & Woman: Quest for Humanity* (Madras: Gurukul Summer Institute, 1992), 104.

[9] For more discussion on this issue see, Camilla Parke, *Dalit Christians: Right to Reservations* (Delhi: ISPCK, 2007).

[10] The issue has been clearly explained in the following works, Godwin Shiri. *The Fights of Christian Dalits* (Bangalore: Asian Trading Corporation, 1997), 109-115; John C.B. Webster, *The Dalit Christians: A History* (Delhi: ISPCK, 1992), 129-189; I.P. Desai (et.al), *Caste, Caste Conflict and Reversions* (Delhi: Ajanta Publications, 1985), 124-137; Sunder Raj, *Conversion Called Confusion* (New Delhi: TRACT, 1986).

[11] There are some joint Christian movements working in state and central level to fight for getting SC/ST benefits to the Lutheran Christians also. Nadar Lutherans are also treated as the

The frame of mind is one of stagnation and disappointment. But in general, they are still struggling to be the faithful Christians.

Lack of political organization and unity is a sign of political weakness which has been responsible for the denial of reservations to them. This Church is in need to produce the reputed politicians and statesmen to serve the society as Lutheran. It may gradually lead them from the receiving end to the negotiating table for issues like reservation. As per the special Constitutional rights granted to them, States in the country can grant non-statutory concessions to some communities. For example, all the Nadars are counted as the backward caste in Tamil Nadu without any religious distinction. Pressure should be exerted upon the Kerala State to get the benefits which are available in other States. They rightly feel that the so-called high caste Christian leaders, those who have great influence in the State, have not done anything to get their genuine grievances redressed.

7.4.2. Setback of Faith and Double Membership Issue

Rejection of profit and constant discrimination by State pressed into a deep and growing sense of disappointment among the Lutheran Christians in Kerala. The Lutherans were disqualified from the eligible class list and were treated as forward class. The Lutheran Christians were not only being deprived of their human rights but often they were rebuked and put to shame whenever they had to approach the authorities and others for their rights. The increasing communalization, which was spreading even to villages, had turned the condition of Lutherans from bad to worse. Thus, the continued State discrimination in the form of the denial of reservation benefits was provoked further by growing communalization in the socio-political life. All these, in general, had created a deep and serious crisis in their lives.[12]

---

forward class thereby alienated from reservation benefits. Nadar Lutheran Welfare society (Register no. T.14/17/2003) was formed and fighting along with the Nadar co ordination committee for the reservation benefits. Now the Nadar – SIUC and Nadar Hindus are getting some benefits. Therefore, one trend is growing among the Nadar Lutherans to keep double membership one as Lutheran and other as SIUC Nadar. Since Hindu Ezhavas are getting high number of reservation the new conversion from this community to Christianity is very few. Moreover they are struggling hard to keep present generation of Ezhava Lutherans under Christian Fold.

[12] Some of the Lutheran pastor's children were reconverted into Hinduism. The TX decided that these pastors should not be elected or appointed on any official posts in TS hereafter (2nd TDS Convention Report, 1958, 6). One of the memorials discussed and passed in the 25th Synod Convention was about the reconversion issue of Lutherans. Resolution no. 13 says: "It is seen that many of the church members in TS have converted as Hindus but such persons are again getting into the committees in congregation, circle and synod levels., and it brings troubles in the congregations so this body resolves: (a) It is welcome to come back as church members those who are converted. (b) But those who have converted , should come back to Christianity with clear proofs and records (Gazette Copy) and they should not get in to any committee in the church, Circle and Synod levels unless and until they do the above." TC. 84/08, Resolution and Decisions 13,25th TS General Convention Minutes, 29, 30 November 1994, 4.

The very fact that if Lutheran has a 'Christian' or 'Biblical' name, he/she is automatically excluded from availing the SC/ST/OBC benefits and it is indeed very alarming. The continued denial of benefits to them had eventually led to socio-economic conditions that were extremely pathetic and beyond recovery. In brief, change of religion did not bring change in their social positions. In such situations most of them were forced to leave the church and return to their old religion. The Lutheran Christians of Kerala once were outcaste by Hindus now experiencing injustice by State, through the denial of reservation benefits to them.[13] In this situation, they were forced to take an option either to fight for their rights while remaining within the Church or leave the Church and reconvert to Hinduism. Therefore, the reversion issue needs more discussion. The great blow from the State to the SC/ST Lutherans when it denied Scheduled Caste benefits to them. In these circumstances, they were forced to take an option either to fight for their rights while remaining within the church or leave the church and reconvert to Hinduism.[14]

A new trend had been started lately to produce a certificate to prove that he/she was a Hindu, in order to get SC benefits. Many of them brought certificates through *Aryasamaj* and Gazette notification.[15] Many *Sambava* Lutherans hid their 'Christian' identity from census enumerators. These people were Christians for church purposes but for all other practical purposes they were forced to project themselves as Hindus. Today, because of the depressed position they are forced to assume a dual identity, a Hindu identity for the sake of getting some State help which is vital for their very survival, and a Christian identity because of their

[13] Walter Alexander wrote: "At least half among the SC/ST Lutheran were reverted back to Hinduism for their personal gains and benefits from government. It seems to me that the present administration encourages such SC/ST Lutherans to revert back to Hinduism. I know well that there are even pastors in our District (SC/ST) who encourage their 'Church men' to convert back with their helps. As you also know there have been at least some pastors who continue as pastors in the IELC at the same time they officially have proclaimed as Hindus through Government Gazettes and receive money and other benefits from Government." Letter from Walter Alexander, to Issac Moon, President, IELC, 29 August, 1998, 3-4.

[14] In Travancore , attempts of re-conversion dates back to the 1920's. The 1921 census figures indicated a surprising increase in the number of Christians. This had caused anxiety and tension among the Hindus. The sudden leap in the numerical strength of Christianity was conditioned by forces inherent in the Hindu social order; which had been irritating causes for mass exodus. The Travancore Temple Entry Proclamation in 1936 was indeed a landmark in the socio-political development of Travancore. It was not because of the zeal for religious reform, but the anxiety to prevent the erosion of the strength of Hinduism. By this, the mass exodus to other faiths ended abruptly and a good number of converts re-converted to their original religion. The All *Travancore Hindu Maha Sabha* and Kerala Hindu Mission were very active in the re-conversion works. (V. Sathyanathan, "Temple Entry Proclamation and reconversion impulse in Travancore", *ICHR 26/1*, June, 1992. 5-20). Therefore, one of the main forces behind reversion was Hindu aggressive mission.

[15] Few See Malayala Manorama, Daily News Paper, 7 November, 2006, 9. Kerala Gazette notification 11/11/ 73, 30/12/1976 and 6/1/89.

faded hope of acquiring a social status.[16] While the church still goes on 'exhorting' them not to revert but to maintain their Christian identity, the vital question of continued existence is forcing them increasingly to take for granted a Hindu identity.

Some of the Lutherans joined other Christian denominations like CSI for getting more respect and material benefits. Few went back to Hinduism for getting benefits such as financial assistances for constructing homes, house plots, girls wedding, hospital treatments, loans, educational scholarships, and reservation benefits. Some felt comforted by joining charismatic groups.

Table 16 shows the opinion about the people who were reconverted to Hinduism or keeping membership in other Christian denominations. Answers given by the respondents are classified below: Too bad (60.3%), it is wise according to present situation (24%) and No comment (15.7%).

	Frequency	Percent	Valid Percent
Very bad	181	60.3	60.3
Intellectual Approach	72	24.0	24.0
No opinion	47	15.7	15.7
Total	300	100.0	100.0

The above table manifests that the Lutheran community in Kerala is not so much serious about the re conversion to Hinduism or keeping more membership with in other denominations which will make available reservation benefits. 24% think it is advisable and an intellectual approach according to the present situation in Kerala. 15% of the people recorded as no opinion. It is also clear how badly the reservation policy of State and Central governments is affecting this Lutheran Community.

In circumstances where non-Christian religious beliefs and practices continued to hold influence over them on one side, the fundamentals of Christian preaching, teaching, sacraments and worship are on the wane in their congregational life on the other side. An important question is whether Christianity still mean anything significant to these people while they hoped for an classless society. Christianity they had to face inequality and at the same time the State had promised them Government benefits if they could become Hindus. In such a situation, is it possible to rightly judge the reversion issue. Re-conversion was mostly for reasons of Government jobs and other benefits and not due to any

---

[16] "It is evident that some left Christianity and now they are vehemently opposing Christian mission. Those who converted without conviction can easily deny their faith. If one converted to Christianity not as 'rice' Christians for economic benefits but by conviction that the Gospel as the means for total liberation, he/she will be able to follow Jesus by bearing the cross." Comment recorded at the time of interview with S. Silvanus (82), on 28 January, 2013.

kind of preference for the Hindu faith.[17] Hence the church needs to pay more and active attention towards this reversion issues.

7.4.3. Crisis in Institutional Management[18]

The higher level of educational identity was achieved by 61 years and above age group, as they received ample opportunities in extending education to their children in which they were lacking. Even though they were not educated, they had high level of self esteem by sending their children to schools and colleges. Now their children have become doctors, engineers and earning members and are holding the values of economic freedom. Church had contributed much in the field of educational emancipation.[19] The evangelists and missionaries had encouraged many people to engage in the educational activities. Missionaries found that illiteracy was the major cause for blind beliefs and inhuman customs. So they felt the need of education for effective communication of the Gospel.[20] Thus, they started elementary schools in almost all evangelistic centers.[21] In some places, they established schools first and then started evangelistic work.[22] In early days, schools were conducted in church buildings. The MELIM missionaries used to hire efficient teachers with better salaries.[23] The Catechists also served as teachers. Needs of the day forced the missionaries to start Nursery schools, Middle schools, High schools, English education, separate boarding schools for boys and girls, teacher training schools, seminary for theological education, and so on. Students enjoyed free boarding and lodging, dress, study materials and all other educational helps.[24] In order to keep the students in school during the working days missionaries introduced noon-meal system for them. The State Government has put this system in practice only in later years.[25]

---

[17] D. Christudas, *Tranquebar to Travancore, op.cit.* 90.

[18] Cf 4:3 Schools and Lutheran Co-Operate Management.

[19] In 1909, 12 youths from Kuttichal and its surroundings were admitted in the MELIM boarding School at Nagercoil even before starting their work at Travancore.

[20] D. Christudas, *Impact of Lutheran Mission among the Sambavars in South Travancore* (Senate of Serampore, Unpublished MTh. Thesis, 2001), 85.

[21] Primary School report (1930-1932), 104; to find the objectives of Educational Mission of MELIM, see Education Committee reports (1953), 1-5.

[22] EHELM, *op.cit.*, 25.

[23] *Primary School Report (1937-1938)*, 2.

[24] The purpose of upgrading schools and need for adding more vocational course were stated in detail in *Current problem in Higher Education* (*1947*), 77.

[25] Report of the Malayalam schools reads as follows: "*The great majority of congregation members are day laborers belonging to the so-called "depressed" class. When the parents go out to work in the field, they wanted the grown up children at house to look after the younger ones. In some cases, the children accompany their parents to the farms to share in the meals given to their parents by employers. In this connection it is worthy of special mention that our Missionaries of Alleppey and Shertallai give noon meal*

With the help of systematic education, in due course there emerged a lot of native *Lutheran* leaders. Besides, a good number of educated men and women became Teachers, Pastors, Evangelists and Catechists. Some of them joined the Government services. Some of them got employment in railways, police, armed forces, mills and factories. Several converts entered into the domestic service of Europeans as attendants, butlers, cooks, gardeners and drivers. Later on, the educated and employed *Lutherans* saved money and they cleared their debts, purchased land and built houses or invested in the education of their children. They began to realize that self-help was the basis of freedom and they slowly learned this lesson. Thus, the Missionaries could open the eyes of this oppressed class to their deplorable conditions and they were made aware of the necessity to better themselves through education.[26] Some educated persons ignore their mother Church and their community. A few are still struggling for their emancipation. Education helped them to overcome the experiences of alienation and gap from their own community and society. This shows the importance of the schools and education in MELIM mission.

But today a lot of schools, boarding homes, TTC School and other educational institutions were closed down.[27] Due to low standard of education level, domination of non Lutheran teaching staff in the Lutheran Schools, ignorance of Christian values and mismanagement in Lutheran schools its reputation and development cut down day by day.[28] Since schools under the Lutheran Corporate management are sinking, its future is very uncertain. Unending quarrel and court cases is another weakness of educational ministry of Lutherans in Kerala.

---

to the unhappy children of those poverty-stricken areas ....". Report of the Lutheran Malayalam Schools (8 September, 1943).

[26] For more details about the educational ministry of MELIM in South Travancore, See, D.Christudas, *Tranquabar to Travancore* (Delhi: ISPCK, 2008), 74-76; D. Christudas, *Malinamakkappetta nanmayude theerangal* (Mal.) (The polluted shores of goodness) in *Aazhangalile Anugrahathinte uravakal* (Blessings from The sources of Depth) (Thiruvalla: CSS, 2009), 93-98.

[27] In 1930, there were 42 schools including one Training School and two Boarding Schools. In 1954, the total number raised to 52. In 1957, it was 29 with 4469 pupils. (2nd TDS Convention Minutes, 14-18 October 1957,4). But in 1971 it decreased down to 24.According to present statistics, there are 24 schools in TDS which include 2 High School, one higher secondary School, 5 upper primary schools and 16 Lower primary schools, with nearly 8000 students and 200 teachers.

[28] The present day education policy of the government is another cause for the destruction of Government and aided schools. The fast growing of private and English medium schools are badly affecting the growth of the rural schools run by government and other Educational Agencies for the benefit of the common people. Those who are running schools as the business are getting more profit. The Protestant Christians in Kerala never enter into the educational mission with business motives. Still they are involving ein the educational ministry as a service. Interview with Rev. Dr. J.W. Gladstone, 10 June, 2013.

The Lutheran Corporate Management of Schools and its administration had been a constant headache to the Lutherans and Kerala State due to the lack of proper policy and rules. The people who responded to the question about the suggestions for a proper administrative structure in school management, all agreed that a genuine effort need to be taken to correct it. People feel that schools are the basic source for the entire crisis and corruption in TDS. Now the schools are not a blessing but seems to be a curse. Some advised that the school manager should be an active IELC member with minimum educational qualification of graduation with administrative skills. Appointing pastors as the school managers which is just a continuation of MELIM policy should be changed. Only the Lutheran Christians should be appointed in Lutheran schools hereafter.

7.4.4. Unending Disputes[29]

There are causes beyond doubt for the increase of court cases in this Church body.[30] It appears that the Court of law has become the first and the last refuge of the Church's leadership and membership to settle even purely ecclesiastical disputes. When the elections are held at the circle level, the district elections could not be held.[31] The politicking is going from bad to worse. Creating confusion and sustaining it for selfish motives has become the style of administration.[32] No doubt court cases are common in society and in politics. Government officials and democratically elected leadership of the country and the States regularly face this challenge. However, in India at the State and Society levels, a functioning administration is in place even when elections are contested and the policies and decisions of the administration are appealed in court.[33]

[29] Cf 4.7.3 Church in the court.

[30] No doubt court cases are common in society and in politics. Government officials and democratically elected leadership of the country and the states regularly face this challenge.

[31] When the church reaches a point where all procedures are completed in two districts, a third one will still be disputing their presidential elections. When everyone thought that the church was ready to meet in convention, it would find out that the term of the officers who were elected in one district had expired. Such unnecessary anomalies have been happening in the IELC.

[32] Rev. T. Joy, An open letter to all members of IELC, 15 June, 1998, 4.

[33] After 1977, the IELC has sought counsel repeatedly from the secular court to run the church mainly because the church's membership and pastors on their own could not agree on principles and values that would best serve the church's mission. Since then the church got used to approaching the secular courts for settling their internal issues. These involved appointments within the system, transfer of properties, hiring and transferring employees including teachers and pastors and so on. There were attempts at making the seminary principal as the final arbiter for settling ecclesiastical litigations. Unfortunately, however, after the first national principal Dr. B.H. Jackayya retired, the appointment to that office of all who followed has been held suspect and critiqued vigorously. Consequently, the neutral and impartial nature of that office was neither acknowledged nor respected fully. This meant that the secular court became the final refuge for both the officers and the membership of the IELC to settle church issues. In this context, some laymen of the Trivandrum Synod filed a "scheme suit" for the entire church seeking in their own

For administrative and leadership directions, the TDS has trusted the courts of the land than any other authority.[34] Experience has shown that those who hold an office in the IELC/Synod could not be trusted. Almost everyone in this Church has been hurt by one problem or another in some manner. Thus the court has become their last refuge, not with the assurance that finally justice will succeed but with the expectation that somehow the conflict will be compromised. Fear and lack of trust of one another control the church's culture.

7.4.5. Administration Crisis[35]

Administrative instability is a chronic disability that has overwhelmed this church for 30 years now. The Synod Executive committee has often become practically non-existent, and is not able to accomplish anything at the service of the church. If committees meet and minutes are written, they are not available for ready reference. The minutes that become available do not necessarily represent the actual resolutions in the meetings. The wording seems to change sometimes on the basis of an afterthought since the meeting. Even call documents and appointment orders are issued employing courtroom language.

There are many comments against the leadership. They are consciously creating chaos and confusion in the Church through their destructive steps to keep stalemate for their vested interests. The political system causes widespread division among the members and destroy the credibility and mission of the Church. Money and caste were misused to control people. The glorious tradition and heritage of this potentially great Church has been spoiled by playing dirty politics and silly tricks. The institutions are in a very bad shape, and not in a position to serve the purpose to which it was established. The schools and even the medical institutions has all become a source of tapping money for political games and personal gains. Those who are in power forget the mission and Christian concerns. They are trying to formulate and impose rules and regulations

---

way the secular court's directions to straighten out the IELC's faulty administration, beginning with the Trivandrum Synod. Experience has shown that the courts do not engage such civil suits with much haste even if there is prima face evidence to sustain such prayers as such issues are not life-threatening or endangering property. That suit was compromised after five years as the LCMS authorized Roger Ellison to aid the IELC in rewriting her constitution. All the hard work that was put in, the series of Church-wide Bible Studies and spiritual life conferences aside, the church was drawn to the court regularly and more frequently since than ever before.

[34] Since 1990 the Church has invited the secular judiciary system to involve in the affairs of the IELC. The absence of a proper Election Commission outside of the administration has decreased the chance of conducting routine elections in any orderly fashion. Court cases have since had a domino effect. When the elections are held at the circle level, the district elections could not be held. When the church reaches a point where all procedures are completed in two districts, a third one will still be disputing their presidential elections. When everyone thought that the Church was ready to meet in convention, it would find out that the term of the officers who were elected in one district had expired. Such unnecessary anomalies have been happening in the IELC.

[35] Cf. 4.7.1 Administrative stagnation.

unreasonably in a non-democratic style. The central payment system has caused a practical disconnect between several IELC Pastors and the congregations they serve. This system has allowed them less time for ministry and more time for politics. Thus the honor and respect due to any office in the church has gradually but steadily begun to fade and to disappear.

7.4.6. Property Negligence[36]

The IELC/TDS has in its custody has material wealth is highly disproportionate to its membership much of which this church has been privileged to own first as huge mission compounds, bungalows, and properties where other charity institutions had been located. Unfortunately, as the Missionaries left India, several of the mission compounds have not been maintained and cared for. Many of the Missionary bungalows have been dilapidated, and many have fallen. Many IELC employees and occasionally pastors themselves do not leave the office or vacate their official residence after their terms end or even after retirement. Families that have rented have stopped paying rent and have claimed ownership of those properties. Neighbors have intruded, nomads have settled in church property and established and claimed right to own these properties. Illegal occupants and encroachers of the Lutheran compounds are increasing.

Selling the mission property for personal gain is another threat which faces Lutherans in Kerala. The authorities often work as the real estate mafia. Since the donor agencies now stop the funding, making money through the selling/leasing of Church properties has become the common phenomena today. The whole church politics are running around this issue.

7.4.7. Struggle for Self Support

The missionaries were social protectors and financial supporters of the early Lutheran Christians. They provided them with the essential necessities of life. Therefore, the life of the people was centered around the missionary (*Saippu*) and his big bungalow, which was located on a huge compound. This kind of mission compound Christianity and the missionary paternalism affected the people negatively.[37] Similarly, the charity-oriented programs of the missionaries

---

[36] Cf 4.6 Trust Association and TDS.

[37] It is quite clear that MELIM had not followed a clear and planned policy in issues like caste, higher education, comity, etc. E.E. Griesse says: *"The Missionary took his stand as a doctrinal point and could not be moved. Doctrine was taught with typical "German bluntness", and was neither understood nor liked by the complacent Hindus".* E.E. Griesse, op.cit, 8. Most of the development programs were missionary centered. When the missionary returned, the project also came to a close. For example, Former Trivandrum missionary A.J. Lutz started different development programs in and around Luthergiri in order to help the most backward class people there out of his personal interest. There was no direct involvement of the Mission Board in this. But all the projects were stopped when he returned home. MELIM missionaries from other districts also had criticized the Mission policy in the Trivandrum District as unjust. E.E. Griesse, *op.cit*; 31. Janaka says, *"A Lutheran Missionary*

made them a dependent community.[38] This means that Missionary-centered development programs of the church never helped them to grow in self-reliance and self-esteem. They expected that the church should help them in every aspect instead of being helped by themselves for their total development. This approach slowly created among them an alertness of their rights and privileges. But strictly speaking, they miserably failed to see their duties and responsibilities in the church and society.[39]

---

*invented a new arithmetical table in terms of caste to the effect that a certain number of Sambavars are equal to one Nadar, a certain number of Nadar is equal to one non-Brahmin caste Hindu, and he is said to assess the value of the converts to the Lutheran Mission accordingly."*He continues, *"The Lutheran Missionaries after all come to the same stock as the British rulers, whose policy has always been 'Divide and rule' whether in the state or in the church, the European wants to be the ruler and would not allow himself to be associated in terms of equality with the Indian without a desperate fight . . . Those modern apostles of Lutheran congregationalism are said to be highly automatic, and to be unwilling to tolerate any independence of thought or action in their converts, in whom slave mentality is sought to be developed a more than anywhere else . . It is really due to a desire to perpetuate the domineering position of the European in the India Lutheran Church."* Janaka, " The Introduction of Untouchability in to Christianity", *Christian Patriort*, 37/13 (September, 1928): 6-9.

P.N. Peter, a critique of missionary attitude writes as follows: *"The Lutherans from America came to work among these poor people. They opened many churches and schools including boarding schools. Their gospel is "you black study Tamil only, if not go away without education". Missionaries opened English schools to Vellalars at Vadakkangulam for recent Christians, but did not allow the old Christians. On asking they said "It is our money and no one has any right to question it".* P.N. Peter, "Depressed Community", *Christian Patriot*, 37/7 (August, 1928): 11. It may be the exaggerations by the non-Lutherans about the Lutheran mission; but the most of the Lutherans viewed the work of MELIM as a liberating force for the subalterns from their age old slavery.

[38] Missionaries at the early stages helped their financially according to their needs and thus made them to repay the age long loans to their masters. They provided money for their day-to-day needs. Besides, they financed them to purchase land and to build houses and church buildings. Missionaries also took initiative for the marriage of their daughters. They introduced lot of schemes to eradicate poverty among them through the economic development services. Some of them even started a number of small-scale industries on personal level to help them. (Interview with M.M. Jacob (83), Karode , on 3 January 2013. M.M Jacob is a retired pastor and former Secretary and administrator of TDS. He lives close to IELC church Karode, Vilappilsala, Trivandrum.) However, the major criticism against the approaches of MELIM missionaries regarding financial uplift may be summed up in the following words of J. Victor. He writes "*Missionaries helped them financially. But it doesn't help them to develop by themselves. In later years they proved that they were very eager to secure their part and rights but they were miserably failed to recognize their responsibilities.*" (J.Victor (79) is a product of Concordia Boarding School. Later on, he became the warden of this hostel. After his teacher and theological training he served as the teacher and Headmaster in Lutheran Schools and also became the General treasurer of IELC. Now he lives at Peroorkada, Trivandrum).

[39] In 1924, the *Sambavar* community tried to organize and fight for their common rights for getting all sorts of religious privileges. The leaders of Christian Sambavars in South Travancore including the MELIM *Sambavars* jointly invited for a meeting of '*Sambava Sabha*'. (P. Daniel Vydhyar, *Sambavar vargathil Ulpetta Sahodararukku oru Apeksha* (Mal.) [An Appeal to the brothers of the Sambava community], 14 October, 1922).

As time passed on, they were grown without proper experience in Christian stewardship. This could be the after effect of their blind dependency. Slowly they were forced to produce more income in order to conduct their church programs. When missionaries left, financial help also began to be declined. Then the dependent nature of this community congregation adversely affected. This being the case, these congregations were forced to become self-supporting, self governing and self-propagating. The World Wars also created financial crisis, as well as dislocation of German Missions. Assistance to the Indian church in the form of missionary personnel and money were stopped unexpectedly.[40] At that time those who were trained to be dependents became confused and unrest. The administration was handed over to the nationals more than a half century before, but this younger Church still struggling hard to be a self-supported church body. Due to poor stewardship, lack of reports and accounts, and misusing the Church money to the Court of the law, the funding agencies has stopped their support.

This Church has been found wanting mainly because it remains ill-equipped and untapped of her strength and distinct nature. Therefore, the focus groups has tried to identify the immediate needs of this typical Christian community to move further.

7.5. Suggestions for the further Growth of this Subaltern Solidarity

To find the opinions of the people about their hopes and dreams towards this unique solidarity for the next century, the present researcher has conducted 10 focus group discussions.[41] One of the questions discussed in the focus groups including suggestions for the further growth of the Lutheran Christian community in Kerala keeping in view of its distinctive nature. The comments are summarized in the following heads along with some personal interview suggestions.

7.5.1. Re-Construction of the Administrative Structure

For an effective administration, a neat administrative set up to suit the present church is required. Administrative stagnation and too many court cases weaken the

---

But the missionaries asked them to withdraw this letter of invitation. The Lutheran leaders from the *Sambava* community who signed in this invitation withdrew their participation stating that: *"We need not to organize and fight for our developments with Government, because our beloved missionary promised that MELIM is willing and capable for giving all our needs."* (M. Paulose Upadesi, *Parayar ennu vilichuvanna Lutheran mission Christheeya Sahodhararkku Oru Apeksha* (Mal.) [An appeal to the Lutheran Christian Brothers who were called as Parayar]. See also the report of the missionary's meeting with Marcus David and Joseph Manuel at the bungalow, 6 January, 1924). It is a clear evident to show that how deeply the native people were depended to the missionaries.

[40] There were 124 MELIM missionaries during 1894 to 1956 and out of that 3 died in India and 12 retired from service. But 96 missionaries resigned from service and returned without completing their term. To see the details about the MELIM missionaries arrival, service and departure, L.W. Meinzen, *Church in Mission*, *op.cit*, 247-251. A detailed study may reveal the real issue behind this.

[41] For the details about the Focus groups see Appendix No. 3.

growth and mission of the church. The credibility and popularity of the Church has become lost due to maladministration and corruption. It is very clear with an experience of a century present structure the Lutheran Church in Kerala cannot move and function properly. Present system is too democratic. The administrative set up should be to re structure to suit the effective administrative requirements and face the contemporary challenges.[42] There should be total cooperation to revise the present constitution and structural change to fulfil the needs of the present challenges and hopes.

7.5.2. Visionaries and Qualified Leaders

The persons who may be elected /appointed to the Church offices should have the qualities of peace making, love and the quest of justice, fair mindedness and neutrality, without partiality to political partisanship. He/she should be the members of his/her family of Lutheran faith and the confessions of IELC. It is recognized that all human beings are sinful by nature and the fact that a candidate may not posses all of the characteristics laid down in Holy Scriptures for leadership in the Church shall not be a bar to office. But the present method of accepting the people who have lost public witness should be avoided in future leadership. Those people who are charged with malpractices and corruption must be disqualified to work together for a new beginning.[43] Executing power and leadership in the church is a service with mutual accountability between the leaders and those served a servant and participatory leadership, characterized by modesty. The present models of leadership have to be reviewed critically as to how far they contribute to structures that allow corruption. Spiritual leadership is based on deep roots in faith that give the inner strength to resist corruption. Bribery during church elections seems widespread. Therefore, approval of a code of conduct for selected and people in governing bodies of churches and church-related institutions are needed. It may be an ethical instrument in addition to the constitutional and legal obligations of a leadership position. Such codes are helpful and improve the credibility not only of top executives, but also of other executive staff and members of governing bodies such as synods and committees. Minimum standard for candidates for elections of positions in churches and church-related institutions is also an urgent necessity. The candidates, or at least

[42] The centralization of power including the bishop system seems to be effective for growth and disciple in most of other denominations. Even the charismatic groups and Christian sects are moving towards the hierarchical system. Believer's Church, Bible Faith Mission, etc., are few examples.

[43] Spiritual leaders committed to servant leadership (1 Pet. 5:1-3) (the office seek the person), seasoned, proven, and respected by fellow clergy's and believers, (2 Thm. 2: 20-26); Apt to listen carefully and to speak the truth in love, with wisdom, justice, compassion and humility (Mic. 2;80, to equip the saints in ministry (Eph. 4;11-16); Committed to God's mission in Christ for the 21st century, to graceful integrity, and to single-mindedness in the use of unrighteous mammon (Lk.16:19). Renouncing influence by money; rooted and being transformed (Rom. 12;1-2) in the love of Jesus Christ, through the living Word by the power of the spirit (Rom. 5:5).

those elected, have to publicly declare their possessions at the beginning and end of their term.[44]

The purpose of the responsible leadership code is to make sure that the leaders of this Church remain accountable to the people. By declaring their assets, incomes and liabilities, leaders can explain to the people that any possessions they have were legitimately acquired and not wickedly acquired. There should be a clear clause to exclude candidates who buy votes, not declare assets and proven dishonest form contesting the elections. This Church needs to grow in the knowledge and skills of church leadership and administration.

7.5.3. New TS Structure

It is well proved that the present structure and constitution is not helpful for a smooth growth and running of the Church. A new and viable church structure should be re-designed to face the contemporary challenges. Some have proposed for the constitutional Episcopal system as an alternate.[45] The revision of Constitution is another pressing prerequisite. In regard to new proposal for a revised structure of the synod, many have agreed that the three circles of Trivandrum, Nilamel and Luthergiri could be separated as a fourth IELC Synod. The nearby circles of Ponvila and Balaramapuram be joined and formed into a separate Synod. Then Malayalam-speaking area will get two synods in IELC. This might be ideal and proportional because there is another two Tamil speaking synods in IELC namely, Nagercoil and Ambur. A few have argued that such an approach would avoid the basic issues of corruption again. But the majority of the respondent was against split in the present Trivandrum Synod according to caste basis.[46]

7.5.4. News Letter

Christiani was a prestigious monthly publication of Kerala Lutherans.[47] After that there was lot of efforts to publish a Lutheran Malayalam news letter. *Lutheran Sabdhom*, a Malayalam publication by a voluntary group is trying to bridge the

---

[44] Many States in the world now have rules for members of parliaments and governments in order to control whether assets during the mandate time have been increased in a legal way or through illegal and corrupt practices. This code is to provide for a minimum standard of behavior and conduct for leaders; to require leaders to declare their incomes, assets and liabilities; to put in place an effective enforcement mechanism.

[45] Even among protestants, the IELC is perhaps the only church in Kerala that elects as its administrative head as president. All other Churches have bishops. In fact, the IELC started out with a General Secretary. They served two year terms. The first president was elected in 1971, for a three year term, re-electable but once. A bishopric till retirement at 65 is worth the pursuit. As the IELC will have a bishop, so will the three synods within it, thus making the Bishop of the IELC the Arch Bishop.

[46] See Table 12.

[47] See 4.4.3. Literature Service.

gap. But the Church needs a written form of official communication which will be reliable, for the Lutherans.

7.5.5. Property Development Policy

Even though Lutherans in Kerala were blessed with lot of huge properties, there is no solid policy for protecting and developing the properties. It was reported that income from many properties are misappropriated by pastors, synod officials and influential lay leaders. The mismanagement of Church properties and selling/leasing church properties should be stopped forthwith at any cost. Relevant and immediate action should be taken by the authorities against the unauthorized occupants of Church properties and efficient management be implemented. The income from Church properties must be used for mission purpose.

It is proposed by the participants of focus group that the local congregations may be entrusted with the movable and immovable properties of the IELC-TA in the respective areas for the up keep, development and protection. It is reported that income from many properties are misappropriated by the influential leaders and by non-Lutheran people. It is proposed that mismanagement of Trust properties be stopped forthwith and relevant action be taken by the Trust and congregation that proper and efficient management be implemented. None of the Church properties will be sold hereafter. With the professional help of real estate development agencies, a master plan will have tobe prepared within a reasonable time and be executed. The income from these properties may be used for nurture and evangelism purposes. All the pastors and church committee may be requested to suggest to the TA how the properties in their area could be developed, source of funds for development such as construction of shops and other buildings, utility of properties and other terms and conditions. Through the income generating projects and running useful institutions, the Church can regain its name and recognition in the society. In short, Lutheran community in Kerala should go back to a mechanism to utilize the available resources of man power and land to provide value addition to the local community. The Church should be flexible enough to take strong decisions to utilize the land and resources to generate economy to strengthen the existing structures and also to focus the establishment of new social project in terms of mission.[48]

7.5.6. Specialized Ministries

Specialized ministries with full time ministers and as separate and permanent department to be instituted at the Synod level, for the benefit of different levels of the members. The main areas of concern may be, children, youth, women and lay ministries, stewardship and evangelism department, Christian education

[48] It is proposed by the participants of focus group that the local congregations may entrust with the movable and immovable properties of the IELC-TA in the respective areas of up keeping, development and protection for the benefit of whole Lutheran community.

and literature works, socio-political action, family and pre-marital counseling, echo club, and so on. Church should select and send for specialized training the right persons and make use of them for the nurture and evangelism field. Administrative stalemate should not affect the growth, nurture and mission of the Church.

7.5.7. Church Discipline

Church discipline is a mark of Christian discipleship. Its use in the Church is a manifestation of Christian love, in response to the command of Christ. Its purpose is to gain the brother/ sister to purity and strengthen the church, to glory of God. Every congregation must exercise Christian discipline to keep order and to promote Christian life among its members. Disciplinary action shall be taken against the pastor or other church worker for gross error in life / or doctrine. Local church members, member congregations and elected / appointed officers also must be aware of the possibility of disciplinary action according to the constitution. But measuring the justice must be with the same and uniform scale without any discrimination. The credibility and public witness of Lutherans in Kerala will be lost due to lack of order and obedience. Any organization or Church without discipline cannot grow, function and survive properly.

7.5.8. Church Court

Corrupt use of power has led to the provocation and litigation. All duly elected / appointed members of the Church bear constitutional responsibility to carry out their duties with love and justice and in conformity with the constitution. To make decisions and take actions to oppress others, is against the interest of the constitution. Corrupt use of power and provoking the people to litigation are thus unconstitutional and the cause of offence to the Gospel and to the name of Christ that shatter the unity of the Church.[49] The ends of the Church discipline are the good of offender and purity of the Church. For discipline within the Church, it shall constitute local and district Church Court to handle the appeals and settle the Church-related issues in a God pleasing manner. If the Church Court can function properly, then the tendency of going to the secular court without seeking the remedies provided in the Constitution may be reduced.

7.5.9. Pastoral Service

Often the authorities are repeating that pastors are the backbones of this Church. But in practice they are the ones who were most ignored in the life of the Church. The struggles today's IELC pastors face in terms of their identity and security in TDS, just continue to be a replay of what their predecessors faced years ago. All ordained/ installed pastors should get voting power in the Church

[49] Ref. Mat. 18:7; Mk. 9:42; Rom. 14:21; 1 Cor. 8:13; 2 Cor. 6:3.

by the virtue of their office. Pastors should not be punished for the mistakes of the parishes where they serve. An endowment fund may be built up until congregations become fully self-supporting. The income of the endowment fund may be used exclusively for mission ministries. It is clear that there is no policy regarding pastoral training, certification, call, ordination and transfer and appointment in TDS. It is obvious that policies differ from one individual to another individual. In order to avoid further confusion, code of procedures and clear uniform policy need to be formulated and followed. The pastor's salary need to be enhanced according to the present living expense ratio. They need full payment of their salary with only statutory deduction. Contribution of the local church to the synod and IELC should not be mingled with pastor's salary. Their average payment is way below that of a low grade school teacher with whose families and children the pastor also needs to raise his family. They receive a pension lower in practical value than what their predecessors received thirty years ago. They have no insurance coverage and health plan. They do not qualify for recognition, nor do their families own something they can lean on once they retire. The pension of the present retired pastors is very meagre and it may be raised to a minimum of 60% of the last salary drawn. In case of death during service, or at the time of retirement a considerable amount should be paid as an ex gratia payment to pastors. Pastoral formation of the ministerial candidates needs to revitalize. The selection of ministerial candidates and their character and public witness should be evaluated from time to time. Those who lost public witness should not be allowed to continue in regular ministry. Church discipline is an expected need for a growing church. The vast majority of them suffer from a very low self-esteem, searching for their own identity, security, and purpose as pastors in the IELC. Encourage the IELC clergy to grow in their self esteem and assume their responsibilities with faith and confidence as respected individuals in the community, enjoying the privileges and capably encountering the challenges of ecclesiastical leadership. This church is badly in need of producing pastors to be the ministers of public witness.

7.5.10. Avoid Corruption

Corruption is increasingly recognized as a threat to good governance and sustainable development. The misuse of public resources and making personal gains with Church fund is a gross sin. Overcoming corruption in churches can be successful if the spiritual, ethical and institutional bases are strengthened. There are still many obstacles to overcome corruption in churches. Those in favour of corrupt practices refine their methods to make them less visible and obvious. Some church leaders hinder and threaten their staff in continuing to fight corruption, and denial of corruption is still a widespread attitude the different efforts of churches show the crucial role of leadership in combating the cancer of corruption. The abuse of entrusted power for personal gain and greed demonstrates the temptation of power. The responsible selection of leaders was always getting key attention for a corruption-free society. Greed is seen as one core root of corruption. Responsible leadership is central to corruption-free churches. Corruption is not only a moral problem of individual behaviour but a structural challenge. Developing a profound understanding of responsible leadership is a central contribution in overcoming corruption. The implementation of a uniform accounting system to all congregations and transparency of accounts in administration will solve a major portion of fraud.

Adapt a payment policy in churches and church-related institutions for all employees, but especially those in leadership positions, in order to pay fair, decent wages – which means sufficient for a modest life in dignity. Salaries in churches are often lower than the comparable market. This sometimes leads to a negative selection of people serving the Church who are not the best qualified. Wealth and access to abundant resources in some other churches can lead to greed. Poverty and greed promote corruption. Therefore, the goal should be to pay which is sufficient, decent and fair, salaries should reduce corruption – even though it is difficult to implement in poor churches and it is complex to define and determine ethically fair wages.

Review and revise rules on expenses and compensation and their implementation under the aspect of good management of limited resources, transparency and overcoming corruption. Establish an annual transparency and anticorruption report in churches and church-related institutions, as a section of the annual report. Protect the Church from the gossips who spread hints on fraud and corrupt practices in churches and church-related institutions. Churches and church-related institutions can nominate an independent office or ombudsman to receive petitions and appeals' and undertake appropriate investigations for suitable disciplinary actions against the defaulters.

7.6. For Further Growth as an Egalitarian Community

The challenge to the mission of the Church is to create the feeling of a just and egalitarian community where the subalterns experience like persons and everyone can relay and live with fraternity and partnership without social intolerance. With this view, the present researcher had asked the members of TDS their suggestions towards this.

Table 17 shows the suggestions to create an egalitarian society among the Lutherans in Kerala.

	Frequency	Percent	Valid Percent
A	48	16.0	16.0
B	76	25.3	25.3
C	59	19.7	19.7
D	67	22.3	22.3
E	22	7.3	7.3
F	1	.3	.3
Total	300	100	100

Code: O= no response; A)=Growth in Christian nurture; B)=Develop a common social psyche; C)=Promote Inter-caste marriages among the Lutherans; D)=Equal and just sharing of resources E)=Proper administrative participation F)=specify any other answer. Along with this questionnaire search, the same question was discussed in various focus groups. They recommended few more points.

7.6.1. Growth in Christian Nurture

The above sample says that 48 (16%) people gave first priority to the need of growth in Christian nurture. Along with that, the majority (76=25.3%) opines to develop a common awareness among the Lutherans for the importance of the cohesion. It may possible only through growth in nurture.[50] Focus groups strongly recommend that the existing ministry to carry out nurture programs among youth, college students and women (eg. VBS, Sunday School, Campus ministry etc,) be effectively reactivated and encouraged to launch out programs with funds embarked for such special ministries. Now the funds are not made available, budgeted or provided. It needs to find funds for such ministries. One specially trained and experienced pastor should be set apart full time as co-ordinator for evangelism and stewardship department. He should be assisted by one pastor from each circle for a certain period. They must begin intensive study and training programs for the congregations. A definite systematic plan is designed in the pastorates, circles and Synod level. After a period the whole program and progress be evaluated for the further improvements and necessary action. Education and empowerment of the local people are an urgent need to revitalize the mission of this Church. Frequent opportunities for fellowship, festival, common worship/ joint Holy Communion and inter dining should be arranged in Circles and Synod level.

[50] While addressing the issue of transform to social structures J. Webster says, "Just as the dalit psyche has been inflicted by long term social relationships of inferiority, subservience, dependency and shame, so also healing and change can come though long term social relationships of respect, systematical reciprocity, closeness, and caring". John Webster, *The Pastor to Dalits, op.cit*, 118.

7.6.2. Develop a Common Social Psyche

124 persons out of 300 suggested (41.3%) to develop a common consciousness through the Christian education. The drive of the Church is to release all them from social behaviours which are opposed to the awareness of the kingdom of God. Here the Church as an agent of unity and communion, should try to discover all possible ways and means that the gospel message becomes leaven in the community to promote communion, peace and harmony among various caste. By that a new Lutheran generation may emerge as Lutherans forgetting their rigid caste background. This means to change a person to enter into relationships with others, a change not for exploitation of liberative process, but combined, recognizing and respecting the dignity of the other. A new awareness may emerge together as a ' community of interests' with a people conscious of a collective identity, of a shared history and destiny to show community witness. In this process, not only the individual psyche has to be considered but also the community aspect. In the liberative progression among the masses who are considered inferior in rank, the Church needs to differentiate the community's needs, priorities, goals, world view and offer the Gospel to its collective psyche.[51] The development of common Lutheran psyche will pave the way to defend their faith and rights and also motivate them to participate actively and jointly in their constant struggles.

7.6.3. Promote Inter-caste Marriages among the Lutherans

Normally marriages and other social interactions are based upon caste considerations.[52] Marriages among the different sects of Christian subalterns continue even after their conversion to Christianity. For example, the Nadar Lutherans look for an alliance from Nadars only, not from Ezhava or Paraiah Lutherans. All of them have became Lutherans, but when it came to give and take, they have strictly followed the old practices continually. But there are lots of families among the Lutherans witnessing the promising signs of inter-caste marriages. 59 (19.7%) persons have proposed to encourage and promote inter-caste marriages among the Lutherans to overcome the caste differences in the society. Lutherans in Kerala can contribute a good model to the society at large by this program. The present researcher was able to meet several inter-caste married families among the Lutherans in Kerala. Late G. Tennyson and his family are the most attractive among them.[53]

[51] L. Stanislaus, *The Liberative Mission of the Church among Dalit Christians* (Delhi: ISPCK, 1999), 327.

[52] One of the most rigorous rules for remaining in good standing within any *jati* is the requirement that one's children marry within that *jati*.

[53] The present researcher was able to meet several inter-caste married people among the Lutherans in Kerala. Kadavil Vasu was a Ezhava Hindu and a progressive thinker influenced by Communism. He tried to fight against the prevailed caste practices among the Hindus. As protest

Lutherans in Kerala is a subaltern Church. There is no meaning to search who are the low and who are the high among the subalterns. A distinct unity among Lutherans must be consciously-created. A new generation with common Lutheran community feeling as well as without any rigid caste bias may emerge through these inter-caste marriages.[54]

7.6.4. Equal and Just Sharing of Resources

Next two answers are related to the administration. Equal and just sharing of resources (67 = 22.3%) and proper administrative participation for all communities (22 = 7.3%) were 29.6% peoples proposal. That means, there is a clear unrest and dissatisfaction among the 22.3% of people who think the urgent need of this Church is equal and just sharing of resources to all caste people for the proper growth with a common identity. There were a lot of complaints and frustrations about the distributions of funds to the local congregations. Compared

---

to the casteism, he decided to join Buddhism where he found not much caste distinction. But he could not meet the proposed Buddha *bikshu* and happened to meet D.S. Schuvala the MELIM missionary. Interaction with him gradually led Vasu to become a Christian and later he converted into Lutheran faith with a new name G. Tennyson. Since he was qualified to be a teacher, he started his carrier as the Lutheran teacher. Then he joined to the seminary for the pastoral class and was worked in Thykkal and Puthanangadi of Trivandrum North station. He was ordained and moved to Wynad mission area in March, 1956. And he served there till his death on 24 December 1971 at the age of 61. His wife was Karthiyani (Sumathi) who died on 6 February 1999. They have 6 children namely, K. Santhan Tennyson, Rev. T. Joy Tennyson, John Tennyson, Esther, Leela, Rev. Prakash Tennyson and Jeyaseela. They all got married from other caste community. Moreover, in their School records in the place of indication of caste consciously Rev. Tennyson marked only as Lutheran instead of caste name. From this family two became Lutheran Pastors and the husband of Esther was also an IELC pastor. Rev. T. Joy married late Rajam, who belongs a mixed family (Father Nair Convert and Mother Syrian Christian) Rev. T. Joy has three children and one among them, Santhosh Tennyson became an IELC pastor. These three were married people from different other caste all are Lutherans. Santhosh Tennyson married a daughter of Lutheran pastor who belongs another caste. Rev. T. Joy also marked his children's (Asha, Santhosh and Soumya) caste as Lutherans in their official records. Rev. Prakash Tennyson married Annie from a different caste background (D/o late Rev. Abisai an IELC pastor). Another beauty is all of the members of this family tree are running families very happily, and there is no caste feelings and issues among them. Rev. Joy believes that there is more possibilities today than his period for the promotion of inter-caste marriages. He shared that, he got an anti caste feeling from his father as an in born character. Christian growth in faith also demands us to forget our caste identities. He opined today there are more flexibility in families about caste differences. Education and economic stability brought more inclusive nature and broad vision. More over a member of this Church who converted to Christianity cannot easy to get marriage alliance from their counterpart Hindu community. Therefore, Lutherans should develop a conscious effort to promote intermarriage between Lutherans forgetting their old caste backgrounds. Lutheran Christians in Kerala can do much better service to create an inclusive and wider society.

[54] According to Indian Christian Marriage Act of 1872 it is legal. It made the children of such marriages legitimate and qualified them for inheritance of property. Pramod Rao, *Religio-Cultural Changes and Communities* (Delhi: ISPCK, 2012), 241.

to other Synods of IELC, the TDS continued to be the most backward. Within the five circles of TDS, Nilamel circle was formed with major people group from the tribal communities are remaining under developed. Those who share the administrative power will share the major part of resources in the past.[55] This creates a great frustration and conflicts among those who were affected. Those who are felt neglected, normally form new groups and try to get into power. Once they get a chance they will also continue the same path of their predecessors. Therefore, the proper system to sharing the revenue to the all people groups may need to be encouraged.

7.6.5. Proper Administrative Participation

Demands for proportionate and adequate representatives from various people groups to the administration in the Church also need to answer. 7.3% mentioned this as an immediate problem to address. Money makes power and power gives money. Thereby the ablest, dedicated and right persons may be excluded from the power politics. Since caste and money play major role in elections, it is quite natural to avoid the pious and poor people and those are in meagre minority in the process of administration. Even in the nominating posts they were not getting their proper participation. The reservation for women in various posts was the constitutional demands, but it seems that, it is reserved for pastor's wives. Constitutional change may not be the remedy for all issues. A new culture of acceptance and love for mission and growth of the Church and accepting each others as the brothers/sisters in Christ must be consciously developed.

7.7. The Needs Identified by the Different Focus Groups[56]

There is a need for overall improvement in the situation so that basic congregational ministry to all people and evangelism and nurture can go on peacefully. There is a need

- for concentration on pastoral ministry in all congregations and adequate arrangements for pastoral care.
- To regain the credibility of pastors as the good shepherds under the Great shepherd.
- Frequent chances to come together for fellowships, study and worship.
- Strong and firm efforts be taken to correct mistakes and to avoid similar mistakes in the future.
- of proper understanding about the pastoral call and a better and uniform method of calling pastors, a method which involves congregations as well as the synod in the process of choosing and calling pastors. It was

[55] In these days this is not a big problem. Due to non transparency and poor stewardship the funding agencies were stopped their donations to this Church.

[56] For the details about the Focus groups see Appendix No. 3.

also felt that a life time call of a pastor in the same congregation is not practical in the present Kerala context and a term call for a period of five years in a congregation may be implemented.[57]

- for practical study of God's word on all levels in order to strengthen the spiritual base of the Church and help the Church to challenge various temptations and obstacles to its growth, peace and unity.
- for more closer link and co ordination between congregations, circles synod and IELC- relationship that are more than mere administrational.
- Ministerial training should be reorganized with emphasis on devotion rather than doctrine.
- Preaching should be less theoretical rather practical to equip the people to celebrate their life.
- Active and conscious lay participation in the administration and mission of the church.
- Christian faith should be practical, expressed in service, forgiveness and dedication.

7.8. Proposals by the Focus Groups

The following proposals were put forth for the better witness and promising growth of this pilgrim community:

- IELC/TDS constitution should be revised and updated accordingly with giving main concern for a structural change.[58]
- The seminary should be improved to concentrate on ministerial formation of the candidates for the holistic mission. A minor seminary should be established in Trivandrum.
- Educated, talented and committed persons should be selected in future for the seminary studies. The ministerial training and pastoral formation of candidates should be renewed to face the contemporary challenges.
- One year catechist course, voluntary evangelist's training and lay training institute should be started with immediate effect.

---

[57] For more than four decades the IELC has been studying the doctrine of the call. The Church has not produced a document on the call, nevertheless. Practically, some pastors called and others are appointed. Some pastors are called by the local congregation and appointed by the Synod. Some who are called by the local congregation are transferred by the Synod to those congregations that did not call them.

[58] According to Lutheran doctrines local churches are divine and autonomous. Circles and Synods are the man made organizations to help the life and ministry of the local church. It has only the vested power from the local church. Therefore, it doesn't support any hierarchical administrative system. People felt this is gradually leading to repeated chaos and administrative stagnation. The local church cannot start major institutions which may be useful to all people. But the short term Synod authorities also incapable to plan long run projects. Therefore, an effective and new structure should be formed.

- Members should be properly educated and should be often reminded to be loyal, honest and humble and to be evangelistic minded throughout their lives.
- Arrange Spiritual awareness conferences, regular Bible studies and Lutheran doctrines should be taught regularly to this extent.
- Churches should be started in all the cosmopolitan cities in India for the Malayali Lutherans.
- Correct whatever irregularities may exist in the Lutheran School Corporate Management and administration of churches with immediate effect.
- Hold back those who have proved to be accountable of misappropriation of funds and serious errors from continuing or holding office in any position for some years.
- Convene a joint, fair, peaceful Trivandrum Synod convention with full representation to discuss, plan and resolve appropriate decisions to move forward further.
- Work out of comprehensive scheme for management of TA properties to assure maximum income and efficient administration.
- Re-construct Trivandrum Synod Pastors conference as a politically free fellowship to do its prophetic mission.
- Discourage groupisms and encourage regular local and synod level gathering together in Christian fellowship to strengthen unity, as experienced in the early days.
- Encourage local level ministry, Bible Study programs and similar efforts for nurture, including circle-level study groups for growth in stewardship, leadership and evangelism training, etc.
- Enhance the salary and pension of pastors according to the present day need with immediate effect.
- Guarantee fair distributions of resources to all those who are really in need and eligible.
- Outsiders from Lutheran community can be welcomed as helpers, not as 'directors'.

7.9. Welcome Signs

In spite of the socio-economic struggles of much of the church's membership, a significant number of the member congregations has taken this challenge rather seriously. Several of them have started their own bank accounts, prepared their own budget, paid their pastor, and some of them sent their synod contribution on a regular basis, and a few of them had their own independent mission going on a side. They sing out loud Christian songs and lyrics during their daily morning and evening family prayers, and they do not hide from their neighbors that they are Christians. When their pastor visits their home they also encourage their non-Christian neighbors to join them for prayer and fellowship.

Mission work has begun in many villages by establishing schools and other charity institutions. During week days the schools impart education for children in the community, and during weekends the school auditoriums have become worship centers for local congregations. New congregations have been added through the daughter church planting method.[59] A group of three or four or five congregations in different locations are to be served by one pastor, sometimes Lutheran school teachers or voluntary evangelists assist him during weekends. The vast majority of them have since become independent, each becoming a pastorate. Several IELC congregations, especially in the urban areas, also run day care centers, the economically poor man's version of the Open Arms Outreach.

Congregations have either on their own, or by partnering with neighboring ones have experimented what used to be called "Hindu Sunday Schools." A few of them in the Trivandrum area have since become full-fledged congregations. Families that have connections with non-Christians through marriage have been God's instruments for bringing over the years a few to faith in Jesus Christ. Youth and children have befriended their friends and classmates and shared with them the love of their Lord. The Second Saturday one-day retreats, laymen's fellowships, and women's fellowships are public testimonies of the faith. Even though Christians are a minority in India, and much of the Church is aware of the not-so-friendly context in which it thrives, in areas where the IELC has preached the Gospel, it is not easily kept under the carpet or hidden in a mass. The people have been ablaze. Under such adverse circumstances, even today through the ministry conversions and adult baptisms do take place. The gospel does have free course. A welcome sign for all to behold the power of the Gospel that frees and unites. The IELC-TDS is not ashamed of the Gospel.

7.10. Conclusion

Lutheran Christian community in Kerala has been built up through several castes and communities from different circumstances. The theology of the Missionaries has also led to their involvement to the depressed sections of people. The MELIM's work in Kerala contributed to the growth and development in the various sphere of the Subalterns life. The Missionaries had a very affectionate heart for all sub caste poor people. Through educational efforts they slowly communicated the Gospel and economically helped them to get rid of poverty and age old slavery. Boarding schools and English education provided them a new social characteristics

[59] Pioneer missionaries followed by indigenous Lutheran teachers, evangelists and pastors started and served multiple congregations in various sites. Such clusters have over the years become pastorates.

and self-respect. Missionaries were their protectors in both financial and social issues. With the help of the MELIM missionaries, they could slowly triumph over slavery and become people of God. Missionaries taught them that they too were the children of God like the high caste. This has given them good hope and self-awareness. Thus conversion was seen as the only possible way for social emancipation.

It is true that their conversion to Lutheran Christianity was not a mass movement. But it was a steady growth by proper teaching. All these point to the fact that the missionaries' attitude, doctrines and strategy that highly influenced their converts both positively and negatively. But the disadvantages of such influences over the *Lutherans* exceeded the blessings that they had received from the missionaries. The Lutherans' understanding of caste is very distinctive. They are not ashamed of keeping their caste identity along with the Christian faith without seeing any contradiction. Among the other Christian denominations they felt the Lutheran mission as a distinctive attempt and as a blessing. Lutherans in Kerala is very accommodative with other caste people and they view their multi caste nature as a blessing. Moreover, they are proud of being called as Lutherans. They are not willing to support a division on the basis of caste. The local congregation welcomes the pastors to serve them without any caste preference.

The caste conflicts and problem faced among the Lutherans in Kerala is not an isolated one but it had similarities in other churches too. Even though they did not lose their caste identity by embracing Christianity, the State has denied them caste benefits due to the acceptance of Christian faith. As familiar in Indian circumstances, by joining Christianity their caste and culture continue to remain. They are also denied privileges that are enjoyed by others in the society. This slowly created caste conflicts between them and other caste Lutherans. Unconstitutionally the State continued to deny the rights of this poor people on the basis of religion. Thus they are alienated both from the Church and Government. By this they are forced to re-convert to Hinduism for Government benefits. Some of them joined other Christian denominations like CSI-South Kerala Diocese where they could enjoy their reservation benefits. By false certificates and open denial of faith, many have left the Lutheran community. They have gone back to Hinduism for getting material benefits. Some feel comforted by joining charismatic groups where they could speak about equality and justice.

Constant administrative stagnation, unending court cases, crisis in Institutional management, negligence of the properties, are identified as the major challenges of this unique Christian community. Since the financial assistance from the mother Church has stopped suddenly, this dependent community is struggling hard to move forward to self sufficiency. They were not properly equipped to tap the power of the Lutheran lay people who are successfully serving society and government in various capacities.

The active participation of the common people towards this study process was promising. They have identified a variety of urgent need of this Church like structural and constitutional change, qualified leaders, development of properties, specialized ministries. They have proposed the revitalization of pastoral and nurture ministry need of frequent opportunities for fellowship and positive measures against the corruption and unending disputes.

Along with the challenges they have recommended possible solutions for the progressive pilgrim journey of this people with their distinctive character. Unless they try to develop a common Lutheran Christian identity freely beyond sub caste identity, they cannot achieve the ultimate goal of the uniqueness of this solidarity. Growth in nurture, development of common social psyche, inter-caste marriages among Lutherans, equal and just sharing of resources and proper administrative participations are also suggested. Specific efforts should be taken to build a Lutheran Community forgetting their individual sub-caste tags. Lutheran community in Kerala teaches that the emerging subaltern identity is a blessing and it is possible to be different cultures and caste diversities can be healthy and mutually beneficial. Attempts must to be made to strengthen their shared co-shared heritage to continue. Presently, promoting the subaltern solidarity is seen as one of the keys to the process of liberation.

Conclusion

Our world is witnessing grave racial conflicts, caste discriminations, denial of rights to the minorities, etc. In this context amalgamation of different unrest caste groups into Lutheran Church in Kerala in the beginning of the 20th century catch our deep attention and appreciation.

The facts recorded in the forgoing pages show that the work of Christian Missionaries resulted in the humanization of the people who were treated as inferior classes in Kerala. It can be explained only against the socio-cultural and historical background of the period of their work. The 19th century was an epoch-making period in the history of Kerala. The political set up prevailing in Kerala in the past days was highly unfavorable to the general welfare of the large majority of her people. Then society was divided in terms of caste. Caste decided the nature of the social relationship of individuals. Its principle made major section of the people mere slaves of the dominant privileged classes. They were traditionally excluded from all positions of power and were subjected to exploitation and humiliation. There is no doubt that the Christian missionaries in South India successfully created an ideological climate which was ideal for the birth of several social justice and social emancipation movements. The 19th and 20th centuries witnessed emergence of a new social order in Kerala under the impact of diverse social, economic and cultural influences. The war against caste disabilities and inequalities was being waged by leaders among the affected people groups. Slowly severe changes took places in and around individuals as well as communities. These particular movements, along with their socio-religious liberation made them as a subaltern people's movements. As a result of these movements, the whole of society became more open to and aware of the needs of each other. A new sense of social awakening, self respect and vision of a new life emerged in the hearts and minds of many people. This openness and awareness led the people towards new realities and changes in Society. The process of change among the depressed classes in Kerala has been gradual and was a purposeful reformation to form solidarity. In this background MELIM entered in the Kerala scene as the latest Christian mission.

Though a Church existed in South India long before one was established in many sections of Europe, the rest of India had to wait more centuries to hear the Good News. The first Protestant Mission in India was begun at Tranquebar by the German Lutherans in the beginning of the 18th century. After the glorious beginning Tranquebar Mission almost went off course and Leipzig Mission took over the challenge. Lutheran Church Missouri Synod financially supported the LELM. Quarrels among missionaries over doctrinal differences distorted the relationship and Missouri Synod started its own Mission Board, the MELIM. MELIM sent their missionaries to Krishnagiri in South India. The main beneficiaries of this Mission were members of the *Subaltern* community.

In South Travancore Protestantism found its growth through Vedamanickam and the LMS missionary Ringaltaube. However, there were Protestant Christians in South Travancore as an extension of Tinnevely and Tranquebar Missions before the conversion of Vedamanikom. The historians of S. Travancore Protestant Christianity so far only acknowledged as, the origin of protestant Christianity in Kerala with Vedamanikom of Mylady and Ringaltaube. Even then, the first protestant Christian, the first protestant missionary, the first protestant church and the first protestant native pastor in Kerala was Lutheran. Yet for the direct Lutheran missionary work, South Travancore had to wait for another century.

Even though the LMS Mission started it work in South Travancore among the *Sambava*r community, the majority of converts were from the *Nadar* caste. Since the *Sambavar* felt that they were neglected by the LMS, they decided to have a separate mission among them. For that purpose, they approached the MELIM missionaries and invited them to South Travancore. They accepted their request and decided to expand their mission in Nagercoil, then part of Kerala. This was the beginning of Lutheran Christian Mission in Kerala in 1911, by Henrich Nau. The noteworthy things in this missionary move were firstly, it was an invited mission not an imposed mission as in the case of the most other mission works in the colonial period. Secondly, here not the missionaries or the mission board found the place and people group for their work, but the people selected the place and the beneficiaries of mission. Thirdly, it was deliberately a mission to the most oppressed people. Fourthly, the first people groups who are involved in this mission were not passive recipients of Lutheranism but active participants of mission. Finally, this was a Christian mission started by the joint invitation of the two subaltern groups which eventually led to the formation of a wider subaltern solidarity in Kerala

The history of Lutherans in Kerala from 1911 to 1956 can be understood as the Missionary era. Trivandrum is the youngest of the Indian Districts of MELIM. From the beginning onwards missionaries tried to reach the different people groups who were socially alienated for ages with the liberating Gospel. Evangelistic work was carried on in many ways. First contacts were established through street preaching, very early in the morning and late in the evening. Schools were used to reach the children and through them the parent and communities. Literature was used to spread Gospel and to foster Christian faith. Medical mission also focused to reach all people in the community. Later special consideration was given to the need of reaching youth, women and the children. Many Indian Bible women were raised to build a healthy church. In late years Sunday school and Vacation Bible School ministry had established a great force in reaching the children. A good number of lay people became instrument to plant the churches and carry out the gospel to their neighbors and friends. Reading rooms and Bible correspondence course also proved as effective means to propagate the Gospel to the non Christian world. The war experiences and the national awakening forced them to learn new lessons like the need of properly trained native workers, formation of an Indian Lutheran Church, and the need of cooperation between Missions and other churches in India. The interest of MELIM missionaries were not only just to evangelize the unreached but to help the Lutheran Christians to be better citizens and help them to develop socially and economically. For this purpose they started many development programs. But such efforts did not bring encouraging results. However, educational mission was one of the major contributions of MELIM to South India. Gradually, new congregations were established among the different people groups. This paved the way for various caste groups to enter into the MELIM's fold. But conversions from caste Hindus did not happen as expected. Yet, emergence of new situations demanded new models of ministry. Thus, the need of training Indian personnel to take over charge from the missionaries was highly recognized, both in theory and in practice. It led to the formation of District Synods.

The present study also makes it clear that the history of fifty years of MELIM in South Travancore was not a history of brilliant achievements by itself. But it was a history of the grace of God to His people. This means that in every sense within a half of the century, members of the MELIM had come to recognize themselves as a Church. Move from Mission to Church had its own challenges. Missouri Evangelical India Mission's Travancore District Conference (TDC) became the Trivandrum District Synod of IELC on 12 October 1956. Formative years of a young Church were vital and challenging. The administrative leadership was changed suddenly from missionaries to the local people without developing a next generation leadership. During the shaping years of the first twenty years, the synod was being led by the national leadership with limited assistance from the missionaries. The period from 1977 onwards may be called as the crisis years. Longing for power, lack of administrative experience and litigations delayed the growth of the young Church.

This study indicates that, unlike many other mission agencies, the MELIM went beyond one caste group and reached out to all subalterns of their fields. People belonging to the marginalized communities largely joined together for their upward social mobility. As a community, society and even as the Church,

Lutherans in Kerala is one Church that has in its membership a large number of castes represented. Lutheran membership in Kerala came from numerous sub-castes, the majority of which were deemed outcastes in the out of date but predominantly omnipresent Hindu caste system. Plurality of caste in the same Church proved to be both a blessing and a problem. The authoritative, parental and missionary centered leadership style was able to hold together all these various communities. The national Church, IELC-TDS was started without capable national leadership. In the determining years this Church started to find the remedies and strength for moving forward with various efforts like Evangelism, Children, Youth, Lay and Women ministries, Literature and Educational ministries and so on. But unfortunately it fell into years of crisis. Peace and reconciliation movements were not able to cure the disease. Administrative stagnation, unending Court cases and State Governments discriminations against the Lutheran Christians weakened the growth and mission of this Church. The issues like maladministration, instability and litigations very badly affected the possibility of collective wisdom and pushed the Church into disunity and failure of vision for mission. Even though there were some positive signs, the present situation necessitates the need of an empirical investigation to find out the various theological, structural and missiological issues behind the situation so that TDS can identify its strengths and weaknesses to move forward with a guiding vision.

The much needed thrust was given to the developments, struggles, tensions and progress of the TDS in its formative years which were directly related to its heritage and with early missionaries. Their ecclesiastical and structural forms were imported from the West. The impact of the Gospel on the lives of people was in diverse type in relation to the complex nature of our Society. Lutheran Christian community in Kerala has been built up through several castes and communities from different circumstances. The theology of the missionaries also led to their involvement to the depressed sections of people. The MELIM's work in Kerala contributed to the growth and development in the various sphere of the Subalterns life. The missionaries had very affectionate heart for all sub caste poor people. Through educational efforts they slowly communicated the Gospel and economically helped them to get rid of poverty and age old slavery. Boarding schools and English education provided them a new social characteristics and self-respect. Missionaries were their protectors in both financial and social issues. With the help of the MELIM missionaries, they could slowly triumph over slavery and become people of God. Missionaries taught them that they too were the children of God like the high caste. This gave good hope and self-awareness to them. Thus, conversion was seen as the only possible way for social emancipation.

Attempts were made to study how far the Subaltern Studies and Subaltern movements paved the way for the new perspectives in historiography. The subalterns were awakened to realize their social position of subordination and made them to be historical subjects capable of active agency. Subaltern people in Kerala were kept under the yoke of the political and hierarchical exploitative social system. While the denial of rights to public space excluded the subaltern subjects from participating in the social scenario with fear weakened the process of emergence of the subaltern subjects in history. Administrative reforms, modern education and Christian Mission, etc., were the guiding force for finding a social space to the subalterns. Kerala society witnessed a lot of mass based social awakenings and movements at the end of the nineteenth and beginning of twentieth centuries. These movements were the form of protest and self affirmation. The communal feelings became more evident among people and each caste or community came to represent a pressure group in the political life of Kerala. However, the subaltern subjects gradually began to affirm their social self. Slowly severe changes took place in and around individuals as well as communities. People were organized under the leaders with definite ideologies to fight for their self hood and identity. Knowledge about their own backwardness and an awareness of their right led these castes to organize themselves under leaders from their own castes. These movements naturally influenced each other. These particular movements, along with their socio-religious liberation made them as a subaltern people's movements. As a result of these movements the whole of Society became more open to and aware of the needs of each other. People were aware that something strange was going to happen in and around their life. A new sense of social awakening, self respect and vision of a new life was emerging in the hearts and minds of many people.

The present study has undertaken to investigate how far, MELIM, as one of the latest Christian mission agencies, planted churches in Kerala as an ongoing experiment. Unlike most other Christian denominations in India, a multitude of castes co-exist in this Church of a hundred years. The organizational structures of the majority of the mainline Christian denominations in India have a certain specific caste orientation. It stands to reason that as such this subculture functions as an infrastructure that has brought certain stability to these churches institutionally, perhaps based on the homogeneous unit principle. This does not mean that other caste Christians are not included in the membership of any particular denomination. They are, although continuing to remain a minority in terms of headcount. Certain particular castes visibly dominate the entire organization and administration of the districts and dioceses of these Churches. Even today there are at least some examples of congregations that maintain their membership with a particular diocese transcending their geographical locations, practically on caste grounds. But, Lutheran Church in Kerala has in its membership a multitude of castes, being a textbook example for all mission Churches of the 21st century. Because for a Church of her size, TDS membership has come from numerous castes and sub-castes, the majority of which were deemed outcaste, practically Hindu caste system.

This study brings forth that the MELIM missionaries accepted the caste system as evil and also as a social reality. Of course, they had not done much to eradicate the caste practices among the converted Lutheran Christians. They thought that a casteless Christianity was not possible and practical in the then Indian context. They permitted them to keep their own caste identity and practices. Along with that they put them to live and stay together with many other caste people as the children of the one living, loving God. This was a unique effort in those days. To belong to a 'community' is to be able to share its resources and communicate with its participants, though this does not mean necessarily accepting all the values and wisdom of those communities. Lutheranism became a locus for the upward social mobility to the subalterns in Kerala. Christian gospel gave this people a sense of freedom and self respect. By ignoring their caste and sub caste barriers an all embracing movement of different people group was possible in history. People from the bottom got identity and history. Even though this people have a one century unwritten history, they were ignored in the pages of both secular and Christian historians.

The study shows that it is true that their conversion to Lutheran Christianity was not a mass movement. But it was a steady growth by proper teaching. All these point to the fact that the missionaries' attitudes, doctrines and strategy highly influenced their converts both positively and negatively. But the disadvantages of such influences over the Lutherans exceeded the blessings that they had received from the missionaries. The Lutherans understanding of caste is very distinctive. They are not ashamed of keeping their caste identity along with the Christian faith without seeing any contradiction. Among the other Christian denominations they felt the Lutheran mission as a distinctive attempt and as a blessing. Lutherans in Kerala is very accommodative with other caste people and they view their multi caste nature as a blessing. Moreover they are being proud of being the Lutherans. They are not willing to support a division on the basis of caste. The local congregation welcomes the pastors to serve them without any caste discrimination.

The analysis and outcome of this research underlines that the caste conflicts and problem faced among the Lutherans in Kerala is not an isolated one but it had similarities in other churches too. All churches in South Kerala have caste conflicts among their members. It is quite natural having caste differences and tendency to keep their own caste consciousness in a multi caste Church which exists in a caste ridden society. As familiar in Indian circumstances by joining Christianity their caste and culture remained the same. The State denied them caste benefits due to the acceptance of Christian faith. They continue to suffer from socio-economic discrimination imposed on them by caste system without even the improvement given to the other subalterns by the constitution and succeeding legislation. The reason is that the government officially regards them as no longer eligible for help on the ground that Christianity does not recognize distinctions based on caste. By treating Lutherans as the Forward Class, Lutherans in Kerala lost their Government reservation. It has bitterly affected the economic system of Lutherans. The Church also failed to support them to fight against this denial of natural justice. They are expecting educational concessions, job opportunities, economic assistance and career guidance from the Church as well as government. Economically, not everyone in this Church has the means to make life's ends meet. This slowly created caste conflicts between them and other caste Lutherans. In other words unconstitutionally the State continued to deny the rights of this poor people on the basis of religion. By this they were forced to re-convert to Hinduism for Government benefits. Some of them joined other Christian denominations like CSI-South Kerala Diocese for getting material profit where they could enjoy their reservation benefits. By false certificates and open denial of faith, many left the Lutheran community. They went back to Hinduism for getting material benefits. Some felt comforted joining charismatic groups where they speak about equality and justice. The efforts made by the Churches in the past to improve their situation by providing basic necessities like housing, land, education and employment, unconsciously created their ability to stand on their own feet and assert their human dignity and fundamental rights. Geographically the Lutherans in Kerala is spread too thin, about 30,000 baptized, and not localized in any one particular geographical district or village. As such this Church is not an entity any politician or a government official will show any interest in. This Church is vulnerable on all sides as an overlooked minority in the community.

The hundred years of pilgrim journey as a unique subaltern solidarity has remained as unrecognized one. The volumes of books published on history of Christianity in Kerala ignored the history of Lutherans in Kerala. The reasons for this rejection may be found within this community and outside the Lutheran Christianity. The findings of empirical study and interviews reveal that even though this Church has a unique history to share, it is facing many challenges to move forward with its uniqueness. Constant administrative stagnation, unending court cases, crisis in Institutional management, negligence of the properties, etc., are identified as the major challenges of this unique Christian community. Further they became a dependent community under the foreign missionaries. Since the financial assistance from the mother Church was stopped suddenly, they are struggling hard to move forward to self sufficiency. They were not properly equipped to tap the power of the Lutheran lay people who are successfully serving society and government in various capacities. The active participation of the common people towards this study process was promising. Along with the challenges they recommended possible solutions for the progressive pilgrim journey of this people with their distinctive character. They identified a variety of urgent need of this Church like, structural and constitutional change, qualified leaders, development of properties, specialized ministries, etc. They proposed the need of frequent opportunities for fellowship and positive measures against the corruption and unending disputes.

Unless they try to develop a common Lutheran Christian identity, beyond sub caste identity, they cannot achieve the ultimate goal of the uniqueness of this solidarity. There is an urgent need for thoroughly revamping it to introduce an effective and integrated pastoral ministry. Growth in Christian Nurture will help the members from various caste backgrounds to live and grow together as one community, as the children of God. Development of common social psyche, inter-caste marriages among Lutherans, equal and just sharing of resources and proper administrative participations, etc., are also suggested as the working models for the further growth of this subaltern solidarity.

Specific efforts should be taken to build a Lutheran Community forgetting their individual sub-caste tags. Lutheran community in Kerala teaches that the emerging subaltern identity is a blessing. And it is possible that different cultures and caste diversities can be healthy and mutually beneficial. Attempts must to be made to strengthen their shared/co-shared heritage to continue. Presently, promoting the subaltern solidarity is seen as one of the keys to the process of liberation. Baptism has been a sacrament of uniting people belonging to different caste/communities. Following the Biblical principle we understand baptism as the event, unique and unrepeatable, by which Christ claims His followers and makes them as his own. The mutual recognition of baptism helps to accommodate the people belonging to different caste/communities.

Lutherans recognize that the Church is a communion in society and as such placed in the world, although not identical with the world. In order to differentiate the Church from the world, the reformation set up marks to point to where in the world this Church as communion could be identified. Church as a gathering of people who are exposed to the dynamics and orientations of social, political, and economic processes is expected to be different from other social units. The presence of Christ can be made available to the world only through communities of disciplined Christians. The reality of communion in Christ must be distinguished from the vision of the way in which this communion is lived out in Church and Society. In the apostolic creed we acknowledge the "communion of saints". We have both communion with Christ and communion with saints. As those who confess Christ, we have confessional communion. The communion that we Christian have with one another transcends death and is therefore important. Although, Christians are divided by language, culture, and denomination, the bond that unites them in Christ is stronger and eternal. There are several factors that try to destroy the communion of believers in Christ. There are people who hinder the Churches coming closer together by stressing uniformity instead of unity. The Augsburg confession provides the minimum requirements needed for unity; preaching the gospel purely and administering the sacraments rightly. Belonging to the protestant tradition Lutherans are aware of Luther's notions of the Church as a communion of justified sinners gathered around word and sacraments.

In the Apostolic Church it was Paul who identified discrimination among fellow believers as a cardinal sin. This that made him, a then high caste Jew, to take such a bold and extreme step to go completely over the side of the gentiles, the then oppressed groups of Christians of scheduled caste and tribe origins, as their apostle. It was also an expression of communal caste resentment against certain disabilities and struggles as they had been unjustly subjected to for long or short periods of time. Therefore, the role of secular factors in the process of conversion of the backward people to Lutheranism should be noticed. Mission offered to this subaltern not only the Gospel of a new religion but also the possibility of secular salvation from the clutches of the tradition which had for centuries burdened them with social disabilities and economic dependence. It is quite clear "a new religion" is consciously 'adopted' by certain groups of people who have their reasons for accepting a new religious tradition. They are united as one body purely on the merits of the grace of God bestowed upon them in Jesus Christ. The faith in Christ liberates everyone from all bondage and through re-birth they all were united in one confession, one body and one spirit; breaking every barrier and crossing all boundaries.

Church exists in a wider society where communal consciousness is quite common. It is quiet natural to reflect this attitude in the members of the Church as part of a larger Society. As a prophetic community here Church must rise as a corrective force to equip the Society with new values and ethics for an egalitarian society. The Lutheran community also needs to create the positive awareness and measures to keep various castes – sub caste groups to live and grow together with a common identity as Lutherans. For that, denying one's own immediate caste identities is not a must, because we believe diversity as God's gift.

There should be a healthy participation of people from different communities. Each community must contribute for the growth and mission of the Church. In this multi-cultural and multi-caste context participatory model has to play a greater role. The leaders should know the diversities and try to trace out unity among the diversity. Each culture should uphold, each tradition should recognize and each one should participate in the holistic mission. Whatever may be the sub-caste name; all subaltern must join together for the common goal. This subaltern solidarity is a gift of God, who through baptism binds many into one, the body of Christ, which transcends but does not replace ethnicity. Creating one Church, one body, and worshiping the one Lord Jesus Christ. Unity comes from the one Spirit, as they confess their faith in one Lord. This solidarity is not from human, but comes from the Lord of all. Recognizing the solidarity between Christ crucified and the 'broken people' of the world, we seek as Christians together to learn to be more deeply a part of this solidarity ourselves. Today, Christians are invited to discover practical ways of Eucharistic living in the world. We are invited to celebrate the efforts of the communities that are oppressed in the world, as they protest against all that enslaves human beings. As Christians committed to greater unity, it is evident that the unity between different castes and communities is an essential part for fullness of life and freedom in the spirit.

Lutheran Christian Mission in Kerala, established by the MELIM Missionaries, was a subaltern's quest for dignity, identity and social empowerment. The idea of a closely-knit fellowship of persons with a sense of belonging together must concord a central place in the life of congregations. Men and women must find security in belonging to one body, become conscious of their worth and realize their interdependence. It is only when the Church, the people of God, can grow into such an oneness that it becomes an effective witness. Among all other Christian Missions, the character of Lutheran community in Kerala is outstanding. Yet, the hundred year's pilgrim journey as a unique subaltern solidarity, history of Lutherans in Kerala is remaining as an unrecognized one.

Bibliography

PRIMARY SOURCES

Ecclesiastical Reports

LMS report for the year1843.

Report of C.M. Zorn, 4 December 1894.

LMS, *One hundred and second report* 1897.

The report of the missionary's meeting with Marcus David and Joseph Manuel, 6 January, 1924.

Ezhava Movement: Ezhava Report No.2, by Zukker F.R. Trivandrum, 27 June 1927. Concordia Seminary Nagercoil, Archives.

Primary School report, 1930-1932, 1937-1938.

Report of the Lutheran Malayalam Schools, 8 September 1943.

Education Committee reports, 1953.

TCDM 1949, 1950, 1951, 1954, 1955.

2nd TDS Convention Report 1958.

4th TDS Convention Working Report, 1959.

Report of the Special Financial Review meeting, TDS, 19/August, 1961.

12th TDS Convention Reports, 1967.

Annual Report of IELC-TA, 22 June 1968.

13th TDS Convention Reports, 1968.

14th TDS convention Working Report, 1969.

Report of Reed Industry - TDS, 11 April 1970, by Martin Jesudas, Social Coordinator.

The work report among the Muslims in Kerala "*Keralathile Musleemngalude idaile pravarthana report"* by Rev. Henry J. Otten, *1971.*

Circle President's Report, Ponvila, 1971.

14th TDS Convention Reports, 1971.

16th TDS Convention Working Report, 1971.

VBS Report by Rose Ziemke, 1972.

17th TDS Convention Work Report, 1972.

Youth Work Report - TDS, by A.R Victor Raj, 5 October 1972.

Report of the President, 18th TDS Convention, Trivandrum 21-23 November 1973.

18th TDS Convention Reports 1973.

19th TDS Convention Work Report, 1974.

Report of the Special IELC Constitution Convention, 1974.

The Strict Confidential Report of the Auditor, J. Daniel, 15 November, 1977.

Report of Special Enquiry Committee, 10 -11 April, 1978.

Report of Special Commission Meeting for Trivandrum Synod matters by L.W. Meinzen, 8-9, January 1979.

Report of Special Commission meeting for Trivandrum Synod matters, 29 January 1979.

Report of the Renewal Conference, Nagercoil: Concordia Seminary, June 24-26, 1982.

Report of the India Evangelical Lutheran Church Renewal Conference, Nagercoil, June 26, 1982.

Work Report of BEF, 2001-2002.

Annual report of LLF 2004, by Titus, D., 30/1/2005.

Annual Report of LLFT, 2006, submitted on 18 February 2007.

24th Annual Meeting Report of BEF, 28 October 2009.

The Annual Reports of LLF, 2008 – 2012.

Annual Report of LLFT, 2010, by Yesudasan, 30 January 2011.

Report on Victor Raj's India Visit, 21 May to 4 June, 2012.

Annual Report of IELC President, 17 July, 2012.

Brief Report of the important work of the IELC Project Department, (nd.) by Ernest.

Report of the TDS School Management Problem - for immediate action, Confidential file, Concordia Seminary Archives, Nagercoil.

Report of the 5th MELIM Conference.

Proceedings

Proceedings of the LCMS 22nd Regular Convention, 1893.

Proceedings of the Missouri Synod, 1893, 1894, 1896, 1902, 1908 and 1912.

Proceedings of the LCMS 22nd regular Convention, 1893.

Government Documents and Records

Proceedings of the Sree Mulam popular Assembly, 1912, 1914, 1916, 1921, 1922, 1923, 1924, 1927, 1928, 1930 and 1935.

Census of India, 1931 Vol. XXVIII, Travancore, Part1, Report. Trivandrum: Government Press, 1932.

Order from the N. Kunjan Pillai, Chief Secretary to Government to the Public Service Commissioner, Order No. R.Dis. No. 893/General 25 June 1935.

Travancore Directory for 1938, Part II.

Travancore Administration Report, 1939-40.

Report of States Re-organization Commission. New Delhi, 1955.

Government of India Ministry of Home Affairs Notification No. 4351/RC/56, New Delhi, 23rd March, 1956.

Administration Report of Kerala State, 1956-57.

Order of the Government of Kerala No. R Dis 26706/57/PD, 14/12/ 1957.

Government of India, Ministry of Home Affairs. No.G.S.R.900, New Delhi, 31st July, 1959.

DPI'S orders of 7/10/1958; 29/9/59; 5/10/59; 25/4/59; 23/6/1960.

DEO's order 17/8/1960; 27/8/1960.

DPI's order no. 56985/ A3/60/Edn. 27/1/1961.

DPI"s order no. D2-137962/60 dated &/4/1961.

Proceedings of the Regional DPI, Trivandrum, Order no. K.Dis. 9082/63/G4.

Nettur P. Damodharan Pillai Commission was appointed by the Government of Kerala for finding the list of socially and educationally Backward Classes of citizens in Kerala for the purpose of Art.15(4) by the Full Bench of High Court direction K.L.T. 266 order No. Go.MS. No. 343/PD17/ 10/ 1967.

Commission Report filed O.S.No.712/71.

Kerala Gazette notification 11/11/ 73, 30/12/1976 and 6/1/89.

GO.R.Dist 26706/57/PD 14/12/1957 G.O. (MS) No. 341/79/GAD 20 June 1979. The same position was repeated in the notification through the political influence of CSI. G.O. (P) No. 409/ 82/ GAD 13 December 1982.

Proceedings No. ET3-3958 /89/ l. Dis. /DPI, 5/6/1989.

Luke Illango Vs IELC, Application nos. 1404 and 405 in C.S. No. 208/89; O.S. no. 67/3 FC 66/65. OS no 129/66 in Neyyattinkara court.

Mandal Commission Report of the Back Ward Classes Commission, 1980: Reservations for Backward Classes, New Delhi: Akalank Publications 1991.

Proceedings No. ET3-35930/91, 16/10/1991.

Proceedings No. ET-119399/91/ DPI, 23/6/1992.

Kaka Saheb Khalelker Commission Report, 1955, quoted in Antony Raj, *Discrimination Against Dalit Christians in Tamilnadu,* Madurai: Ideas Centre, 1992.

General Education (F) department G.O. (Rt) No. 241/94/G. Edn. Trivandrum, 19/1/1994.

Order no. ET/ 44008/95/ K.Dis., 6/2/96.

Gazette notification issued by Government of India, No. 71, 4/4/2000, *Hindu* daily, 17/3/2000.

G.O. (P) No. 36/2000/SC/ST DD(F) 27 May 2000.

GO (RT) No. 3959/2/ DPI, dated 12/11/2002.

Order no. G4-6656 /72/ R. Dis., 16/5/1975. B4-33320/2002 Education, DPI, Trivandrum, 1/1/2003.

G.O. (Rt) No. 4794 /03/ G. Edn. 21/11/2003; GO. (Rt) No. 3959/02/ G. Edn. 12/11/2003.

Common Judgement dated 22/1/2003 in OP.Nos. 37000/02 and 37712/02.

Hearing note to KSCBC no. 1232/ 95/ C/KSCBC, 11 February 2005.

Proceedings of the additional Director of Public Instruction (General) Proceedings of Administration, to all congregations and pastorates, 29 October 2005.

G.O. (MS) 104/2009/SCSTOP, 21/11/2009.

Order no. ET4/ 52533/11/ DPI/ D.Dis. Thiruvananthapuram, dated 2/3/2012.

Court Cases

Christudas, J., V. Yesudasan, G.E. Abraham, Chellappan, I.A. no. 2257/80 in OS No.1 of 1980.

Christudas, J., V. Yesudasan Vs Trivandrum synod of IELC, O.S. Appeal No. 1368 of 78 at the Munsif Court of Trivandrum. 17 October 1980 (OS. 1368 of 78),

Simon, A. & A. Masillamony Vs IELC, OS Appeal No. 194-196 of 1992 in the division bench of Madras High Court.

Revision petition from S. Johnson, 5/7/1992.

Poomaniraj, M.S. Vs IELC, C.S. No. 674 of 1997 in the Division Bench of Madras High Court, 6/5/1995.

W.P (C). No. 7897 of 2004Vs Kerala State and Others, 23/2/2004; O.S.No.244/2002 dated 26/4/2002.

Kailasom & Girija Vs Kallayam Pastorate and others, O.S.A. Nos. 265 of 2003 dated nil.

Kallayam Pastorate vs P. Jeyasing Peter, Election officer, O.S. No. 265-272 of 2003.

Nelson. I. & others Vs Kallayam Pastorate & others, Civil Appeal No. 4124 and 4122 of 2006, by Supreme Court of India at New Delhi, 14/9/2006.

The appeals O.A. Nos. 1115 and 1116 of 2010 in C.S. No. 879 of 2010, 9 February 2010.

Court Orders

Order No. S2-15238/50/ CS 17/9/ 1952.

Madras High Court Division Bench on OSA Nos. 125 and 126 /89 dated 26th April 1989.

Additional Munsif of Thiruvananthapuram on O.S.362/1989, 31/1/1992.

CMP No. 194-196 of 1992, by Madras High Court, 10/3/1993.

O.A. Nos. 688 and 689 of 1997 in C.S. No. 674 of 1997.23/11/1999.

Madras High Court, in O.A. Nos. 688 & 689 0f 1997 in C.S. No. 874/97.

Madras High Court Nos.3370 to 3372 of 2000 in C.S. No. 674 of 1997.

Kerala High Court judgement 4/2/02, O.P. No. 3590/02.

Order from District Judge S9/67792/2002, 7/12/2002.

Madras High Court, in application Nos. to 1311 to 1319 of 2002 in C.S. No. 674 of 1997, 6.5.2003.

Madras High Court, O.S. No. 265 to 272 /2003, 9/9/2003.

Madras High Court, in OSA Nos. 265-272of 2003, 31/12/2003.

Additional Munsiff, II, Neyyattinkara on the injunction appeal by IELC-TA, 30 September 2003.

Additional Munsiff, II, Neyyattinkara against Kerala Synod, OS/720/2002, 30 September 2003.

Madras High Court, in CMP Nos. 17563 to 17572 of 2004, 22 December, 2004.

Additional Munsiff I. Neyyattinkara upon the case OS. 656/2002 between Kerala Synod and Mohan dated 31 March 2005. O.S. No. 190/2004, CMA 2/2003, CMA 9/2006, AS No. 325/2003.

High Court of Madras, OSA. No. 265 to 272 of 2003, 21 July 2004.

High Court of Judicature at Madras O.S.A. nos. 265 to 272 of 2003, 22 December 2004.

High Court of Ernakulum in W.P.(C) 37459 of 2003, 21 May 2004.

Additional District Judge, Thiruvananthapuram, in Salim Brothers Vs IELC, on A.S. 242/2000; O.S. 1829/1996 on 29 March 2006.

Kerala High Court, Asha Gregarious Vs State of Kerala & others, WP(C) 5878/05Y, 29 March 2006.

Minutes

Minutes of the Local Conference, 1923 and 1924.

Minutes of the 13th Nagercoil District Council, April 8, 1928.

Minutes of the 14th Nagercoil District Conference, 10 October 1928.

Minutes of the Trivandrum Synod Executive Committee 60:07, 71:9; 72:140, 73:136, 67:106, 66:18, 66:9, 69:36, 59/09, 60/27, 80:65, 80:73, 7/04, 6:56, 73:96, 12:73, 77:36, 87: 95, 73:191, 66: 175, 177, 265, 67:93, 68:10, 110, 60/36, 69:204, 70:75, 33:78, 66/129, 65/89, 64/88, 73:123, 73:194, 65:124, 69:21, 74:182, 77: 03, 77:33, 4/91, 77/70, 65:74, 66:36, 80/54, 85:17, 39, 77:95, 77:116, 77:123, 87:93, 7/2004

IELC Trivandrum Synod. Minutes of the 1st Synod Convention, 1956.

IELC Trivandrum Synod. Minutes of the 2nd Synod Convention, 14-18 October 1957.

India Evangelical Lutheran Church. Minutes of the 2nd General Convention, 1960.

Minutes of the 5th Trivandrum District Synod Convention, 1960.

Minutes of the 8th Trivandrum District Synod Convention, 1963.

India Evangelical Lutheran Church. Minutes of the 3rd General Convention, 10-12 January 1963.

India Evangelical Lutheran Church. Minutes of the 4th General Convention, 24-25 February 1964.

Minutes of the 11th Trivandrum District Synod Convention, 1966.

Minutes of the 12th Trivandrum District Synod Convention, 1967.

Minutes of the 13th Trivandrum District Synod Convention, 1968.

India Evangelical Lutheran Church. Minutes of the General Missionary Conference, 18-20 April 1968.

India Evangelical Lutheran Church. Minutes of 6th General Convention, Bangalore, 25-27 April 1968.

Minutes of the 14th Trivandrum District Synod Convention, 1969.

Minutes of the 15th Trivandrum District Synod Convention, 1970.

Minutes of the 16th Trivandrum District Synod Convention, 1971.

Minutes of the 17th Trivandrum District Synod Convention, 1972.

Minutes of the United Christian Organization Executive Committee, 3 April, 1972.

Minutes of the 18th Trivandrum District Synod Convention, 1973.

Minutes of the 19th Trivandrum District Synod Convention, 1974.

Minutes of the Trivandrum District Synod Convention, Nov. 21-22, 1978.

India Evangelical Lutheran Church. Minutes of the Meeting of the Church Council, 78:6, 78:81 (1978); 79:6 (1979).

India Evangelical Lutheran Church. Minutes of the Board for Literature 81:13, 29-30 November 1985.

Minutes of the 13th IELC Triennial Convention, July 1989.

Minutes of IELC Ad-hoc Committee, 8 June 1993.

IELC Trivandrum Synod. Minutes of the General Convention, 29 and 30 November 1994.

Minutes of the 25th General Convention, 29-30 November 1994.

Minutes of the Gospel Work Committee: 66/12, 66/14, 66/15.

Minutes of the First Executive of LLF, 20.2.2005.

Minutes of the IELC Trust Association, 65/17.

TC. 84/08, Resolution and Decisions 13.

Constitutions

IELC Constitution and By-laws.
IELC-Trust Association Constitutionsand By-laws.
Trivandrum District Synod Constitution and By-laws.
Bethel Evangelism Fellowship Constitution and By-laws.
Nadar Lutheran Welfare Society Constitution and By-laws.
Kerala Lutheran Backward Synod Constitution and By-laws.
Constitution of Lutheran Employees Fellowship.
The Constitution of Rev. Dr. James Canjanam Gamaliel Endowment.

Agreements and Certificates

The Certificate of Incorporation No.4583 of 1961, Madras on 8 September 1961 under Companies Act, 1956 (No.1 of 1956).

The lease agreement between IELC-TA and Keltron Projectors, 4 page stamp paper document, 27 December 1995.

Registration certificate OF Lutheran Laymen's Fellowship -Trivandrum on order no T.2070 on 11 August, 2004.

Notices/Protests/Appeals/Memoranda

The Deputy Secretary of the Government of India Home Affairs, New Delhi, Letter No.18/4/58-SCT-IV, 23 July 1959 to all State Governments and Union Administrations.

Action Council, IELC Avasa Christhavarude Avakasa Prakyapanam (Declaration of rights of IELC Backward class Christians) Printed Notice, 6 September, 1971.

Action Council for IELC Backward Churches, *Is it need to us to continue to be as the member churches of present TDS administration?.* Printed notice, 11 November 1971.

Titus, Paul and P.D. Martin. A special notice to the Backward Community Lutheran Churches of IELC, 3 February 1972.

Kunju Kunju, C., Meenkulam, Convenor, action group for Nilamel circle, "Adarsamellam Pinnokkakaranum Adayamellam Munnokkakaranum." (All dreams to Backward people and All profits to forward people) 9/11/1973.

Joy, T., A.R. Victor Raj, S.D. Jayaprasad and J. Christudas. Njangal Prathishethikkunnu (We protest), 4/9/1977.

Abraham, G.E. Convener, Lutheran Church Action council, Memorandum submitted to the Chief Minister and Home Minister of Kerala, 17/11/1977.

Jnan enthu cheyyendu karthave (What shall I do, Lord). Letter to all members of TDS, *Christiani Magazine*, 18 August, 1979.

Acquisition notice served by Government of Kerala, No. LA3- 1906/85 dated 20/9/1985.

John Hus, D., Appeal to the Honorable Minister, KSEB-Kerala, 15/10/1985.

Sunder Raj. Conversion Called Confusion. New Delhi: TRACT, 1986.

Robinson David. Backward Lutheran Churches are on struggle, 24 January 1988.

Kuttichal, Mambally and Thachancode churches, Protest Fast Notice, dated 23/1/1991.

The churches and pastors of Ponvila circle, An open appeal to the members, officials, pastors, Institutions and local churches of IELC, 22/3/1993.

Joy, T. An open letter to all members of IELC, 15 June, 1998.

Walter Alexander. Letter to Issac Moon, President, IELC, 29 August 1998.

Soosappan and 22 others. Letter to the notice of all churches of TDS, 5/6/2000.

Memorandum to Trivandrum Synod Executive submitted by Congregations denied of voting right in Trivandrum Synod, January, 2003.

LLF, Trivandrum, memorandum submitted to IELC on 14/9/2003.

Trivandrum Circle, An appeal, 23/9/1997, An appeal on behalf of 10 congregations in Trivandrum Circle to the IELC and LCMS officials, 24/1/2003.

Resolution submitted by the churches and pastors of IELC-TS to LCMS officers through Dr. Herbert Hoefer 12/6/2004.

Paul Durai, P.K., Chief Election Commissioner of IELC, Election notification from the office of the Chief Election Commissioner to all congregations, 24 April 2007.

Neethikkay Anicheru (Join for Justice) circular No.1 published by NLWS.

Letters and Correspondence

Madhava Rao, T., Dewan of the Durbar. Letter No. 895 to Lieutenant General W. Cullen, British Resident of Travancore, Trivandrum, and 17 May 1859.

Jesudasan, J. to Heubner, 12 June 1907.

Seminary Board, 3 September 1937.

Jesudasan, J. to R.M. Zorn, 5 October 1941.

Nagercoil District Conference to Jesudasan, 5 December 1941 and April 1942.

Jackayya, B.H., General Secretary IELC to all churches, regarding 5% subsidy cut by Home Board, 5 May 1958.

Arputharaj, S. No.18/4/58-SCT-IV from the Deputy Secretary of the Government of India Home Affairs, New Delhi, 23 July 1959 "Christian Minority in India."

Zorn, R.M. to D. Vedamanickom, 11 October 1961.

Meinzen, Larry. to B.H. Jackayya, R.M. Zorn and H.J. Otten, 17 October 1961.

Markose, J. Open Letter, 20 October 1961.

Manasseh, D. to B.H. Jcakayya, 29 October 1961.

Jackayya, B.H. IELC General Secretary to D. Vedamanickom, President, TDS, 6 and 11 November 1961.

Yohannan, M. to B.H. Jackayya, 13 November 1961.

John Thampi, N. to B.H. Jackayya, 13 November 1961.

Jackayya, B.H., IELC General Secretary to all workers of TDS, 27 November 1961.

Paul, M.N., Secretary Convener, Malabar Circle. Open letter, 7 December 1961.

Sainudheen, A. to J. Ezekiel, General Secretary of IELC, 20 July 1964.

President, TDS. to Secretary, Malabar Circle, 19 August 1971.

George, P.K., Secretary, Malabar Circle. to TDS President, 30 August 1971.

Manager, Lutheran School. to DPI, Thiruvananthapuram, 7 April 1975.

Thomas Edward, G., President IELC. to the Officers of TS, 13 April 1978.

Thomas Edward, G. President, IELC. to TDS Executive Committee, 13 April 1978.

Thomas Edward, G., President IELC. to the Members of Peace Committee, 5 February 1979.

Trivandrum Synod Officers. to the Convener, Interim Committee for TS Administration, 16 February 1979.

Lutheran Action Council to Roger L. Ellison, Palm Sunday, 1982.

Westcott, Edward A., Executive Secretary LCMS to the Membership of IELC, 15 March 1982.

Edward Westcott to the membership of IELC, 29 April 1982.

Ellison, R. to L.W. Meinzen, 30 April 1982.

Meinzen, L.W. to A.R. Victor Raj, 25 January 1985.

Secretary-Treasurer, IELC Trust Association to the Members of the Managing Body, 2 May 1985.

Devadas, G., Trust Member TDS to the Secretary-Treasurer, IELC-TA, 10 June 1985.

Victor Raj, A.R. to L.W. Meinzen, 28 June 1985.

Dearmun, E.B. to all Pastors and Leaders of IELC, 2 October 1985.

Victor Raj, A.R. to all pastors, 2 December 1985.

John Hus, D. to Executive Engineer, KSEB, 3 May 1986.

KSEB. to IELC-TA, No. DB.45/PKDA/2006, 17 April 1986 and 225, 25 April 1986.

BEF. Easter letter, 25 March 1988.

Soosappan, M., President TS to D. John Hus, President IELC, 25 July 1988.

Walter Alexander to Issac Moon, President, IELC, 29 August 1998, 3-4.

Vedamanickom, D. to Edward Westcott, Executive Secretary, LCMS and Louis Y. Nau, Asia Secretary – BFMS-LCMS, 4 November 1988.

John Hus, D., President IELC. to the Officers of IELC, Church Council Members of IELC, Election Commission, Synod Officials and Unit Heads, 15 December 1988.

Victor, J. Former General Treasurer IELC to P. Joshua Siromony, 15 October 1992.

Tennyson, Prakash. President, Trivandrum Circle to A. Sundaram, IELC Trust Secretary, 2 March 1989.Rajayyan, K., Convener, Lutheran Action Group. Open letter, 18 November 1993.

Joy, T. An open letter to all members of IELC, 15 June 1998.

Victor, J. Former General Treasurer IELC to Alice Brauer, Secretary-Treasurer IELC-TA, 26 March 2001.

Concordia Lutheran Church, Perurkada. An Appeal to the Secretary-Treasurer, IELC Trust Association, 1 September 2002.

NLWS. to J. W. Gladstone CSI, Bishop, 18 August 2003.

NLWS. to Vincent Samuel, Bishop of Latin Catholic Diocese, 18 August 2003.

Victor, J. to T. Joy, 29 August 2003.

NLWS. to Chief Minister of Kerala, 22 September 2003.

Yovel, J. Secretary, Trivandrum Synod. to DPI, 12 May 2004.

Manikom, M. District Registrar, to S.M. Samlanglin, No. 11438/E/2010, 15/12/2010; No. 589/E/2012, 17/2/ 2012.

Appukuttan, D. to the researcher, 22 May 2012.

Victor, J. to the researcher, 2 January 2013.

Lazar, L. to E.B. Dearmun, n.d.

Interviews

Bhanu Samuel (51), Presbyter, CSI-SKD. Chennai, 19 February 2012.

Yovel, J. (68), Former Comptroller, IELC and Secretary, TS. Kallayam, 11 July 2012.

Albert, C. (87), Former Treasurer, TDS. Kavadithalakkal, 8 July 2012.

Pavithrasingh, L.T. (45), BPLT Member, TS. Neyyattinkara, 8 July 2012.

Grace M. Joseph, (67), First Theologically trained woman, Trivandrum Synod. Manakadu, 11 July 2012.

Yesudasan, D. (64), President, Lutheran Laymen Fellowship. Trivandrum, 12 July 2012.

Titus, D. (63), Convener, Lutheran Laymen Fellowship. Peroorkada, 12 July 2012.

Vasu, K.K. (80), First convert in Ernakulam. Peroorkada, 13 July 2012.

Sony Lawrence (33), Secretary, LLF-T. Vattappara, 14 July 2012.

George, N.C. (70), Editor, Lutheran Sabdam. Kariavattam, 15 July 2012.

Santhosh Raj, P.R. (37), Pastor, Lutheran Church, Idinjar, 15 July 2012.

Sarala Paras (68), Treasurer, LVS. Kuttara, 15 July 2012.

Suma Chrispin (36), Deaconess. Luthergiri, 15 July 2012.

Betzy M. Joseph, (65), President, Kerala Lutheran Vanitha Samajam. Vazhayila, 18 July 2012.

Ambrose, Y. (83), Former President, Lutheran Church, Ponvila, 12 August 2012.

Krishna Panickar (87), Former President, Lutheran Church, Cheruvallur, 12 August 2012.

Parameswaran, P.K. (82), Retired Pastor. Cheruvalloor, 12 August 2012.

Justus, K.M. (80), President, Lutheran Church, Sreekariyam, 13 August 2012.

Joshua, Gifton E. (70), Former Comptroller, IELC. Sreekariyam, 13 August 2012.

Silvanose, Y. (76), Advocate, Kumarapuram. 13 August 2012.

Enose, A. (88), Retired Teacher. Marayamuttom, 14 August 2012.

Joy, T. (74), Former Principal, CTS. Chenkavila, 14 August 2012.

Suseelan, K. (86) Retired Pastor. Chenkavila, 14 August 2012.

Robert, P.J. (76), Former Church Council Member. Sreekariyam, 14 August 2012.

Jacob, M.M. (86), Former Secretary, TS. Vilappilsala, 15 August 2012.

Prakash Tennyson (63), Pastor, Calvary Lutheran Church, Perurkada, 15 August 2012.

Rachel Abraham (65), TX Member, Sreekariyam, 15 August 2012.

Thimetheus (90), Former President, Lutheran Church, Thundathil, 15 Aug. 2012.

Dipu Raj, D.S. (27), President, Youth League. Peroorkada, 4 January 2013.

Ebrai (75), Member, Calvary Lutheran Church, Peroorkada, 4 January 2013.

George, S. (78), Former Church Council Member, Kavadithalakkal, 4 January 2013.

James Raj, D. (73), Former Church Council Member. Peroorkada, 4 January 2013.

John Prasad, T. (37), Pastor, Lutheran Church, Kariavattom, 4 January 2013.

Kanagamma Thompson (86), Member, Concordia Lutheran Church, Peroorkada, 4 January 2013.

Moses Swamidas (64), Bishop, Bible Faith Mission. Parasuvaikkal, 4 January 2013.

Nesamma (90), W/o Late Rev. P.G. Sathianesan, Peroorkada, 4 January 2013.

Isaac, E. (76), Former Secretary, Ponvila Circle. Marayamuttom, 16 February 2013.

Shibu Stephen (30), Secretary, Lutheran Church, Neyyattinkara, 16 February 2013.

Thankaraj, H. (64), Member, IELC-TA. Kottaikal, 16 February 2013.

Usha Vijayarajan (58), President, Vanitha Sangam, Ponvila, 16 February 2013.

Justus Enose (77), Secretary, TS. Nanthancode, 17 February 2013.

Robinson, M. (57), President, TS. Aryanad, 17 February 2013.

Yovas, J. (79), Former President, TS. Katchani, 17 February 2013.

Daisy Appadurai (63), President, KLVS. Trivandrum, 18 February 2013.

Das, J. Paramananda (64), Professor, CTS, Nagercoil,18 February 2013.

Nair, N. Vasudevan (58), Pastor. Devicode, 18 February 2012.

Bernard, D.V. (65), Principal, CTS, Nagercoil, 28 February 2013.

Stanley, D.J. (50), Pastor, Lutheran Church, Nilamel, 20 March 2013.

Gladstone, J.W. (69), Former Bishop, CSI-SKD. Uriyacode, 10 June 2013.

SECONDARY SOURCES

Books

Abhimanyu. *Ayyankali* (Mal.) Trivandrum: Kerala Samskarika Vakuppu, 1990.

Abraham, K.C. *Liberative Solidarity*. Thiruvalla: CSS, 1996.

_______. *Transforming Vision: Theological – Methodological Paradigm Shifts*. Thiruvalla: CSS, 2006.

Agur, C.M. *Church History of Travancore*. New Delhi: Asian Educational Services, 1930 (1903).

Aiya, V. Nagam. *The Travancore State Manuel, Vol.1.* Trivandrum: Government Press, 1906.

Amaldass, Anand (ed.). *Christians Thinkers in India,* vol 3. Chennai: Satya Nilayam Publications, 2007.

Aprem, Mar. *Indian Christian Who is Who*. Bombay: Parish Church of the East, 1983.

Asan, Mahakavi Kumaran. *Brahmasree Narayana Guru.* Kottayam: Lalu Books, 1997.

Athyal, Abraham P. and Nyce Dorathy Yoder (eds.). *Mission Today: Challenges and Concerns.* Chennai: Gurukul, 1998.

Athyal, Jesudas M. *Relevant Patterns of Christian Witness in India.* Thiruvalla: CSS, 2000.

_______. *The Community we Seek, Perspective of Mission.* Thiruvalla: CSS, 2003.

Ayyar, L.A. Krishna. *Social History of Kerala, vol. 1. The Pre-Dravidians.* Madras: Book Centre Publications, 1968.

Azariah, Masillamony. *A Pastor's Search for Dalit Theology*. Delhi: ISPCK, 2000.

Baepler Walter A. *A Century of Grace: A History of the Missouri Synod, 1847-1947.* St. Louis: CPH, 1947.

Bainton, Ronald H. *Studies on the Reformation.* London: Hodder & Stoughton, 1963.

Balakrishnan, P.K. *Narayana Guru.* Kottayam: NBS, 1963.

Banerjee, Brojendra Nath. *Struggle for Justice to Dalits Christians.* New Delhi: New Age International (P) Limited, 1997.

Bevans, Stephen B. and Roger P. Schroeder. *Constants in Context: A Theology of Mission for Today.* Maryknoll, New York: Orbis Books, 2005.

Bosch, David J. *Transforming Mission: Paradigm Shifts in Theology of Mission.* Maryknoll, NY: Orbis Books, 1991.

Bosch, David J. *Believing in the Future: Towards a Missiology of Western Culture.* Valley Forge, Penn: Trinity Press International, 1995.

Bunkowske, Eugene W. (ed.). *The Lutherans In Mission.* Fort Wayne: Lutheran Society for Missiology Book Series, 2000.

Camilla Parke. *Dalit Christians: Right to Reservations.* Delhi: ISPCK, 2007.

Carr, Dhyanchand. *God's Mission Towards a Community of Communities.* Thiruvalla: CSS, 2002.

Chaldwick, Owen, *Reformation.* Baltimore: Penguin Books, 1964.

Chentharassery, T.H.P. *Poikayil Sree Kumara Guru Devan* (Mal.). Trivandrum: Navodhanam Publications, 1979.

_______. *Pampady John Joseph* (Mal.). Thiruvalla: Backward Peoples' Development Corporation, 1989.

_______. *Ayyankali.* Trivandrum: Prakasam Printing Co., 1979.

Cherian, C.V. *A History of Christianity in Kerala.* Kottayam: CMS Press, 1973.

Chirakkarodu, Paul. *Dalith Cristhavar Keralathil* (Mal.) (Dalit Christians in Kerala). Thiruvalla: CSS, 2000.

Christudas, D. *Tranquebar to Travancore.* Delhi: ISPCK, 2008.

Christudas, D. *Aazhangalile Anugrahathinte Uravakal.* (*Source of Blessings from the Depths*). Thiruvalla: CSS, 2007.

Cook, George Wood, *Kerala, A Portrait of the Malabar Coast.* London: Faber & Faber, 1967.

Cook, Robert E. *Half a Century Divine Leadings and 37 Years of Apostolic Achievements in South India.* Cleveland: Church of God Foreign Department, 1955.

Desai, I.P., et.al. *Caste, Caste Conflict and Reversions.* Delhi: Ajanta Publications, 1985.

Dev, C. *Christhava Sabha Erupathu Noottandukaliloode* (Mal) (The Christian Church Through Twenty Centuries). Pathanamthitta: GLS, 2003.

Dharmatheeram, John. *Sree Narayana Guru Devan.*Trivandrum: St. Joseph's Press, 1965.

Dumont, L. *The Caste System and its Implication*. Delhi: Vikas Publishing House, 1970.

Elert, Werner. *Structure of Lutheranism.* St. Louis: CPH, 1962.

Evers, George. *The Churches in Asia.* Delhi: ISPCK, 2005.

Fernandez, Walter (ed.). *The Emerging Dalit Identity: The Reassertion of the Subalterns*. New Delhi: Indian Social Institute, 1996.

Fenger, J. Fred. *History of the Tranquebar Mission.* Madras: M.E. Press, 1906.

Firth, C.B. *An Introduction to Indian Church History.* Madras: CLS, 1992.

Fisher, G.P. *The History of Christian Church.* London: Hodder & Sloughter, nd.

Forrester, Duncan B. *Caste and Christianity.* London: Curzon Press, 1979.

Forrester, Duncan B. *Caste and Christianity: Attitudes and Politics in Caste of Anglo-Saxon Protestant Missions in India*. London: Curzon Press, 1980 (1979).

Gawthrop, Richard L. *Pietism and the Making of Eighteenth Century Prussia.* Cambridge: University Press, 1993.

George, Jacob. *Religious Life of the Ilavas of Kerala - Change and Continuity*. Delhi: ISPCK, 1995.

George, Keerankeri and V.P. Srivastava (eds.). *Taking Text to Context*. Delhi: ISPCK, 2011.

George, M. *Christianity in India through the Centuries*. Hyderbad: Authentic, 2009 (2007).

George, N.C. *Phalangal Mundirivalliyil* (Malayalam) (Fruits in the wine). Trivandrum: IELC, 1975.

Gladstone, J.W. *Protestant Christianity and People's Movement in Kerala: A Study of Christian Mass Movements in Relation to New-Hindu Socio-Religious Movements in Kerala, 1850-1936*. Trivandrum: Seminary Publications, 1984.

Gnanadasan, Joy. *Forgotten History.* Madras: Gurukul Publication, 1996. (1994).

Godwin Shiri. *The Fights of Christian Dalits.* Bangalore: Asian Trading Corporation, 1997.

Gomez, M. *Thullal Purayil Ninnu Thudakkam* (Beginning from an Occultist's shed). Nalanchira: Jayamatha, 2011.

Goyal, Shankar. *Recent Historiography of Ancient India*. Jodhpur: Kusumanjali Book World, 1997.

Gritsch, Eric W. and Robert W. Jenson. *Lutheranism.* Philadelphia: Fortress Press, 1976.

Gross, Andrew, Kumaradoss Y. Vincent and Liebau Heike (eds.) *Halle and the Beginning of Protestant Christianity in India: Communications between India and Europe.* vol.iii. Halle: GmbH, 2006.

Guha, Ranajit (ed.). *Subaltern Studies1: Writings on South Asian History and Society.* Delhi: Oxford University Press, 1982.

Guru, Nataraja. *The Word of the Guru.* Ernakulam: Pai & Co., 1968.

Hallmann, David G. *A Place in Creation.* Toronto: The United Publishing House, 1992.

Hambye, E.R. *History of Christianity in India*. Bangalore: CHAI, 1997.

Hedlund, Roger E. (ed.). *Christianity is Indian: The Emergence of an Indigenous Community.* Delhi: ISPCK, 2000.

_______. *Quest for Identity: Indian Churches of Indigenous Origin: The "Little Tradition" in Indian Christianity.* Delhi: MIIS/ISPCK, 2000.

Hoefer, Herbert, (ed). *Debate on Mission.* Madras: Gurukul, 1979.

Hudson D. Dennis. *Protestant Origins in India, 1706-1735.* Cambridge: W.B. Eerdmans Publishing Company, 2000.

Hunt, W.S. *The Anglican Church in Travancore and Cochin, 1816-1916.* Kottayam: CMS, 1968.

Hutton, J.H. *Caste in India.* Delhi: Oxford University Press, 1946.

Jacob, George. *Religious Life of the Ilavas of Kerala-Change and Continuity.* Delhi: ISPCK, 1995.

Jacob, John A. *A History of the LMS in South Travancore, 1806-1857.* Nagercoil: Diocesan Press, 1990.

Jaganathan, Milton (ed.). *Mission Paradigm in the New Millennium.* Delhi: ISPCK, 2000.

Janice, Kerper Brauer (ed.). *A Rainbow of Saris.* St. Louis: LWML, 1996.

Jeyakumar, Arthur. *History of Christianity in India, Selected Themes.* Madurai, TTS, 2007.

Jeyakumar, Vijayalayam. *Sree Narayana Guru Oru Samagra Patanam.* Kottayam: NBS, 1995 (1993).

Jayaraj, Daniel (ed.). *Ordination of the First Protestant Indian Pastor Aaron.* Madras: Gurukul, 1998.

Jeyaraj, Daniel A. *German Exploration of Indian Society: Ziegenbalg's "Malabarian Heathenism."* Delhi: MIIS & ISPCK, 2006.

Jeyaraj, Daniel A. *Bartholomaus Ziegenbalg: The Father of Modern Protestant Mission.* Delhi: ISPCK & GLTCRI, 2006.

John, K.J. (ed.). *Christian Heritage of Kerala.* Cochin: L.M. Pylee Felicitations, 1981.

Jose, N.K. *Vaikunda Swamikal: Kerala Samuhya Navodhanathinte Margadarsi* (Mal.) (Vaikunda Swamikal: Forerunner of Kerala Social Reformation). Thiruvananthapuram: Bahujana Vartha, 2008.

Joseph, M.P. (ed.). *Mission and Solidarity.* Bombay: Urban Industrial League for Development, 1995.

Joseph, P.C. *Poikayil Sree Kumara Guru: Jeevithavum Darsanavum* (Mal.) (Life and Vision of Sree Poikayil Sree Kumara Guru). Thiruvalla, 1994.

Kangazha, Vijayan. *Sree Kumara Guru Devan: Biography.* Trichur: 1978.

Kariyal, Anthony. *Church and Society in Kerala: A Sociological Study.* New Delhi: Inter Cultural Publications, 1995.

Kawashima, Koji, *Missionaries and a Hindu State Travancore, 1858-1936.* Delhi: OUP, 2000 (1998).

Keinath, Hermann O.A. (ed.). *Documents Illustrating the History of the Lutheran Churches in America: With Special Emphasis on the Missouri Synod.* Illinois: Concordia Teachers College, 1947.

Kim, Sebastian C.H. *In Search of Identity: Debates on Religious Conversion in India.* New Delhi: Oxford University Press, 2003.

Kohlhoff, Elizabeth A. (compiler). *Pastoral Symphony – The Family and Descendents of J.B. Kohlhoff.* Richmond: University of Western University, 1989.

Kolb, Robert and Timothy J. Wengert. Eds. *The Book of Concord.* Minneapolis: Fortress Press, 2000.

Kooiman, Dick. *Conversion and Social Equality in India: The London Missionary Society in South Travancore in the 19th Century.* Delhi: Manohar, 1994 (1989).

Koshy, Ninan. *Caste in the Kerala Churches.* Bangalore: CISRS, 1968.

Kretzmann, Martin L. *Lengthening the Cords, A Survey of Expansion Plans in the MELIM for the Next Five Years.* Nagercoil: MELIM, 1953.

Kshirsagar, R.K. *Dalit Movements in India and its Leaders, 1857-1956.* New Delhi: MDP, 1994.

Kumar, Prem, M.P. *Kadampakalkkappuram* (Malayalam) (Beyond Boundaries). Calicut: UESI, 2005.

Kumaran, M.K. (ed.). *Sree Narayana Yugaprabhavam.* Varkala: International Sree Narayana Guru Year Commemoration Committee, 1978.

Kumaran, Mukorth. *Sree Narayana Swamikalude Jeeva Charithram.* Talassery: Saraswathy Vijayam Press, 1930.

_______. *Sree Narayana Guru.* New Delhi: National Book Trust, 1988.

Kuriakose, M.K. *History of Christianity in India: Source Materials.* Delhi: ISPCK, 1999.

Kusuman, K.K. *Issues in Kerala Historiography.* Trivandrum: University of Kerala, 2003.

Kutty, T.S. Samuel. *The Place and Contribution of Dalits in Select Pentecostal Churches in Kerala from 1922-1972.* Delhi: ISPCK, 2000.

Lehmann, Arno E. (ed.). *Handbook of Lutheran World Missions.* Germany: LWF, 1952.

_______. *It Began at Tranquebar.* Madras: CLS, 1956.

Lindsay, Thomas M. *Luther and the German Reformation, Vol. III.* Edinburgh: T & T Clark, 1935.

Logan, William. *Malabar.* New Delhi: Asian Educational Services, 1995.

Lohse, Bernhard. *Martin Luther.* Philadelphia: Fortress Press, 1986.

Longchar, A. Wati. *The Tribal Religious Tradition in North East India: An Introduction.* Jorhat: Eastern Theological College, 2000.

Longchar, A. Wati. *An Emerging Asian Theology; Tribal Theology: Issue, Method and Perspective.* Assam: Tribal Study Centre, 2000.

Luden, David. *Reading Subaltern Studies: Critical Histories, Contested Meaning and the Globalization of South Asia.* Delhi: Permanent Black, 2002.

Luekening, F. Dean. *Mission in the Making.* St. Louis: CPH, 1964.

Mackenzie, G.T. *Christianity in Travancore.* Trivandrum: Travancore Government Press, 1902.

Manickam, Sundararaj. *The Social Setting of Christian Conversion in South India.* Wiesbaden: Franz Steiner Verlag, 1979.

Massey, James (ed.). *Indigenous People: Dalits.* Delhi: ISPCK, 1994.

_______. *Dalits in India: Religion as a Source of Bondage or Liberation with Special Reference to Christians.* New Delhi: Manohar, 1995.

_______. *Downtrodden: The Struggle of India's Dalits for Identity, Solidarity and Liberation.* Geneva, WCC Publications, 1997.

_______. *Towards Dalit Hermeneutics.* New Delhi: Centre for Dalit Studies, 2002.

Mateer, Samuel. *The Land of Charity.* London: John Snow & Co., 1871.

Meinzen, E.H. *Fifty Years.* Unpublished History of Nagercoil District Conference 1907-1957.

Meinzen, L.W. *A Church in Mission.* Vaniyambadi: Concordia Press, 1981.

Menon A. Sreedhara. *A Survey of Kerala History.* Kottayam: DC Books, 2012 (1967).

_______. *Social and Cultural History of Kerala.* New Delhi: Sterling Publishers Pvt. Ltd., 1979.

_______. *Kerala History and its Makers.* Madras, 1990.

Menon, K.P. Padmanabha, *History of Kerala.* New Delhi: Asian Educational Services, 1993.

Menon, P. Shangoonny. *History of Travancore from the Earliest Times.* New Delhi: Asian Educational Services, 1985 (1878).

Menon, T. Madhava. *Hand book of Kerala* vol.1. Thiruvananthapuram: The International School of Dravidian Linguistics, 2000.

Meyer, Carl S. (ed.). *Moving Frontiers.* St. Louis; CPH, 1964.

Mingana, A. *The Early Spread of Christianity in India.* Manchester: University Press, 1925.

Muller, Max. *Chips from a German Workshop, Volume 11*. New York: Charles Scribner and Company, 1869.

Mundadan, A.M. *Indian Christians' Search for Identity and Struggle for Autonomy.* Bangalore: Dharmaram Publications, 2003.

Nalunnakkal, Geevargees Coorilose. *Ethical Issues: Subaltern Perspectives.* Thiruvalla: CSS, 2007.

Nau, Henrich. *Vanji Bhumi* (German). St. Louis: CPH, 1913.

Nirmal, Arvind P. *A Reader in Dalit Theology*. Chennai: Gurukul Lutheran Theological College and Research Institute, 2007.

Nisar, M. and Kandasamy Meena. *Ayyankali: A Dalit Leader of Organic Protest.* Calicut: The Other Books, 2007.

Nossitier, T.J., *Communism in Kerala: A Study in Political Adaption*. Bombay: OUP, 1982.

Oddie, G.A. (ed.). *Religion in South Asia-Religious Conversion and Revival Movements in South Asia in Medieval and Modern Times.* New Delhi: Manohar, 1991.

Oommen, George and C.B. Webster John (eds.). *Local Dalit History.* Delhi: ISPCK, 2002.

Oommen, George and Iversen Hans Raun (eds.). *It Began in Copenhagen.* Delhi: ISPCK, 2005.

Panikkar, K.K. *Sree Narayana Paramahamsan.* Alleppey: Vidyarambam Press, 1985.

Patrick, G.P. *Religion and Subaltern Agency.* Chennai: Department of Christian Studies, University of Madras, 2003.

Paulus, Masillamony. *Life History of M. Paulus.* Autobiography, Unpublished Manuscript, 5th June 1928.

Podipara, Placid. *The Thomas Christians.* Bombay: St. Paul Publications, 1944.

Polack, W.G. *Fathers and Founders.* St. Louis: CPH, 1938.

Pothen, S.G. *The Syrian Christians of Kerala.* Bombay: Asia Publishing House, 1963.

Pramod K. Nayar. *An Introduction to Cultural Studies.* New Delhi: Viva Books, 2008.

Rai, Lala Lajpat, *Young India.* Delhi: Publication Division, 1965.

Raj, Sunder, *Conversion Called Confusion.* New Delhi: TRACT, 1986.

Rajasekhar, V.T. *Christians and Dalit Liberations.* Bangalore: Dalit Sahithya Acadamy, 1987.

Rajendran, G., *The Ezhava Community and Kerala Politics.* Trivandrum: The Kerala Academy of Political Science, 1974.

Rao, Pramod, *Religio-Cultural Changes and Communities.* Delhi: ISPCK, 2012.

Richter, Julius. *A History of Missions in India.* New York: Fleming H. Revell, 1908.

Rongpi, Solomon, ed. *Mission and the Local Congregations.* Delhi: ISPCK/NCCI, 2011.

Russel, R.V. and Hiralal. *Tribes and Castes of the General Provinces of India.* Delhi: Cosmo Publications, 1984.

Sandegren, J. *The Song of Tranquebar*. Madras: CLS, 1955.

Sarosh T. Jacob, ed. *Kerala Sabha Chratithra Nigandu* (Mal.) (Dictionary of Kerala Christian Church History). Pathanapuram: Spiritual India Publications, 1999.

Schmidt, O.H. *Globe-Trotting for the Gospel.* New York: Vantage Press, 1962.

Schwiebert E.G. *Reformation Lectures.* Indiana: Letter Shop, 1937.

Selvaraj, A. *Christianity and Social Transformation: The Kerala Story.* Trivandrum: ICRO, 2002.

Shiri, Godwin. *The Plight of Dalit Christians – A South Indian Case Study.* Bangalore: Asian Trading Corporation, 1997.

Singh, Brijraj. *The First Protestant Missionary to India, Bartholomaeus Ziegenbalg 1683-1713*. Oxford: University Press, 1999.

Siromony, Joshua. *Comprehensive Vision and Transforming Mission: The Evolution of the Religious Thoughts of Sree Narayana Guru and its Practical Implications.* Delhi: ISPCK, 2005.

Smith, Geoffry Nowell (ed.). *Selections from the Prison Note Books of Antonio Gramsci*. Chennai: Orient Longman, 1988, 52-53.

Sobhanam, B. ed. *A History of the Christian Missions in South India.* Thiruvananthapuram: Kerala Historical Society, 1996.

Spitz, Lewis W. *The Protestant Reformation.* New York: Harper & Row, 1985.

Stanislaus, L., *The Liberative Mission of the Church among Dalit Christians*. Delhi: ISPCK, 1999.

Swamidas, Moses. *Conversion and Reconversion in India: A Study of the Experience of Dalit Christians in the Context of the Ministry of the Bible Faith Mission.* Parasuvakkal: Bible Faith Mission Publication Series, 2001.

Swavely, C.H. (ed.). *The Lutheran Enterprises in India.* Madras: FELCI, 1952.

Thekkedath, Joseph. *History of Christianity in India*, Vol.II. Bangalore: TPI, 1984.

Thomas, M.M. *Salvation and Humanization.* Madras: CLS, 1970.

Thomas, V.V. *Understanding Subaltern History: Theoretical Tools.* Bangalore: BETSSC/SATHRI, 2006.

________. *Dalit Pentecostalism.* Bangalore: Asia Trading Corporation, 2008.

Thomas, Saju. *Kerala Pentacostal Charitram* (Mal.) [The History of Pentecostals in Kerala]. Kottayam: Good News Publications, 1994.

Umaithanu, C. and Udayan P. Kasi. *Bhagavan Vaikunda Swamikal Varalaru* (Tamil). Nagercoil: 1966.

Vaidiyan, V. Bhargavan. '*Ente Gurudeva Smaranakal*' (Mal.) (*My Memories About Gurudev*). Quilon: Sree Narayana Guruvarsham Smaraka Grandham, n.d.

Vaidyar, C.R. Kesavan. *Sree Narayana Chinthakal.* Kottayam: NBS, 1972.

Vajta, Vilmos (ed.). *The Lutheran Church: Past and Present.* Minnesota: APH, 1977.

Vanchiyoor, Appa. *Ayyankali Padathalavan* (Mal.) (Ayyankali the Captain). Trivandrum: Kerala Harijan Sahithya Pravarthaka Co-operative Society, 1984.

Vargees, George. *Malankara Nasranikalude Jathyaulkristyavum Rajayasevana Nirathayum* (Mal.), [The Civil Service and Caste Nobility of Malankara Nasraniees]. Kottayam: MOC Publications, 1988.

Velupillai, T.K. The *Travancore State Manuel, Vol. I,* Trivandrum: Kerala Gazetteers Department, 1996 (1940).

Vethanayagamony, Peter. *It began in Madras.* Delhi: ISPCK, 2010.

Victor, Vinod, et al. (ed.). *Ecumenism: Prospects and Challenges.* Delhi: ISPCK, 2001.

Vincent, Thomas. *Relevance of Latin American Church to Indian Ecclessiology*, Calcutta: RNB, 2000.

Viswanathan, Susan. *The Christians of Kerala.* Delhi: OUP, 1999.

Walker, Williston. *A History of the Christian Church.* New York: Charles Scribner's Sons, 1958.

Walpole, Beth. *Venture of Faith: A Brief Historical Background of the Church of South India.* Madras: CLS, 1993.

Webster, John C.B. *The Christian Community and Change in Nineteenth Century North India.* Delhi: Macmillan, 1976.

_______. *The Dalit Christians: A History*. Delhi: ISPCK, 1992.

_______. *Religion and Dalit Liberation: An Examination of Perspectives.* New Delhi: Manohar, 1999.

Wilfred, Felix. *On the Banks of Ganges: Doing Contextual Theology.* Delhi: ISPCK, 2002.

Wilson, K. *The Twice-Alienated: Culture of Dalit Christians.* Hyderabad: Booklinks Corporation, 1982.

Wolf, L.B. *Missionary Heroes of the Lutheran Church.* Philadelphia: The Lutheran Publication Society, 1911.

Yesudhas, R.N. *A People's Revolt in Travancore: A Backward Class Movement for Social Freedom.* Trivandrum: Kerala Historical Society, 1975.

_______. *British Policy in Travancore, 1805-1859.* Trivandrum: Kerala Historical Society, 1977.

_______. *The History of London Mission Society in Travancore (1806-1985*). Trivandrum: Kerala Historical Society, 1980.

Zachariya, Zachriya (ed.). *Herman Gundert: Keralolpathiyum Mattum* (Mal). Kottayam: DC Books, 1992.

Articles and Journals

Aranzazu, Maria Agnado. "Mission Spirituality and Care for Creation: An Introduction." *IRM* 99/2 (November, 2010).

Arnold, David. "Gramsci and Peasant Subalternity." *The Journal of Peasant Studies* V.11 (July 1984): 155-177.

Ayrookuzhiel, Abraham A.M. "Dalits Challenges to Religious Systems: A People Ignored by the Church History." *ICHR* XXXIII/2 (December, 1989): 115-131.

Das, J. Paramananda. "Almenikalude Arangettam." (The Emergence of Laymen's). *Christiani*, Golden Jubilee Special 57/2 (February, 1976): 35-38.

David Immanuel. "History of Christianity in India: Changing Perspectives." *ICHR*: XX/1(June, 1986): 5.

David, M.D. "The Problem of Caste." *ICHR* 18/2 (December, 1984): 141-153.

David, M.D. "Social Background of Basal Mission Christians: The Problem of Caste." *ICHR* XVIII/2, (December, 1984): 141.

Dominic George. "Mandal Commission and the Future of Dalits." *Religion and Society* XLI/1(March, 1994): 61.

Downs F.S. "History of Christianity in India" *CHAI* I/5. Bangalore, 1992.

Elizabeth, V.S. "Inevitability of Re-writing Indian History from a Feminist Perspective." *Journal of Dharma* 28/2 (April-June, 2003): 232-245.

Gamaliel, J.C. "Bethel Evangelism Fellowship - A Short History." *BEF Souvenir* (January, 1995): 1-4.

George, N.C. "Adhiyathe Anchu Varshangal." (Mal.) "The First Five Years." *Christiani 52/11* (November, 1976): 70-75.

Gladstone, J.W. "19th Century Mass Movement in South Travancore - A Result of Social Liberation." *ICHR,* X/1 (June, 1976): 53-66.

________. "Christian Missionary Work and Socio-Religious Movements in Kerala 1850-1910." *ICHR,* XX/1 (June, 1986): 30-42.

________. "Christian Missionaries and Caste in Kerala." *Dalit Theology,* ed. M.E. Prabhakar. Delhi: ISPCK, 1989.

________. "Theological Research: History of Christianity." *SATHRI Journal* I/1 (January, 1991): 63-73.

________. "Mission and Evangelism in India- A Historical Perspective." *Paradigm in the New Millennium*. Ed. W.S. Milton Jeganathan. Delhi: ISPCK, 2000.

Gladstone, J.W. "Ecumenism and the People of God in India." Victor Vinod, et.al., ed. *Ecumenism: Prospects and Challenges*. Delhi: ISPCK, 2001. 193-201.

Gyan, Prakash. "Subaltern Studies as Postcolonial Criticism." *The American Historical Review*, 99 / 5 (December, 1994): 1475-1490.

Hedlund, Roger E. "Indian Christians of Indigenous Origins and their solidarity with Origin Groups." *Journal of Dharma* 24/1 (1999): 13-27.

_______. "Indian Instituted Churches: Indigenous Christianity Indian Style." *Mission Studies*, XVI/1/31 (1999): 26-41.

_______. "Approaches to Indian Church History in the Light of New Christian Movements." *ICHR* XXXIV/2, December, 2000. 153-170.

Hoefer, Herbert. "But it work? Unintended Social Consequences of a Perfectly Good Theology." *Missio Apostallica Journal of the Lutheran Society for Missiology*, XI/1/23 (May, 2004): 49.

Hospital, Clifford G. "Cloths and Caste in Ninetieth Century Kerala." *ICHR* XIII/2, 1979.

Huebner. "Nagercoilil Sthapikkappettittulla Namathu Missionin Arambha Charithram." ("History of the origin of our Mission at Nagercoil"). *Sathia Satchi* 24/8: 162-173.

James, Woba. "Methodolgical Issues in the Writing of the History of Christianity in the 19th and 20th Centuries with Special Reference to the Post Colonial Theory." *SATHRI Journal* 1/1 (January, 2006): 151-168.

Janaka "The Introduction of Untouchability into Christianity." *Christian Patriot,* 37/13 (September, 1928): 6-9.

Jesudason, G. "Extension of work of the Missouri Evangelical Lutheran Mission in India." *The Lutheran Witness* 26 (17 October, 1907): 157.

Kalapura Jose. "Christianity and Marginalized in India: A Subaltern Historical Overview." *ICHR* XLIII/I (June, 2009).

Kuppaswamy, T.V. "Reflections on the Genesis of Kerala." *Journal of Kerala Studies, Vol.1* (March, 1975).

Manickam Sundararaj. "Origin and History of the Christian Dalits in Kerala and Tamil Nadu." *Religion and Society* XXXIV/3 (September, 1978).

Massey, James. "Christian Dalits: A Historical Perspective." *Religion and Society XXII*/2 (July, 1990): 56.

Meinzen, Luther W. "The Structure of the Congregation in Mission." *The Gospel Witness*, LXV/1-3 (January-March, 1970): 6.

Mohan, P. Sanal. "Keezhala Patanangalum Dalit Charithravum." (Subaltern Studies and Dalit History), *Malayalam* Weekly, 15/52 (25 May, 2012): 48-58.

Mohan, Shanta. "New Education Policy – Its Relevance to Woman." *Religion and Society* Vol. XXXVI/3 (September, 1989): 3.

Naumann, Martin. "Life of Missionary K.G. Theodore Naether." *Concordia Historical Institute Quarterly*, XXXIX (January, 1967): 184.

Oddie, G.A. "Christian Conversions in the Telugu Country 1860-1900: A Case Study of One Protestant Indian Movement in the Godavery-Krishna Delta." *Indian Economic and Social History Review*, XII (January-March, 1975): 61-79.

Oommen George. "Dalit Conversion and Social Protest in Travancore 1854-1890." *Bangalore Theological Forum* Vol. XXVII (September-December, 1996): 69-84.

_______. "Historiography of Indian Christianity and Challenges of Subaltern Methodology." *Journal of Dharma*, 28/2 (April-June, 2003): 230-231.

_______. "Christianization or Dalitization: The Twentieth Century Experiences of the Dalit Christians in Kerala." ICHR, Vol. XXXVI/1 (June, 2003): 1-22.

_______. "Strength of Tradition and Weakness of Communication – Central Kerala Dalit Conversion." in GeoffreyA. Oddie, ed., *Religious Conversion Movements in South Asia: Continuities and Change, 1800-1900*. Richmond: Curzon Press, 1997. 79-95.

Otten, H.J. "Aathmika unarvinte Anugrahangal." (Blessings of Spiritual Renewal). *Christiani*, 52/10 (October, 1977): 14-17.

Panikkar, K.N. "Alternative Historiographies: Changing Paradigms of Power." *Jeevadhara*, Vol. XXXII (January, 2002): 11.

Prakash Gyan. "Subaltern Studies as Post-Colonial Criticism." *American Historical Review* (December, 1994): 1475-1490.

Peter, P.N. "Depressed Community." *Christian Patriot* 37/7 (August,1928).

Prabhakar, M.E. "Christian Dalits." *Religion and Society* 34/3 (September, 1987): 3.

Rash, A. "Ordination of M. Paulus at Trivandrum." *The Lutheran Witness*, 51/8 (August, 1930): 307.

Raj, A.R. Victor. "Justification Only through Faith." Doctrinal Essay Presented at 21st TDS Convention, 1977, *Christiani*, 52/11, Trivandrum, 1977, 61-66.

Rajarigam, D. "Tamil Churches and Caste, A Historical Sketch." *Religion and Society*, XV, September 1968.

Robinson, Gnana. "Solidarity as Missionary Principle." in Jeganathan W.S. Milton (ed.) *Mission Paradigm in New Millennium*. Delhi: ISPCK, 2000, 58-93.

Samuel, Simon. "A Post Colonial Historiography; Toward a Post Colonial Approach to Reading the Discourses of a Colonial Subject Community." Doon Theological Journal 1/1 (January, 2004): 5-19.

Sathyanesan, V. "Temple Entry Proclamation and Reconversion impulses in Travancore." *ICHR* 26/1 (June, 1992): 5-20.

Spivak, Gayathri Chakravarthy . "Can the Subaltern Speak?" *Colonial Discourses and Post-Colonial Theory: A Reader.* Patrick Williams and Laura Chrisman (eds.). New York: Columbia University Press, 1994, 66-111.

Thomas, V.V. "Subaltern Historiography and Post-Colonial Theory: The Case of Dalit Pentecostalism in Kerala." *Religion and Society*, Vol.49, Nos. 2 & 3 (June & September, 2004): 124 -127.

_______. "Challenges to the Mission of the Church in India Today." Samson Prabhakar (ed.), Bangalore: BTESSC/SATHRI, 2006.

_______. "Post Colonism, Post Modernism, and Post Pentacostalism - Challenges and Perspectives." Samson Prabhakar (ed.). Bangalore: BTESSC / SATHRI, 2007.

_______. Women Contribution to the Indian Church with Special Reference to the Women among the Pentecostal Churches in India." *Kerala Historical Review,* I/1 (February, 2009): 51-68.

Victor, J. "Kodukkunnathil nam Valaruka." (Let us grow in giving). *Christiani*, 52/11 (November, 1976): 2.

Zeimke, Rose M. "Sabhayile Vanitha Pravarthana Prasnam." *Christiany*, 34/6 (June, 1958): 138-141.

Zorn, H.M. "Relation between MELIM and LMS." *ICHR* 1/2 (December, 1967), 133-143.

Presentations

Christudas, D. "Contributions of MELIM in South Travancore." Paper, presented in Seminar on "The Contributions of IELC towards Socio-Cultural Empowerment, Educational, Medical and Health Services, Organized by Chair on Christian Studies, Manonmoniam Sundarnar University and IELC at Concordia Seminary, Nagercoil, on 29 June 2011.

Christudas, D. "Akshara Sushrushayil Lutheran Christhavarude Sambhavanakal-Oru Avalokanam" ("Literary contributions of Kerala Lutheran Christians in Kerala - An Appraisal"). Paper presented on The Annual Seminar of Lutheran Voice at Perurkada Trivandrum on 24 November 2011.

Grum, M.H. "The Church and Social Service." Paper presented in the IELC Convention, Pernambut, IX 61/ 172 (June 1961).

Manohar, Chandra Prasad. "Dalit Theology: Methodological issues as contextual theology of liberation." Paper presented on the D.Th. Methodology Seminar. Bangalore: SATHRI, 2008.

Mayer, J.W. "The Church as the People of God United in the Word of God." General Conference Doctrinal Essays - Trivandrum, 1960.

Oommen, George. "Dalit Liberative Identity as Amalgam: Pulaya Christians, Missionaries, Caste Associations and Labour Union Movements in the 20th Century." Paper presented in International Seminar on Missionary Foundations of Indian Renaisance, at Vasco Da Gama Research Institute of Cochin (VGRI). 22-24 September 2011, 6.

Snaitang, O.L. "Methodoloical and Historiographical Issues in the study of the History of Christianity in India." Paper presented at D.Th Methodology Seminar, Bishops College, Kolkatta, 12 May 2010.

Suseelan, K. "Royal Priesthood and Lutheran Confessions." Essay presented in 9th Triennial Convention of IELC, Ernakulam, 26-28 February 1976.

Thomas, V.V. "Subaltern Historiography& Postcolonial Theory: The Case of Dalit Pentecostalism in Kerala." Paper presented in CHAI Conference, Secunderabad, Oct. 26-29, 2000.

Newspapers

Travancore Daily News, 2 January 1925.

Times of India, 20 March 1957.

Malayala Manorama, 14 June, 2003; 12 August 2003; 22 August 2003; 23 August 2003; 8 October 2003; 26 November 2003; 16 January 2004; 3 March 2004; 10 April 2004; 15 February 2006; 7 November 2006; 4 December 2009; 1 April 2011, 2011 July Sunday.

Thani Niram, 4 February 1979.

Mathrubhoomi, 18 March 2000.

Madhyamam, 9 January 1989.

Magazines

Homiletic Magazine, 48/7 (July 1924).

The Lutheran Witness Vol. LX1V, 14 July, 1908; 60/10 (September, 1921).

Sathia Satchi (January-December, 1932).

Christian Patriot 37/7 (August, 1828).

Yuva Sabdhom, 1/2 (December, 1969); 1/5 (November, 1970).

Christian Patriot 37/7 (August, 1828); 37/13 (September, 1928).

Youth Digest 2/5 (June, 1972).

Christiani, 4/7 (1928); 5/5, 5/10 (1929); 6/1 (1930); 19/5, 19/7 (1943); 34/5 (May, 1958); 34/9 (September, 1958); 34/10 (October, 1958); 39/12 (December, 1963); 48/9 (August, 1967); 49/11 (November, 1968); 55/9 (July, 1974); 56/9 (September, 1975); 52/11 (November, 1976); 54/6 (July, 1973); 55/79 (July, 1974); 56/8 (August, 1975); 57/1 (January, 1976); 57/2 (February, 1976); 57/11 (November, 1976); 54/3 (March, 1978).

The Travancore Times 81/5 (25th June 1952).

Concordia Historical Institute Quarterly, XXXIX (January 1967).

Travancore Daily News, 2 January 1925.

Theses and Dissertations

Anderson, Lemuel. "A Study of the Constitution of India Evangelical Lutheran Church with reference to select relevant litigation." M.Th. Dissertation, UTC, Bangalore, 1999.

Bernard, D.V. "A Historical Study of the Origin and Growth of the Lutheran Church in Kerala up to Present Time." Unpublished B D thesis, UTC, Bangalore, 1974.

Christudas, D. "Impact of Lutheran Mission Among the Sambavars in South Travancore." M.Th. Thesis. Senate of Serampore, 2001,

Griesse, Elmer. "Lutheran India Missions." M.A. Thesis. St. Louis: Washington University, 1945.

Sunil, T. "Changes in the understanding of mission among Pentecostals in Kerala with a Special Reference to the Indian Pentecostal Church of God since, 1934." MTh. thesis, Senate of Serampore, 2008.

Thomas, Alex. "Problems and Prospectus of Dalit Mar Thoma Christians: A Socio-Historical Survey since, 1888." MTh. thesis, Senate of Serampore, 1997.

Thompson, Sam. "Evolving an Ethical Critique in relation To the leadership crisis of IELC with particular reference to the Trivandrum synod." Unpublished MTh. Thesis, UTC, Bangalore, 2008.

Bulletins

Bethel Evangelism Fellowship Bulletin, 13 March 1993.

Awake, and Awake for the Church, 12/4/1999.

BEF Bullettin, 13 March 1993.

Newsletters

BELL News Letter of BEF, 5/2001.

News Letter, LLF, Trivandrum, August, 2011.

Souvenirs

CSI Paruthipalli, 170th Annual Souvenir, 2010.

Sree Ayyankali Smaraka Puthuvalvilakom L.P.S. Platinum Jubilee Souvenir. Vengannoor, 1980.

BFM Platinum Jubilee Souvenir, October 1988.

BFM Souvenir, 1995 and 2006.

James Town CSI Church, Bi-centenary Souvenir, 16/5/2010.

Others

Life history of M. Paulus, Autobiography (manuscript), 5th June 1928.

The Regulations and Proclamations of Travancore, Vol.1X, Trivandrum, 1936.

Current problem in Higher Education, 1947.

Kretzmann, M.L., *The India Mission 1947-1950.*

"Mutual Agreement Paper" Between LCMS and IELC, Nagercoil, 1982.

"Protocol Document" between LCMS and IELC, Nagercoil, 1982.

Code of Conduct for members of IELC, 1892.

NLWS Representation to Kerala State Commission for Backwards Classes, 15 May 2004.

Divakaran, J. *BFM Charithravum Velluvilikalum* (Mal) (BFM - History and Challenges) *Prayanam* of a persecuted Community, BFM Souvenir, Published in connection with the consecration of the first bishop Moses Swamidas, 13 March, 2006.

Manorama Year Book 2011, Kottayam: Manorama Publications, 2011.

Devadas, Sukumaran. On Myself (Autobiography) vol.11. Manuscript.

Jesudasan, J., *Biography.*

Paulose Upadesi, *Parayar ennu vilichuvanna Lutheran mission Christheeya Sahodhararkku Oru Apeksha* (Mal.) [An appeal to the Lutheran Christian Brothers who were called as Parayar].

Raj, Victor A.R. Pastor's Communion Document.

Questionnaire

Dear friends,

*I am doing a doctoral level research under South Asia Theological Research Institute(SATHRI- Senate of Serampore College) on the title, "**An unacknowledged Subaltern Solidarity: History of Lutherans In Kerala From 1911 to 2011**". To find the uniqueness and challenges of this Christian Solidarity, this questionnaire is sent to you as a part of research methods. The questionnaire is exclusively for an academic purpose. I request you to answer the questions to the best of your knowledge. Your answers, sincere opinions, suggestions or supplementary comments will be gratefully appreciated. I assure you that all the information gathered from you will be kept strictly confidential.*

Thanking you.

D. Christu Das

Personal Details

A. Age B. Gender: **Male / Female**

C. Caste Background: 1) ***SC*** 2) ***ST*** 3) ***OBC*** 4) ***Forward Class***

D. Educational Qualifications: Secular Theological

E. Marital status: ***Married/Un- Married*** ***Widow/Widower/Separated***

F. Occupation

G. Administrative office held in, if any with number of years

Congregation Circle Synod IELC

I.If you are a ***Pastor/Retired Pastor/Church worker/Deaconess***

Designation Years of service

(Please ***tick the appropriate answer***)

1. Are you proud of being a Lutheran Christian? ***Yes/No***

2. Is your local congregation multi- caste community? ***Yes/No***

3. Do you like to have a pastor from other caste to your local church? ***Yes/No***

4. Do you think one can be a Christian along with keeping his/her own caste identity? ***Yes/No***

5. How many caste people are in your church?

   a) ***Below 3*** b) ***4-5 Castes*** c) ***above five***

6. Do you think TDS needs a bifurcation according to the caste basis? ***Yes/No***

7. How do you evaluate the multi- caste nature of the Lutheran Church in Kerala?

   As a blessing/confusion

8. Do you think MELIM mission in Kerala was a unique attempt among other Protestant missions? ***Yes/No***

9. Is there any caste crisis among the Lutheran Christians in Kerala? ***Yes/No***

10. What is your opinion about the people reconverted to Hinduism or keeping membership in other denominations?

    Too bad/it is wise according to present situation/No comment
    (*Please number the answers according to the priorities*)

11. As a Christian how you view the problem of caste?

    ....***Caste is a sin***.............***Caste is a social and cultural reality***

    .... The caste system is an affair of this world and not a contrary factor for salvation

    ....for the time being we must be patient with caste system

12. In your opinion what makes Lutheran Christian community in Kerala as a unique movement?

    ...... Confessional Lutheranism .... Evangelical approach......... Mission to low castes .... Lutheran heritage .... Subaltern solidarity .... Social concern

    Specify if any other.............

13. In your opinion , why the one century history of Lutherans in Kerala were not noticed so far? Because:------

    .... **Lutherans ignored its importance**

    .... **The other historians ignored this history**

    .... **Lutherans may not provide the details about themselves to others**

    .... **Due to lack of social/political involvement**

    Specify if any other..................

14. If there is a caste crisis among the Lutherans in Kerala, what will be main causes?

    .... **Lack of understanding of Christian doctrine**

    .... **Failure of practising Christian faith**

    .... **Due to Church politics and secular factors**

    .... **Due to natural socio-cultural phenomena**

    .... **Due to satisfy the financial interests**

    Specify if any other..............

15. What will be your suggestions to create an egalitarian society among the Lutherans in Kerala?

    .... ***Growth in Christian nurture***

    .... ***Develop a common social psyche***

    .... ***Promote Inter-caste marriages among the Lutherans***

    .... ***Equal and just sharing of resources***

    .... ***Proper administrative participation***

    Specify if any other..............

Kindly return to: *Rev. D.Christu Das, Concordia Theological Seminary, Nagercoil, 629001.*